Olympic National Park

OLYMPIC NATIONAL PARK

A Natural History
Revised Edition

Tim McNulty

UNIVERSITY OF WASHINGTON PRESS *Seattle & London*

Copyright © 2009 by the University of Washington Press
All photographs are copyrighted to the photographers credited.

Original edition published by Houghton Mifflin Company in 1996
Reissued by Sasquatch Books in 1999
First University of Washington Press edition published, with corrections, in 2003
Revised edition published in 2009
Design by Thomas Eykemans

Printed in the United States of America
14 13 12 11 10 09   5 4 3 2 1

LIBRARY OF CONGRESS CATALOGING-IN-PUBLICATION DATA
McNulty, Tim.
Olympic National Park : a natural history / Tim McNulty.—Rev. ed.
    p. cm.
Includes bibliographical references and index.
ISBN 978-0-295-98887-0 (pbk. : alk. paper)
 1. Natural history—Washington (State)—Olympic National Park.
 2. Olympic National Park (Wash.). I. Title.
QH105.W2M37 2008
508.797'98—dc22   2008046289

The paper used in this publication is acid-free and 90 percent recycled from
at least 50 percent post-consumer waste. It meets the minimum requirements
of American National Standard for Information Sciences-Permanence of Paper
for Printed Library Materials, ANSI Z39.48-1984.

Frontispiece photo by Janis Burger.

To Polly Dyer, friend, mentor,
and longtime defender of Olympic wildlands.

Contents

Preface

MUCH has changed in the dozen or so years since I wrote the original edition of *Olympic National Park,* the first comprehensive natural history of this remarkable coastal wilderness. Global warming was a concern among many of the scientists I interviewed then; now it is widely seen as a significant factor influencing environmental conditions throughout the park. Intensive studies of Blue Glacier on Mount Olympus are measuring the pace of climate change in the Olympics. And the plight of several threatened Olympic salmon stocks may be linked to climate-driven changes in mountain snowpack and river conditions.

Pioneering field research has brought Olympic wildlife populations into clearer focus: endemic Olympic marmots, black bears, and a number of small mammals are among the species whose new stories are told here. Studies have been undertaken to assess the prospects for reintroducing wolves into the Olympics. Fisher, the only other species extirpated from the Olympics, was reintroduced early in 2008. New data are unlocking the mysteries of migratory salmon, steelhead, and bull trout in Olympic rivers, and salamanders in mountain streams. Recently arrived barred owls are affecting the status of threatened northern spotted owls in Olympic's ancient forests. On the coast, seabird populations are in dynamic flux with shifting currents and weather patterns. Bald eagles and peregrine falcons have recovered from dangerously low numbers, and a burgeoning population of sea otters is pioneering new territories and rejuvenating coastal ecosystems.

On the human side of the story, new archaeological discoveries are filling in critical gaps in our understanding of early people on the peninsula. The renaissance in Native American cultures described in the earlier edition continues to unfold, with the Makah Tribe reasserting its treaty right to hunt whales and the Elwha Klallam Tribe hosting the largest intertribal canoe gathering in memory to celebrate the rediscovery of an ancient village on the Port Angeles waterfront.

The project to restore the Elwha River has made significant strides toward the eventual removal of two salmon-blocking dams, and important salmon recovery efforts are under way across the peninsula. At the same time, the convergence of global warming, new endangered species listings, and unsustainable land-use practices have raised new conservation concerns and posed questions about the future viability of the Olympic ecosystem.

The mountains and rivers remain "timeless," but our understanding of the life-forms that inhabit them—and the effects our actions have on their future—is an ongoing, ever-deepening story. It is my hope that this new edition recasts that story in a current light and brings readers even closer to the heart of this wild and spectacular corner of the earth.

TIM McNULTY
November 2008

Acknowledgments

A NY attempt to tell the story of a place as wonderfully diverse as Olympic National Park is dependent upon the expertise and generosity of a host of scientists and researchers working in the field. Many knowledgeable individuals took time from their work to help me understand aspects of the Olympics' natural history, point me toward new research, or review revised sections of this manuscript. I owe them all a debt of gratitude. Any inaccuracies, of course, are entirely my own.

At Olympic National Park, biologists Steve Acker and Ed Schreiner shared their knowledge of Olympic's plant communities; Patti Happe and Kurt Jenkins shared insights into the park's wildlife; Pat Crain and Sam Brenkman shared their knowledge of Olympic fisheries; and Scott Gremel was generous with his research and insights on spotted owls. Kim Sager shared her pioneering work with black bears. Pat Loafman shared insights from fieldwork on Olympic amphibians. Steve Fradkin explained some of the mysteries of currents, tides, and intertidal communities. Jerry Freilich shared insights into long-term monitoring of the Olympic ecosystem. Brian Winter was a great help in understanding the process of the Elwha River restoration. Paul Gleeson, David Conca, and Jacilee Wray shared perspectives on peninsula archaeology and early ethnography. Roger Hoffman assisted with map preparation and contributed insights into bird populations on the peninsula, and Cat Hawkins Hoffman shared perspectives on park resource issues.

Former Olympic National Park biologists Bruce Moorhead, Doug Houston, Paul Crawford, Shelly Hall, Erran Sharpe, and John Meyer shared a wealth of experience and insights gleaned from years of work in the Olympic ecosystem. And Russ Dalton provided a unique perspective on the early history of the Olympics.

Special thanks are due to Michael Smithson, former chief of resource education for the park, who was supportive of this project from its inception and helped facilitate research. Park museum curator Gay Hunter provided access to numerous scientific papers and reports. Janis Burger and Sharon Wray assisted with historical photographs, and Janis also shared her considerable knowledge of native plants.

I also wish to thank Howard Conway, Megan Dethier, Jerry Franklin, Jim Kenage, Philip Mote, Julia Parrish, Bob Van Pelt, Joseph Vance, and Andrea Woodward of the University of Washington; Nalini Nadkarni and Ted Whitesell of The Evergreen State College; Suzanne Cox Griffin of the University of Montana; and the late Ed Tisch, formerly of Peninsula College, for their invaluable assistance and advice. Thanks, too, to Keith Aubrey, Jan Henderson, Robin Lesher, Catherine Raley, and David Shaw, researchers with the U.S. Forest Service; Ed Bangs and Ulrich Wilson (retired) of the U.S. Fish and Wildlife Service; Gretchen Blatz, Steve Jeffries, Greg Shirato, Anita McMillan, and Jim Watson of the Washington Department of Fish and Wildlife; Ed Bowlby and Bob Steelquist of the Olympic Coast National Marine Sanctuary; Pat Gearin, and Bob DeLong of the National Marine Fisheries Service Northwest Marine Mammal Laboratory; Bill Lingley and Jeff Cederholm of the Washington Department of Natural Resources; Melissa Peterson of the Makah Cultural and Resource Center; Kathy Duncan of the Jamestown S'Klallam Tribe; and Frances Charles, Carmen Charles, and Jamie Valadez of the Elwha Klallam Tribe.

I'd also like to thank Barbara Blackie, the late Nelsa Buckingham, Al Charles Jr., Welden Clark, Tim Cullinan, Delbert Gilbrow, Dick Goin, Jerry Gorsline, Ed Grumbine, Ruth Kirk, Keith Lazelle, Dennis Lewarch, Jim Lichatowich, Carsten Lien, Pete Schroeder, Autumn Scott, Fred Sharpe, Dave Shreffler, Jimmy Swingle, Roland Tabor, and the late Robert L. Wood for their assistance.

A big thanks goes to my agent, Anne Depue, and to Pat Soden, Marilyn

Trueblood, and Kathleen Pike Jones at the University of Washington Press for their professionalism, enthusiasm, and support.

Lastly, I wish to thank my wife, Mary Morgan, for her patience and encouragement throughout the rather lengthy process of revising of this book.

Olympic National Park

An Island of Rivers

I WATCHED them form as I followed an elk trail high above a timbered basin: light, feathery clouds that clung to the peaks as though the mountains had grown wings. Now, hours later, they had thickened and melded into a high plane that spread over the snow-streaked summits of the Olympic Mountains like a quilt. I'd seen the pattern before—the slow dance of mountain and cloud as moist air from the Pacific draws up over the heights of the range—and I knew what was to come.

Letting go of my destination, I climbed to an aerielike camp on a favorite ridge. From there I'd have a splendid view as the pageant of weather once more laid claim to this coastal mountain wilderness. Though I might grouse a bit, I never seriously complain about the weather. It was ocean-borne rain and snow that sculpted these mountains over time, and the ever-present breath of moist marine air continues to stir them to life.

The Olympic Mountains form the backbone of Washington's Olympic Peninsula, that angular thumb of land that juts into the Pacific at the northwest corner of the United States. The heart of the peninsula, more than 1,400 square miles of rugged mountains, heavily forested river valleys, and spectacular wilderness coast, has been preserved as Olympic National Park.

Olympic is one of the premier wilderness parks in the United States, and it harbors one of the richest old-growth forest preserves in the world. The park also protects the core of a larger ecosystem that surrounds it.

Mount Olympus becomes shrouded in clouds as moist marine air from the Pacific rolls up the Hoh River valley, rises, and cools. At just under 8,000 feet in height, Mount Olympus receives some 240 inches of precipitation annually, mostly in the form of snow. PHOTO BY JANIS BURGER.

Simply stated, an ecosystem is a complex of interacting plants and animals large enough to support the habitat needs of all the species it contains. The Olympic ecosystem is a living fabric that stitches the movement of tides over storm-worn coastal reefs to windblown drifts of snow at the heights of mountain peaks. Within this tapestry lies a wealth of interdependent plant and animal communities flourishing in a landscape of timeless beauty.

Olympic National Park was established only about seventy years ago, but its story reaches back much further than that. The character of the Olympic Mountains, their unique plant and animal species, and the startling natural diversity found here all trace their evolution to the shifting climate and profoundly changing landscapes that culminated during the Pleistocene ice age.

For thousands of years during the Pleistocene, the Olympic Peninsula was isolated from the rest of North America's mountain ranges by continental glaciers that advanced repeatedly from the north. The alpine plant and animal communities that adapted or evolved during this time remained separated from mainland ranges by the inland seas the glaciers left in their wake. Today Puget Sound, the Strait of Juan de Fuca, and the deep valley of the Chehalis River to the south continue to isolate this coastal range, lending an islandlike character to the peninsula's ecosystem. Though not an island in the geographic sense, the Olympic Mountains and the life communities they support can be seen as an island of rivers, separate in a way, but bound to seas and skies, flyways and migratory routes. Lifted up quite recently and weathering down in time, the Olympics are a window into the long and lovely story of the passage of life over the earth, an island where those primal forces still hold sway.

South of my perch, the glacier-clad slopes of Mount Olympus rise out of the forested headwaters of the Hoh River in broken sweeps of rock and ice, the summit just tasting the clouds. Ascending nearly 8,000 feet in elevation less than forty miles from the Pacific, Mount Olympus is the tallest peak in the Olympics. Spilling down its flanks, blue-white in the overcast light, are massive rivers of ice that hearken back to that earlier time of the Pleistocene. These glaciers, and more than sixty other named glaciers in Olympic are a reminder that the 12,000 to 14,000 years that separate us from the last great ice age are a geological blink of an eye. They also serve as a benchmark, revealing the dire changes human society is imposing on the earth's atmosphere and climate.

The glaciers of Mount Olympus visible from my ridgetop, the Hoh, the Blue, the White, and Ice River glaciers, are fed by some 240 inches of precipitation each year, mostly in the form of snow. By contrast, less than thirty-four miles to the northeast, in the rainshadow of the range, Sequim Prairie in the Dungeness Valley receives fewer than twenty inches. Spruce and hemlock forests of the coast give way to pines and junipers in the upper Dungeness, and Dungeness Valley farmers irrigate their crops. The diversity of habitats and plant communities born of this climatic variation contributes to the biological richness of the Olympics and deepens their beauty.

Below me, a tongue of coastal fog has worked its way up the Hoh Valley. Like the ghost of a glacier, it rises and subsides against the upper reaches of forest. As winds stir the fog layer, the muted thunder of the river rises and falls with the cadence of a distant sea. Low clouds and fog,

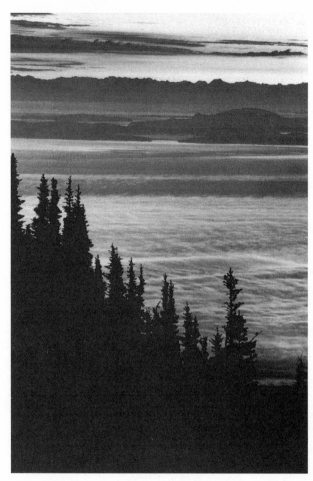

Morning fog lingers in the Puget Sound lowlands as seen from Deer Park in the northeast Olympics. The Cascade Range in the distance forms the eastern edge of the Puget Sound basin; Washington's San Juan Islands, in the middle ground, lie within the rainshadow of the Olympic Mountains. PHOTO BY JANIS BURGER.

so characteristic of these coastal valleys, are an essential part of the famed temperate rain forests of the Olympics. Beneath the cloud layer, through miles of unbroken valley forest, the moss- and lichen-draped limbs of rain forest trees sift the fog, letting a fine rain fall on shaded forest floors. Somewhere in the valley, herds of Roosevelt elk browse the lush understory of ferns and shrubs, and Douglas squirrels cut cones for their winter stores.

For more than a century, the rain forest valleys of the Olympics were prized by lumbermen and naturalists alike for their record-size trees. Sitka spruce, western hemlock, western red cedar, and Douglas fir all reach giant proportions here. Only during the past half-century have scientists begun to understand and appreciate the ecological complexity and

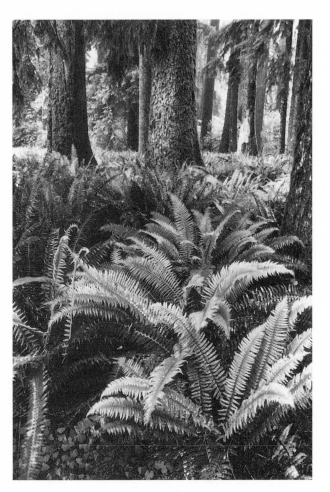

Olympic's cool, wet coastal climate nurtures lush temperate rain forests in west-side valleys. By a measure of biomass per acre, these forests are the most productive in the world. PHOTO BY JANIS BURGER.

richness of these forests and the number of species that depend on them for habitat.

Today, more than 85 percent of the ancient forests that once mantled the lowlands of the Pacific Northwest, including much of the lowland Olympic Peninsula, have been destroyed by logging. But as land managers turn their attention toward ecological restoration and sustainable resource use, the ancient forests protected by Olympic National Park and the genetic information and ecosystem functions preserved here are proving invaluable. In the meantime, the majestic forests of Olympic continue to offer solace, inspiration, and time-worn perspective to millions of visitors each year.

The isolation of the Olympic Peninsula was a fortunate accident of geography that allowed its forests to survive the nineteenth-century assault of mining, trapping, logging, and railroad building that altered so much of the western landscape. As a result, the Olympic Peninsula entered the twentieth century with its forests, wildlife communities, and watersheds wonderfully intact. To this day no through roads cross the Olympic Mountains, and more than sixty miles of wild, rugged coastline remain free of roads and developments. The rivers that slice their way out from the interior mountains follow their restless courses to the Pacific, the strait, or Puget Sound largely unfettered. And some valley farmers still have to repair fences after the elk move through.

But all places, even those we treasure most, are but points on a continuum, brief moments in the passage of time through a changing landscape. To appreciate a place like Olympic National Park is to understand the natural processes that created it and brought it to life. It is to understand, too, that the landscape and its life communities will continue to evolve and change. Ancient forests succumb to windstorms and fire, plant communities to changes in rainfall and climate. Because of their mobility, wildlife populations are susceptible to activities occurring outside the national park; Olympic's wild salmon runs are affected by logging and road management, as well as commercial fishing pressures on the high seas.

Until the past century, the land was its own best protector. Early park and national forest designations helped conserve much of the peninsula's resources. But road building and clear-cutting increased dramatically on public as well as private lands in recent decades, and as the human population increases, pressures to develop rivers, shorelines, and habitat areas persist. As conflicting pressures mount on land managers and public officials, it falls to each of us to assume stewardship for places like Olympic National Park. While natural forces continue to shape the evolution of the Olympic ecosystem, concerned and informed citizens have an increasing say about human-caused impacts to national park resources. Citizen involvement transformed the forest service's management of its remaining ancient forests. Informed public opinion has a similar role to play in land-use decisions affecting the larger ecosystems that surround and support our national parks.

The native cultures who occupied the Olympic Peninsula for thou-

More than 60 miles of rugged, undeveloped coastline are protected within the park. Offshore sea stacks and islands provide nesting habitats for thousands of seabirds as well as haul-outs for resident and migratory sea mammals. PHOTO BY JANIS BURGER.

sands of years lived in dynamic balance with the natural bounty that surrounded them. The coastal cultures of the Pacific Northwest are considered to be among the most sophisticated and highly developed native cultures north of Mexico. Several ancestral native villages still flourish along the Olympic shoreline. They remind us that humans living sustainably with the natural environment have always been a part of the Olympic ecosystem. Their cultural practices serve as models as we look for sustainable ways to live and work here today.

As I sip my tea, Mount Olympus and its retinue of peaks have fallen to the descending cloud layer, and valley clouds from the Hoh River rise to join other clouds creeping across ridges to the north and east. Soon I'll be seeing only my boot tips perched on a rock ledge over the void. Rain will be rattling against my tent before dark—already the wind has drowned out the river's distant song—and tomorrow will be much the same. Though I know it's probably futile, I'll give it a day or two before packing up and hiking out. I always do.

As I rummage through my pack for a sweater, two chestnut-backed chickadees land in a shrubby tree beside me, utter their chittery three-note song, puff up, and appear to hunker down. It's an old adaptive trait in these mountains: settling in to a turn in the weather. It helps keeps us honest. And when the skies clear, as they eventually do, we all emerge, as from a chrysalis of cloud, and dry our wings in the sparkling light of a world newly made.

Part 1

THE MOUNTAINS

CHAPTER 1

Shuffled Texts of Stone

THE Olympic Mountains must have come as a shock to the early European explorers who sailed the west coast of North America. For a thousand miles the coast ranges rose in gently folded hills, sere and treeless to the south, progressively greener and more deeply forested as seafarers sailed north. Suddenly, just past the forty-seventh parallel, the coast hills erupted into a high, rocky jumble of snow-clad summits, ice fields gleaming in the windy light.

Though explorers had plied Pacific Northwest waters since the mid-sixteenth century, the first sighting of the Olympic Mountains wasn't recorded until 1774. On a clear day in August that year, Spanish seafarer Juan Perez sighted the ice-bound summit of the Olympics' highest peak and recorded it in his ship's log as El Cerro de la Santa Rosalia. Fourteen years later, in 1788, British sea captain John Meares spotted the same peak from the Strait of Juan de Fuca to the north. Remote and hidden behind a retinue of ridges and peaks, the mountain struck the captain as a suitable dwelling place for the gods of this new land, and he named it Olympus after the mountain that was home to the gods of Greek mythology. British captain George Vancouver, who explored the inland waters of Puget Sound four years later, extended the name to the range of mountains that surrounded Meares's Olympus, and the title stuck.

Since "Mount Saint Rosalie" was the first geographic feature to be named by Europeans in what is now Washington State, one might suspect the Olympic Mountains would be among the first in Washington to be explored. Instead, the mystery that shrouded the mythic Greek Mount Olympus prevailed in this far corner of the New World for most of the next century. It wasn't until the late 1880s, at the close of the American frontier, that systematic explorations of the Olympic Mountains got under way. Although the native people who lived on the peninsula had developed a rich body of myths recounting the creation of this land, the veil of mystery surrounding the geological origins of the Olympic Mountains would remain until quite recently.

In his 1888 report to the secretary of the interior, Washington Territorial Governor Eugene Semple included a section on the Olympic Peninsula:

> The mountains seem to rise from the edge of the water, on
> both sides, in steep ascent to the line of perpetual snow, as
> though nature had designed to shut up this spot for her safe
> retreat forever. . . . In tradition alone has man penetrated its
> fastness and trod the isles of its continuous woods.

The *Seattle Press* picked up the call for an expedition that would at last unlock "the mystery which wraps the land encircled by the snow capped Olympic range," and the following year, a group backed by the *Press* began a celebrated exploration of the Olympics. It was not the first party to venture into the heart of the interior Olympics, nor the best organized or equipped, but the members of the *Press* party achieved lasting notoriety for their dogged and persistent traverse through the heart of the range during one of the worst winters on record. Three grueling months after starting up the Elwha River in December 1889, expedition leader James Christie and Captain Charles Barnes slogged through deep snow to a ridge crest north of Mount Wilder and at last laid eyes on the interior mountains. Barnes described the scene in his journal: "Range after range of peaks, snow-clad from base to summit, extended as far as the eye could reach, in splendid confusion."

The confusion was more Barnes's than the mountains'; his party had just spent weeks ascending a tributary divide only to realize they had to descend 3,000 feet back to the main valley of the Elwha. But his words would prove prophetic in more ways than the captain could know. A splendid confusion reigned among geologists banging away at Olympic rocks for the better part of the next century.

Field geology, like all natural science, is a process of building on past knowledge, evaluating new data, reexamining assumptions, questioning earlier hypotheses. The knowledge that geologists have gained to date about the origins of the Olympic Mountains, though extensive, is certainly not the last word—as new dating techniques applied to Olympic rocks have recently shown. Nonetheless, the past few decades have proved a watershed in our understanding of the geologic story of the Olympics. The plate tectonics revolution of the 1960s shattered prevailing theories of the Olympics' origins—as it did all of theoretical geology—and the pieces are still being reassembled. Its impact on geology at the time was equal to that of Darwin's theories on nineteenth-century biological science. Suddenly, the young, rough-hewn rocks of the Olympic Mountains were seen through a new lens, and the deeper story of this rugged range, so recently added to the North American continent, began to come to light.

Geologists now know that the Olympic Mountains were formed of sedimentary and volcanic rocks, both laid down over millions of years on the abyssal plain of the ocean floor and submerged continental shelf. Seafloor sediments were rafted in, crumpled against the volcanics, and the whole mix plastered onto the edge of the continent like a massive barge running aground on a quiet shoal. But how we've come to know this story, and the painstaking work by which geologists pieced together the scrambled puzzle of the Olympics' orogeny, is as compelling as the sheer heights and shaded canyons of this long-hidden range. That story opens a window into the depth and beauty of these mountains as surely as an evening alone on a ridgetop, listening for the first star.

PIECES OF THE GEOLOGICAL PUZZLE

Early observers in the Olympics assumed that, like many other mountain ranges, bedrock of the mountainous core of the Olympics must be made up of granite and gneiss. These rocks were commonly found as pebbles and boulders in streams flowing north and east out of the mountains. The *Press* party explorers brought back a first glimpse of the real story; Barnes in particular was able to correctly identify much of the core rock

Mount Constance and the rugged east Olympics are carved from marine lavas that flowed onto the continental shelf and seafloor during the Eocene. As the ocean plate collided with the continent, these lavas and associated sedimentary rocks were upended and shoved against the continent's edge to form the Crescent Formation.
PHOTO BY JANIS BURGER.

as slate and sandstone. But the specimens they had gathered and packed during months in the mountains were lost when their raft hit a logjam and capsized in the Quinault River. Barnes somehow managed to save his field notes.

From such inauspicious beginnings, the story of the origin of the Olympics slowly began to unfold.

In his 1888 report, Governor Semple had described the "continuous array of snow-clad peaks" that bordered Hood Canal to the east and the Strait of Juan de Fuca to the north as composed of basalt, a tough, dark, volcanic rock common to ocean floors. Bulbous "pillow" structures the size of giant watermelons in the eastern Olympics suggest that the lava that formed these rocks erupted underwater and cooled quickly. By the 1930s, Charles Weaver, a geologist from the University of Washington, had identified these basalt rocks as part of the Crescent Formation, a thick horseshoe of basalt that rings the mountains on their north, east, and south sides and extends from Central Vancouver Island in British Columbia south into Oregon. Crescent Formation basalts form the bedrock of some of the Olympics' most visible and dramatic peaks: Storm King, Mount Angeles, and Tyler Peak to the north; Mount Constance and the double summits of the Brothers on the east; and Mount Tebo and Colonel Bob to the south.

By piecing together the Crescent basalts with the sedimentary rocks of the interior Olympics and the younger sediments that lie outside the basalt horseshoe, Weaver reasoned that the Olympic Mountains formed an anticline, that is, a giant upward fold in the earth's crust that also tilts down toward Seattle. Subsequent erosion "unroofed" the Olympics, exposing the sedimentary rocks of the interior. This theory neatly explained how the basalt horseshoe of the Crescent Formation formed around what were believed to be the older rocks of the interior. Fossils found in the Crescent rocks dated to the Eocene epoch, about 45 million to 60 million years ago, but no fossils had been located in the sedimentary core rocks. Weaver's anticline theory of the Olympics' formation, the mountains' folding and uplift caused by "tectonic forces deep in the earth's crust," would remain intact for the next forty years. But throughout that time, the story became increasingly complex, and continuing field research brought almost as many questions as answers.

Natural oil seeps, first noted in Olympic sea cliffs in 1881, touched off an oil rush at the turn of the twentieth century. All of the more than a hundred wells drilled were unsuccessful, but company geologists located fossil foraminifera in the sedimentary rocks. These microscopic, chambered protozoa were ubiquitous in the earth's oceans over a long period of time, and they evolved rapidly. This enabled paleontologists to date layers of marine rock with a high degree of accuracy. The age of these fossils showed that some of the core rocks were actually younger than the Crescent basalts. This finding cast doubt on the anticline theory. If the theory was to hold, it would need serious modification. The plot was beginning to thicken.

Studies of the Olympics' rocks intensified in the years leading to World War II when manganese was in great demand. With work done by Charles Park Jr. of the U.S. Geological Survey, additional pieces of the puzzle began to fall into place, and an improved geologic map of the Olympics was developed. Park found even younger fossils in the core rocks. They dated from the Oligocene epoch, around 22 million to 38 million years ago. The core rocks were incredibly faulted, broken up, and restacked, so geologists assumed the basalts were that way too. Park's work and research done later by Wilbert Danner and other geologists from the University of Washington established the age and distribution of many of the Olympics' rocks. Scientists now knew what the mountains were made of, how the rocks came to be, and when some of them were deposited. Some of Barnes's splendor was beginning to wear off the confusion. But the larger story of how the mountains were born remained hidden.

THE FLOOR OF AN ANCIENT SEA

Throughout Tertiary time, which began about 60 million years ago, the coast of North America was located farther to the east than it is now. The area that was to become the Olympic Peninsula lay quietly beneath the waves of a coastal sea. Rivers pouring off the western edge of the continent carried silt, sand, pebbles, and rocks. Rivers, or perhaps a great single river—an ancestral Fraser or Columbia—eroded the low mountains of old northwestern North America. Where rivers met salt water they slowed, dropped their load of materials and formed deltas on the continental shelf, just as they do today.

As river deltas stacked higher and steeper, earthquakes regularly triggered massive collapses. Undersea landslides of sediments peeled off deltas and flowed out over the shelf onto deep ocean floors in dense riverine slurries called turbidity currents. These undersea rivers formed channels and fans across the deep ocean floor. Propelled by the density of sediment-heavy water, they flowed in some cases for hundreds of miles. The current Cascadia channel, fed by the Fraser, western Olympic and Columbia rivers, extends 1,300 miles across the Pacific Ocean basin. Depending on the frequency and nature of the submarine landslide events, most sands settled out in thick beds in deep channels. Some sands, silt, and mud overflowed the channels and fanned out over miles; these became interbedded with layers of finer sediments as they settled through calm water. As the process repeated over millions of years, and layers thickened in the cold depths of the sea, sedimentary rocks formed. Sands compacted into sandstone, finer sediments into siltstone and shale. Occasionally slurries would contain pebbles, forming conglomerate, or broken chips of mud and rock, which became breccia. These black chips are ubiquitous in sandstone pebbles scattered over western Olympic rivers and beaches.

Thick, erosion-resistant beds of sandstone in "fossil" sea-bottom channels have been tilted on end and now compose the bedrock of the highest peaks of the Olympics' inner core, including Mount Olympus, Mount Anderson, and most of the Bailey Range.

Between the turbidity channels, thinner, weaker beds of sandstone, siltstone, and shale stacked up in layers. These formations are more subject to erosion, but evidence of these rhythmic beds is found today throughout the mountains. Particularly noticeable outcrops appear on Blue Mountain along the Deer Park Road. Sandstones, made up of grains of quartz, feldspar, and mica can be easily distinguished. Shales, made up of clay minerals, are composed of grains much too fine to see. Very few of the sedimentary rocks of the Olympics were buried deep enough or long enough for intense metamorphism to occur. It is estimated that sedimentary rocks accumulated on the seafloor off the continental coast in the area to become the Olympic Mountains were five miles deep.

Geologists working in the Olympics marveled at the intensity of deformation in the sedimentary core rocks. Instead of neat beds stacked up chronologically like the rocks of the Grand Canyon, strata laid out horizontally along the ocean floor were bent, broken, smashed, smeared, and restacked as though kneaded by a very large baker. Rarely do rocks become this deformed without having undergone extensive metamorphism. The degree of deformation of the Olympic rocks bears witness to the tremendous forces that built these mountains. But before plunging into that part of the story, we'll need to step back a few decades and revisit the state of geological knowledge as it stood in the 1950s.

THE PLATE TECTONICS REVOLUTION

World War II has been described as a technological piñata. Among other breakthroughs, sensitive technologies developed for locating German submarines proved a windfall for oceanographers mapping the ocean floor. In the years that followed the war, detailed topographic maps of the sea bottom revealed some fascinating features. Long mountain ranges marked by central rift valleys traversed the centers of most ocean floors. Seafloors rippled off along either side of these ridges, then dropped into deep trenches that bordered the edges of continents. Geologists were able to measure the orientation of the earth's magnetism as recorded in ocean floors. They discovered some surprising patterns.

Ocean floors are composed of basalt, and basalts are rich in iron. As molten lava cools to form basalt, its iron-oxide magnetite crystals align with the earth's magnetic field. Scientists have long known that the earth reverses its magnetic field every several hundred thousand years; the last magnetic reversal was about 720,000 years ago. Cooling basalt retains the magnetic polarity of the earth at the time it solidifies. Scientists working in the north Pacific discovered a striped pattern of magnetic reversals spreading out symmetrically along both sides of the ocean ridges. The north-south-running patterns were identical to each other. Geologists identified similar magnetic reversals within older lavas on land. Later core dating showed that ocean floors became progressively older the farther one progressed from midocean ridges, with the oldest dates near the edges of continents. But the ocean floor dates in general were curiously young. At 150 million years, the oldest dated seafloors proved much younger than the oldest rocks on the continent, which are 3.8 billion years old. This raised an obvious question: What happened to the older seafloors?

By the mid-1960s, an explanation emerged. It became clear that seafloors are formed along central spreading ridges by lava upwelling from the earth's mantle. As ridges form, new seafloor spreads out along either side, creating plates. These ocean plates interact with other plates also floating on the earth's mantle; there are about a dozen worldwide. Some plates are continents; some are part continent, part ocean floor. Some plates override each other; some collide, giving birth to mountain ranges; others split apart to form new oceans. Earthquakes measured along the coastal margins of some continental plates, including in the Puget Sound area, indicate that the denser and heavier ocean plates are bending down under the lighter continental plates in a process called subduction. As subducting seafloors descend beneath continental plates, they are metamorphosed into even denser rock, then melt to form lava. Some of this lava returns to the surface through faults and conduits in the earth's crust

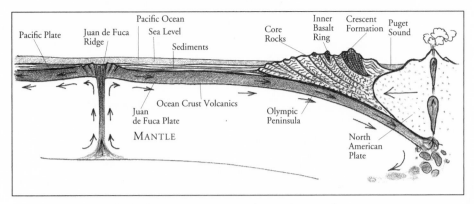

A cross section of the Olympic Mountains and Juan de Fuca Plate.
DRAWING BY DIANE GUSSET.

as volcanoes; some remains deep beneath the surface to form batholiths and sills. Volcanic chains and arcs commonly form inland of subduction zones. The Cascade volcanoes bear this relationship to the subducting Juan de Fuca plate, which lies off the Northwest coast. Similar volcanic arcs make up other parts of the "Ring of Fire" that circles the Pacific Ocean, delineating the boundaries of the subducting Pacific plate as well as numerous small plates.

Scientists are uncertain as to what drives the plates, but a growing consensus seems to favor the earth's primary force: gravity. The earth's crust, whether continent or ocean bottom, floats on a semiliquid or plastic mantle that surrounds the planet's molten nickel core. As molten material rises along ocean ridges and new rock is added to ocean floors, the warm, new ocean crust tends to float high on the upper mantle. Older, cooler parts of the plates, when encountering lighter, drifting continents, may be pulled back down into the mantle by gravity.

But in the area of the Northwest coast that was to become the Olympic Peninsula, the process became complicated.

FORMATION OF THE OLYMPICS

Geologists are still reconstructing events that led to the formation of the Olympic Mountains, and new research is giving rise to slightly differing interpretations. For now, this much is accepted. Around 60 million years ago, two large ocean plates were colliding with the westward drifting

North American plate. The fast-moving Kula plate was pushing north against the continent's edge at about six inches per year. Just south of it, the Farallon plate was striking the continent due northeast. The oblique angle of the Kula plate, as it encountered the dogleg formed by the north-west-trending edge of Vancouver Island and the north-trending edge of the Cascade Mountains may have weakened, stretched, and torn the edge of the continent. This created a deep marine rift basin parallel to the continent's edge. This long rent in the continent's margin allowed massive plumes of lava to erupt into the submerged rift basin. Accumulating over a period from about 45 million to 60 million years ago, these lavas eventually built a chain of volcanic seamounts that stretched from present-day Ucluelet on Vancouver Island to Coos Bay, Oregon. The volume of lava that erupted was stupendous, as much as 25,000 cubic miles.

We know by the presence of pillow lavas and marine fossils that nearly all the basalts erupted beneath the sea. But rare exposures of columnar basalt palisades in the upper part of the Crescent Formation along Hood Canal indicate that some lavas topped out above sea level. Today the marine basalts of the Crescent Formation form the foundation of the Washington and Oregon Coast Range.

Sedimentary rocks continued to accumulate and deepen on both sides of the basalts, filling coastal basins and spreading out in channels and fans across the deep ocean floor. The Kula plate pushed north to disappear beneath Alaska, but the subducting Farallon plate continued to raft its massive load of deep-ocean sediments against the continent's edge. Softer and more pliable, the sedimentary rocks jammed against the tough metamorphic rocks of the continent and were scraped off like earth before a bulldozer.

Geologists estimate that over the past 45 million years, as much as 3,000 miles of seafloor subducted beneath the North American plate. The layers of sedimentary rocks carried with it were bent, broken, smeared, and plastered against the edge of the continent like a slow, multicar collision.

Then, beginning about 20 million years ago, the sedimentary rocks and basalts, previously mangled by intense thrust faulting, folding, and deformation were subjected to further abuse. For 5 million years most of the older rocks were up-folded into a giant, eastward-plunging arch. The

Upended beds of sedimentary rocks alternate with ribs of volcanic breccia on the shoulder of Mount Angeles. The breccias formed as lava flows picked up fragments of existing rock. Mixed beds like these show that Olympic rocks formed close to the continent's edge. PHOTO BY JANIS BURGER.

arch, first noted by Weaver in the 1930s, extends 125 miles north to south and stretches eastward from the west-central Olympics almost to Hood Canal. It is characterized by, and ultimately responsible for, the open-to-the-west horseshoe shape of the Crescent Formation basalts. In 1975, U.S. Geological Survey geologist Rowland Tabor, the most respected and prolific of Washington's geologic mappers, reasoned that the arch formed as a result of continued plate interaction at the Vancouver Island–Cascade Range dogleg in the continent's edge. Although subsequent hypotheses linking erosion rates and mountain-building processes have been developed, Tabor's elegant explanation is still favored by many geologists.

As the plate drove its conveyor belt of rocks against the concave coastline, continual thrust faulting—during which sheets of rock bent, broke, and overrode each other—pushed the Olympics rocks, including the basalts, upward and southwestward over the ocean plate. It's not surprising that one geologist described the whole Olympic range as standing up on end. In retrospect, it's a small wonder that early geologists were able to make any sense of these rocks at all.

Today, the boundary where the sedimentary core rocks ran up against the upended base of the basalt ridge and were thrust beneath it is marked by the Hurricane Ridge fault. Beginning at Cape Flattery in the northwest corner of the peninsula, the fault extends eastward behind Mount Angeles and Blue Mountain before bending south to trace the western wall of the rugged line of east Olympic summits from Buckhorn Mountain to Mount Washington and Mount Ellinor. From there, a southern extension of the fault bends westward to the Lake Quinault area. On one side of the fault lie the Crescent basalts, on the other the sedimentary rocks of the core. A series of roughly parallel thrust faults echoes through the interior Olympics, where the core rocks themselves broke and were thrust beneath each other.

But as one might expect in the Olympics, the seam isn't quite that clean. With all the folding and faulting accompanying subduction, large sections of Crescent Formation or younger basalt were sheared off and placed within the eastern core rocks. This "inner basalt ring" rears up in the jagged spires of the Needles above Royal Basin and Sawtooth Ridge at the headwaters of the Hamma Hamma River. These formations were far more resistant to erosion than the sedimentary rocks around them. Today they offer some of the best rock climbing in the Olympics.

At some point, between 10 million and 20 million years ago, the Olympic Mountains began to rise. Almost immediately, as the ancestral Olympics emerged from the sea, the erosive powers of running water and gravity began working on the young rocks, inscribing the outlines of the mountains and river valleys we know today.

CARVING OF THE MOUNTAINS

The same sea that cooled lavas and sorted out sands and silts brought forth the weather that began to reclaim the Olympic rocks grain by grain. Rainfall and melting snow moving across the surface of rocks found weaknesses: faults softened by grinding and pressure, the less resistant siltstones and shales. Aided by gravity and the abrasive power of the silt, sand, and gravel they contained, streams quickly began to carry the mountains away. As the Olympics rose higher and intercepted more moisture from the sea, streams and rivers swelled in size. Larger streams carried more materials, gradients steepened, and the cutting powers of streams increased. The rivers of the western Olympics, the ancestral Hoh, Queets, and Quinault rivers, carving into strike-slip faults along weaker sedimentary rocks, captured larger watersheds than the streams draining the more resistant basalt bedrock to the east. The Elwha River, which flows north, captured the largest watershed in the Olympics, eventually cutting into the heart of the uplifting mountain mass. But the finish work, the final sculpting of the Olympic peaks and ridges and deep valleys of today, came only with the turn in the earth's climate that ushered in the Ice Age. In the meantime, vast amounts of rock were eroded off the uplifting mountains and carried out to the continental shelf and ocean floor, laying down the grains and strata for ranges of mountains yet to be born.

The Olympic Mountains continue to rise today—not much in laypersons' eyes, but very rapidly by geologic standards: one-hundredth of an inch per year. The most recent pulse of uplift followed the retreat of the continental ice sheet about 13,000 years ago. The Farallon plate that gave birth to the Olympics has almost totally subducted. A remnant of the old plate, renamed the Juan de Fuca plate, remains off the Northwest coast. About 300 miles in width, it is presently sinking beneath the continent at a rate of about two inches a year. Research has linked that process not only to our currently active Cascade volcanoes, but to major earthquakes that in the not-too-distant past have shaken the region to its foundations.

The Juan de Fuca plate meets North America along the 800-mile Cascadia subduction zone, the largest thrust fault in the continental United States. The colliding plates jam and "stick," sometimes for centuries. When the subducting plate breaks loose and the continental plate recoils, it rocks the Northwest with a magnitude eight or nine "megathrust" or subduction earthquake. In 1987, U.S. Geological Survey geologist Brian Atwater discovered evidence of the most recent subduction quake along the Washington coast 300 years ago. Spruce forests were inundated by seawater in coastal estuaries. Upland forests subsided

Geological map of the Olympic Peninsula, adapted from Tabor, 1978.

MAP PREPARED BY OLYMPIC NATIONAL PARK.

and large deposits of wave-driven sand flooded inland. Tree ring dating showed the flooding took place in 1700. Historical records indicate that coastal fishing villages in Japan experienced a series of earthquake-triggered tidal waves, or tsunamis, at that time, washing away houses and boats and flooding rice paddies. Calculations placed the date for the subduction quake at January 26, 1700. This was nearly a century before European contact with the Northwest coast, but stories passed down among coastal tribes describe shaking, jumping, and trembling of the earth and huge waves that washed canoes into the trees.

Geologists have calculated that the North American plate is thrust faulted over the Juan de Fuca plate, causing a subduction quake every 200 to 1,000 years. Different earthquake patterns in Puget Sound suggest the Juan de Fuca plate might be pulled apart every twenty years as it grinds deep beneath the continent. Meanwhile, Mount Saint Helens is erupting anew, and small earthquakes throughout western Washington and British Columbia suggest that big things are afoot beneath this restless corner of the earth. The window the Olympic Mountains offers into the deep tectonic processes of the earth's past may also provide glimpses of tectonic changes to come.

READING THE ROCKS TO HURRICANE RIDGE

The seventeen-mile drive to Hurricane Ridge provides an easy glimpse into the foundation of the Olympic Mountains and the processes that formed them. The Hurricane Ridge Road leads from the lowlands along the Strait of Juan de Fuca up through the undersea lavas and related sediments of the Crescent Formation and out onto the high, windy edge of the mountainous core. From its lower end in Port Angeles, the escarpment of Mount Angeles lifting abruptly out of the upper forests announces the Crescent Formation basalts. As the road gains elevation, it enters a series of tunnels cut though cliffs of pillow basalt. The "pillows," each about two feet in width, formed as the surface of erupting lava cooled quickly in shallow seas, giving the rock face a lumpy, doughlike texture. Higher up, on the mountain's northeast shoulder, upended flows of volcanic breccia alternate with layers of shale to form a series of vertical fluted chimneys. The chimneys record intermittent lava flows that picked up chunks of sedimentary layering on the seafloor. During lapses between the flows, silt sifted down out of turbid ocean water to form the interbedded shale. The softer shale eroded more quickly, leaving these pronounced fluted chimneys.

Past the tunnels, the Hurricane Ridge Road cuts through a shoulder of Klahhane Ridge, where beds of rare red limestone, sandstone, and siltstone are interspersed with darker basalts. The limestone formed as microscopic skeletons of plankton and shells of foraminifera rained down over centuries onto the soft muds of quiet ocean floors. Their red color

As lava spilled out onto the ocean bottom, it cooled rapidly, forming lumps or "pillows." Pillow lavas can be seen throughout the northern, eastern, and southern Olympics. PHOTO BY JANIS BURGER.

comes from iron oxides in the basalt. Not long before reaching the top of Hurricane Ridge, the road passes the Hurricane Ridge fault, that major juncture between the peripheral rocks of the Crescent Formation and the sedimentary rocks of the core of the Olympics. Here, the thin-bedded sandstones and mudstones that underlie the Crescent basalts become bent, twisted, sheared, and deformed where the core rocks were thrust beneath the basalts, upending them and forcing them against the continent's edge.

The text of that process—the awesome forces that crumple up mountains and build continents—is written indelibly into bedrock of the Olympic Mountains, scraped clean by glaciers, and readily accessible. As we've seen, the Olympics have been a thorny text to decipher, and geologists are just beginning to glean the range's deeper secrets. What they find will not only provide us with a more accurate picture of how the Olympics came to be; we also may be given a clear snapshot of that eternal dynamic by which the earth's youthful seafloors and the ancient bones of the continents give birth to rough new lands.

The northern Bailey Range from Hurricane Ridge. Core rocks of the interior Olympics are composed primarily of marine sediments. Siltstones, sandstones, and shales were laid down on the ocean floor by rivers beginning about 65 million years ago.
PHOTO BY JANIS BURGER.

Past the Hurricane Ridge fault, the rocks become increasingly more deformed—and confusing—as one ventures into the core. But once the road swings around Hurricane Ridge and the interior Olympics sweep into perspective, the problems of geology give way to the grand view. A chiseled sea of mountains, crest after ragged crest, leaps into view, a more splendid confusion of ridges, canyons, and peaks than a pilgrim could ask for. To the southeast, the bare broken summits of the eastern core are dominated by Mount Anderson in the distance. To the south, the deep, timbered valley of the Elwha River carries the eye into the heart of the mountains where the snowcapped peaks of the Bailey Range stretch away in a high, broken wall. Behind them, a slight bit hazy with distance, the summit of Mount Olympus breaks through its perpetual snowfields and glaciers, distant, blue, and implacable.

The mountains seem poised at the crest of a wave. And in a sense they are: cast in from the sea, lifted briefly to their wintry heights, and brought down inevitably by the agents of gravity. The Olympic Mountains make up only a tiny corner of earth, battered by winds and washed with ocean rain. Yet this small, rugged range encloses the beauty of a newly born earth, and like the brushstrokes in a painting by Sesshu or van Gogh, traces the magic by which it was brought to life.

A LONG VIEW OF AN EPHEMERAL RANGE

On a cool, drizzly day in August, I visited the Hurricane Ridge fault with geologist Rowland Tabor. Tabor spent ten years mapping the fine points of Olympic geology for the U.S. Geological Survey. His 1975 book, *Geology of Olympic National Park,* is still the classic guide to understanding Olympic rocks and serves amateurs and seasoned geologists equally.

We walked the length of the Hurricane Ridge fault, following the near-vertical strata, pecking discreetly at the rock (in a chapter on the Olympics published in the *Geological Society of America Centennial Field Guide,* Tabor advises his colleagues to keep their rock hammers concealed "to prevent misunderstandings" with park rangers). At the fault, where sedimentary rocks were thrust against the Crescent basalts, and beyond it into the core, the rocks were twisted and bent almost beyond recognition. Tabor explained that the intensive deformation of the core rocks was part of the reason these sediments were scraped off onto the continent rather than subducted under the crust. "It all happened in such a short time that the Olympic rocks never got buried deep enough for serious metamorphism to occur," he said. "That's why, unlike the Cascades, there's no gneiss or schist in the Olympics." He explained that the big peaks in the interior, such as Mount Olympus and Mount Anderson, were primarily sandstone, the weaker shales and siltstones having dropped out and eroded away. Because of the sedimentary nature of the Olympic Mountains, Tabor refers to them as "ephemeral." It was only later that day, as we indulged in a bit of speculation on the long-term future of the Olympics, that I learned what he meant by that.

We were walking back to the car just below Hurricane Ridge. Green, forested slopes swept up into rocky ridgetops. I asked Tabor how long it will be before the spreading Juan de Fuca plate propels the Olympic Peninsula onto the continental mainland, where it can take its rightful place alongside its earlier tectonic arrivals: the Northern Cascade and

Okanogan subcontinents. He answered with his usual depth of perspective.

"Like all the coast ranges, the Olympics are an ephemeral welt," he explained. "These mountains will erode away and disappear long before they can become part of the geological record of the continent." He looked around him, smiled, then added, "We're lucky to be around to appreciate them."

CHAPTER 2

Legacies of Ice

I T was late spring, still early in the climbing season for Mount Olympus, and the weather was that familiar mix of low overcast and high wind that climbers call "unstable." Two friends and I had left a chilly camp at Elk Lake and followed a route by flashlight up through Glacier Meadows to the moraine above Blue Glacier. The trail was still deeply buried in winter snow, and a litter of limbs, needles, and lichen blown down from the forest canopy further darkened the route. We reached the moraine just as the overcast sky began to brighten, roped up, strapped on crampons, and began to thread our way up the broad frozen slope of the glacier.

As dawn broke, a wintry landscape of snow and ice fields spread out before us. Dark shapes of cliffs rose into the cloud ceiling, and the occasional *schush* of snow and pebbles whispered down shallow gullies. Light flurries ghosted in on the wind, and the summit remained hidden in cloud.

This was my first visit to the icy realm of Mount Olympus, and though I've returned often in the years that followed, those initial sensations remain crystal clear. As we passed beyond the last shapes of alpine trees, we had the distinct sense of stepping back into an earlier time. That sense deepened as we climbed the crystalline slope that led to the crest of the Snow Dome. The high, sloping shelf of the dome spilled its burden of snow and ice in an icefall to the glacier below. As the ceiling lifted, the lower shoulders of the summit rocks drifted into view: snow dusted, rimed with hoarfrost, and whistling faintly in the mountain wind.

At 7,965 feet in elevation, Mount Olympus and the retinue of peaks that surround it carry the aura of an arctic island in the temperate sea of Olympic's forests. Fueled by relatively warm, moisture-laden winds from the Pacific Ocean a mere thirty-five miles away, Mount Olympus receives up to 240 inches of precipitation each year, the highest amount in the lower forty-eight states. It falls mostly as snow, more than a hundred feet of it in the course of a winter. The snowpack feeds a prodigious system of glaciers on Olympus—the third largest in the contiguous United States. Nine alpine glaciers descend from the upper snow slopes into the headwater valleys of the Hoh and Queets rivers. They hold nearly 80 percent of the glacier ice in the Olympic Mountains. Given the amount of snow that falls on these mountains, it's not surprising that the glaciers of Mount Olympus form at a lower elevation and descend farther into their valleys than anywhere else in the lower forty-eight states. Blue Glacier is the largest of the Olympics' 266 glaciers; it descends two and three-quarters miles to as low as 4,049 feet in elevation, where it pours its opaque, glacier flour–laden stream into the headwaters of the Hoh.

The Blue Glacier is a stunning contemporary example of the shape and dynamics of a force that thoroughly transformed not only these mountains but much of the northern landscape of North America. It is also one of the most intensively studied glaciers in the country.

In geologic terms, glaciers are a recent phenomenon in the Olympics, appearing only over the past 2 million years. When considering them, we need to hone our sense of geologic time—from thinking in terms of millions of years to thousands. In the case of the Little Ice Age, we can further reduce that time scale to mere centuries—barely time for the dust to settle on the page of an open book.

In the relatively short geological life span of the Olympics, the recent 1.8-million-year period of the Pleistocene epoch was a brief interval, the shadow of its passing still upon us. But its effect on the rolling meadowlands and smooth, water-carved preglacial Olympics was profound. Had it not occurred, the Olympic Mountains might resemble the gentle, folded hills of the Coast Ranges to the south. And the unique biological diversity so characteristic of these mountains would surely never have developed.

However recent and brief their tenure here, glaciers marshaled incredible force in shaping the face of the Olympic Mountains as we know them today. From serrated ridges and steep mountain walls to rounded foothills and broad valley floors, evidence of the Olympics' glacial legacy is carved irrevocably into the breadth and texture of the land. Not only did alpine glaciers sculpt the present shape and character of the landscape; large ice sheets advancing from the north wielded immense power in sculpting and forming the character of the entire region. That the Olympics form a peninsula today, wreathed by seawater and isolated by a deep, wide river valley to the south, was largely the work of the Cordilleran ice sheet pulsing south from its chill northerly realm. And with all the grace of a hundred thousand D-8 Cats with an ocean of diesel to burn, it changed things around some.

DAWN OF THE PLEISTOCENE

The forces that ushered in the glacial epoch are complex, involving grand-scale interactions among continents, oceans, the atmosphere, and the solar system itself. It's evident from the geological record elsewhere that there have been successions of glacial ages in the past, as far back as 2.3 billion years ago, each lasting tens of millions of years. Climatologists suspect that these events were triggered by a combination of the earth's tectonic forces (movements of continental plates, collision and uplift, and the birth of oceans), and their resultant effects on atmospheric circulation and ocean currents. Scientists generally agree that for an ice age to occur, much of the earth's continental landmass must be located in the higher latitudes, a condition certainly present in the late Cenozoic, which preceded the Pleistocene. As plates collide and ranges are uplifted, as they were in western North America and central Asia during the Cenozoic, continental crust is exposed above the level of soil and plants, and continents reflect more of the sun's warmth, reducing the amount of solar energy available at critical northern latitudes. Higher ground also collects more snow. It's also clear that reduced summer melting rather than increased winter accumulation of snow is key to the formation of ice caps, from which continental glaciers are born. Once perpetual ice becomes established, it reflects more of the sun's warmth away from the earth, and a ripple effect spreads through the atmosphere and ocean currents, leading to feedback loops of cloudier skies, less warmth—and more ice.

Once a glacial age begins, cyclical variations or glaciations within it are triggered by subtler factors involving the earth's pattern of rotation and tilt and the solar cycles of the sun. We also know that unlike today, two critical greenhouse gases, carbon dioxide and methane, were less plentiful in the atmosphere during glacial times, allowing radiant energy from the earth's surface to escape into space, but it's unclear why. The ice ages that spawned the glaciers that changed the face of the Olympics began with a gradual cooling of the earth's climate around 2.5 million years ago.

Whether an alpine glacier flowing into a valley or a continental ice sheet grinding down from the north, glaciers are formed and behave in essentially the same way. Simply stated, glaciers form in regions when winter snowfall exceeds summer melt. In the Olympics today the snow line (the elevation where snow lingers from year to year) occurs at a relatively low 5,500 feet, slightly higher in the dryer eastern Olympics. By contrast, snow line in the northern Rockies, with that region's warmer summers and lower precipitation, lies at around 10,000 feet. Closer to home, the snow line in the Cascade Mountains occurs at about 8,000 feet. Above the snow line, the process whereby winter snow compacts into glacial ice is gradual but complete.

During the warming days of spring, individual snowflakes are melted, compacted, and recrystallized into rounded granules, or corn snow. As compaction increases, a hard, permeable crust of firn snow develops. Under the weight and pressure of continued compaction, air is driven from the firn, and snow granules melt at point of contact, meltwater then refreezing between them. The interwoven, crystalline ice grains that result become further deformed as a glacier becomes "plastic" and under the pressure of weight and gravity begins to flow downhill.

This formative process, the birthing of glacier ice, requires a year and at least a 100- to 200-foot accumulation of snow. It also mirrors, in microcosm and in a radically telescoped time scale, the formation of sedimentary rocks. Snow is an eolian sediment. Deposited by wind, layered and compacted, firn snow resembles sedimentary rock. Glacier ice, having recrystallized under tremendous pressure and stress, shares similarities with metamorphic rock. Deep ice melting against substrate mimics deeply buried rock strata melding with the earth's mantle.

Today, these big, pliant, blue-white rocks abound on Mount Olympus, where annual snow accumulation more than accommodates them, as well as on many other high summits in the interior Olympics. Glaciers fare less well in the dryer eastern Olympics, but this wasn't always the case. The scene that greeted my friends and me that chill morning on Mount Olympus was fairly common throughout these mountains on several occasions throughout the Pleistocene, and evidence of glacial carving can be seen everywhere throughout the range. Few are the Olympic peaks whose symmetry and lines do not reflect the sculpting hand of glacier ice. And fewer still are the river valleys left unshaped by glaciers moving their slow trains of rock-bound ice into the lowlands.

FINAL SCULPTING OF THE OLYMPICS

The Olympic Mountains were affected not only by repeated advances of alpine glaciers, but also by the Cordilleran ice sheet, which pushed south into the area from the Coast Mountains and inland ranges of northern British Columbia at least six times over the last 2 million years. The tracks of alpine glaciers are a bit more difficult to read, as successive glacial advances tend to erase evidence of earlier glaciations. Geologists studying the moraines of alpine glaciers on the west side of the Olympics have identified four major alpine advances, but core samples from ocean sediments indicate there were more than twenty periods of increased glaciation throughout the Pleistocene. It was during this time that the final sculpting of the Olympics took place.

As with most mountain ranges, the alpine glaciers that carved the Olympics tended to follow drainage patterns already incised by rivers and streams, primarily along strike-slip faults. But where the gentler hands of flowing water tended to bend, meander, and flow around resistant strata or formations of rock, the freight trains of glaciers roared right through. As a result, alpine (now valley) glaciers tended to widen and straighten preexisting stream-cut valleys in the Olympics, shaving back spur ridges and flattening river bottoms into characteristic U-shaped valley floors. This is most evident today in the large western Olympic river valleys such as the Hoh, Queets, and Quinault. In contrast, stream-cut valleys have a marked V shape. As glaciers flowed down the Olympics' valleys, rocks as well as river cobble, gravels, and sand frozen into the bottoms of glaciers acted like huge rasps scouring the bedrock. Large boulders and flakes of rock also became frozen into glaciers and were plucked and carried along.

When summer melting exceeded winter accumulation, valley glaciers receded, leaving behind their load of rock and debris. Piles of talus and rockfall that accumulated on the tops of glaciers sloughed off their sides to become lateral moraines. Recent lateral moraines are prominent along the northeast side of Blue Glacier and in several deglaciated alpine basins such as those at the head of Royal and Cameron creeks in the Dungeness watershed. The cross-valley piles of rock dumped off the stationary or retreating terminus (or snout) of a glacier are terminal moraines. Quinault Lake in the southwest corner of Olympic National Park formed behind a terminal moraine of the Quinault Valley glacier.

Tremendous amounts of rock and rubble were transported from mountains to valley floors by Olympic glaciers. Materials sorted into rough layers of sand, gravel, and boulders by glacier meltwaters are referred to as *outwash*; unsorted materials are called *drift*. Both are easily seen along the cutbanks of lower rivers or in storm-cut sea cliffs along the Olympic coast. Outwash plains resemble alluvial fans often found at the mouths of steep mountain canyons, though the vast majority of ice-age outwash plains in the Olympics have been reshaped by rivers and are now well hidden beneath valley forests. Nonetheless, most of what we have come to know of the behavior of valley glaciers in the Olympics has been pieced together by studying moraines, outwash plains, and sea cliffs.

Glaciers were also the principal agents in shaping the character of the rugged mountainous uplands of the Olympics. Unlike the headwaters of nonglaciated streams that fold themselves gradually, tributary by tributary, into a lower valley, the headwaters of Olympic valleys often end abruptly in steep-walled cirques. These high mountain basins, carpeted with meadows and scattered copses of subalpine trees, often cradling a still mountain tarn at their base, compose some of the most stunning alpine scenery in the Olympics. The ice-free cirque basins of upper Royal Creek, Grand Creek, and the Sol Duc River are among the most popular backcountry destinations in Olympic National Park.

Mount Ferry Basin in the Bailey Range presents a classic glacier-carved landscape. Ice-sharpened ridges give way to a broad glacier-carved cirque floor and snowmelt tarn. PHOTO BY JANIS BURGER.

Cirque walls are roughly carved and cliffy. As firn and ice along the upper end of a glacier melt away from a rock headwall, a deep *bergschrund* forms. In late summer such "schrunds" become the bane of climbers, often requiring dicey acrobatic passages from glacier to summit rock. As meltwater freezes in cracks behind exposed blocks of rock in the headwall, the blocks loosen and clatter down into the bergschrund to become part of the glacier's load. These angular blocks increase a glacier's cutting power and help it grind down the floor of a cirque, further steepening the cirque walls. The cutting power of upper glaciers is also increased by loads from snow cornices collapsing from windblown ridges above, or icefalls spilling onto it from an adjoining peak. There is no doubt a cirque of magnificent proportions being carved at the head of Blue Glacier today.

While alpine glaciers grind away at cliff sides, gravity and frost action whittle the upper ridges, sharpening ridge crests, steepening relief, and generally sprucing up the neighborhood. Cameron Basin, one of the most beautiful subalpine parklands in the Olympics, presents a stunning example of a glacier-carved mountainscape. A large cirque broken by glacier-smoothed cliffs and ridges and veined with gently undulating moraines, the basin is a classic glacial landscape. A hike to Cameron Pass at its head reveals the marked contrast between the steep, glacier-cut basin to the north and the gentle, nonglaciated slope falling away to Lost Basin to the south.

Valley glaciers descended all of the major river valleys in the Olympics, carving wide U-shaped troughs in the sedimentary core rocks and narrower slots in the more resistant basalts of the Crescent Formation to the north, east, and south. Radiocarbon dating of a peat bog below a terminal moraine on the Hoh-Bogachiel divide suggests that the maximum advance of alpine glaciers in the Olympics occurred between 30,000 and 60,000 years ago, well ahead of the most recent advance of the Cordilleran ice sheet into the Olympics. Moraines indicate that the Quinault Valley glacier escaped the confines of its valley walls at this time and may have coalesced with the Queets Valley glacier at one point, forming a small piedmont glacier on the southern coastal plain. The maximum advances of the Hoh Valley glacier and the Dosewallips Valley glacier to the east most likely reached present-day sea level; it is unlikely that any of the Olympic glaciers reached the much lower sea level of that time. Glacial till (drift that hasn't been reworked by meltwater) is present in sea cliffs south of the Hoh River, suggesting that the terminus of the Hoh Valley glacier reached at least that far.

Though difficult to read, sea cliffs reveal a remarkable record of the past. For example, sea cliffs south of the Hoh River show lower outwash strata that seem to be tilted more than the more recent strata above them. Geologists interpret this to mean that uplift of the Olympics continued well into the glacial era. Similar evidence can also be found along older river terraces, and these are presently the subject of intensive study.

While terminal moraines of valley glaciers can be found in the western Olympics, evidence of the maximum advance of east-side valley glaciers is harder to find. This is due to the singular fact that all of the northern and eastern lowlands were completely buried and dramatically reshaped beneath thousands of feet of Cordilleran ice.

THE COMING OF CONTINENTAL ICE

Although the arrival of the Cordilleran ice sheet was almost an after-thought, a final gloss on the geological history of these mountains, no event would have as profound an effect on the ecology of the Olympics. At least six times during the 1.8 million years of the Pleistocene, a vast ice sheet descended from western British Columbia into the neighborhood of the Olympics. On at least four of those glaciations, the ice sheet surrounded the Olympic Mountains on two sides. With outwash streams surging around the southern end of the peninsula, the Olympic Mountains were effectively isolated from the nearby Cascades and Coast Range mountains at least four times during their history. This isolation, combined with the topography and geographical isolation of this islandlike range, was a critical factor in determining the patterns of life-forms that presently grace the Olympics.

Like alpine glaciers in the Olympics, the Cordilleran ice sheet was also born in snowy mountain cirques, only these were far to the north in the Coast Mountains of British Columbia. Ranging between 10,000 and 13,000 feet in elevation, the Coast Mountains are much higher than the Olympics and present a formidable barrier to moist air flowing in off the Pacific. Even today the Coast Mountains support sizable ice caps. Alpine glaciers flowing west from these mountains coalesced into a piedmont glacier in the coastal lowlands. While the northern end of the ice sheet flowed west into the Pacific, its southern expanse ran up against the Insular Mountains of Vancouver Island. Picking up additional mass from the glaciers flowing east from the island mountains and west down the Fraser Valley, the ice sheet turned south.

The earliest identifiable advance of the Cordilleran ice sheet into the area of the Olympic Mountains, the Orting glaciation, occurred about 2 million years ago. When it reached the peninsula, the ice sheet split against the basalt prow of the northeast Olympics. Like the twin wakes of a bow wave, one lobe flowed west, initiating the carving of the waterway that would be known as the Strait of Juan de Fuca, and one lobe flowed south along the eastern Olympic front into the Puget trough.

As world climate fluctuated throughout the Pleistocene, the Orting

The extent of the Fraser glaciation on the Olympic Peninsula shows the estimated extent of alpine glaciers during the Evans Creek stade (around 19,000 years ago) and the extent of Cordilleran ice sheet during the Vashon stade (around 15,000 years ago). MAP PREPARED BY OLYMPIC NATIONAL PARK.

glaciation was followed by three other advances of the ice sheet: the Stuck, the Salmon Springs, and, most recently, the Fraser glaciations. Each of these was in turn marked by pulses or "stades" as the ice pushed forward and melted back in response to climatic conditions. Glaciologists are still sorting out dates and areas affected by various glaciations; the date of the Salmon Springs glaciation, for example, was recently bumped back a half million years. Most easily read, however, and evident throughout the northern and eastern Olympics, is the most recent glacial advance into this area, the Vashon stade of the Fraser glaciation.

Beginning a mere 17,000 years ago, the Vashon was one of the most extensive glaciations to affect the Olympic Peninsula. Like the Orting and earlier glaciations, it split into two lobes. Hemmed by the northern scarp of the Olympics, the Juan de Fuca lobe ground west, curving around the northwestern end of the mountains to the Quillayute Prairie north of the present town of Forks, and completing the carving of the Strait of Juan de

Low clouds fill the Elwha and Lillian valleys, a common occurrence during winter in the Olympics. This view suggests the Pleistocene landscape of 18,000 years ago when alpine glaciers flowed down into river valleys. PHOTO BY JANIS BURGER.

Fuca. The Puget lobe flowed south through the Puget lowland along the east face of the Olympics. Advancing between 200 and 500 feet per year, it reached as far as the Black Hills, fifteen miles south of Olympia, and left in its wake the lovely inland sea of Puget Sound. Swollen by the melting valley glaciers of the east Olympics and west slope of the Cascades, the vast braided outwash stream of the Puget lobe cut southwest around the Black Hills and out to the Pacific along the present course of the Chehalis River, leaving a channel vastly oversized for the modest stream that occupies it today. The Cordilleran sheet had reached this far at least once before, maybe more, but each successive advance tended to work over earlier tracks pretty thoroughly. In the Olympic Mountains, however, evidence of this most recent passage of the Cordilleran is easily seen by even the most casual viewer.

Blocks and boulders of telltale light-colored granite lie scattered like Easter eggs in riverbeds and on forested mountain slopes up to nearly 4,000 feet in the northeast Olympics. Since granite is not found in the bedrock here, all of these "erratics" were carried south from the mountains of western Canada by the continental ice sheet and dropped off as the ice melted, some riding ice floes far up flooded valleys. The ice sheet reached its highest point at 3,800 feet on Blue Mountain and tapered off in height as it split off west and south. The Puget lobe was about 3,200 feet thick over Seattle and 1,500 feet over Olympia; erratics are plentiful throughout middle and lower elevations.

It's hard to envision what it must have been like in the Olympic Mountains during the Vashon ice sheet's reign. The Malaspina Glacier that flows out of the Saint Elias Mountains in Alaska today probably provides the closest analogy, but climate and conditions here were far different. The alpine glaciers of the Olympics had reached their maximum advance during the earlier Evans Creek stade of the Fraser glaciation between 22,000 and 18,000 years ago. By the time of the Vashon stade they had retreated partway up their valleys, leaving a drift of bouldery cobbles and outwash. As the Vashon ice sheet dammed the northern and eastern river drainages, valley lakes were impounded and filled with runoff from the receding valley glaciers. Large fjordlike lakes stretched tens of miles up the Sol Duc, Elwha, Dungeness, Dosewallips, Duckabush, Hamma Hamma, and Skokomish river valleys. As chunks of Cordilleran ice calved off into the lakes, erratic rocks frozen into the ice were rafted on floes and dropped far up valleys. Overflow streams cut new channels along the margins of the ice sheet, and fine, clay-forming silt settled over lake bottoms. Numerous unstable valley slopes, slides, and road failures in the Olympics today hearken back to these flooded valleys.

The Vashon ice sheet may have enclosed the northern Olympics for 1,500 years, reaching its maximum extent some 15,000 years ago. The Juan de Fuca lobe melted and broke up first, allowing the impounded lakes to drain north and Olympic rivers to resume their preglacial courses. Seawater flooded the glacier-carved basins. By 12,500 years ago, the ice had left the strait and Puget Sound; the world's climate ameliorated and marine waters filled the troughs left in the ice sheet's wake. Vegetation recolonized the denuded glacial slopes, and large mammals such as the mastodon—as well as their two-legged hunters—ventured into the northern lowlands. But the signature of ice was indelibly inscribed in a vastly altered landscape. Rounded foothills and spur ridges, kettle lakes and scattered wetlands and bogs attest to the heavy hand of the ice sheet.

Puget Sound, the Strait of Juan de Fuca, and the long glacier-carved fjord known as Hood Canal mark its track, as do some of the park's most pristine lowland lakes, such as Crescent and Ozette. If glacier-bared ground is difficult to envision beneath the lush mantle of lowland forest, it doesn't take much digging with a shovel to bring the past alive. The ubiquitous presence of glacial till (known locally as hardpan), gravels, moraines, and rocky drift that underlie the lowland landscape soon make themselves known. For the observant, it's possible to read the geological past by marking the kinds of vegetation and the forest and plant associations that thrive in this area today.

ADAPTATIONS OF ICE AGE PLANTS AND ANIMALS

With the effects of global warming becoming alarmingly acute over the past decade, scientists look to the climatic upheavals of the past for clues as to how natural biological communities may fare in years to come. By studying the ways in which plants and animals responded to the fluctuations of Pleistocene and more recent Holocene climates, biologists and resource managers might better prepare for the inevitable changes to come.

The record for Pleistocene animal life in our area is sketchy; glaciers did a pretty good job of smudging out most traces of Ice Age fauna. Marine fossils from this time suggest a colder and generally more northern marine environment than is found here today. Remains of land-dwelling animals indicate that bison, elk, caribou, woolly mammoth, and mastodon found their way into adjoining lowland areas during interglacial periods. The most complete picture of early postglacial animal life on the peninsula came in 1977, with a remarkable discovery about six miles south of Sequim.

Emanuel Manis was digging a duck pond in a peat bog on his land when he turned up two "logs" that resembled tusks. As it turned out, they were, and the site eventually yielded the nearly complete skeleton of a mastodon (*Mammut americanum*) estimated to have died more than 13,000 years ago. More remarkable than the completeness of the skeleton were signs that it may have been butchered for meat by humans. A spear point was embedded in one of the animal's ribs. The site also showed signs of human encampment and tool use. The Manis site was studied intensively by archaeologists from Washington State University. It presents an intriguing view of human and animal interactions as well as the condition of the natural environment on the northeast Olympic Peninsula in the centuries following the retreat of the ice sheet.

Scientists studying the plants that lived during the various stages of the glacial age have turned up a much more continuous and complete record. By examining pollens found in the sediments of glacial peat bogs and interglacial (and postglacial) lake beds, as well as identifying ash layers from known volcanic eruptions and radiocarbon-dating plant remains, a fascinating picture has emerged of the Olympic Peninsula and Puget Sound area over the past 20,000 years.

Drawing on the work of others as well as her own research, paleoecologist Cathy Whitlock describes conditions that preceded the most recent Vashon glaciation. The Laurentide ice sheet had advanced to its farthest extent over the northern third of North America, and its presence caused a general cooling in the Pacific Northwest. The Laurentide also split the jet stream, shifting winter storm tracks to the south and reducing precipitation throughout the Northwest. Cold, dry easterly winds from the great ice sheet further deepened the cool and arid conditions here.

As the Cordilleran ice sheet began its advance and alpine and valley glaciers were well into their retreat from the Olympic lowlands, the western Olympic Peninsula was covered by a mosaic of parklands, muskeg and sedge communities, and subalpine forest reflecting a moderating marine influence. Scattered forests of spruce, pine, mountain hemlock, and alder suggested forest communities found at higher elevations in the Olympics today. Lowlands on the east side of the Olympics were similarly open but colder and dryer. Grasses, sagebrush, and alpine plants covered open areas between scattered stands of such continental tree species as Engelmann spruce—which today is found mostly in mountains east of the Cascade crest as well as in scattered sites in the Olympics—lodgepole pine, subalpine fir, and Pacific yew. The environment may have resembled the subalpine forests of the northern Rockies.

As the Cordilleran sheet reached its maximum extent, around 15,000 years ago, the climate had already begun to warm. More familiar lowland forest species such as Sitka spruce and western hemlock began to appear in the coastal Olympics. Conditions probably became wetter during this time, because of the recession of the Laurentide ice sheet and a return to "normal" winter storm patterns. Temperatures were still three and a half to eleven degrees Fahrenheit colder than today's.

As the Puget and Juan de Fuca lobes receded north from their moraines and outwash plains around 14,000 years ago, the first tree species to colonize the rocky outwash soils was lodgepole pine. The pollen record shows that it was 2,000 to 4,000 years before the pines were joined by Sitka spruce, Douglas fir, western hemlock, and alders to form a closed-canopy forest in these areas. In the arid rainshadow of the northeastern Olympics, open communities and herbs and shrubs persisted until about 10,000 years ago, although prairie and oak woodlands had colonized the coarser outwash soils as early as 12,000 years ago. Pollen from core samples taken in southern Puget Sound, beyond the margin of the ice sheet, show that high-elevation species and lowland forest species commingled following the glacier's retreat between 10,000 and 11,000 years ago.

The warming trend in the earth's climate that led to the rapid retreat of the ice sheets and the subsequent rising of sea levels continued for several thousand years, reaching a time of maximum warming in the Northwest between 9,000 and 10,000 years ago called the Hypsithermal period or climatic optimum. An increase in the tilt in the earth's axis and its position relative to the sun at this time intensified the solar radiation reaching the earth. This led to near-Mediterranean conditions of higher temperatures, lower precipitation, and extreme summer drought that prevailed until about 6,000 years ago. Evidence of the Hypsithermal warming is evident in the pollen record on the Olympic Peninsula as fire-responsive species such as Douglas fir, red alder, and bracken fern became more abundant within the older, moisture-loving spruce-hemlock forests. As wildfire played an increasingly important role in the ecology of the area, prairies expanded in the lowlands, and plant communities of the Puget basin began to resemble the open savannas of the Willamette Valley in Oregon. Precipitation in the Puget trough may have been 40 to 50 percent lower than today, and temperatures two to six degrees warmer. It was during this time that trees more common to southern climates, such as the lovely Pacific madrone and golden chinquapin, may have found their way to the Olympics, adding to the beauty of our lowland forests.

Sometime between 5,000 and 6,000 years ago, the intensity of summer droughts began to abate and the "grandfather tree" of Northwest coastal people, the western red cedar, became plentiful along streams and coastal lowlands. The return of red cedars was a momentous event for the Olympic Peninsula. Not only would this tree provide the material foundation for a highly developed Native American culture, but by falling into streams and creating pools and riffles, it prepared the way for salmon to flourish in peninsula rivers. The red cedars were soon followed by western hemlock, Sitka spruce, and western white pine, a return to forest communities similar to those found on the peninsula today.

Not long ago, it was assumed by many ecologists that forest and plant communities, along with their associated wildlife, "migrated" north and south along elevation gradients and mountain ranges with the advance and retreat of glaciers. Appealing as this idea may be, careful analysis of the pollen record shows that plants responded to climatic change and disturbance in subtler and more complex ways. For instance, during the time of maximum Cordilleran advance, temperate plants were thriving close by and trees were present on nearby uplands. Indeed, the quick return of Douglas fir to the peninsula and nearby areas during the Hypsithermal (less than 500 years after conditions grew warmer) and the rapidity with which other forest trees responded to late glacial changes suggest that complex adaptations were at work. To understand these processes, to explain some of the wonderful diversity of the Olympics' plant communities, and to explore the significant role the Olympics played in preserving biodiversity in the Northwest forest ecosystem, let's look into the idea of biological refuges.

THE OLYMPICS AS BIOLOGICAL REFUGE

Ecologists call them *refugia*, places where plants and animals can escape extreme conditions. They can be cool bogs or upland areas in hot conditions; streamsides, lakeshores, and wetlands during arid times; or ice-free places during periods of glaciation. As we've seen, in just the past 20,000 years the Pacific Northwest experienced a wide range of climatic extremes, including the prolonged visits of an Arctic ice mass. It was a period in which no millennium has been exactly like any other. For a *refu-*

gium to harbor a variety of plants and animals through these changing conditions—as well as throughout the 2 million years of the Pleistocene—it would have to contain an incredible diversity of habitats, microclimates, elevational ranges. It would have to be unique.

To the late Nelsa Buckingham, a botanical researcher and inspiring presence to natural history enthusiasts across the Olympic Peninsula, the picture was clear. And she found supporting evidence everywhere in the kinds of plants and animals that are found—and not found—on the Olympic Peninsula today. Buckingham, along with scientists in a number of fields, believes that the Olympic Mountains served as such a *refugium* for plants, not only through the ice ages of the Pleistocene, but as far back as the late Miocene, 5 million to 15 million years ago. To illustrate, Buckingham pointed to a number of biological characteristics that make the Olympic Peninsula unique. Though the peninsula shares most of its plant species with other areas of western Washington, it lacks some species, such as noble fir, that are common elsewhere in the state. The peninsula also hosts a surprising number of endemic plant species, plants that occur here and nowhere else. There are eleven of these Olympic Peninsula endemics; another six occur only here and on Vancouver Island to the north, and three more are found only here and on Saddle Mountain on the Oregon coast. Just as fascinating to Buckingham are the Peninsula's "disjunct" plant species, those found here as well as some distance away but missing from areas in between.

Other aspects of the story intrigued Buckingham as well. Though the peninsula occupies only 9 percent of Washington State, it harbors 27 percent of the plants listed as rare by the Washington Natural Heritage Program. Add to that the high number of endemic animal species and subspecies found in the Olympics (five mammals, one amphibian, three fish, five insects, two mollusks, and a number of near endemics that occur also on Vancouver island), as well as the twelve mammals common to the Cascade Mountains but historically *absent* from the Olympics, and it becomes obvious that significant evolutionary forces have been at work here.

A number of factors contribute to this unique situation. Topographically, the abrupt relief of the mountains (less than ten miles from tidewater to the alpine summit of Mount Angeles, for example) has created a range of elevational life zones in close proximity. Climatically, the same

Mean precipitation in inches for the Olympic Peninsula. Differences in precipitation create an abundance of habitat niches in a relatively small area. MAP PREPARED BY OLYMPIC NATIONAL PARK.

moisture-laden southwest winds that dump 240 inches of precipitation on Mount Olympus are wrung dry by the mountains, sprinkling a mere 18 inches on the rainshadow area of Sequim, less than thirty-four miles away, and creating one of the steepest precipitation declines in the world. This combination of climatic and topographic diversity creates an extravagance of habitats and niches. During times of severe climatic change, alternative habitat sites for plants as well as animals are likely to be close by.

Perhaps the most significant factor leading to the uniqueness of the peninsula's biotic communities is its topographical isolation. The Olympics comprise an islandlike cluster of mountains separated from neighboring ranges by a lowland river valley and inland sea. We know the peninsula was also isolated for extended periods by continental ice sheets and large outwash channels during the long millennia of the glacial age. This isolation tended to limit the ranges of a number of peninsula plants, possibly allowing distinct subspecies and varieties to evolve. It also hindered the repopulation of a number of wildlife species, particularly those keyed to mountain habitats, after the ice had receded.

As far back as the Miocene, the Olympics shared the subtropical vegetation that stretched from the Pacific Coast east to the Rockies. The uplift of the modern Cascade Range between 2 million and 7 million years ago blocked the easterly flow of moist marine air and gave rise to vast arid scrublands east of the Cascades. Olympic Peninsula plants were further isolated by the repeated advance of the Cordilleran ice sheet over the past 2 million years as the ranges of many plants to the north and east were erased by the ice. Since, at the height of glaciation, only the northern and eastern margins of the peninsula and the glaciated upper valleys were covered by ice, most of the landscape, including a large area between the Dungeness and Elwha rivers—and a wide coastal plain exposed by the lower sea level (as much as 400 feet below current levels)—remained an ice-free refuge for plants.

To illustrate this for me, U.S. Biological Survey botanist Ed Schreiner brought up a series of range maps for Olympic plant species on his computer. Based largely on the work of Buckingham and others, base maps of the North American continent showed the disjunct ranges of plant species, such as sticky oxytropis (*Oxytropis viscida*). It occurs on the peninsula, but its next closest range is in the mountains of northeastern Oregon. Another eastern disjunct is long-stalked draba (*Draba longipes*), whose nearest kin lies more than 300 miles distant in northeastern British Columbia. Northern grass-of-Parnassus (*Parnassia palustris*) has a similar range; it is found here and in the northern interiors of northwest Canada and Alaska. Mountain owl clover (*Orthocarpus imbricatus*) graces meadows in the Olympics and Vancouver Island but isn't found again until one travels to the mountains of southern Oregon. Many plants, including Cooley's buttercup (*Kumlienia cooleyae*), appear to be at the southern extent of their ranges along the Pacific Coast in the Olympics. It's logical to suspect that the ranges of all these species were once joined to the Olympic Peninsula but that tectonic events, climate change, and the movements of Pleistocene ice separated them. Following the glaciers, the spread of closed-canopy forests in the lowlands may have further isolated these and many other disjunct species.

Schreiner thinks the ranges of these and other disjuncts present a clear case for the Olympics as an ice-age refuge. He compares the Olympic Peninsula to the land bridge islands to the north, the Alexander and Queen Charlotte archipelagos and Vancouver Island. All were connected to the mainland during parts of the Pleistocene, and all are now isolated. Endemic and disjunct plants as well as "missing" plant and animal species are characteristic of islands, land bridge islands, and island habitats like the Olympics worldwide, but it's the particular assemblage of plants and animals found here, says Schreiner, that stamps the peninsula as unique.

Questions certainly persist. Did the endemic plant species of the Olympics—plants such as the stunning Piper's bellflower and delicate Flett's violet—evolve here (neoendemics), or are they the relicts of once wider-spread populations (paleoendemics)? Schreiner suggests that the Olympics have both. How did—and how do—the Olympics interact with other land bridge islands farther north? One thing is certain: the ice ages and the climatic upheavals that preceded them have reshuffled the deck of plant and animal communities wildly in the Olympic Mountains. It's characteristic of glacial *refugia* that plant species tend to be all mixed up—alpine and subalpine species mixing willy-nilly with lowland plants and varieties. The pollen record confirms this for most of western Washington. When climatic shifts occur on the order of centuries, species get by where they can. Nelsa Buckingham liked to point out that 75 percent of the nearly 1,200 vascular plant species, subspecies, and varieties native to the Olympics occur from the lowlands to the subalpine, and those that don't are usually confined to specialized habitats such as lakes and shorelines. Her conclusion was that not only have the Olympics served as a *refugium* since the late Miocene; these mountains remain a refuge today.

Certainly the Olympics hold a key position in the region's evolutionary history and they may prove vital to its future. With the well-accepted prospect of a four to eight degrees Fahrenheit global warming facing us this century, diverse habitats and healthy functioning ecosystems such as those of the Olympic Peninsula and the species richness they harbor will prove essential to the continuing process of evolution.

THE LITTLE ICE AGE

When we view the climatic fluctuations of the past, we tend to do so from the supposed "norm" of our current climate. The recent decades of our interglacial age have given us a mistaken sense of climatic stability; the very phrase "ice ages" summons images from a primordial past. But as recently as a few centuries ago, world climate was in the midst of a tenuous half-step back toward that earlier time of ice. The evidence of this global cooling, along with its very recent aftermath, was recorded quite clearly by the alpine glaciers of the Olympics.

Since the Neoglacial or Little Ice Age occurred during the historic era in Europe (roughly from the fourteenth to the nineteenth century), its evidence abounds throughout the historic record. Lithographs and paintings dating to the sixteenth and seventeenth centuries show glaciers lying close upon alpine villages in Europe; historic documents confirm that the villages of LaRosiere and Argentier in France were overrun. Within a decade, temperatures dropped four degrees Fahrenheit cooler than today's. Grain crops failed, leading to famine, disease, and population loss. Wheat prices in Europe escalated between 1250 and 1350, then again in the 1600s and 1800s, correlating with cycles of cold weather. Wine production in Austria and northern Europe slumped to the point of driving the population— and their descendants in the U.S. today—to beer. In the 1400s, Vikings found sailing routes to their Greenland colonies blocked by ice; by 1450 the colonies had failed. Closer to home, Francis Drake's 1579 voyage to find a Northwest passage was beaten back near the Canadian border by biting winds and freezing rain—in June. Captain Vancouver, exploring the Northwest coast in the late 1700s, recorded that Alaska's Glacier Bay was filled with ice. In 1816 a five-day blizzard fell on New England, ruining crops—in August.

Alpine glaciers extended worldwide, and the glaciers of the Olympics were no exception. Though nearly all of the Olympics' alpine glaciers

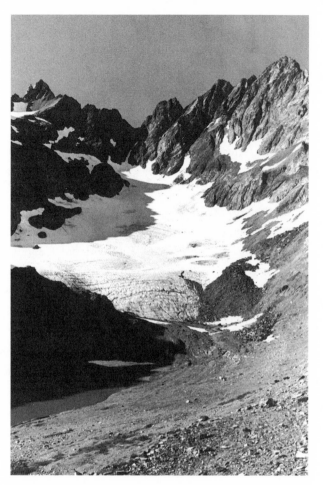

Mount Anderson and the recently deglaciated basin of the Anderson Glacier. Photographs taken early in the 1900s show the entire foreground covered with ice. Such evidence of the "Little Ice Age" and subsequent global warming can be found throughout the high mountains. PHOTO BY JANIS BURGER.

most likely disappeared during the Hypsithermal period of global warming, the large glaciers on Mount Olympus may have lingered. Scientists were able to determine the approximate age of moraines left by the Blue Glacier on Mount Olympus by dendrochronology—counting the rings on trees growing on them. Early Neoglacial advances of the Blue date to 1250 and 1650. Blue Glacier reached its maximum Neoglacial advance into the upper Hoh Valley in the early nineteenth century. By 1815, it had already begun its retreat up the valley, but for the rest of the century it would continue to cascade down a spectacular icefall below its present terminus.

The booming of the great river of ice down this cliff face, still visible in photographs taken in the early 1900s, may have given rise to a Hoh Indian version of the coastal legend of Thunderbird. It was believed that

Thunderbird got angry whenever hunters approached his "house" at the foot of Mount Olympus. He thundered his complaint, sending ice cascading out his door and crashing down the mountainside. Not surprisingly, the legend goes, "no one would sleep near that place over night." The story was "confirmed" by observers visiting the area in the late nineteenth century, who reported low rumbling interspersed with booming crashes. The glacier began to retreat from the cliff face during the 1920s, and by the late 1930s the cliff was ice free, as it remains today.

Studies of Blue Glacier began in earnest with the creation of Olympic National Park. Beginning in 1938, park naturalists measured and photographed the terminus of Blue Glacier every year. More intensive studies launched during the "International Geophysical Year" of 1957–58 have continued to the present. The result—the longest record of continuous data for any glacier in North America—makes the Blue an excellent laboratory for studying relationships between weather patterns and the growth and shrinkage of glaciers.

Blue Glacier continued to recede from the late 1930s through 1953. But as a result of cooler weather and a heavier snowfall that began in the late 1940s, more than three decades of retreat, measuring more than 800 feet, temporarily ended when the glacier stabilized in 1954. The following year it took a halfhearted lunge forward, but by 1960 Blue Glacier had receded farther up the valley than it had since the early nineteenth century. Then, in 1965, Blue Glacier began to advance again. With cooler weather and heavier snows in the late 1960s and early 1970s, it continued its advance, regaining more than 500 feet in length by 1980. That advance was brought to a halt by drought conditions that prevailed from 1977 to 1981. The glacier remained relatively stable over the next five years; then in 1986, the Blue began a steady retreat. It has been receding at an average of more than 50 feet per year since then.

Current research on Blue Glacier correlates "mass wasting" (the amount a glacier loses by melting relative to its annual gain from precipitation) with local weather conditions. Since glaciers filter out short-term climatic fluctuations, only long-term data are preserved. Measurements show a significant loss in Blue Glacier's mass since 1976. National Weather Service data from nearby Quillayute indicate a warming trend over the past century, with annual temperatures at the 5,000-foot elevation increasing more than two degrees Fahrenheit since 1948. The most profound increase occurred during winter months. Since this elevation represents the snow accumulation zone for Blue Glacier, the trend does not bode well for the glacier's future. Already over the past century, snow accumulation has decreased by more than twenty inches at the glacier's terminus. Precipitation there falls mostly now as rain.

University of Washington glaciologist Howard Conway points out that this level of warming could be critical for temperate glaciers like the Blue throughout the Northwest. The South Cascade Glacier, like other glaciers in Washington's Cascade Range, has lost a third of its mass over the past half-century. In the Rockies, a dozen glaciers have disappeared from Glacier National Park over the past forty years; the rest could be gone by 2030. Some predict mountain glaciers around the world could disappear by the middle of this century.

Blue Glacier and other closely watched glaciers throughout the world are now proving what climatologists have been pointing to for decades. The earth is growing warmer. 1995 was the hottest year on record. Then it was surpassed by 1997, then 1998, then 2001, and every year thereafter through 2006. In the Pacific Northwest, at the elevation of the Olympic and Cascade mountains, more and more winter precipitation is falling as rain rather than snow. More frequent and more intense winter floods have taken tolls on roads, bridges, and trails, not to mention salmon.

Average global temperatures rose 1.1 degree Fahrenheit over the past century, accompanied by a sea level rise of six to nine inches. In the Northwest, winter temperatures have increased 2.7 degrees since 1950. Current climate predictions suggest a four-degree rise in temperature in the Northwest over the next half-century. These temperatures will mean more winter rain and less snow in the Northwest, particularly at middle elevations. Analyzing projections from around the world and using the last century as a benchmark, the University of Washington's Climate Impacts Group predicts a 59 percent reduction in winter snowpack in Washington and Oregon by 2050. Philip Mote of the climate group confirms we are already progressing at that rate. Warming since the 1970s has exceeded any period in the instrumental record. With so large an area of the Olympics close to the winter freezing level, Mote explains, even a slight rise in winter temperatures can shift the balance from snow to rain.

A change of one degree in the average annual temperature corresponds to a 300-foot rise in the snowline. Subalpine meadows will certainly diminish. Dryer forests in summer will increase the frequency and intensity of wildfires. More frequent floods, earlier runoff and late summer droughts will spell bad news for salmon. Changing flow regimes and shifts in winds and currents may affect upwelling of nutrients in nearshore areas, altering plankton blooms, which has impacts that can reverberate throughout the marine food chain.

Will the Olympics revert to an early Holocene climate of prolonged droughts and frequent wildfires? It's too early to tell. But there is no longer any doubt that human-caused carbon dioxide buildup in the atmosphere is a factor in global warming. Nine of the ten warmest years on record occurred since 1995, and the trend continues. In 2007, the Intergovernmental Panel on Climate Change of the United Nations reported that without drastic changes in human carbon outputs, global climate will probably warm by four to eight degrees Fahrenheit over the course of this century, with an accompanying rise in sea level of seven to twenty-three inches—not taking into account the melting of glaciers on land. At even a modest rate of increase in greenhouse gases, temperatures are predicted by the end of this century that the earth has not seen in the last 125,000 years. The implications for water supplies, ecosystems, and biological diversity, not to mention agriculture, fisheries, and the world's industrial economy are impossible to fathom.

We know from pollen cores that the Olympic ecosystem passed through times of extreme climatic shifts in the past 20,000 years, but the pace and scope of changes facing us are unprecedented. The critical question of whether humans can reduce carbon dioxide emissions on a global scale in time to head off the worst scenarios of a warming world remains unanswered. But every scientist I've spoken with agrees on the critical importance of maintaining and restoring healthy functioning ecosystems to cope with the magnitude of coming change.

In his 2006 book *An Inconvenient Truth,* Al Gore wrote: "This isn't an ideological debate with two sides, pro and con. There is only one Earth, and all of us who live on it share a common future. Right now we are facing a planetary emergency, and it is time for action."

Endemic Plants of the Olympic Peninsula

Olympic Mountain milkvetch	*Astragalus australis* var. *olympicus*
Piper's bellflower	*Campanula piperi*
Spotted coral-root	*Corallorhiza maculata* var. *ozettensis*
Flett's fleabane	*Erigeron flettii*
Thompson's wandering fleabane	*Erigeron peregrinus* ssp. *peregrinus* var. *thompsonii*
Quinault fawn lily	*Erythronium quinaultensis*
Olympic rockmat	*Petrophylum hendersonii*
Olympic Mountain groundsel	*Senecio neowebsteri*
Olympic cut-leaf synthyris	*Synthyris pinnatifida* var. *lanuginosa*
Olympic Mountain dandelion	*Taraxacum olympicum*
Flett's violet	*Viola flettii*

Endemic Mammals

Olympic marmot	*Marmota olympus*
Olympic chipmunk	*Tamias amoenus caurinus*
Olympic snow mole	*Scapanus townsendii olympicus*
Mazama pocket gopher	*Thomomys mazama melanops*
Olympic ermine	*Mustela erminea olympica*

Endemic Amphibians

Olympic torrent salamander	*Rhyacotriton olympicus*

Endemic Fish

Olympic mudminnow	*Novumbra hubbsi*
"Beardslee" rainbow trout	*Oncorhynchus mykiss irideus*
"Crescenti" cutthroat trout	*Oncorhynchus clarki clarki*

Endemic Insects

Hulbirt's skipper butterfly	*Hesperia comma hulbirti*
Olympic grasshopper	*Nisquallia olympica*
Mann's gazelle beetle	*Nebria danmanni*
Quileute gazelle beetle	*Nebria acuta quileute*
Tiger beetle	*Cicindela bellissima frechini*

Endemic Molluscs

Arionid slug	*Hemphillia dromedarius*
Arionid jumping slug	*Hemphillia burringtoni*

CHAPTER 3

The High Country Year

T HE air is cool and patches of snow linger in the draws as I climb the trail through a mountain forest of western hemlock and silver fir. It's late spring back in the lowlands; the delicate trillium and red currant blossoms have already begun to fade. But here, queen's cup has just opened its small white petals, and beadruby lifts slender clusters of cream-colored flowerets over leaves still damp with morning rain. It's this first freshness of spring that draws me to the high forest long before the mountain meadows open into the lush wildflower gardens of summer.

In the years I worked in these mountains, planting trees and clearing trails, I'd follow the advance of spring as the tattered edge of winter snow retreated up the mountain slopes. We'd start work in February most years, when the first blooms of Indian plum brightened the lowland forest. Late May would find us working the upper edges of the mountain forest. Above us, the meadows of the subalpine zone, where trees give way to open parkland and rocky cliff, were still deep in snow. Beyond that, the high, open ridges of the alpine zone, well past the limit of trees, were raked by icy winds. Some years a late snow would sweep down and send us trundling back to the lowlands with our hats pulled over our ears.

No longer out on a daily basis, I now trace the season's progress by the bloom of wildflowers along familiar trails. Trailside plants along with subtle changes in forest composition also let me know how high I've wandered. Usually, at this time of year, the reappearance of the snowpack

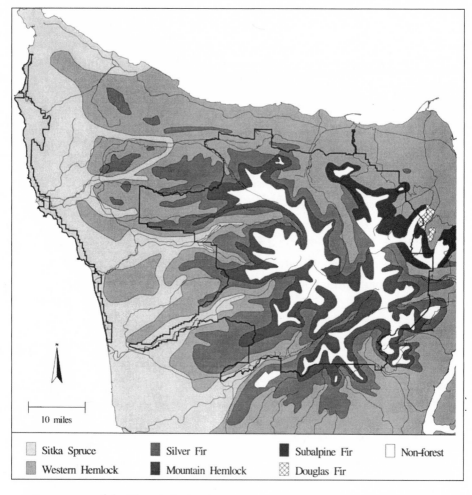

Forest zones of the Olympic Peninsula.

MAP PREPARED BY OLYMPIC NATIONAL PARK.

Legend:
- Sitka Spruce
- Western Hemlock
- Silver Fir
- Mountain Hemlock
- Subalpine Fir
- Douglas Fir
- Non-forest

10 miles

flashes the signal that I've entered the subalpine forest. But later in the season, or if the winter has been mild, as is often the case in recent years, I might wander past the first subtle shift in the upper forest without seeing it. Then, somewhere around the 3,500-foot level, I'll look up and notice that the forest is grading almost imperceptibly into the smaller mixed stands of mountain hemlock or subalpine fir that mark the lower reaches of the subalpine zone, the portal of the Olympic high country.

High subalpine forests, sunlit wildflower meadows, and flashing snowmelt streams define the Olympic high country: snowfields and rock cliffs edged with gnarled scraps of forest, or wide rolling meadowlands broken by scattered copses of subalpine firs and stilled with blue alpine tarns. Here, as everywhere in the range, the beauty and richness of these mountains springs from the marriage of a varied and broken topography with the perennial gift of coastal weather.

Because of the heavy snowfall that buries the high country in winter, subalpine and alpine zones occur at lower elevations in the Olympics than in continental ranges such as the Rockies or the Sierras. These lower elevations and the abundant moisture translate into less severe conditions for Olympic alpine communities: temperatures are moderate, ice storms rare, and drying summer winds less common. Even subtler factors such as soil temperatures and the degree of ultraviolet radiation are moderated by elevation and climate. All of this, combined with ample summer moisture from melting snow, has bequeathed to the Olympics' high forests and meadowlands an extraordinary lushness. And just as precipitation patterns have created diversity among the lower forests of the Olympics—from western rain forests to dry, rainshadow forests of Douglas fir and lodgepole pine—prevailing weather patterns shape the nature of the Olympic high country. This becomes apparent to anyone who explores the high forests of Olympic National Park.

THE SUBALPINE FOREST

From Hurricane Ridge, the Bailey Range rises up out of the deep canyon of the Elwha River in a long southeasterly sweep of snowy summits. The range encloses the headwaters of the peninsula's major west-flowing rivers and, along with the high Olympus massif to the west, intercepts the brunt of weather systems moving in from the Pacific. Because of prevailing wind patterns, the mountains northeast of the Baileys receive much less rain and snow than the western and southern Olympics. At higher elevations throughout the range, where most of this precipitation falls as snow, the composition of subalpine forests and meadow communities and the kinds of wildlife they support are keyed to the amount of winter snow and how soon it melts in spring and summer. Other factors contribute, but the amount of moisture available during the short growing season shapes the alpine ecosystem.

Subalpine fir copses alternate with meadows in the eastern Olympics. Copses result from layering, as lower limbs take root and grow new stems. In the western Olympics, mountain hemlock is the principal subalpine zone tree.

PHOTO BY JANIS BURGER.

West of the Bailey Range, the upper forests are dominated by mountain hemlock mixed with silver fir at its lower reaches. Alaska cedar is frequently found here, along with understory shrubs of oval-leaf huckleberry and white rhododendron. In spring, avalanche lilies pop up through receding snowbanks, and white-vein pyrolas and sidebells nod over damp mossy floors. Mountain hemlock (*Tsuga mertensiana*) is well adapted to wet, snowy mountains and is commonly found in coastal ranges where winter snows exceed ten feet. It is easily recognized by its full crown of dark green needles (uneven in length), stout limbs, and brown, furrowed bark. Near timberline, mountain hemlock's gnarled, shaggy shape stands in bold profile against a snowfield or glacier.

In the drier northeastern Olympics, mountain hemlock–silver fir forests are replaced by more open forests of spirelike subalpine firs, with Douglas fir and lodgepole pine occupying the driest south-facing ridges and rare stands of whitebark pine in the high, windy passes of the rainshadow. Because of the lighter snowpack and generally more continental conditions on the east side (cooler winters and warmer summers), subalpine fir forests develop at higher elevations here—around 4,200 feet rather than the 3,500 feet for mountain hemlock—and they extend higher, to nearly 6,000 feet in elevation. In the central Olympics, habitats are mixed; subalpine firs favor south slopes, while silver fir–mountain hemlock forests occur on the cooler north sides. Winter snow—and resulting summer moisture—affect tree growth differently east and west. Along Deer Ridge in the northeast Olympics, tree line is higher on north slopes, where lingering snow nurtures summer growth, while along High Divide in the central Olympics, tree line is higher on south slopes because heavy snows inhibit tree growth on north sides.

Not surprisingly, the elevation of tree line is less than constant throughout the range; in fact it's hardly a line at all. Rather it's a mosaic of meadows and clumps and ribbons of trees that weave along peaks and ridges throughout the subalpine forest zone, either as small glades within groves of trees or as large openings. Some meadows result from lightning-caused fires and are maintained by heavy snows that kill tree seedlings or by scorching summer drought. Heavy winter snows can also sweep away forests along steep avalanche tracks. Thick tangles of Sitka alder and shrubs thrive in these areas between ascending tongues of subalpine trees. Together, the alpine and subalpine zones are a broad belt covering nearly a third of Olympic National Park. To a hiker, they are a montage of fluidly shifting environments that seem to change with each turn of the trail.

The emblematic tree of the high Olympics—as well as the high forests of most of the mountain West—is the subalpine fir (*Abies lasiocarpa*). To breathe the rich balsamy scent of subalpine firs is to taste the essence of the high country. Extending from southeast Alaska and the Yukon as far south as New Mexico and Arizona, it is the most widespread true fir in North America, yet its elevational range is highly specialized. Unable to regenerate in the dense silver fir–western hemlock forests, subalpine fir pushes its upper ranges to the most windswept ridges. There, a few eke out a marginal existence as dwarfed and twisted *krummholz* shrubs ("crooked wood" in German). They may be centuries old and serve as habitat for the hardy southern red-backed vole and dusky shrew. Their more common spirelike form, however, is wonderfully adapted to the cold, snowy mountain environments in which they thrive.

The combination of snow, icy winds, a short growing season, and summer drought have given rise to some remarkable adaptations in subalpine firs. Notable at a distance across mountain meadows, their distinctive narrow symmetrical spires are well adapted for bearing up under heavy loads of snow. Their tough, short limbs, thick with brushy blue-green needles, cluster densely around their trunks, shedding snow like a steeply pitched roof. Snow-laden limbs provide insulation as well as a protective shield against blistering, wind-driven snow and ice. Subalpine firs are limbed to the ground. The lower limbs often form skirts that, insulated beneath accumulations of snow, may take root in the moist duff-covered soil in spring, send up leaders, and form a cluster of new trees. This "layering" provides an additional means of regeneration not shared by mountain hemlocks or silver firs, and copses of close-growing subalpine firs also absorb more of the sun's warmth. Such clustered tree islands are common at tree line in the Olympics. Surrounded by blue-leaf huckleberry, the trees provide shade and cover for blacktail deer as well as a number of bird species in summer. Over time, the parent trees die back, leaving ring-shaped clusters of firs scattered amid the mountain meadows.

Like Douglas firs, subalpine firs are able to close off the stomates in their needles when the soil dries out in summer, shutting down photosynthesis and making themselves extremely tolerant of drought. But unlike Douglas firs, they're also frost tolerant, suiting them to alpine conditions. Though their low limbs and thin, resinous bark make them susceptible to wildfire, they can regenerate successfully under a variety of conditions. During the warm Hypsithermal period between 6,000 and 10,000 years ago, subalpine firs were common throughout the Pacific Northwest; the high stands at tree line today may be remnants of that earlier time.

When traveling through subalpine fir stands in summer, it's common to hear the deep territorial booming of a male blue grouse from its drumming log. Grouse frequently nest beneath the branches of downed trees, nestling their clutches of brown-flecked, buff-colored eggs in shallow scrapes. Later in the season, hikers can't help but notice the large cylindrical cones of subalpine firs: purple hued and glistening with pitch, cradled in nests of boughs. Understory shrubs in these forests include white rhododendrons on north slopes and common junipers on south slopes, with showy polemonium, Scouler's harebell, and delicate starflowers brightening the forest floor.

Subalpine firs and mountain hemlocks are currently playing an important part in research on global climate change being conducted by the park service. Studies are under way to determine how vegetation changes in response to a changing climate. Scientists are monitoring the edges of alpine meadows where these trees are extending their ranges. Such ecotones (areas of transition between different environments) are natural laboratories; they can be seen as "tension zones" where plants test the limits of their habitats. Research conducted by Andrea Woodward of the U.S. Geological Survey's Olympic Field Station has shown that different species in different microclimates extend their ranges during different climatic periods. For instance, during the first half of the twentieth century, milder winters and drier summers allowed mountain hemlocks to successfully colonize alpine meadows in the central and southern Olympics. In this part of the mountains, where winter snowpack limits tree seedling survival, a period of less snow and warmer summers permitted mountain hemlock seedlings to become established in nearby meadows and to thrive there. Conditions in the northeast Olympics, however, proved quite different. Here, the major factor limiting the reproduction of subalpine firs is summer drought. Consequently, the firs didn't extend their range during the first half of this century, but beginning in the mid-1940s, increased winter precipitation and cooler, wetter summers allowed subalpine firs to advance into adjacent meadows. With a shift in conditions in the mid-1980s, the invasion ceased. Much like the study of alpine glaciers over time, the study of plants along ecotones such as the upper edge of forest and meadow can help us learn a good deal about the recent history of climate change and possibly assess future trends.

MOUNTAIN MEADOW COMMUNITIES

It's nearly summer by the time the high meadows of the Olympics begin to slough off their winter burdens of snow and begin their short, intense growing season. Depending on the depth of the winter snowpack, snow melts back from different alpine environments at different times, creating a mosaic of blossoming meadowlands that unfolds along mountain

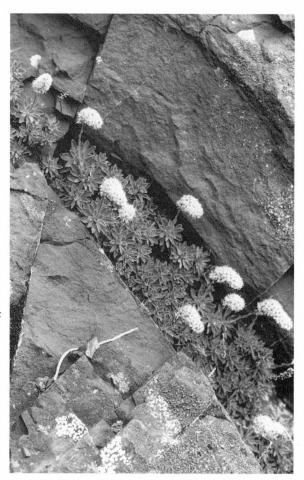

One of eleven plants endemic
to the Olympic Peninsula,
Olympic rockmat blooms
in mid-summer and prefers
clefts in steep rock faces.
Several near-endemic plants
grow only in the Olympics
and on Vancouver Island to
the north. PHOTO BY JANIS
BURGER.

slopes and basins throughout the summer. It's a glorious time to visit the
Olympic high country. It's a time of intense activity for the small mammals that graze on emerging plants as they forage for food in preparation
for the winter and keep a wary eye out for predators—eagles, hawks, cougars, coyotes—that cruise the high meadows in search of them. Blacktail
deer taste the morning mist on newly greening huckleberry shoots, and
bees hum loudly among heather blossoms. Dark-eyed juncos arrive from
the lower forests, working the edges of meadows for seeds and hawking
insects for their nestlings. Rare golden eagles cruise the cirque basins,
alert for an unwary marmot. Gray jays and pine grosbeaks call among
subalpine firs, and Clark's nutcrackers frequent the high whitebark pines.
It's a brief interlude, barely five months from subalpine spring to winter—

the first snows usually dust the high meadows by October; the first permanent snows fall by early November. But within this short window an unimaginable loveliness unfolds across the high country like an embroidered tapestry spread over a garden of stone.

More than 1,050 native plant species occur in the Olympic high country, including most of the Olympics' endemic and disjunct species. But these plants group themselves in different ways. Botanists working in the high Olympics have noted that certain plants tend to grow together as various microsites—open slopes, basins, swales, and such—emerge from winter snow. While keyed to the time of emergence from snow and availability of summer moisture, these communities are also shaped by elevation, aspect and degree of slope, soil depth, exposure to wind, and frequency of disturbance. Like their lowland counterparts, alpine and subalpine ecosystems are fluid and dynamic, making delineation of plant communities an inexact science at best. But by looking at plants in the associations in which they frequently occur, we get a fuller sense of the diversity and complexity of the Olympics' alpine areas.

After a mild winter, high, windswept alpine ridgetops and steep south-facing slopes around Hurricane Ridge and Blue Mountain begin to melt out by late April. The only real alpine tundra in the Olympics occurs in this northeastern corner of the range, most notably on Elk Mountain east of Hurricane Ridge, Gray Wolf Ridge, and the high ridges of Buckhorn Wilderness. In these remote spots are found the cryptobiotic crusts common to alpine tundra and cold, dry desert shrub-steppe. Composed of lichens, mosses, cyanobacteria, and fungi, these crusty layers carpet rocky ridgetops in delicate patinas of black to gray-green. Scattered among them are a few hardy alpine plants such as sedges, snow willows, and sandworts. Except for these few isolated spots along ridges and mountaintops, the alpine zone is limited by the Olympics' relatively low elevation, the steepness of the high peaks, and the presence of permanent ice and snow. Lacking the high rolling ridges common to alpine areas of the Rockies, alpine plants in the Olympics are confined to narrow meadows along ridgetops and clumps of cushion plants on stable rocky slopes. On less stable scree slopes facing south or west, these plants tend to grow in long down-sloping ribbons or stripes.

Their early emergence from the snow exposes the plants that grow in these areas to extensive spring freezing and thawing, as well as severe summer drought. As a result, alpine plants evolved unique strategies for coping with extreme conditions. Nearly all the flowering plants of the alpine and subalpine areas are perennials. Rather than growing new plant structures to reproduce by seed each year, they merely add to their plant tissue and survive quite handily, not flowering at all if conditions are unfavorable. Plants such as the lovely spreading phlox that graces many of the Olympics' rocky slopes form cushions, as do delicate fronds of silky phacelia and the endemic Olympic Mountain synthyris. Their dense, low cushion shapes minimize exposure to the elements and insulate plants against winds and extreme temperatures. Cushion plants catch and hold blowing dirt and debris, which absorbs moisture and stabilizes their growing sites, as well as the seeds of other plants, such as western wallflower and alpine timothy, giving them a place to grow. Some plants that are found only in this community, such as smooth douglasia, grow in low mats. Less compact than cushion plants, mats commonly root by layering, which anchors them firmly to loose gravelly slopes. Thread-leaf sandwort, mountain lover, and small-flowered blue-eyed Mary are also found in these early emerging communities; so is one of the few nesting birds of the alpine, the horned lark. Horned larks have been known to build their nests beneath the cover of overhanging cushion plants. They can scratch and dig through snow for seeds, and their newly hatched young are seen some years as early as June.

By mid-June, visitors to Hurricane Ridge will notice prairielike bunch grass meadows melting out along south- and west-facing slopes. Tufted thatches of Idaho fescue are soon followed by showy blossoms of thread-leaf sandwort and bluebells of Scotland. Blue spires of broad-leaved lupine crowd the edges of subalpine forests here, and scalloped onion and spreading phlox colonize the lightly eroded areas. The Olympic snow mole, an alpine subspecies of the Townsend mole and an Olympic endemic, can sometimes be seen here; its diggings are evident among the grasses. Many of the plant species in this bunch grass community are also common to the sagebrush steppe of eastern Washington. Botanists suspect that this community, like the subalpine firs that border it, was much more widespread during the warm Hypsithermal period.

By late June in the northeast Olympics, even the shallow gullies and swales have become free of snow, but snowmelt streams and moist ground persist. The meadow communities that have developed here include conspicuous stands of American sandwort and cow parsnip, which partially shade understory plants such as waterleaf and pioneer violet, as well as ground creepers like American vetch. These robust multilayered communities are also home to the only known alpine colonies of Aplodontia or "mountain beavers" in the Pacific Northwest, and the meadows are frequently riddled with their burrows.

A similar but wetter meadow community develops on steep east- to northeast-facing slopes that melt out later in July. Dominated by Sitka valerian, which lifts a tall stem to a cluster of pink-white flowers with long, lashlike stamens, fringed with showy sedge with its fuzzy flower spikes, and crowned with the subtle elegance of chocolate lilies, this may be the most elaborate of the Olympics' subalpine communities.

Along with these meadow communities, observant hikers can find a wealth of small wildflower gardens as specific plants appear in microsites throughout the mountains. Small seeps provide habitat for the insectivorous common butterwort. Parsley-fern clings to rock outcrops. Alpine willow herbs and bright yellow monkey-flowers colonize wet sites along streams while extravagant elephant's head and delicate bog orchid breathe life into pocket wetlands. Part of the joy of discovery while roaming the high meadows is recognizing old friends tucked away in unexpected neighborhoods.

As summer progresses, the high meadows and basins of the central Olympics melt out from the snowpack, and a different, wetter series of plant communities greets backcountry hikers. Among them, heather meadows are probably the best known, or at least the most easily recognized, subalpine plant community in the Pacific Northwest. The juniper-like foliage and small, bell-shaped red and white blossoms of heather grace the high country of Mount Rainier, the North Cascades, and the Coast Mountains of British Columbia. In the lower-elevation subalpine areas of the Olympics, heather meadows are found mostly in the glacier-carved basins of north-facing cirques, where conditions approximate those of higher ranges. Heather meadows are not expansive in the Olympics, but they occur throughout the range—from Grand Valley and Appleton Pass in the northern Olympics to Hart and Marmot lakes and upper Lena Lake to the south. The scenic meadowlands of Seven Lakes Basin below High Divide are among the richest heather meadows in the mountains. Here the sweet greens of avalanche lilies and blue-leaf huckleberry—tastiest of all huckleberries—abound, making them as popular with deer and black bears as with people. But don't search here for heather voles; they're common in most other alpine habitats—they love huckleberry—but I don't often find them in heather.

Given the dramatic settings of heather meadows in glacier-carved cirques, it's not surprising that the worst damage done to these meadows comes from backcountry campers. The woody stems of heather hold up well under the weight of heavy snows, but continual trampling from lug-soled boots takes a toll. Olympic National Park managers are restoring damaged meadows by closing some sites to overnight use and raising subalpine plants from seed to revegetate damaged areas. The effort has been successful, but continued education about the nature and fragility of alpine communities and cooperation among the increasing numbers of park visitors is necessary to protect existing and newly restored heather meadows.

Snowbanks linger longest in low swales and sinks, often within cool, north-facing heather meadows. Many of these sites do not melt out until August, some not until September. The black alpine sedge meadows that develop here are usually small and the plants low-growing. Sedges, pussytoes, thick fields of avalanche lilies, and the twin pink-lavender blossoms of alpine willow-herb are common. Dusky shrews are known to favor sedge meadows, where they skitter about secretively in search of insects. The black alpine sedge community also has a wide distribution in North America, suggesting these plants were formerly more common. But in these postglacial times, they persist only in the coolest sites on high mountains.

The most common type of meadow encountered by hikers throughout the Olympics is characterized by lush fields of tufted showy sedge. The singular white tufts of American bistort, bright yellow fan-leafed cinquefoil, and lavender beds of broad-leaved lupine flourish in the deep, moist soils of showy sedge meadows. These meadows hug the north slopes and level ridgetops in the dry northeast Olympics but elsewhere carpet west- and south-facing slopes. At Honeymoon Meadows on the West Fork

Dosewallips, showy sedge grows waist high along the trail. In sites like this there's not much diversity; showy sedge outcompetes nearly everything else. Still, this is the most productive community in the subalpine, producing as much as six times more biomass than the bunch grass communities in the rainshadow. Showy sedge meadows are central to the ecology of the high country for another reason as well. Along with the bunch grass, valerian, and black alpine sedge communities, they form the heart of habitats preferred by the most gregarious and conspicuous of Olympic's alpine residents, the Olympic marmot.

THE OLYMPIC MARMOT

Even after the snowiest of winters, when mountain meadows are buried beneath May drifts of ten feet or more, one sure sign of spring is the skittery tracks of marmots newly emerged from their winter-long sleep. Their tracks are the first signs of life I see in the high country when I make early season climbing trips, and the mere sight of them never fails to delight me. The sharp, piercing whistle of a marmot's warning call seems to wake the whole subalpine community, and the animal's loping gallop across the spring snow lets me know that the world still ticks true. Marmots are incredibly social mammals; their early tracks frequently lead to a deep burrow in the snow, then directly down to another entrance in the colony. How these creatures find them beneath ten feet of snow is a mystery, but they rarely miss.

The endemic Olympic marmot (*Marmota olympus*) is one of six North American marmot species—those large members of the ground squirrel clan—and the most social. They greet each other morning and night with nuzzling, nibbling, and play-wrestling. Extended families of about a dozen individuals share common colonies, feeding and resting together, exchanging sentry duties to guard against predators, and tolerating infants and yearlings much more than their cousins in the Rockies, the yellowbelly marmots. This behavior may be influenced by the long, seven- to eight-month hibernation period necessitated by the Olympics' heavy winter snows and the consequently short summer. During that season marmots must mate, rear young, and pack on enough fat to sustain them through their winter hibernation. Maximizing cooperation and

The Olympic marmot evolved into a separate species during the long isolation of the Pleistocene. Recent studies have shown that Olympic marmot populations are in decline. Endemic subspecies in the Olympics include: the Olympic chipmunk, Olympic snow mole, Mazama Pocket gopher, and Olympic ermine. PHOTO BY JANIS BURGER.

minimizing aggression seems a wise evolutionary imperative under such conditions.

A typical marmot colony is made up of an adult male, two adult females, yearlings, occasional two-year-olds, and the summer's infants. Females do not mature until their third year and then, in most cases, breed every second or third year, an adaptation that may reflect the short summer feeding period. During years with optimal conditions—early meadow emergence and an abundance of food—females have been known to breed for two (and in one case three) consecutive years. Mating usually takes place in May; two to five young are born in June and emerge from their grass-lined nursery burrows in late July.

One of the many traits I've always admired in marmots is their fondness for wide front porches. Nearly every burrow complex is outfitted with one at its main entrance, and the sight of a marmot relaxing there in the morning sunlight brings to mind a cup of tea and the morning paper. Other burrows scattered across a typical five-acre colony afford quick escapes from predators. Most mornings are spent feeding in a group—the better for safety. Midday brings them back to their burrows for a long rest (another admirable habit) before evening feeding. As the summer unfolds, feeding activity increases.

Marmots have excellent taste in habitat. Nearly all marmot colonies in the Olympics are located in mosaic meadow complexes where three or more plant communities are intermingled. Marmots prefer newly emerging plants with tender immature flowers. These plants are higher in calories and proteins—and digestibility—than older plants. Since different plant communities emerge from the snow at different times, such mosaic habitats offer the highest productivity and the best chances for winter survival. Foraging marmots move systematically from bunch grass communities in June to showy sedge and valerian communities through July and August. By mid-August most years, marmots are wrestling less and concentrating their feeding activities in the late-emerging black alpine sedge communities, adding to their fat reserves every day. By October, when the meadow plants have died back, the marmots have safely sealed the entrances to their grass-lined hibernation burrows and snuggled in for another long nap. Barring a light snowpack or midwinter thaw, they'll wake to tunnel through deep snow in mid-May, popping up like scraps of cinnamon toast, ready for another summer's frolic in the high meadows.

More than any other alpine mammal, the Olympic marmot embodies the coevolution of a native species with its environment. In the geographic and Ice Age isolation of the Olympic Mountains, the Olympic marmot evolved into a separate species with distinctive behavior and an ecology shaped by the nuances and seasonal variations of its subalpine environment. Similarly, the presence of marmots—burrowing and selectively feeding—has influenced what kinds of plants grow in the meadows where they live; areas grazed by marmots are known to support more species than ungrazed areas. These relationships, honed and deepened over millennia of adaptation and change, give us a glimpse of the wisdom and magic that lie at the heart of a wilderness ecosystem. Like the elk herds and their rain forest valleys, marmots are an inseparable part of their alpine world. By observing them, a trace of the elegant stitchwork that underlies the beauty of these mountains comes to life.

Just to the north, on Canada's Vancouver Island, endemic Vancouver Island marmots are not faring well. Their population has crashed from about 300 animals in the 1980s to less than 30 animals in the wild today. An intensive program of captive breeding and reintroduction is currently under way on the island. The fate of Vancouver Island marmots and the prospect of climate-driven landscape changes have raised concern over the status of Olympic marmots. A multiyear study begun in 2002 by Suzanne Cox Griffin of the University of Montana has documented a significant population decline in Olympic marmots as well. Griffin and her research team surveyed twenty-five historic marmot colonies in the northeast and north-central Olympics that were occupied as recently as 1989. By 2006, fifteen were vacant. The high, dry meadows from Hurricane Ridge to Obstruction Point supported more than 100 marmots in the 1960s. There were 12 in the spring of 2004. Marmot numbers are also in decline in other areas of the park. For every two occupied colonies, researchers found one that had been abandoned. Birth and death rates for marmots recorded over the course of the study are similar to those found on Vancouver Island, clearly indicating a population in trouble.

Reproductive success rates vary season by season of course, and climate change is an unknown factor. Researchers looked at a number of possible causes for the decline. They found the presence of humans was not a significant factor, nor was winter mortality, even during winters of extremely light snowpack. Of all the marmots monitored, none died during hibernation. But one constant that persisted throughout the study was predation. Lactating females seemed particularly vulnerable; female mortality is at 30 percent per year. Golden eagles, cougars, bobcats, and coyotes are known to prey on marmots. But in some survey sites, the number of marmots that appeared to be taken by coyotes was alarmingly high. Early naturalists noted the absence of coyote among the native fauna of the Olympic Peninsula. As wolves were eliminated from the peninsula, coyotes began to fill their niche. By the 1930s coyotes had populated the logged-over lowlands around the peninsula. Today researchers report their presence throughout the high country as well. Researchers also found that, during summer, marmots are known to make up 10 to 20 percent of these coyotes' diet.

Impacts from other predators and the long-term effects of global warming on subalpine meadow habitats remain unknown. Biologists continue to monitor marmot populations in the park, and conservation measures such as relocating marmots to former colony sites and selectively controlling coyotes are being discussed. In the meantime, the familiar warning whistles of marmots that ring across high meadows might also be sounding an alarm for the future health of the alpine ecosystem.

NATIVES AND NON-NATIVES

Though Olympic marmots are closely watched in their alpine environs, we know less of the lives and ecology of the other mountain-dwelling mammals endemic to the Olympics: the Olympic yellow-pine chipmunk, Olympic snow mole, Olympic Mazama pocket gopher, and Olympic short-tailed weasel. These animals may have evolved into distinct subspecies in the geographic and Ice Age isolation of the Olympic Mountains, and the ecological webs and niches they occupy are now part of the fabric of a unique ecosystem. Genetic research being conducted by Jim Kenagy of the University of Washington's Burke Museum has confirmed that the Olympic chipmunk and Olympic pocket gopher are indeed disjunct populations widely separated from their nearest relatives, which are found at Mount Rainier and in the southern Olympic lowlands, respectively. Kenagy's researchers also found that the Olympic snow mole shares its alpine habitat with the coast mole (*Scapanus orarius*), previously unreported from the Olympic high country. Further genetic work will be required to confirm whether either of these is an isolated population, but heather voles, found throughout the Olympic high country, may be as well. Alas, the Olympic ermine, which are widespread throughout the Olympic Mountains—and much of North America—may be misnamed. Olympic snow moles, pocket gophers, and heather voles remain active all winter beneath the deep mountain snowpacks. It's unknown how changing winter snowpack conditions will affect these and other alpine and subalpine species.

As important as these endemics in defining the character of the Olympic ecosystem is the historical absence of a number of mammals common to the Cascades. These "missing dozen," as they became known, included grizzly bear, wolverine, lynx, pica, mountain sheep, mountain goat, and smaller mammals: golden-mantled ground squirrels, water voles, and northern bog lemmings. Over the past several decades, a few of the missing dozen—porcupine, red fox, and coyote—have naturally colonized parts of the peninsula. As mentioned, coyotes took advantage of a niche left by the wolf. Eliminating this top predator from its home in Olympic valleys was an early human blunder, a product of ignorance and limited understanding of ecological processes and relationships. But early mistakes weren't limited to extirpating species from the ecosystem. Long-lasting problems and resulting damage to alpine and subalpine environments have also resulted from a species introduction.

In the 1920s, before the creation of Olympic National Park, some 20 mountain goats from British Columbia and Alaska were introduced into the Olympic Mountains by hunting interests. The goats flourished in the moderate coastal climate of the Olympics, and by the mid-1980s, their numbers had increased to an estimated 1,100 animals. Long before that, as early as the 1960s, mountain goat damage in the form of extensive cropping of subalpine meadows and large barren wallows where goats dusted themselves became obvious. Studies begun in the 1970s showed that goats occupied much of the alpine country of the park as well as adjoining Olympic National Forest. Their preferred range overlapped the ranges of the Olympic marmot and other endemic mammals. More worrisome was that their range and forage requirements overlapped the ranges of several rare or endemic plant species, such as Piper's bellflower, Olympic Mountain milkvetch, and Olympic Mountain groundsel. Because goats tend to overgraze their favorite plants, other plant species that favor disturbed areas moved in, altering the composition of the park's alpine and subalpine meadow communities. Since these communities evolved in the absence of large rocky-outcrop herbivores, including mountain goats, it was determined that the goats posed a threat to the ecological integrity of the park.

In the 1980s, the park service began an experimental management program that involved tagging, capture and removal, sterilization, and killing some mountain goats for research purposes. Some 400 goats were removed from the park by 1989. Research showed that sterilization was ineffective, and by 1990, the park service was forced to stop capturing and removing goats because safety concerns limited helicopter operations in the high country. Increasing goat mortalities and limited capture successes as goat numbers declined also demonstrated that further live-capture was unfeasible. In 1995, the park service released a draft plan to remove remaining non-native goats by the only effective means available, aerial shooting. The decision struck some as drastic and unwarranted, but research has shown that even one goat returning to a wallow seriously retards recovery. National Park Service management policies state that parks will manage exotic species whenever they threaten park resources and when control is prudent and feasible.

Two independent science panels reviewed the park's research. A 1992 study concluded that mountain goats alter plant community structure, increase bare soil, and pose a risk to rare plant species. A later review, conducted after the draft environmental statement was released, disagreed. It conceded that mountain goats were not native to the Olympic Peninsula and acknowledged that damage had occurred to subalpine plants and soils. But it found that park studies failed to distinguish the damage goats caused from natural factors such as erosion, the effects of other animals, and human trampling.

A survey competed during summer 2004 found a mountain goat population estimated between 260 and 320 animals, a number similar to census estimates over the previous decade. Goat numbers showed a decrease on the east side of the park but an increase on the west side. Goats are also known to persist on Forest Service lands along the park's eastern boundary, home of some of the highest concentrations of rare plants on the peninsula.

No management actions have taken place since late 1989, nor has a final environmental statement on goat management been released by the park. While Olympic goat populations remain stable, native mountain goat populations in other parts of Washington State have been in steep decline. Olympic's goat population is now part of a statewide study attempting to find the cause for the decline. One contributing factor may be overhunting. Most native mountain goat populations in other parts of the state have been subject to sport hunting, while the majority of non-native goats in the Olympics are protected in Olympic National Park. Mountain goats have posed a continual dilemma to park managers at Olympic, but national park service management policies on exotic species

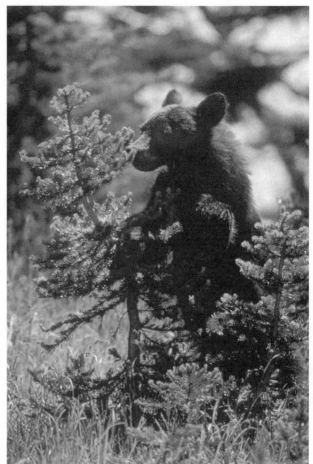

Black bear cub and subalpine fir. Olympic's black bears are known to migrate to subalpine meadows in summer to feed on tree bark, plants, roots, grubs, and berries. They feed voraciously in summer and fall in preparation for their seven-month winter denning season. Cubs are born in the den in mid-winter. PHOTO BY JANIS BURGER.

are clear. Non-native burros were removed from Grand Canyon National Park, European boars from Great Smoky Mountains, and feral goats from Haleakala. Ultimately, if the ecological integrity of the Olympics' irreplaceable alpine and subalpine plant communities is to be preserved, the bitter pill is that non-native goats must be removed from all jurisdictions in the Olympics and damaged alpine areas allowed to heal.

A more natural, longtime visitor to the Olympic high country is the black bear. Black bears (*Ursus americanus*) are seen frequently in the high meadows in late summer, most often snout down in a patch of huckleberries. During such times, the normally shy bears seem oblivious to passing hikers as they pack on fat that will sustain them through their five to seven months of winter denning (females den up earlier and emerge later than males). Black bears feed voraciously in late summer and fall, gaining three to five pounds per day and piling on up to four inches of fat before entering hibernation dens in October or November. While in the den, in late January or February, one to three young are born. Weighing only twelve ounces at birth, the cubs are nursed by their mothers and gain weight rapidly. At only eight weeks they weigh in at five pounds. One of the reasons is that bears' milk is incredibly rich, containing 33 percent fat and 15 percent protein (human milk, by comparison, contains 3.5 percent fat). Nursing sows can lose 40 percent of their weight by spring, so late-season feeding in the high country is critical not only to their survival but to the bears' productivity as well.

A recent study of black bears conducted in the Olympics found that male black bears are incredibly wide ranging—and become a significant part of the subalpine community in late summer and fall. Of twelve bears captured and radio collared in the Elwha valley, all dispersed to the high country in summer to feed on the lush growth of meadow plants and ripening berries. From the Elwha, bears traveled to subalpine basins in the Quinault, Sol Duc, Dosewallips, Hoh, Queets, and upper Elwha watersheds. More surprising, the bears wasted little time in their movements. In less than a day, one radio-tagged male traveled from Hurricane Ridge down to the Elwha valley bottom, then to the near top of Mount Wilder in the Elwha headwaters, a distance of more than fifteen miles upvalley. Typical home ranges for male black bears in the Elwha valley were measured twenty-five miles north to south along the valley drainage, fourteen miles east to west. Mean territories for males encompassed fifty-five square miles; female territories were about one-third that size. Inevitably, home territories include subalpine meadows. By mid-July most of Olympic's black bears are enjoying a high-country feast that will last through September. As the cold weather sets in they return to their favored valleys and prepare dens for a long winter's residence.

AUTUMN IN THE HIGH COUNTY

The lid on my water bottle was frozen shut, and my cooking stove was rimed with frost. But morning sun already reached the far edge of the meadow, stirring mist like steam from slowly warming broth. Yesterday, the edges of a high lake near camp still held ice in midafternoon, and last night's rain whitened the ridgetop above me. This was my last visit to this high basin before winter locked the country in white, and I drew out my stay as long as I could. I didn't want to leave without a last glimpse of the elk that had been browsing this basin throughout the late summer and fall. I had seen fresh sign everywhere, but for the past few days the elk had eluded me, and I was afraid they had already returned to the lowlands. One more range through some high basins and I'll head down too, I told myself, reluctantly as always. It's a crime to leave a camp like this in good weather.

In late summer and fall, the high forests and meadows fairly ring with the bugling of Roosevelt elk. As soon as the high country is free of snow, elk migrate up from surrounding valley forests to partake of the summer growth. By fall the bulls have herded their "harems" together, and their bugling echoes across cirques and basins. Black bears arrive in the high meadows to fatten themselves on the huckleberry crop, and Cooper's and sharp-shinned hawks have left their nesting areas in the deep forest to join other hawks, larks, and owls feeding on the late-season flush of band-winged grasshoppers. In these creatures the arms of the forest reach up to gather the bounty of the high sunlit slopes before drawing back into winter. In them, the singular wholeness of the ecosystem shines through.

Fall is my favorite time in the Olympic high country. There's a crisp cleanness to the air, and fresh winds rustle the seed pods of summer wildflowers. It's a time when the meadows exchange the exuberant hues of summer blooms for the burnt sunset colors of fall. As the late peninsula botanist Ed Tisch has written: "At upper levels . . . where open forest gives way to meadow, the arrival of autumn is not simply the end of summer, but a brilliant culmination where color streams from dying leaves and straggling flowers."

Now that brilliant culmination was upon me. The leaves of white rhododendrons along the upper edges of tree line have turned golden with the first frosts, and mountain ash leaves kindle a bright, fiery orange. Closer to the ground, the leaves of thin- and blue-leaf huckleberries run from burgundy to a stunning bluish rose, a color matched only by the twilight sky. The sheer intensity of the summer season burns on in the alpine fall like the embers of a dying fire.

On my last day in the high country, I followed an elk trail that traversed a series of high basins. Toward noon I stopped at a windy pass and finished my lunch as the inevitable clouds began to build against the summits above me. The open basin below was empty of wildlife; not even the whistle of a marmot broke the windy silence. Just as I made ready to go, I noticed some movement in the timber far below. And there, across a low finger of meadow, came a large bull leading a band of elk. The bull waited while the elk followed across the narrow bottom of a cirque, then moved singly and by twos and threes, a river of buff rump patches, up a talus slope and back into a fringe of trees. Through my field glasses I tried to count them, but ultimately gave up and watched as they disappeared, swallowed up by the arms of the forest. Then, like a watchman closing a gate, the bull turned and stepped slowly into the trees.

Part 2

THE FOREST

CHAPTER 4

The Rain Forest

SPRING comes early to the rain forest valleys of the western Olympics. That may be part of their magic. Tucked beneath a blanket of winter clouds and rain, lush beds of mosses and liverworts—which cover nearly every horizontal surface here—awake and begin their growing season. More than 1,000 mosses, lichens, and liverworts make their home in these valleys, but theirs is a subtle bloom. More vivid are the small blossoms of spring-beauty and evergreen violet that glint from damp forest floors some years as early as March. By April, rufous hummingbirds have returned to the early salmonberry blossoms. Curled white petals of trillium float leaflike and immaculate above the moss and oxalis, and soon the cream-white blossoms of bunchberry fringe the buttress roots of huge rain forest trees.

Rising amid the gold-green of new maple leaves, the rainforest trees are what most capture my attention. Giant Sitka spruce, western hemlock, western red cedar, and Douglas firs lift like pillars into a cathedral canopy of green and broken light. There's something in the stature and grace of these old trees that never fails to slow my pace and alter my perspective. Conifer forests mantled much of the earth 200 million years ago, before the world was transformed by flowers. To enter an ancient forest is to step into an ongoing story as old as life itself. As I breathe the sweet, oxygen-rich air, something inside me knows I'm part of that story, and I recognize the forest as home.

Early maple leaves lend a golden hue to this moss-green world, and scarves of clubmoss and aerial fronds of licorice fern sway gently in the valley breeze. The rain forest is awash with life. Even the moss-carpeted logs that litter the forest floor support gardens of blooming wildflowers. Dense thickets of forest seedlings crowd the broad shoulders of other logs, suspended above the thick growth of the forest floor like stranded sailors clinging to a life raft. Stumps sprout lavish caps of huckleberry and moss, and waist-high fern fronds glisten with recent rain.

The temperate rain forest is the most spectacular of the old-growth forests that mantle the lowland valleys of Olympic National Park. It represents a coastal forest type that stretches more than 2,000 miles from northern California to southeast Alaska. The Sitka spruce–western hemlock forests that dominate these low-lying coastal areas, like the redwoods that grow to the south, are bound by a narrow coastal fog belt that rarely extends more than a dozen miles inland. Sitka spruce is a coastal tree, wind hardy and keyed to ocean fog. Its salt-tolerant needles can extract minerals and nutrients from moist marine air. That this forest type reaches its maximum potential in the inland valleys of the western Olympics is the fortunate result of a number of factors. Over time, these lucky accidents have given rise to a magnificent forest community, one that boasts some of the largest trees and the greatest biological productivity in the world.

The stage for the Olympic rain forest was set during the Pleistocene, when alpine glaciers repeatedly bore down west-flowing river courses, carving deep, flat, U-shaped troughs. As glaciers retreated, valley floors were filled with glacial rubble and debris. The deep, long valleys that resulted— the Hoh, Queets, Quinault, and to a lesser extent the Bogachiel—are aligned with the prevailing southwest winter storm track. In consort with the abrupt rise of their surrounding mountains, these valleys funnel prodigious amounts of precipitation into their upper reaches. While Kalaloch on the coast receives 90 inches of precipitation each year, the Hoh Visitor Center, less than 30 miles inland, molders beneath 140 inches. A dozen or so miles farther into the mountains, Mount Olympus tops the charts at 240 inches. As this weather pattern held during the climatic fluctuations that followed the Pleistocene, alpine glaciers have continued to pulse forward and melt back. Drift from these recent glacial advances left a series of terraces in the valleys. Outwash from meltwaters as the glaciers retreated carved through them, resulting in a series of gentle stepped terraces along valley floors. The age of these terraces in turn influences the types of vegetation they support. The mix, from young disturbance species along gravel bars and bottom lands to the ancient stands of upper terraces, offers a diversity of habitats for the numerous wildlife species that make the rain forest home.

During the brief, relatively dry months of summer, blankets of coastal fog funnel up rain forest valleys and are strained through the myriad needles of tall conifers to fall through forest canopies and onto forest floors as "tree drip." This booster shot of summer moisture, which can add as much as 30 inches of precipitation to the rain forest annually, moderates summer drought and greatly reduces the chance of serious wildfire. Steep, glacier-carved valley walls also provide protection from the frequent windstorms that ravage coastal forests elsewhere. This mix of protection from natural disturbance and an optimal climate has allowed the Olympic rain forest to achieve great age and complexity. And it has produced some exceptionally large trees.

TREES OF THE RAIN FOREST

Sitka spruce (*Picea sitchensis*), the tree most emblematic of the rain forest, has sharp, bluish green needles that grow brushlike from the twig, and scaly, purplish brown bark. Mature spruces rise from their fluted bases in straight untapering cylindrical trunks to heights of 250 feet or more. Spruce trees five to eight feet in diameter are not uncommon in the rain forest. A large spruce near the Hoh Visitor Center is thirteen feet in diameter; one in the Queets valley is fifteen feet, and one rain forest giant growing near Lake Quinault was measured at nearly eighteen feet. Other tree species also reach huge dimensions here. Some of the largest Douglas firs in the world grow in the Hoh, Queets, and Quinault valleys, and three of the five largest known western hemlocks are found in western Olympic valleys. The current record red cedar, nearly twenty feet in diameter, grows on the north shore of Lake Quinault. Of course these records change as new trees are found and former champions lose their tops or fall. But given the extent of past logging in the peninsula's coastal forest, most of it along the productive, low-elevation coastal plain, it's doubtful that the true record trees were ever measured.

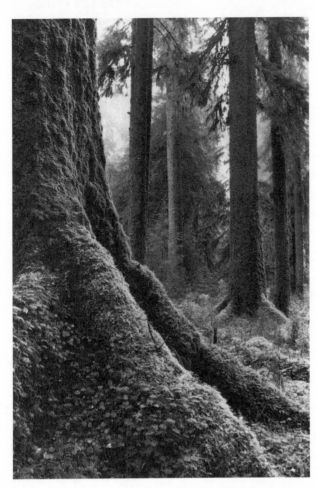

Sitka spruce is a fog-loving coastal tree that grows along a 2,000-mile belt from Oregon to Alaska. It reaches its greatest development in the temperate rain forest valleys of the Olympics; spruces here have attained diameters of 18 feet and heights approaching 300 feet. PHOTO BY JANIS BURGER.

Sitka spruces, like the western hemlocks (*Tsuga heterophylla*) that share dominance in the rain forest, are shade tolerant. Both are able to reproduce beneath the shade of the old-growth canopy. Because of this, they seed in readily beneath early succession trees such as red alder and Douglas fir, which require freshly disturbed ground and ample sunlight. Eventually, spruces and hemlocks come to dominate older rain forest stands. Lacking major disturbances such as windstorms, river meanders, or fires, the spruce-hemlock community can perpetuate itself indefinitely. But disturbances do occur; trees are toppled by windthrow or succumb to insects or lightning fires. That's when Douglas firs seed in to newly exposed soils. Less common than spruce or hemlock in the rain forest, Douglas fir is unable to reproduce in forest shade. The towering firs that grow along scarps and terraces stand as witness to fires, windstorms, and river cuts that disturbed the forest centuries ago. Sitka spruce can also survive on freshly disturbed soils, but in deep forest shade, western hemlock has the edge over spruce. Eventually, hemlock comes to dominate most lowland forests elsewhere in the Northwest. That a coastal species like spruce continues to hold its own in these inland valleys no doubt is due largely to generous amounts of rain and coastal fog. But another factor in spruce's success may be elk. Resident herds of Roosevelt elk that browse these valleys shun prickly spruce seedlings, but they find hemlocks irresistible.

Other trees are also woven into the fabric of the rain forest: red alder, northern black cottonwood, bigleaf maple, and western red cedar are most noticeable. Where and how thickly they grow in the forest can tell us much about how the rain forest community develops over time. In the near absence of major windstorms and fires, the prime disturbance factor in these forests may well be the rivers. A recent study of the Queets River indicates that the river reworks valley-bottom forests completely about once every 900 years. As they braid and meander across their floodways, rain forest rivers carve at forested banks, create logjams, shore up new gravel bars, and flood bottom lands, leaving behind layers of fine, sandy soil. These activities intensified over the past 1,000 years with the glacial advances of the Little Ice Age. The resulting valley terraces and the plant communities they support offer a glimpse into the stages of rain forest succession—the procession of plant species through time that leads toward stability or "climax."

RIVER TERRACE COMMUNITIES

In the Hoh Valley, a sequence of communities on progressively aged river terraces corresponds with periods of recent glacial advance. To wander across these terraces, from the river bank to valley walls, is to pass through the successional stages of the temperate rain forest and see how this ancient community develops over centuries, from simple pioneering species to the complex structure of an ancient forest.

Red alder and willow thickets begin to crowd young gravel bars along the river the first few years after they form. As they grow, these dense, young stands are used as cover by elk, especially during calving. As the river migrates back across its floodway, mature alders come to dominate these areas; grasses carpet the understory and Sitka spruces begin seeding into the young soils. These alder bottoms, open and airy, are favorite camping spots along the river; they are also havens for songbirds and important feeding areas for valley elk, particularly during spring and summer.

The first terraces, just above the alder flats, are slightly older, having been deposited by the river about 400 years ago. Here, the spruce seedlings of the alder flats have grown into mature stands, while the short-lived alders have dropped out. Western hemlocks also appear on these terraces, mostly as smaller trees and seedlings on fallen logs. Bigleaf maple and black cottonwood trees are abundant, and a few older Douglas firs linger from earlier disturbances. Grasses that dominated the alder flats are giving way to shamrock-like oxalis, enchanter's nightshade, sword fern, and mosses. Low, spreading limbs of vine maples seek sunlight in the dense forest shade.

On the second terraces, older trees are dying, allowing the canopy to open. Sitka spruce and hemlock are codominant here, forming a climax community. The spruces reach ages of 500 and 600 years. Vine maples grow in thick tangles, and salmonberry and huckleberry shrubs are common. Sun-loving grasses have all but disappeared now, and ferns, mosses, and beds of oxalis cover much of the ground. Mossy groves of bigleaf maples occupy the disturbed sites of old landslides and the alluvial fans of side streams, where they're joined by the graceful, fluted columns of western red cedars.

The third and oldest terraces are closest to the valley walls. Laid down by the alpine glaciers of the Pleistocene, more than 15,000 years ago, they support the deepest soils and the oldest valley forest communities. Most of the trees are ancient hemlocks, and a low growth of oxalis, foamflower, bracken, and mosses blanket the ground. Beyond them, valley walls host an entirely different forest type, where rain forest communities give way to montane forests of the upper slopes.

NURSE LOGS AND THE FOREST FLOOR

Among the signature characteristics of the temperate rain forest— large tree size, abundant mosses, lichens, and liverworts, and multilayered canopies—is an abundance of dead and down logs. As much as 20 percent of the forest's biomass (which totals nearly 250 tons per acre) is retained in standing snags and down trees. Many of the latter serve as "nurse logs," fallen trees that act as nurseries for forest seedlings. Seed germination on the rain forest floor is scant because of the thickness of the moss and herb layer. Either seedlings can't compete or fallen seeds remain suspended above the soil. Nurse logs offer a head start for seedlings, providing nutrients, moisture, and in some instances, protection from browsing elk. Nearly all the trees in the rain forest had their beginnings on nurse logs, upturned root wads, or broken-off stumps.

Soon after a tree falls, it's attacked by bark beetles and wood borers. They bore first the soft tissue of the cambium layer and later into the carbohydrate-rich sapwood and heartwood. Species such as ambrosia beetles, and the microbes and fungi that accompany them, are pioneers. They initiate a complex community of consumers, predators, and scavengers. Mites, termites, and carpenter ants eventually follow; over decades they will return the nutrients and organic materials of the fallen tree to the soil. Recent research suggests that up to a third of the nitrogen in Northwest forest soils may come from nitrogen-fixing processes within decomposing logs. Sitka spruce, western hemlock, and true firs decompose relatively quickly, but Douglas fir and western red cedar can last almost as long on the forest floor as they stood in life—700 or 800 years for a fir, 1,000 for a red cedar. Throughout the process of decomposition, fungi growth drains nitrogen from these logs, and the logs provide habitat for a plethora of organisms from fungi and bacteria to spiders, mites, millipedes, and snails. Even vertebrates such as salamanders, shrews, and voles use downed logs for feeding, cover, and travel routes over the crowded forest floor. The complex interactions between plants, animals, and nutrients in decomposing logs are a critical link in the energy cycle of old-growth forest ecosystems.

While most of these functions are hidden from view, nurse logs provide a poignant glimpse of new life springing from old. The moss growing in the bark crevices of newly fallen trees creates a secure and moist environment for tree seeds. Hundreds, if not thousands, of seedlings may crowd along the length of a nurse log, but only a few will develop into mature trees. Their survival ultimately depends on their roots reaching the soil. Some roots gain advantage by finding their way into insect borings and tapping the moist, decomposing wood inside the nurse log. But these early starters face intense competition from other seedlings, as well as crowding by the deepening moss layer, sliding off with sloughing bark, and toppling by snow and wind. Browsing elk and summer drought can also take a toll. Within a decade, only one in ten seedlings will survive; only one in thousands ever becomes an old-growth tree. Still, evidence of trees' nurse-log beginnings is apparent throughout the rain forest, from "stilted" trees that had their start atop stumps and root wads, to rows of mature trees or "colonnades," roots still clutching the hollow ghost of a vanished nurse log. There are few places where the eternal cycle of life drawing from death is more strikingly apparent.

THE ROOF OF THE FOREST

While the cycle of life is easily seen in nurse logs and colonnades, much of the life of the rain forest is less apparent to visitors because it goes on above their heads. A profusion of mosses, lichens, liverworts, and ferns drape the limbs and trunks of rain forest trees. More of these species found in the Olympics occur in the forest canopy. Virtually all canopy plants are epiphytes, plants that grow on other plants without parasitizing them. Drawing their nutrients from the atmosphere, rain, blowing dust and detritus, and fog drip passing through the canopy, these epiphyte communities serve a number of functions beneficial to the health and maintenance of the forest ecosystem.

Easily the most noticeable of these communities are the luxurious hanging mosses that drape the limbs of bigleaf maples. These aerial gardens benefit from an absence of the trees' leaves in winter to develop to a lush extravagance. Moss mats six to ten inches deep and trailing up to six feet below the cushioned tree limbs are common. The long, draping fronds are the clubmoss *Selaginella oregana*. Closer in structure to a fern than a moss, selaginella forms willowy hanging scarves from bigleaf and vine maples. Cat-tail moss (*Isothecium stoloniferum*) is an olive-green moss that dominates the lower limbs of rain forest trees. Higher in the canopy, feathery hanging moss (*Antitrichia curtipendula*) forms soft mounded pillows. These are joined by dozens of other mosses, as well as liverworts,

Epiphyte mat and licorice ferns. Such canopy plants do not harm their host trees. In fact, research has shown that some rain forest trees may benefit from these epiphyte mats by sprouting roots into them and gaining extra nourishment. PHOTO BY JANIS BURGER.

lichens, and licorice ferns. With a minimum collective dry weight of a ton or more per tree, moss mats have twice the biomass of the understory plants that grow on the forest floor and are four times heavier than the trees' own foliage. For years, scientists thought that bigleaf maples and other rain forest trees served only as toeholds for these epiphyte communities, but studies conducted in the 1980s proved otherwise. Scaling climbing ropes into the canopies of bigleaf maples, Nalini Nadkarni made a remarkable discovery. She found tree roots growing in the organic soil that had developed at the base of epiphyte mats. The large bigleaf maples, and vine maples and cottonwoods to a lesser extent, as well as some rain forest conifers, tap into their moss mats with roots identical to the roots the trees put down into forest soil. This strategy enables them to garner extra nutrients from these newly forming soils, and completes a symbiotic relationship between the trees and their epiphyte gardens.

Throughout the old-growth forests of Olympic, the canopy is home to a rich assortment of invertebrates, birds, and small mammals, as well as a complex community of microorganisms whose importance to the health of the forest ecosystem is only now beginning to be understood. More than 130 epiphytes have been identified in the Hoh Valley alone, the great majority of them lichens. Lichens are formed of a partnership between fungi, which provide structure, and algae, which photosynthesize sunlight. One group of canopy lichens provides the valuable function of "fixing" essential nitrogen from the atmosphere and making it available to the forest ecosystem. These cyanolichens, as they are called, are capable of producing two to six pounds of nitrogen per acre each year—a considerable portion of the total nitrogen needs of the forest. Some cyanolichens, like the common *Lobaria oregana*, which can make up a fifth of the canopy's biomass, are blown down in winter storms and provide a nutritious and easily digestible food for elk and deer. Another group, the alectorioid or pendulous lichens, like wispy, yellow-green old man's beard, are extremely sensitive to air pollution and serve as excellent indicators of air quality. Chemical analyses of some of these lichens in the Hoh Valley indicate that the Olympic rain forest has some of the cleanest air in the world.

Various groups of lichens occur at different stages of forest development. For instance, important cyanolichens and alectorioid lichens do not appear until younger forests begin to age, and they do not dominate canopies until forests reach 400 years. Lichens and other epiphytes also arrange themselves in zones in the forest canopy. Fog drip, rain, and snowmelt filter through the canopy as "throughfall," which becomes chemically altered as it leaches through each successive layer. The resulting solution, a nutrient-rich brew loaded with nitrogen and phosphorus, is an important source of nutrients for forest plants, including the trees themselves.

The old-growth forest canopy has been called the "last scientific frontier." Early research suggests that a wealth of new invertebrate species is likely to be discovered there. Studies conducted in the Quinault Valley found that arthropod communities—mites, springtails, millipedes, and spiders—are less numerous in the canopy than in the forest soil, but there are a number of canopy specialists that are not found on the forest floor. A more extensive study taking place in the canopy of a similar forest in Vancouver Island's Carmanah Valley has yielded an astounding 15,000 arthropod species, including 500 that are new to science. The highest densities, including elaborate predator-prey relationships, were found in the oldest canopies. We're accustomed to hearing of this kind of diversity in tropical rain forests; that our own temperate forests could also contain this level of richness should be reason enough to preserve the last unprotected remnants of ancient forests. If we don't, we'll never know the extent of what we've lost.

THE RAIN FOREST ELK

In fall, the rain forest valleys echo with the high whistling calls of elk. During the fall rutting season the great bulls stomp and pace back and forth through the forest clearings, warding off challengers and attempting to keep their "harems" intact. This is my favorite time to watch them, keeping downwind, in the cover of nearby trees. Their tan, muscular shoulders, polished antlers, and blond rump patches flash among the subdued greens and scarlet-edged golds of the autumn forest. The darker fur of their necks and legs blends with the shadows of forest trees. Where shafts of sunlight penetrate the canopy, their breath explodes in clouds of steam.

Elk are known to have been a part of these forests for at least 3,000 years, and evidence of their continued presence, from scat and tracks in churned-up mud to browsed shrubs and ferns, is everywhere you look. Though elk can be elusive in summer, when some of the herds migrate to high meadows and others favor the shade of dense valley growth, the frenzy of the autumn rutting season brings them front and center. I would have trouble imagining these valley forests without them.

The Roosevelt elk of the Olympics (*Cervus elaphus roosevelti*) are a distinct race of elk found in the Pacific coastal region from California's Russian River north to Vancouver Island in Canada. They are the largest of North American elk and the second largest animal (after moose) in the deer family. Bulls can weigh up to 1,000 pounds, or about four times the size of the blacktail deer that share their range. Olympic National Park protects the largest population of Roosevelt elk in the world.

One of the most conspicuous inhabitants of the rain forest, Roosevelt elk may help shape the character of the forest as well. The open, parklike appearance of rain forest valleys is largely the result of browsing by elk herds. PHOTO BY JANIS BURGER.

Nonmigratory elk in the Hoh Valley, those that remain year-round, typically live in herds of fifteen to twenty-five, occupying home ranges of four to ten square miles. After a summer of feeding on the lush growth of the forest floor, elk are in peak condition. Following the fall rutting season, which lasts four to six weeks in September and October, the mature bulls disperse and the herds return to their matriarchal social patterns. Herds commonly include older cows, their female offspring, and their calves. Upon reaching maturity, bulls generally drift away singly or in small groups.

The forest provides winter food in the form of hemlock boughs, alder buds, sword ferns, and lichen, as well as cover and shelter from winter storms. During periods of heavy snows, elk may leave their favored valley bottoms and gather nearby on low south-facing slopes, where warmer temperatures and less snow mean better forage. In February and March, herds begin to frequent more open alder bottoms, where increasing sunlight ushers in the first spring growth. Calves are born in May and June when food is abundant. Migratory herds, those usually occupying the upper portions of valleys, make their way into the high-country meadows in the weeks that follow. There they graze on the rich summer growth and seek the shelter of subalpine trees or snowbanks during midday heat. Valley bottom herds favor north-facing toe slopes during these warm summer days. Herds typically stay together throughout the summer months, either in subalpine range or in valleys. By September the bulls have grown new antlers and once more begin to assemble sizable harems and sound their shrill whistles and guttural grunts across meadow and forest.

When I view these animals in their natural environment, it strikes me that the tremendous productivity of these forests has contributed to the Roosevelt elk's impressive size and stature. More intriguing is the way elk have shaped the character and structure of the rain forest. In several different studies, biologists attempted to quantify elk's effect on forest vegetation by constructing fenced exclosures that prevented elk and deer from browsing small samples of valley forest. Two larger exclosures were built in the South Fork Hoh Valley in 1980. The contrast between vegetation inside and outside the fence is stunning. Outside, the open grassy "parklike" character of the forest floor is broken only by low clusters of ferns and shrubs. Inside the fence is a jungle. Salmonberry and thimbleberry bushes grow profusely, as do huckleberry and waist-high sword fern. Many herbs that grow small and sparse outside the exclosure loom large and vigorous inside, and the grassy glades that roll to the fence line are nowhere to be found within it. Young saplings such as vine maple and hemlock are much more numerous inside the exclosures than in the surrounding valley forest.

In 1990, park service biologists conducted a survey of twenty-two older exclosures along with the two built in 1980. Surprisingly, they found that there were actually more species growing outside the exclosures than inside, and the total cover of grasses and forbs was much greater. By limiting the growth of shrubs and ferns through browsing and trampling, elk help create and maintain the groomed appearance of the forest floor. This in turn results in an increase of the grasses and forbs that elk, as well as other herbivores, such as deer, mice, voles, and snowshoe hares, prefer for food. This is particularly true on the floodways and younger river terraces most frequented by elk.

But the story doesn't end there. Along with shaping the character of the forest floor, browsing elk may also influence the structure of the forest itself. Observations of the South Fork Hoh exclosures suggest that the abundance of Sitka spruce in the rain forest may be due in part to browsing elk's taste for hemlock seedlings and avoidance of Sitka spruce. This kind of mutuality in an old-growth forest system is striking. The coevolution of the elk and the rain forest is yet another window into the complexity of a wilderness ecosystem. Even when no elk are to be seen, their presence permeates the beauty of the rain forest.

It wasn't too long ago that this story nearly took a sharp turn for the worse. By the turn of the twentieth century, the Olympics' elk herds had been decimated by overhunting. Elk were killed first for their meat and hides; later, they were shot purely for their upper canine teeth, prized as watch fobs by members of the Benevolent and Protective Order of Elks. By 1905, the estimated elk population on the peninsula was reduced to fewer than 2,000 animals. Public outcry over the carnage led President Theodore Roosevelt to create Olympic National Monument in 1909. The monument protected a core area of elk habitat in the central mountains. Along with hunting restrictions put in place earlier by the state of Washington, this allowed elk numbers to rebound. The population increased to between 5,000 and 7,000 by 1914, followed by severe winter die-offs between 1915 and 1917. Nonetheless, by the mid-1930s wildlife biologists were reporting "overbrowsing" of the peninsula's elk range. Extended elk hunting seasons were opened again in 1936.

The following year, 4,000 hunters descended on the western peninsula. More than 800 elk were killed, many left lying in the woods. Two hunters were also killed in the melee, and several more were injured. The excesses of the 1937 elk hunt proved a powerful argument for the creation of Olympic National Park the following year. The park was created in part "to provide suitable winter range and permanent protection for the herds of native Roosevelt elk and other wildlife." It included much more of the elk's rain forest habitat than the original monument, and it remained closed to hunting. By the 1950s, the Olympics' elk population had stabilized at its present level of 4,000 to 5,000 animals. Some 3,000 thrive in the park's western rain forest valleys, a number well within the carrying capacity of their environment. Typically, 25 calves are produced per 100 elk in these valleys, compensating for natural mortalities. Olympic is one of the few areas in the world where a large population is controlled naturally without hunting.

These conditions are less prevalent in the Queets River corridor, a narrow band of protected river valley closely bounded on both sides by managed state and private timberlands where hunting is common. And it doesn't hold true at all for migratory east-side elk populations. The small bands of elk that inhabit the steep, narrow valleys of the Dosewallips, Duckabush, Hamma Hamma, and Skokomish rivers that drain east into Puget Sound spend only part of the year in Olympic National Park. The Dosewallips and Duckabush herds have been known to migrate fifteen to twenty miles, climbing nearly 5,000 feet in elevation to reach summer ranges in subalpine meadowlands of the park. In winter, however, these animals descend the mountains and leave the park to forage on adjoining forest service, state, and privately owned timberlands and valley farms. Large tracts of this winter range have succumbed to logging and residential development over the past few decades, and hunting pressure has increased dramatically. As a result, east-side elk numbers plummeted.

A moratorium on hunting east-side elk seems to have halted the decline. Currently, some 200 elk inhabit the eastern valleys. But the long-term future of this population remains uncertain. Studies of elk that use logged lands as well as park lands along the Queets corridor on the west side have shown that elk generally avoid the dense, even-aged plantations that replace natural forests in the wake of clearcut logging. Rather, they prefer old-growth forests, along with younger clearcuts that somewhat mimic natural openings, and young alder flats along valley floors. As with the east-side elk, the long-term survival of the Queets corridor elk will depend on sensitive management of state and private forest lands outside Olympic National Park.

Meanwhile, elk populations in western valleys outside the park have plummeted. Intensive clearcut logging of state and corporate timberlands through the 1960s and '70s resulted in an elaborate network of roads through dense, young tree plantations. Roads provide easy hunting (and poaching) access, and crowded stands of young, even-aged trees offer little in the way of habitat. Elk numbers on these lands declined from an estimated 10,000 in 1980 to about 6,000 today. It's worth noting that the "unmanaged" herds in the old-growth forests of the park remained stable throughout this time.

COUGAR AND WOLF

Elk and deer are major prey for that most secretive and solitary hunter of Olympic forests, the cougar. The large cat is the ghost of the forest, reclusive and silent. Unlike the more visible black bear and coyote, which are primarily scavengers of winter-killed elk and deer, cougars usually shun carcasses, preferring to take their meat on the hoof. Though little is known of the cougar population in the Olympics, evidence of the animal's presence—tracks and the scented scratch mounds in the dirt that mark their territories—is plentiful on backcountry trails, and cougars are believed to be common here. Males are known to cover ranges of more than fifty square miles. In more than three decades of wandering Olympic trails, I've seen only one, but it was an unforgettable experience. A large, tawny, and singularly graceful animal with distinctive facial markings, it slipped only partway into the brush ahead of me, then paused briefly to peer back before disappearing into the forest.

Cougars, or mountain lions (*Puma concolor*), are highly skilled and efficient hunters, perhaps the most adept large carnivore in North America. Unlike wolves, who hunt in packs, a cougar usually hunts alone, advancing on its prey stealthily, with slow, fluid, snakelike movements, before launching a carefully timed attack. It reaches its quarry in a bound or two, pouncing on its back with a twenty- to thirty-foot leap. A single gripping bite to the neck with the cougar's long incisors and powerful jaws can suffocate an elk or deer or sever its spinal cord with surgical precision. Though such acts of predation are rarely observed in the wild, a researcher tracking a radio-collared cougar in the Rockies arrived at a fresh kill site where a 150-pound cat had just taken down a 1,000-pound bull elk. The elk's neck was broken and its antlers driven nine inches into the ground.

The antlers and hooves of a large elk can inflict crippling or fatal injuries to cougars as well, however. There are numerous reported instances in which an elk was wary or a cat's timing was off, and the battle went the other way. Thus, where cougars prey on elk herds, they don't select quarry at random. Rather, they tend to go after more vulnerable or exposed animals, the tired or weak, sick, aged, or young. A cougar can take on average one large animal every twelve to fourteen days, more when a mother is feeding kittens (a growing family can devour a deer overnight).

Though such persistent hunting does affect populations of elk and deer, cougar predation is not usually a major factor determining herd size. The amount of habitat and quality and availability of winter range are far more important.

Females breed every other year, and young cougars spend most of their first two years with their mother. They're nursed for the first eight weeks, then taken to kill sites to eat small amounts of flesh. Gradually they learn how and what to hunt as they sharpen their skills in preparation for a solitary life as an adult. After twelve to twenty months, most young cougars disperse, often over long distances, and find their own territories, a process that may take years. During this transient period they are especially vulnerable. They may be killed by other cougars defending territories, or as has been more common recently, they may wander into areas occupied by people.

Several encounters between humans and young adult cougars on the peninsula in recent years have ended badly for the cougars. As the human population increases and more people move into previously wild areas, cougars may be losing some of their instinctive fear of humans. In 1994, Olympic National Forest reported its first instance of a young cougar attacking a child. Fortunately, the child's father and other adults chased the cat off. The only documented instance of a cougar fatally injuring a person in this state occurred more than seventy years ago.

Still, incidents such as these have been increasing throughout the West. There have been seventy-three cougar attacks on humans in the United States and Canada between 1991 and 2003; ten were fatal. Park rangers advise visitors hiking with children to keep them close by. Hikers who come upon a carcass that might be a fresh kill are advised to give the area a wide berth. Those few who may suddenly meet a cougar should not flee, but stand their ground or back slowly away, giving it a chance to leave. As forest lands outside the park are converted to residential development and civilization continues to encroach into formerly wild habitats, encounters between humans and cougars will likely continue. As is inevitably the case in such trends, it will be the wild animals that pay the price.

Historically, Roosevelt elk and blacktail deer in the Olympics were also preyed upon by another efficient though less solitary predator, the wolf. Before settlement, gray wolves coexisted with elk herds in most valleys of the Olympics. In 1861, ethnologist James Swan found "innumerable quantities of wolves" on Sequim Prairie. Their howling kept him up all night. Wolves were reported as common as late as 1894. But by the early twentieth century, following decimation of elk herds and after a program of systematic extermination by settlers and federal trappers, wolves disappeared from the Olympics. In 1919, Amos Cameron caught a wolf in a bear trap in the upper Gray Wolf River drainage. It was one of a pack of six following a herd of elk through snow. The following year, settler Grant Humes trapped a male wolf on the Elwha River. It was the last documented animal of its kind in the Olympics.

A few bounties were paid over the next few years, but a study conducted by noted wildlife biologist Adolph Murie in 1935 made it official. Wolves had been extirpated from the Olympic Mountains. By the time the park was established three years later, there were no wolves left to save. Murie's report also contained something unusual and quite visionary for its time. He recommended that when a national park is established in the Olympics, wolves be restored to Olympic valleys. Seventy years later, his recommendation is still pending.

As of this writing, the gray wolf is listed under the 1973 Endangered Species Act. The act directs federal agencies to insure the preservation and recovery of any species threatened with extinction in "all or a significant portion of its range." In 1981, a National Park Service advisory board nominated Olympic as one of the two best wolf reintroduction sites in the national park system and recommended planning and information programs be undertaken. Olympic National Park echoed this recommendation in a 1974 management plan. In the meantime, the other recommended site, Yellowstone National Park, began a successful wolf reintroduction program in 1996. A decade later, the presence of fifteen wolf packs has revitalized the Yellowstone ecosystem. A resulting decline in Yellowstone's northern elk population has allowed aspen groves and streamside stands of willow and cottonwood to recover. Tree shade cools waters for trout. Songbird numbers have increased and beaver colonies have returned to Yellowstone streams. The park's coyote populations have fallen by half, resulting in an increase in rodents, a boon for red foxes and hawks. The return of a keystone species, Yellowstone's top predator, has sent waves of renewal cascading throughout the greater Yellowstone ecosystem.

In the wake of the early success at Yellowstone, the U.S. Fish and Wildlife Service conducted an extensive feasibility study for returning wolves to Olympic National Park. The study, released in 1999, found that it was biologically feasible to restore wolves to the Olympic ecosystem. It concluded that the park and surrounding forest service wilderness areas could support a healthy population of about fifty-six wolves distributed in six to seven packs in river valleys. The primary habitat that would be used by wolves is almost entirely (98 percent) in public ownership, and the likelihood of wolves coming into contact with humans, pets, and livestock, the study concluded, would be insignificant. Wolf predation on elk and deer would reduce populations at the most about 17 percent, well within population viability, though concern was expressed for isolated, east-side elk populations.

Nevertheless, opposition to reintroduction ran strong in the resource towns of the western peninsula. A series of contentious town hall meetings in three of these towns—only weeks before the feasibility study was released—was enough to kill the proposal. Ironically, a survey conducted a year earlier showed that more than six out of ten Puget Sound area residents favored introduction. On the Olympic Peninsula a majority supported the idea. The reason is obvious: restoring the top predator to one of America's premiere wilderness areas and old-growth forest preserves is simply the right thing to do.

In the rain forest valleys of Olympic National Park, it's possible to step into the profound beauty and ecological wholeness of a landscape essentially unaltered by modern man. Here, wildlife populations still exist within the ancient cycles and dynamics of the forest, and processes of evolution continue uninterrupted. How much more stirring it would be for us to have the haunting music of wolves returned to these valleys. Wolves would add a singular note of wholeness to the persistent music of Olympic rivers. And as in Yellowstone, their return would restore a remarkable and dynamic ecosystem to wholeness.

CHAPTER 5

The Old-Growth Forest Community

I T'S a warm morning in late spring and a biologist friend and I have
hiked deep into the old-growth forest of the Sol Duc Valley. We're
looking for a pair of owls known to inhabit this reach of forest to
see if they are nesting. We climb through an open forest of silver fir and
hemlock. A half-hour after leaving the trail, at a little over 3,000 feet in
elevation, we traverse the slope. Within minutes, we find the nest tree, a
broken-off hemlock snag about three and a half feet in diameter. We're
still unpacking equipment when the owl swoops down over our heads and
lands on a nearby limb. From this distance, the northern spotted owl is a
striking bird. A stippled brown and white breast fluffs out beneath a dark
oval face ring surrounding soft gray feathered brows and alert dark eyes.
The owl's interest is piqued as my friend places a small mouse on a limb,
but the owl remains aloof on its perch. Nearly fifteen minutes pass before
the owl sweeps silently down, grasps the mouse in its talons, and flies to
a perch nearer the nest. From there it whistles a contact call and hoots to
its mate, a muffled *who-who-who-who*, with the mouse still in its beak.
She answers, and the owl disappears into the nest cavity and reappears
seconds later, sans mouse.

That's a good sign. It means the female is probably with her young.
The previous year proved a poor one for owl reproduction on the Olympic
Peninsula, which is frequently the case, but this breeding season is show-
ing improvement. Throughout the summer, park biologists will monitor

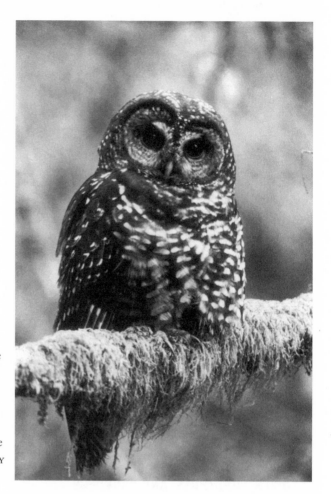

Listed as threatened under the Endangered Species Act in 1990, northern spotted owls have continued to decline in Olympic forests. Past logging outside the park and displacement by bared owls throughout the peninsula's forests are seen as causes. PHOTO BY JANIS BURGER.

53 owl territories in the park, assessing population levels and determining reproductive success. It's estimated that between 200 and 250 spotted owl pairs inhabit the 6,200 square miles of the Olympic Peninsula; the majority, about 175 pairs, reside in Olympic National Park.

In 1990, the northern spotted owl was listed as threatened throughout its range by the U.S. Fish and Wildlife Service. Since the peninsula lies near the northern extent of the owl's range, and the population here is isolated from owls in the Cascade Range to the east, there is concern over the spotted owl's long-range viability in the Olympics. But it's not just the health of this singular species that fuels concern, it's the health and viability of the old-growth forest ecosystem the owl has come to symbolize.

Spotted owls were thrust onto center stage in the ongoing controversy over the fate of remaining old-growth forests. Estimates vary, but it's generally agreed that at the beginning of the twentieth century, 19 million acres of old-growth forest covered the coastal hills and valleys of the Pacific Northwest. Less than 10 percent remains. Spotted owls need old-growth forests for nesting and feeding habitat. That's why forest service biologists chose the northern spotted owl (*Strix occidentalis caurina*) as an "indicator species" for the entire old-growth ecosystem. Plucked from the obscurity of its deep forest home, the spotted owl now serves as a kind of canary in the coal mine. By monitoring the owl's population trends, biologists attempt to assess the health of the old-growth community.

The largest preserve of temperate old-growth forest in the Northwest, Olympic National Park offers scientists an opportunity to study a relatively intact old-growth ecosystem. Owl studies and other old-growth research conducted here could prove critical to future recovery and restoration of previously logged forests elsewhere in the Northwest. More than 430 species of birds, mammals, amphibians, reptiles, and fish are known to inhabit the Olympic Peninsula as permanent or seasonal residents (another 50-odd bird species appear from time to time). All rely to some extent on the healthy functioning of this diverse forest ecosystem. For the past two decades, the spotlight has shown most glaringly on spotted owls.

OWLS, SQUIRRELS, AND TRUFFLES

Nesting in cavities near the broken tops of old-growth trees, spotted owls can range great distances in search of their favored prey, northern flying squirrels, bushy-tailed woodrats, and snowshoe hares. These prey species tend to be less abundant in the Olympics than in coastal forests farther to the south, which may account for the larger home ranges of Peninsula owls—from 3,000 to 33,000 acres per pair. Spotted owls can maneuver deftly in the winding canyons and multistoried layers of the old-growth forest canopy; the same canopy hinders the larger great horned owls that prey on spotted owls. Flying squirrels, which make up a large part of spotted owls' prey on the peninsula, also prefer the forest canopy, except when they're drawn to the forest floor to feed on truffles. The spotted owl/flying squirrel/truffle story is a perfect example not only of the kinds of specialized interactions that have evolved in these ancient communities, but of the complex web of mutually beneficial interconnections between species that form the heart of the forest ecosystem.

It's somehow appropriate that spotted owls, one of the most prominent members of the old-growth community, should be intimately connected with one of the forest's most hidden fruits. Truffles are the spoor-laden fruiting bodies of certain fungi. Unlike their aboveground cousins the mushrooms, truffles grow just beneath the surface. Fungi are everywhere in these forests; their slender, nearly invisible mycelia permeate and cover every vertical foot of it, from canopy needles to root hairs. In the canopy, fungi join algae, yeasts, and bacteria to form a microscopic community on and within the needles that scientists call simply "scuzz." Some of these fungi are toxic to needle-grazing insects; others fix nitrogen from the atmosphere, while others serve as food for a number of arthropod species such as mites and springtails—as well as spiders and other predators who eat them. These predators in turn keep other leaf-eating insects in check.

Fungi also play a critical role in forest soils, where they form mycorrhizal relationships with the roots of trees. The mycelia, the vegetative, nonfruiting parts of these fungi, grow on and penetrate tree root tissues. Their threadlike hyphae, which are about one-hundredth the diameter of a typical root hair, easily penetrate the interstices between soil particles and greatly enhance a root's ability to absorb moisture and nutrients. These fungi house nitrogen-fixing bacteria beneficial to both fungus and host tree. They also stimulate root growth and inhibit harmful pathogens and root grazers. For their part, trees feed sugars and amino acids—products of photosynthesis—to the fungi, which cannot photosynthesize. Mycelia networks also allow trees to exchange carbon and nutrients among themselves, a wonderful function that allows understory trees to benefit from the photosynthesis of larger trees in the canopy above them. Most plant roots are colonized in this way, including all Northwest trees. Foresters have found that in the absence of fungi, trees do not grow as well, and many forest seedlings will not survive. Fungi play an equally important role in cycling nutrients back to the forest from dead and decaying wood and plant matter.

Mushrooms are familiar to all of us, truffles less so. But their sharp, pungent aromas are well known to forest creatures and are irresistible to a number of small mammals. In the old-growth forests of the Olympics these include Douglas squirrels, Townsend's chipmunks, deer mice, red-backed voles, and flying squirrels—not to mention elk and deer. Fungal spores survive in the intestines of many small mammals, where they combine with bacteria and yeast, which makes them easily used by tree roots. The fecal pellets of small mammals scurrying about the forest are thus an important means of distributing these spores, especially in newly disturbed areas, where they prepare exposed soils for new tree growth. Although flying squirrels spend most of their time in the forest canopy, gliding deftly from tree to tree and feeding on lichens, the lure of truffles draws them frequently to the forest floor, especially during the spring to fall fruiting season. There, busily digging into the soil for these tasty treats, they become easy targets for spotted owls swooping down on silent wings.

Protected from habitat destruction, spotted owls have had few natural threats in Olympic National Park, but just as concern was beginning to mount about the species, a new competitor appeared in Olympic's forests. Today it poses a significant threat to spotted owls.

Barred owls (*Strix varia*) are a slightly larger, more aggressive, and more adaptable cousin of spotted owls that do not require old-growth habitat. Historically, barred owls inhabited forests east of the Rockies. They extended their range west across Canada over the past century and made inroads into western Washington by the mid-1970s. The first barred owl was noted on the Olympic Peninsula in 1985. Since then they have made incursions into spotted owl habitat, displacing the native owls throughout the Olympics. Biologists believe they are a major factor in spotted owl declines here. Spotted owl numbers in the park have dropped from an estimated 230 pairs in 1995 to about 175 pairs a decade later. Many of the owls that remain have retreated into more marginal, higher elevation habitats. Adult survival rate appears to be declining. In Olympic National Forest, spotted owl numbers have fallen by nearly half over that period. No one knows how many barred owls have made their way into Olympic Peninsula forests, but their rate of detection by biologists increases by about 15 percent per year. If the trend continues, spotted owls could disappear from the northern part of their range.

By closely monitoring spotted owl populations in the Olympics, biologists keep a necessary finger on the pulse of the forest ecosystem. It's not only the species of the old-growth forest that are of concern, but the vital processes and interrelationships that have evolved in this ancient and complex realm.

THE ARCHITECTURE OF AN OLD-GROWTH FOREST

"Old growth" is a condition that develops over time in the coniferous forests of the Northwest. The major elements of the old-growth community were in place here when the climate stabilized about 5,000 years ago, but the finely tuned relationships between species and their environments suggest associations that reach back much farther than that, possibly through the climatic fluctuations of the Pleistocene. It may be that the genetic wisdom encoded in the ancient forest ecosystem includes the ability to respond and adapt to natural disturbances and dramatic shifts in climate and weather patterns we newcomers have yet to witness in the Northwest. We know the old-growth ecosystem has thrived through repeated episodes of wildfire, wind, volcanic eruption, and glacial advance. Whether it can survive the onslaught of human design remains a troubling question.

It takes between 175 and 250 years for old-growth characteristics to begin to appear in most forest stands in the Northwest (that's more than a century longer than cutting rotations on most industrial tree farms). A 250-year-old stand is still "young" for old growth. Large trees are certainly an important part of an old-growth forest, but so are large standing snags and downed trees in various stages of decomposition. The uneven, partly open canopy that results when old trees fall and understory trees reach to fill the void is part of the old-growth story, as are the sunny glades that usher in a diversity of plants during the often decades-long interim. As is dramatically evident in the rain forest, an abundance of epiphytic plants, lichens, liverworts, and mosses also characterizes this unique forest community.

These conditions, combined with the moderate climate (cool in summer, warm in winter) and the long-term stability found within these centuries-old forests, have created a specialized habitat that nurtures a richness of species and complexity of relationships extending well beyond the

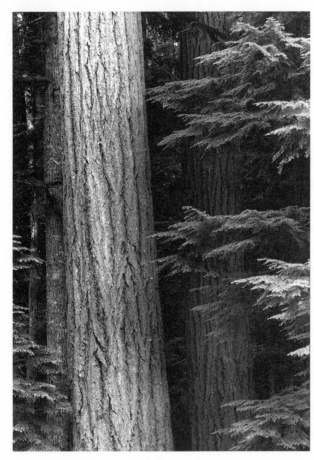

An old-growth forest of western hemlock and Douglas fir (Douglas fir is easily recognized by its deeply furrowed bark). Unlike Douglas fir, hemlock can seed in and thrive in the shade of an existing forest. In the unlikely absence of natural disturbances such as windstorms and wildfires, western hemlock will eventually dominate a stand. PHOTO BY JANIS BURGER.

spotted owl. At least seventy species of birds, thirty small mammals, and twenty amphibians are known to be associated with old-growth forests. One researcher noted that forty wildlife species that use old-growth or mature forest for primary habitat cannot meet their habitat needs outside this forest type. Debate continues over the number of species that actually depend on old-growth forests as habitat. Some, such as pileated woodpeckers and northern goshawks, seem to do well in younger natural or unmanaged forests (which usually still contain a biological legacy of old growth: snags, downed logs, a mix of species). Others, like marbled murrelets and Vaux's swifts, appear to be solely dependent on this forest type. Still others, such as the endemic Olympic torrent salamander and Cope's giant salamander, are only rarely found outside old-growth forests.

LIVES OF THE OLD-GROWTH FOREST

Until recently the marbled murrelet (*Brachyramphus marmoratus*) remained the most mysterious of seabirds. It was the last of North America's breeding birds to have its nest discovered. Ornithologists searched for the nest of this quail-sized seabird for the better part of a century. There were plenty of clues to their whereabouts, however. Murrelets were frequently seen flying inland from the ocean, sometimes carrying fish, and their calls were often heard as the birds passed over coastal forests. They were so common early in the twentieth century that loggers working in coastal forests dubbed them "fog larks." Chicks occasionally turned up on the floors of old-growth forests, but it wasn't until 1974 that a nest was finally discovered in California. It was in a depression on a moss-covered limb high up in an old-growth Douglas fir. Since then, hundreds of nests have been found in coastal forests, on the Olympic Peninsula and elsewhere, some as far as fifty miles inland from the coast.

Nearly all nests found south of Alaska have been located in the upper canopy of large old-growth trees. Murrelets choose broad, horizontal conifer limbs covered with a thick layer of epiphytic mosses and lichens for nest sites, usually hidden beneath the shelter of low overhanging foliage. Females lay a single egg in a shallow depression in the moss, and the parents take turns incubating, usually for twenty-four-hour stretches. After the chick hatches, both parents make the lengthy ocean-to-forest commute to feed it, sometimes as often as four times a day.

When fledging time approaches, usually after thirty to forty days, young murrelets pluck the remaining down from the tips of their feathers, exercise their wings, and are ready to fly. The parents usually stop bringing food at this time. Remarkably (for young murrelets seem aerodynamically unintended for flight—one researcher likened them to flying potatoes), the hungry fledglings leap from their nest and fly directly to salt water, where they land and begin to fish.

Though forest nesting is unusual for a seabird, it offers marbled murrelets some unique advantages. The cool environment is compatible to a bird accustomed to the chill waters of the north Pacific. The forest offers shelter from coastal storms and protection from coastal predators such as bald eagles and gulls. Some biologists suspect this nesting strategy reaches back to a time when giant dawn redwoods mantled the coast from California to the Aleutian Islands. If so, the strategy served murrelets well for some 15 million years. But it was no advantage when industrial logging entered the picture.

The decline of marbled murrelets following the destruction of old-growth forests on the Pacific Coast was pronounced. Breeding populations are no longer found in areas where coastal old-growth forests have been logged, and it's estimated that about 20,000 birds remain along the California, Oregon, and Washington coast. In 1992, after years of foot dragging, the U.S. Fish and Wildlife Service belatedly listed the marbled murrelet as threatened in those three states. Four million acres of critical habitat for the species' recovery was designated, predominantly on federal lands. Viable populations still exist in the northern parts of their range along the Gulf of Alaska, where, in the absence of ancient forests, some birds nest on the ground. Murrelets also remain relatively abundant in British Columbia. In the United States, however, despite endangered species protections on federal lands, marbled murrelet numbers are in decline. That is a shame, for murrelets, like the wild salmon that return to their natal streams beneath forest trees to spawn, embody the unity of forest and sea and attest the health of a functioning ecosystem.

Vaux's swifts also rely almost exclusively on old-growth forests. True to their names, these small, streamlined birds are astounding fliers and spend most of their lives in flight, cruising the high forest canopy and devouring insects on the wing. They can fly as much as 600 miles in a single day. Vaux's swifts construct their nests in the large, hollow, often burned-out snags of old forests. They nest and roost in colonies, but unlike their eastern cousins the chimney swifts, Vaux's have not warmed up to chimneys for nest sites. Studies show that Vaux's swifts are much more abundant in old-growth than in younger forests, no doubt because of the availability of suitable snags.

Another distinctive snag dweller common to peninsula forests is the pileated woodpecker. Largest of the woodpeckers after the ivory-billed, pileateds sport flashy red crests and long, chisel-like beaks. They feed primarily on larval and adult carpenter ants, and the staccato drumbeat of their jackhammering on snags to get at them is unmistakable. Pileateds excavate roosting and nesting cavities in large snags two feet or more in

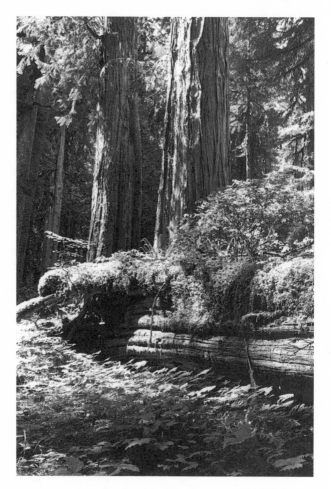

Western red cedar grows throughout the lowland forest, usually favoring streamsides, seeps, and swamps. Native Northwest cultures found a myriad of uses for red cedar, and its clear, rot-resistant wood is still prized for roofing and siding. As a result, most old-growth cedar stands outside of the park have been logged. PHOTO BY JANIS BURGER.

girth. Many of these cavities, roomy, dry, well insulated, and lined with wood chips, are later put to use by Douglas and flying squirrels, owls, bats, and martens for nesting and roost sites. Wood ducks and fishers also favor cavities in large snags, and larger mammals such as bobcats and even bears are known to "hole up" in them. As snags age and soften with decomposition, they become easier to work. By then, some 35 to 40 percent of the bird species common to Northwest forests may have used them for nest sites. Raptors such as goshawks and sharp-shinned hawks favor snags for perches and for plucking posts, where they pluck and eat their kills. A number of bats, including long-eared and long-legged myotis as well as silver-haired and hoary bats, find optimal breeding habitat beneath the loose sheaths of bark that clothe old Douglas fir snags.

Though not dependent on the peninsula's old-growth forests, Douglas squirrels, or chickarees, are found throughout the Douglas fir forest, and their territorial chatter punctuates almost any walk in the woods. Chickarees do reach their highest abundance in old-growth forests, however, and they're all but absent from clearcuts. Their busy, gray-brown shapes, brightened by orange underparts and eye rings and often crowned with their bushy, upturned tails, are a common sight in Olympic forests; the cone husks of their middens decorate many a downed log or stump. Autumn in the silver fir zone can be a particularly hazardous time for hikers, as the stout, pitchy cones cut by squirrels rocket to the forest floor like small mortars. Douglas fir cones cached for the winter and forgotten have proved important seed sources following fires or other natural disturbances in the forest. Chickarees are also important dispersers of fungal spores throughout the forest. Because they harvest and store so much food, Douglas squirrels remain quite active through the winter, and they're not above spending precious energy harassing trespassers from the safety of a limb. Quick as they are, squirrels do serve as prey for owls, hawks, and martens, among others. But the presence of these predators hasn't lessened the squirrels' brashness, nor has it seemed to put a nick in their population.

Martens and fishers, both sleek and accomplished hunters, are members of the weasel clan. The marten, the smaller of the two, prefers montane forests, where it hunts a number of small mammals relentlessly and effectively. Its yellow-brown coat, low rounded ears, and orange throat patch are unmistakable. Though martens can hunt in the canopy (they share with spotted owls a taste for flying squirrels), winter frequently brings them to the forest floor, where they search among the downed logs of old-growth forests for rodents. They are also known to use logs, well insulated with snow, for winter resting spots.

Marten numbers are in steep decline in the Olympics, and sightings of them, or their tracks, have become extremely rare. The last confirmed martin sightings here were in the early 1990s. But fishers have made a recent and dramatic comeback. The fisher (*Martes pennanti*) is a sleek, dark brown, catlike animal with short legs and a long, stout tail. Fishers are consummate predators of mature and old-growth forests, quick and efficient hunters of snowshoe hares, squirrels, small mammals, and birds.

Douglas squirrels or "chickarees" are common residents of most Olympic forests, nesting in trees and feeding mainly on conifer seeds. Chickarees can often be seen gathering and storing cones in late summer and fall. Like many rodents, they also have a taste for fungi and are important agents in disseminating spores. PHOTO BY JANIS BURGER.

They once hunted forests across the United States and Canada, but their fur, often compared to Russian sable, was prized for its deep luster. It led to the fisher's undoing. Through the nineteenth and early twentieth centuries, fishers were trapped relentlessly. In 1920, with their pelts commanding as much as $120 each, thirty-seven fishers were trapped in the Queets Valley. Another twenty were taken from the Quinault the following year. By the 1940s they were eliminated from most of their range in the United States. The last documented fisher on the peninsula was a female trapped near Lilliwaup Swamp in the eastern Olympics in 1969.

Fishers prefer to hunt in mature and old-growth forests of low- and mid-elevation valleys and slopes; they use snags and down logs for denning and resting. Unfortunately, these are the same forests that sustained the heaviest logging on the peninsula and elsewhere. Population surveys conducted in the 1990s confirmed that fishers had been extirpated from Washington. In 1998, the fisher was listed as endangered by Washington

State. More recently, studies conducted on a reintroduced fisher population in Oregon's Rogue River valley assessed habitat requirements for fishers in Northwest forests. A feasibility assessment conducted by the Washington Department of Fish and Wildlife identified the northern and western forest valleys of Olympic National Park as the best suitable habitat for fisher reintroduction in the state. In 2007, the park service, in cooperation with the Washington Department of Fish and Wildlife, released a plan to return fishers to Olympic. And early in 2008, eighteen fishers were released in the snowy forests of the park's Elwha and nearby Morse Creek valleys. The animals were captured in British Columbia, where healthy populations still exist, and examined and cared for prior to transport. When they were released into the park, they bolted out of their wooden pens and into the winter forest without looking back. Over a three-year period up to a hundred fishers will be released into lowland forest areas from the Elwha to the Quinault valleys. The animals will be closely monitored to evaluate success of the reintroduction. In the first few weeks following the release, fishers are exploring habitats from the Dosewallips and Gray Wolf watersheds in the east Olympics west to Lake Crescent. They have been seen hunting mountain beavers in the lowlands and snowshoe hares below Hurricane Ridge. Reintroducing fishers, one of only two mammal species missing from Olympic National Park, is a major step toward restoring the wholeness of this incredible forest ecosystem.

Along with charismatic predators like the marten and fisher are a number of less conspicuous dwellers of Olympic's old-growth and late-succession forests. Goshawk and merlin are swift and effective hunters of the forest. They are seldom seen, but their presence is felt in the quickness and alertness of their favored prey, small mammals and forest birds. The brown creeper, an inconspicuous forest bird, blends so well with the bark under which it nests that it can evade predators simply by freezing in place. Winter wrens stay low in the forest among ferns and brush, their presence made known by their mellifluous singing. Townsend's warblers hawk for insects all summer in the high forest canopy, where they nest, and frequently linger into fall and early winter. Chestnut-backed chickadees and red-breasted nuthatches are found in the forest year-round, as are golden-crowned kinglets, whose winter flocks are often seen high in the canopy. Hidden in downed logs and in burrows beneath the ground, red-backed voles dine almost exclusively on truffles, while several types of shrews rustle about busily in search of beetles and other invertebrates. Even the ubiquitous white-footed deer mouse shows higher numbers in old-growth than in younger forests. These and countless other species are as integral a part of the fabric of the old-growth ecosystem as spotted owls or Roosevelt elk.

THE LOWLAND FOREST

Whether hiking the trails or driving the Olympic Highway, travelers heading east from the rain forest valleys of the western Olympics to the drier northern and eastern slopes of the peninsula will notice the lowland forest taking on a distinctly different flavor. The western hemlock and Douglas fir forest of the northern and eastern Olympics lacks the rain forest's lush extravagance of mosses, ferns, and epiphytes, for instance, as well as its abundance of nurse logs and resulting colonnades. East of the Sol Duc River, the domed crowns and deep green foliage of grand fir (*Abies grandis*) replace Sitka spruce in the lower valleys and floodplains, and pines become noticeable throughout the forest. Large western red cedars still grace moist areas and stream banks, places where they have escaped the frequent wildfires, but the crowning glory of the lowland forest is the Douglas fir.

This striking tree was first described in 1791 by Archibald Menzies, the naturalist who sailed with Captain Vancouver; it was more than a century later that David Douglas collected the seeds of this tree and sent them back to England. Not a true fir, it was known variously as a pine, a "yew-leafed fir," and a spruce. Taxonomists finally settled on "false-hemlock" (*Pseudotsuga menziesii*) or, as it's commonly known, Douglas fir. Simply stated, Douglas fir is a magnificent tree. Found in a number of different forest types throughout the West, it reaches its greatest size in the old-growth forests of the coastal Northwest.

The deeply furled, rust brown, often fire-charred bark of ancient Douglas firs always catches my eye in the shade of a mixed forest. As early morning or evening light threads its way through the columns of trees, an old Douglas fir can seem as luminous as a softly glowing lamp. Its coarse-textured, moss- and lichen-flaked bark seems to invite the hand, and a few old giants alongside popular trails show evidence of years of "hugging."

Olympic National Park harbors some of the finest stands of old-growth Douglas fir remaining anywhere. Outstanding examples can be found at Barnes Creek on the shores of Lake Crescent, along the Sol Duc Road and the short trail to Sol Duc Falls, and throughout much of the Elwha Valley. The upper end of this valley, where the Elwha begins to bend west above Godkin Creek, supports an exceptionally beautiful forest with trees reaching diameters of eight feet or more. Protected in their valley bottom enclave in the heart of the mountains, some of these giants may date to wildfires that burned through the area in the early 1300s. The Skokomish River valley in the southeast corner of the park also supports stunning Douglas fir forests; some may be easily seen from the short Shady Lane Trail at Staircase. A magnificent Douglas fir grove on forest service land can be viewed along the Rain Forest nature trail on the south shore of Quinault Lake.

Taking in one of these grand old Douglas firs from broad base to distant crown never fails to lift my spirit; the first stout limb emerges 80 or 100 feet up the trunk, and the whorl of limbs beyond fades into the splintered green light of the upper canopy. Looking out over a valley or mountain slope thick with the ragged, broken crowns of ancient firs suggests that all is right with at least one corner of the world, so there must be hope for the rest.

Though it is among the longest-lived northwestern trees, capable of reaching 1,000 to 1,200 years in age, Douglas fir is not the climax tree species of the lowland forest. It can successfully reproduce only after a major disturbance clears standing forests and exposes mineral soils. Once established, though, it is vigorous and quick to grow, outcompeting other tree species and dominating young stands. Individual trees can eventually reach heights greater than 250 feet and diameters of more than 12 feet. The clear, strong, straight-grained wood of old-growth Douglas fir built the timber industry in the Northwest, and it remains the prime commercial timber species on the world market today.

Since Douglas firs are unable to reproduce in dense shade, western hemlock is considered the climax tree species of the lowland forest. In the absence of large disturbances, a Douglas fir forest will be slowly replaced by shade-tolerant hemlocks and western red cedars. But this textbook ver-

One of the hidden jewels of the forest, Calypso orchid or fairy slipper brightens mossy trailsides. Fairy slippers rely on the presence of certain fungi in the soil to successfully reproduce. PHOTO BY JANIS BURGER.

sion of forest succession actually occurs only rarely, in the wetter parts of the forest. Elsewhere, the lowland forest proves itself a much more dynamic system. Not only do catastrophic wildfires and windstorms "recycle" forest stands, but river cuts, mass slumping, ice storms, diseases, and insect infestations also take their toll. Even where forests are left undisturbed, long-lived Douglas firs continue to loom over the younger forest like proctors in a schoolyard. In the rainshadow of the northeastern Olympics, where the fire frequency is compounded by scarce rainfall, Douglas firs maintain climax communities on a few exposed south-facing sites, but such stands are rare, amounting to less than 1 percent of the forest.

Like the temperate rain forests of the western Olympics, rainshadow forest communities of the northeast are another essential part of the Olympic ecosystem. They represent an adaptation to a much harsher, drier environment—conditions common to the intermountain West, east of the Cascade crest. In the rainshadow of the Olympics one can encounter trees typical of southern Coast Range or Rocky Mountain forests, and a number of understory shrubs and plants thrive here that occur rarely, or not at all, in west-side forests. Oxalis, that shamrocklike ground cover that carpets forest floors of the western slope, disappears in the rainshadow. In its place, the tough, low-growing shrub salal and the spiky leaves of Oregon grape crowd the forest floor. Baldhip rose is much more abundant, and the prolific pink blossoms of Pacific rhododendron serve as the signature of the dry-side forest. The pale blossoms of Pacific dogwood and bitter cherry trees also add brightness to the spring woods. Two members of the heath family typical of drier climates, the shrubs kinnickinnick and manzanita, are also common to rainshadow forests, as are the shrubs snowbrush ceanothus and ocean-spray.

A tree that stands out among the lowland forests of the rainshadow is a graceful hardwood, the Pacific madrona (*Arbutus menziesii*). The only broad-leaved evergreen tree found in peninsula forests, madrona retains its dark, shiny leaves in winter. Instead of dropping leaves, it sheds its thin outer bark to reveal wonderfully sinuous tan to purplish brown limbs. Clusters of pink-tinged, cream-colored flowers in spring yield bright orange-red berrylike fruits in autumn, making this one of the loveliest of woodland trees.

Such continental tree species as quaking aspen and Engelmann spruce put in rare appearances here, as does common juniper, which forms a shrub at higher elevations. A rare Rocky Mountain juniper woodland can be found in the upper Dungeness country, and dense stands of lodgepole pines reminiscent of the northern Rockies grace high south-facing slopes. Whitebark pines form a timberline tree in the open meadows of the upper Dungeness, just as they do along the high, windswept ridges north of Yellowstone.

The lower forest also follows patterns common east of the Cascades. In the lowlands of Dungeness Valley near Sequim, there is a second timberline. Rainfall drops below fifteen inches a year, and forests give way to prairie. Growing among the unmitigated sprawl of the town of Sequim, the last remnants of a Garry oak woodland attest to an arid, presettlement savanna landscape similar to Oregon's Willamette Valley or the historic prairies south of Puget Sound. Sequim Prairie, along with other extensive rainshadow prairies here and on nearby islands, was maintained by Native American burning for the past 3,000 to 4,000 years. Some eighty plants common to Sequim Prairie are known to have been used by native people in the Northwest, and camas bulbs, found only in prairies, were a staple of Native Americans' diets. Some of the same species found in remnant prairies today also grow on rocky south-facing slopes of the Dungeness uplands, suggesting the mountains' role as a biological refuge during the ice ages. Sequim Prairie was known to early settlers for its abundance of game animals and was hunted heavily. "Beside elk and wolves, deer abound," noted James Swan in 1861, "and vast numbers are annually killed by settlers and hunters either for their own food or else for the Victoria market." In some ways the Dungeness valley was a small Serengeti, a wonderfully rich assemblage of open prairies and woodlands, grazing herbivores, and their predators. Today, a few native prickly pear cacti (*Opuntia fragilis*) can still be found in undisturbed corners of the Prairie, but agriculture and urban and commercial growth have altered the landscape irrevocably.

These unusual arid-ground plant communities found throughout the northeast rainshadow of the Olympics are astounding for their proximity to one of the wettest spots in North America. More than a reflection of this area's low rainfall and active fire history, they are the botanical legacy of the region's long-term climatic history. As we face the certainty of global warming, these drought-tolerant, fire-adapted communities are critical genetic reserves deserving of careful management and protection.

FIRE AND THE FOREST COMMUNITY

In the wet, temperate rain forests of the peninsula's west-side valleys, wind plays the dominant role in forest disturbance. These forests succumb to major wildfires barely once every 500 to 900 years, while severe windstorms hit the coast on an average of once every 20 years. Elsewhere on the peninsula, it's a different story. Wildfire has been the major catalyst shaping forest ecosystems from lowland valleys to subalpine meadows. Before settlement, large lightning-caused fires swept through the forests of the Olympic Peninsula countless times. Evidence of past fires—in the rings of old-growth trees and layers of charcoal in soils and bogs—shows at least three periods of intense fire activity in Olympic forests over the past 1,000 years. They were probably characterized by large-scale climate fluctuations bringing a combination of summer drought and drying east winds.

The first period culminated in the year 1308, when a large fire swept across millions of acres in the western Cascades and Olympics, burning about half the forests on the peninsula. Conflagrations like these are referred to as stand-replacement fires, because they kill most trees on burned sites and open the ground to new seedlings. In the thick, densely forested old-growth stands of the Olympics, large, infrequent stand-replacement fires are the rule. The Douglas firs that seeded in on charred soils in the wake of the 1308 fire are now 650-plus-year-old giants and can be found today scattered throughout the park. A second series of intense wildfires scorched the Olympics from the mid-1400s until about 1538. These fires swept through mountainsides and valley bottoms across the Olympics, often reburning areas recovering from the earlier fire. Large expanses of forest in the Washington and Oregon Cascades also burned at this time.

The last great series of wildfires to hit the peninsula swept through on dry east winds around 300 years ago, culminating in 1701. Those fires burned more than a million acres of lowland forest along the eastern and northern slopes of the Olympics from tidewater to middle and upper elevations. The great lowland Douglas fir forests that greeted early settlers and became the basis for the peninsula's early timber economy had their beginnings in the ashes of this fire. The late nineteenth and early twentieth centuries saw a rash of smaller fires, largely the result of early land clearing and the reckless logging practices of the day. The Dungeness fire of 1890–91 burned 30,000 acres of dry rainshadow forest. The Sol Duc burn of 1907 covered 13,000 acres in the Sol Duc Valley, and the 1951 Forks fire, triggered by a train in logging slash, burned 33,000 acres, nearly destroying the town of Forks.

Unlike clearcut logging, natural disturbances like wildfires and windstorms are selective in what they take. As was seen in the 1988 Yellowstone fires, wildfires commonly burn in patches, leaving ribbons and islands of standing green trees, even in the most heavily burned areas. The thick, corky bark of older Douglas firs insulates them from most light and moderate fires and some high-intensity fires as well. Surviving trees serve as seed sources for the new forest, further selecting for this fire-resistant trait. Moist areas along streams, draws, and wetlands are frequently spared, allowing red cedars and other moisture-loving forest plants to survive. Large downed logs that have absorbed water like big sponges provide cool, moist islands during fires where small mammals, amphibians, and invertebrates can survive. Downed logs also protect fungi needed to form mycorrhizal relationships with new tree seedlings. Fire-killed trees that remain standing serve important habitat needs for a number of snag-dependent wildlife species.

The forest has evolved with these disturbances, and they are essential in maintaining ecosystem function and diversity. The pattern of small clearings, alpine meadows, and different-aged forest stands that result from wildfires overlay topographic differences in rainfall, elevation, and slope exposure to create a biologically rich mosaic of natural forests across the Olympic landscape.

THE MONTANE FOREST

Farther up the mountain slopes, beginning at about 1,000 feet in elevation in the western Olympics, higher east of the Bailey Range, the lowland forest grades into mountain forests of Pacific silver fir. Silver fir, or "lovely fir" (*Abies amabilis*) as it's known to science, is a tall, stately conifer with resinous silver-gray bark and deep green foliage. The fires that raged through much of the western hemlock–Douglas fir forest over the last 700 years have largely missed this cool, wet forest zone, making silver fir–hemlock stands among the oldest forest communities (if not the oldest trees) in the Olympics. Western hemlocks of the lowlands persist upslope to become part of this zone, but silver fir's extreme tolerance to dense shade leads to its eventual domination of the montane forest. Conversely, silver firs can also be found at low elevations, particularly on north slopes and draws where pockets of cool air flow down from higher slopes. The floors of west-side silver fir forests are usually carpeted with damp beds of oxalis and moss. In the eastern Olympics, this forest type is confined to narrow bands along cool, mid-elevation stream bottoms, and huckleberry shrubs and five-leaved bramble grow below. In the dry heart of the rain-

Montane forests of Pacific silver fir occupy a wide elevational band between 1,000 and 3,000 feet in the western Olympics but are mostly confined to cool, moist stream bottoms on the east side. Pendulous lichens that cover these trees down to the average winter snow depth are an important seasonal food for flying squirrels. PHOTO BY JANIS BURGER.

shadow, the silver fir zone drops out completely. In its place, fire-generated forests of Douglas fir and hemlock, mixed liberally with a few species of pine, juniper, and yew, extend all the way up to high, windy stands of subalpine fir. Throughout the rest of the Olympics, the silver fir forest finds its upper limit in shaggy, snow-loving forests of mountain hemlock.

But anyone who spends time hiking in the Olympics knows that forest types really don't stack up that neatly. The way we group species reflects our human need to classify as much as it does natural processes. Mountain species such as Alaska yellow cedar and lowland giants such as Douglas fir both appear throughout the silver fir forest, and any turn in the trail, any rocky outcrop or creek gorge can yield something new. During the years I worked the trails of the Olympics, I wondered at the large, old Douglas firs I'd find scattered throughout the upper reaches of the silver fir forest; so much larger and obviously older than the trees of the montane forest that surrounded them, they seemed out of place. It wasn't until years later that forest ecologist Jan Henderson unlocked the mystery for me. Henderson had spent a decade completing a comprehensive ecological survey of Olympic National Forest. For him, the silver fir zone is a living legacy of the forest's response to 1,000 years of climatic change.

Henderson explained that those venerable 700- to 900-year-old Douglas firs scattered high in the silver fir forest are the last remnants of an earlier climate. Douglas fir forests seeded in following large fires that marked the end of a thousand-year-long climatic warming. During that time the Douglas fir forest had extended its range far up the mountain slopes, and the silver fir zone was a narrow band above it; a similar zonation exists in the Oregon Cascades today. Beginning around 700 years ago, with the onset of the global cooling trend known as the Little Ice Age, shade-tolerant silver firs worked their way downslope in a series of steps, eventually replacing the older Douglas fir forests. The silver fir forest took its last downward step between 150 and 200 years ago, just as the Little Ice Age was coming to a close. These montane "pioneers" that ventured into the lower forest aren't faring well under current climatic conditions. Succumbing to disease and insect infestation, they experienced serious die-offs in the 1950s. Today, the survivors describe a ragged line that marks the tail end of the Little Ice Age. Like the ancient Douglas firs above them, these silver firs bear witness to that elegant dynamic by which an intact ecosystem responds to climatic and environmental change.

Olympic harbors a wealth of pristine forest lands unequaled in any other national park. Nearly a quarter million acres, a quarter of the park's land, is crowned with the productive, diverse, and habitat-rich old-growth forests. These forest communities extend up river valleys on all sides of the park, weaving the biological wealth of the lowlands into the mountainous heart of the ecosystem. Outside Olympic National Park, logging and human-caused fires have destroyed more than 95 percent of the old-growth Sitka spruce and Douglas fir forests that once crowned peninsula lowlands. The valley forests that remain on park, national forest, and state-owned lands are a resource of planetary significance. Stitched together by the rivers that link the mountains to the sea, they form the heart of this coastal ecosystem. Within them, an extended family of spotted owls, flying squirrels, elk, salmon, and humans share a relationship far older than the oldest of trees.

CHAPTER 6

The Lives of Olympic Rivers

O F all the seasonal wildlife movements that knit together the strands of the Olympic ecosystem, the fall and winter migrations of salmon up the forested rivers must be the most dramatic. Salmon climb nearly every stream on the peninsula, but to me the ascent of coho salmon into the deep mountainous reaches of the upper Sol Duc River is the most spectacular. Gold-brown needles litter the forest floor, and high winds usher in the first fall storms. For days rains have saturated mountain slopes, and tributary streams pulse with runoff. The river has risen in its bed, sweeping the summer's leaf litter from gravel bars and burying boulders beneath cascading blue-green waves. It seems an unlikely time for the ocean to deliver gifts to the inland forest; the headlong rush in the valleys is seaward. Falls and rapids churn, and low limbs of streamside trees bob and tug in the runoff. But a visit to Salmon Cascades, a short falls where the Sol Duc River narrows and spills over a tough ledge of basalt, brings me to the heart of this yearly exchange. With the coming of fall rains, the cascades have erupted into a white-water torrent. For weeks, a run of coho salmon that entered the river in August has been working its way up the low boulder-strewn channel and has stacked up beneath the falls. Now is that amazing time in the river's annual cycle when the "summer-run" coho take flight.

As I lean against the wet rail of the overlook beneath dripping trees, first one, then another, then three salmon at once leap from a sudsing pool

With the first heavy fall rains, coho salmon begin to leap the torrent of Salmon Cascades on the Sol Duc River. Once past the cascades, they spawn beneath old-growth forest upstream from Sol Duc Hot Springs. PHOTO BY JANIS BURGER.

at the base of the falls. Kicking wildly, they fling themselves in arcs above the white rush of the torrent. Their dark flashing shapes, lit with a red underglow, seem to float almost motionless before falling and being swept back downstream. Above the falls in calm, spring-fed pools beneath a forest of Douglas fir and red cedar lay the spawning gravels of their birth. It seems, amid the tumult of falling water, that few if any will make it past this barrier. But with thousands of years of adaptation to the dynamics of this very stream behind them, nearly all of them will. With them, the salmon return a wealth of marine-derived nitrogen, carbon, phosphates, and other nutrients from the ocean to the forest. Recent studies suggest that between 20 and 40 percent of these nutrients in rivers and streams may come from spawned salmon.

No one knows why the summer-run coho enter the river so much earlier or climb farther upstream than other wild coho. Coho salmon (*Oncorhynchus kisutch*) are common in the Olympics, where they spawn in small streams, tributaries, and the side channels of most major rivers. But by entering the mouth of the Quillayute River during the low flows of August, the salmon are forced to contend with the shallow, rocky flow of the river for fifty miles inland. Along the length of their route they are preyed upon by black bears, bald eagles, and those sleek, efficient hunters of the waterways, river otters. Like others of their kind, they have just spent two to four years in the vast waters of the north Pacific, feeding and growing strong on its plentiful marine resources: smelt, herring, rockfish, and sand lance, as well as smaller salmon. By eating voraciously during their final spring and summer, they have doubled or tripled their weight and entered the river at peak physical condition. Now, not having fed for as long as two months in the river, they must surmount this final barrier and still maintain the strength to spawn. It is a cycle repeated throughout the rippling waters of peninsula rivers, a ritual both sacrificial and heroic.

Upon reaching their spawning grounds, females excavate their nests, or redds, in clean, washed gravel with great kicking sweeps of their tails. Males contend for each available female, lunging and biting with hooked snouts and jagged teeth, emblems of their spawning stage. When a female is ready to spawn, a dominant male approaches and swims close beside her. Seen from above, they articulate a single graceful motion. Crouching low in the redd, the female releases her eggs and the male his milt simultaneously. Then the female moves just upstream and covers the eggs with gravel from her next redd. Spawning gravels must be large enough to allow a flow of cold, oxygenated water to bathe the eggs during the three to five months of incubation and protect them from predators as well as heavy flows. As many as 3,000 eggs may be laid in several redds by a single spawner (large chinook may lay as many as 5,000).

The salmon are battered and weakened by their long journey inland. White fungus covers the scars of their upstream passage, and fins and tails are beaten and frayed. Their last reserves of ocean-gleaned energy nearly spent, females guard their redds while males summon strength to spar for the last available females.

Within days the ritual is complete, and the salmon die. Carcasses litter gravel bars and logjams and catch on brush that borders the stream. A pungent smell of decaying fish hangs in the chill air. Beneath the gravel, encoded within the soft pink quarter-inch eggs, is the genetic information that will insure that enough spring fry survive their first perilous year in the stream and two more in schools at sea to successfully navigate the river and spawn in these same sheltered waters.

Olympic is one of the most important wild salmon sanctuaries in the world. It is the only national park outside Alaska that hosts such generous runs of wild anadromous, or ocean-running, fish. Throughout the park's rivers, tributaries, and small coastal streams, some seventy stocks of the five species of Pacific salmon native to the Northwest as well as steelhead repeat this cycle. A stock is a genetically distinct population of fish that spawn together in a single stream. Like the summer-run coho of the Sol Duc, each stock is perfectly keyed to the geological character, climatic variables, disturbance history, and flow regimes of its native stream. Wild salmon cycle from river to ocean and back to stream, carrying in their genetic makeup the evolutionary wisdom of their watersheds. The clean, cold forested rivers of Olympic National Park provide some of the most productive spawning habitat on the Northwest coast. Salmon and steelhead stocks native to the Olympics represent an irreplaceable resource as much a part of this islandlike ecosystem as the old-growth forests in which they evolved.

To me, salmon embody the essential unity of mountain, forest, and sea. In the downstream flow of minerals and nutrients, they are agents of renewal and return. The evolution of Pacific salmon, their adaptation to postglacial streams—and the forests that lent them structure and stability—is a miracle of reciprocity. A timeless cycle of death and rebirth informs their migrations, and the beauty of these seafaring creatures resonates through the forests, rivers, and streams like a slow and silvery pulse.

WILD OLYMPIC SALMON

Rarest of the peninsula's salmon is the sockeye. Adapted to lake environments, juvenile sockeye emerge from the gravel and spend a year in Olympic's coastal lakes before migrating to the ocean for another one to four years. On their return they often summer in lakes before spawning. Sockeye salmon have been badly hurt by hydroelectric dam construction in the Northwest; it's estimated that 96 percent of sockeye habitat in the Columbia River basin alone has been lost. Only a few wild runs are left in Washington State, and two occur in the park. A large run spawns in Quinault Lake and its tributaries in late winter and early spring. In the early 1900s nearly a million sockeye returned to Quinault Lake. In spring and early summer a much smaller run enters Ozette Lake on the park's northern coastal strip and spawns in the lake and its tributaries in winter. Ozette sockeye numbers have dropped to the point that the stock was listed by the federal government as threatened in 1999. Ozette Lake and Lake Crescent also support smaller, landlocked forms of sockeye called kokanee.

Largest of the wild swimmers, chinook, or king, salmon spawn in cobble-sized gravels in the main channels of the peninsula's larger rivers. Small spring runs occur in the Hoh and Quinault rivers, where they favor the headwater reaches (swimming as much as forty-five miles up the Hoh), as well as the Gray Wolf River in the northeastern Olympics. Low numbers for the spring Queets chinook run have raised concern among park biologists. Summer runs also enter the Hoh and Queets rivers, as well as the Quillayute system, and spawn in the middle reaches. Both spring and summer chinook remain in the rivers throughout the summer, where they're prized by sport fishermen. Chinook can spend up to seven years at sea, where they reach impressive sizes; seventy pounds is not uncommon. The majority of chinook enter rivers in fall and spawn near the coast. Fall Chinook are found in all the park's coastal rivers.

Because coho, or silver, salmon (all salmon have at least two names) spawn in tributaries, spring creeks, side channels, and the upper reaches of main rivers, they are found virtually everywhere on the peninsula. But their ubiquity subjects them to some severely degraded habitats outside the park. Small streams, wetlands, and side channels are critical habitats for coho, but they are also among the most heavily roaded, logged, and developed habitats on the peninsula. And since coho spend their first year in streams before migrating to the ocean, they are further susceptible to winter floods and summer droughts. As a result, coho runs are depressed in many areas of Puget Sound, the Strait of Juan de Fuca, and the southern Washington coast. Coastal coho are listed as threatened in Oregon. With prime coho habitats such as the upper Sol Duc, the park protects some of the best remaining spawning and rearing habitat remaining on the Northwest coast.

Ironically, the two most abundant Pacific salmon, chum and pink salmon, are uncommon on the northern Washington coast (though chum are relatively abundant in Grays Harbor and Willapa Bay to the south). Pinks return to Olympic streams in the fall of odd-numbered years and spawn in the lower rivers, where their eggs are subject to being washed away by floods. This problem is compounded in watersheds that have been heavily logged. A unique pink salmon stock reminiscent of the Sol Duc coho enters the Dungeness River system in early summer and climbs well up the Gray Wolf to spawn, some of them reaching the park. In 2001, this run set near-record returns. Small numbers of chum salmon spawn in the Queets, Ozette, and Quillayute rivers. Diminishing numbers also return to the Dungeness and other east side-streams, where they have been listed as threatened. Newly hatched chum fry do not linger in rivers but swim downstream to rear in coastal estuaries. There were historic chum runs in the Elwha, and thousands returned to the Queets and Quinault rivers as recently as the 1950s. Chum remain extremely rare in the Olympics today.

On the other hand, the peninsula has become justly famous among sport fishermen for its winter runs of wild steelhead, or sea-run rainbow, trout. Steelhead spend an average of two years in freshwater and two years at sea. Unlike other salmon, they can return to spawn two or three times. Steelhead grow large, up to thirty pounds in coastal rivers, and though smaller than chinook salmon, they are vigorous fighters and have a reputation for being notoriously difficult to land. A much smaller population of summer-run steelhead climb well into the park up the Hoh, Queets, and Quinault rivers, but they have declined precipitously throughout the Pacific coast region. Compared to other portions of their range, winter steelhead runs remain relatively healthy on Olympic's coastal rivers, but steelhead in east Olympic streams are in trouble.

A 1992 report by the Washington Department of Fish and Wildlife and the Western Washington Treaty Indian Tribes lists winter steelhead stocks as depressed on the Dungeness, Dosewallips, Duckabush, and Skokomish rivers. The greater portions of all of these east-side watersheds lie outside of Olympic National Park, where they have been subject to intensive road building, logging, and development. During heavy rains, roads dump silt and pollutants into streams; logging removes large trees needed for log-jams (when they fall) and shade for streams, and destabilizes slopes. And residential development introduces a stacked deck of wild cards into the stream environment—from poorly maintained septic systems and leaky automobile crankcases to lawn and garden chemicals. Summer-run steelhead, as well as coho salmon, are also faring poorly on the Dungeness

River, which is tapped for irrigation in the arid Sequim Prairie. Dungeness chinook salmon is also listed as critical. Chinook numbers were so low in the 1990s that returning fish were trapped in weirs and their eggs reared in a hatchery to maximize survival. Captive rearing has shown some success, and chinook numbers have climbed steadily since 2001.

Streams that drain the rainshadow of the Olympics are subject to chronic low flows during dry summer months, making them extremely susceptible to degradation from shoddy land-use practices. The condition is likely to worsen as global warming reduces winter snowpacks—and summer flows. Five of the twelve salmon stocks listed as critical in Washington State are found in the northeastern Olympics. So are high percentages of depressed stocks, including pink salmon in the Dosewallips and coho in the Duckabush rivers. In 1999, the National Marine Fisheries Service added Puget Sound chinook and Hood Canal chum to the endangered species list. In 2007, Puget Sound steelhead were also listed as threatened under the Endangered Species Act. The agency is now working with other management entities to develop and implement recovery plans for these stocks as well as federally listed bull trout and Ozette Lake sockeye. The plans guide government efforts to return these stocks to biological viability, that is, self-sustaining generations of salmon produced in their native streams. They identify factors that limit salmon recovery and guide agency, tribal, and community efforts to fix them.

Many of the most endangered Olympic salmon runs are important precisely because they have adapted to stressed and marginal environments. Noted fisheries biologist Jim Lichatowich compares the spectrum of wild salmon stocks to the more than 400,000 varieties of plants our government invests tens of millions of dollars each year to conserve because of their genetic importance to commercial agriculture. The difference is that wild salmon can't be housed in a climate-controlled warehouse; to save their genetic diversity it's imperative to protect their habitats.

Degraded habitat isn't the only threat facing Olympic's wild salmon. Even runs that spawn entirely within the park can be subject to overfishing at sea. This becomes a major threat to wild salmon when hatchery-produced fish are figured into the allowable catch. The plight of the wild coho that leap Salmon Cascades illustrates the problem.

The threats hatchery fish pose to wild salmon are now well understood. Large numbers of hatchery-reared fry released into streams tend to school up, as if waiting to be fed. They can't read territorial cues and displace native fry from feeding stations. They also compete with wild fish for resources at sea. Bred in close quarters, hatchery fish have also been known to carry diseases that can infect native salmon. But a larger problem develops when hatchery fish return to river mouths along with wild fish. Washington state officials commonly set commercial fishing limits based on the expected hatchery return, which is often many times greater than the wild return. This was the case with the Sol Duc coho. Of the 20,000 coho that returned to the Sol Duc in 1980, for example, only 1,800 were wild fish. But they were fished just as heavily as the hatchery fish offshore and in the Quillayute River. The state has since attempted to address this problem by cutting back on the allowable catch, but hatcheries remain a serious threat to depressed wild stocks, particularly in the smaller rivers of the eastern Olympics.

For decades, bull trout were a mystery fish among other, higher-profile river spawners. But their federal listing as threatened throughout their range in 1999 focused intense research on the species. Radio-telemetry studies of bull trout in the Hoh River and Kalaloch Creek that began in 2002 have revealed a startling life history unlike that of any other Pacific salmon or trout. Bull trout (*salvelinus confluentus*) are large (up to ten pounds or more), feed entirely on other fish, live as long as thirteen years, and can spawn multiple times. They require the cleanest and coldest waters of any salmonid in North America. Bull trout on the Olympic Peninsula show complex migratory patterns with variable periods of residence in streams, nearshore marine waters, and in other rivers. One tagged fish swam from the Hoh River out to the Pacific, more than ten miles south to Kalaloch Creek, and up that stream. Others ascended multiple streams. Hoh River bull trout also migrated to the Clearwater, Queets, and Quinault rivers. More than half of the fish monitored migrated to the ocean, and nearly a quarter of those ascended other streams. Some even returned to the Hoh to spawn deep in the park. Clearly, more mysteries remain to be unlocked regarding this unique and threatened species.

Lake Crescent, home to at least five fish species has mysteries of its own. The 600-foot-deep lake was gouged by the Cordilleran ice sheet then isolated by a series of landslides at its eastern end. This geological history has given rise to some unique fish. Genetic testing has shown that the famous, robust Beardslee and crescenti trout that inhabit the lake are unique subspecies of rainbow and cutthroat trout, respectively, with life histories keyed closely to their singular environment. Beardslee trout, which can reach twenty pounds, spawn in a very short stretch of the lake's outlet stream, the Lyre River. Crescenti, which can weigh up to twelve pounds, spawn in Barnes Creek and other Lake Crescent tributaries as well as the Lyre River outside the park, and a section of lake shoreline. Both were in serious decline in the 1990s, primarily due to a century of overfishing (there were at one time as many as eleven fishing resorts operating on the lake). In 2000, the Beardslee population was estimated at less than a hundred. New catch-and-release regulations and gear limitations were put into effect in 2001, and surveys in recent years indicate increased spawning. Biologists express continuing concern for these emblematic fish, however, and populations are closely monitored. Olympic's only endemic fish species, the Olympic mudminnow, is also a species of concern. Little is known of this tiny inhabitant of small streams and wetlands, one of only four species in a unique family. It is federally listed as a threatened species.

Unlike seagoing steelhead trout, resident rainbow trout are found upstream from falls or other natural barriers. Native cutthroat tend to spawn high in small tributary streams above other salmon and trout but are found throughout park waters, from river estuaries and side channels to beaver ponds and small streams. Rainbow, cutthroat, and brook trout found in high mountain lakes are virtually all non-native fish, descendants of trout planted by sportsmen, a practice no longer sanctioned by the park.

Taken together, the wild runs of salmon and steelhead that return to Olympic rivers each year represent an incalculable resource, not only to tribal, commercial, and sport fishermen, but to the terrestrial ecosystems that receive their bounty, and to the productivity of the streams themselves. No one knows the size or extent of the historic wild runs that once thronged Olympic rivers, but they must have been staggering. Early homesteaders reported salmon choking small streams on the peninsula. Settlers on the Elwha described droves of spawning salmon so thick they spooked horses attempting to ford the river. The historical record offers a wider picture.

Records for canneries operating on the Hoh, Queets, and Quinault rivers indicate that during the years 1911 to 1927, canneries processed an average of 76,500 salmon and steelhead per year—and more than double that number in the best years. Calculations based on similar records for Oregon canneries during that time suggest that a million coho salmon alone returned to Oregon coastal streams each year. Aside from its value to humans, this kind of yearly return represents a motherload of nutrients to freshwater aquatic and terrestrial ecosystems.

SALMON AND THE FOREST COMMUNITY

Concern over the decline in historic salmon runs in the Northwest and the implications for forest and wildlife communities on the peninsula prompted researchers to embark on some groundbreaking studies. Scientists wanted to see how and to what extent spawned salmon carcasses were used in the upstream reaches of spawning streams. Their findings shed new light on the ecological ties that bind the mountains and forests to the sea.

In a study conducted in Olympic National Park in the late 1980s, researchers distributed nearly a thousand tagged coho salmon carcasses on sections of several spawning streams, including the upper Sol Duc. A number were fitted with small radio transmitters to track their dispersal. Movements of the salmon, both within and outside the stream were carefully noted. Since the tributary streams used by coho are subject to frequent flooding in fall and early winter, it was assumed that most spawned salmon carcasses were flushed downstream. Researches found the opposite. A large percentage of carcasses remained in the spawning areas. They were caught in logjams or in the limbs of submerged trees or stranded in pools and eddies formed by fallen logs. A large number were dragged by animals into the adjoining forest and only partly eaten.

One of the study's most surprising findings was the high percentage of carcasses that were consumed by wildlife. On the upper Sol Duc, for instance, the figure is eight out of ten. Most were eaten by black bears, but no fewer than twenty-one other wildlife species were observed feeding on the salmon carcasses as well. Bears, river otters, and raccoons dragged carcasses from pools, ate part of them and left the rest. Over the days and weeks that followed, a company of smaller mammals and birds tidied up. Among the guests at the banquet were coyotes, mink, skunks, bobcats, squirrels, deer mice, and several shrews. Bald eagles, red-tailed hawks, ravens, and crows flocked to river corridors to join them, as did Steller's and gray jays. Dippers, those small riverine songbirds who usually dine on invertebrates and fry, couldn't resist the spread, nor could those shy, diminutive singers of the underbrush, the winter wrens. All in all, just over half the total species of mammals and birds inventoried along the streams partook of the spent salmon. Only mole, beaver, cougar, and elk abstained. Other studies have indicated that even deer may venture an occasional nibble.

A more recent study examined the relationships between salmon and 605 species of terrestrial and marine mammals, birds, reptiles, and amphibians in Washington and Oregon. Researches found that 119 species interacted with salmon in saltwater and terrestrial environments. Eighty-eight species, including 25 mammals, 60 birds, 2 amphibians, and 1 reptile, were characterized as having routine (though in some cases indirect) relationships with salmon. For these species and for untold numbers of invertebrates, salmon are a significant part of the complex web of life that sustains them.

For many wild residents of Olympic river valleys, the seasonal largess of salmon comes when other sources of protein may be scarce, and it immediately precedes a time of extreme stress for many wildlife species here. Spawned salmon may make the difference between death and survival for some animals during severe winters. It's extremely likely, with historical spawning levels of coho estimated at ten times current numbers, that past runs supported much higher levels of wildlife than are found in parts of the Olympics today.

Virtually all members of the aquatic community benefit directly from spawning coho salmon—from aquatic plants and invertebrates to resident fish. Even the "shredders" (snails, stonefly nymphs, and other insects that break coarse organic material down into finer particles) are enriched by salmon-derived nutrients. Growth rates for young coho salmon are known to double during the winter following spawning, while cutthroat trout in a nearby stream without spawning salmon show no winter growth at all.

Salmon add important nutrients to the entire spectrum of life in a stream and increase aquatic diversity. Not surprisingly, the elimination or reduction in number of spawning coho salmon in small coastal streams puts the entire stream community at risk.

The benefits of spawned salmon to streamside forests are also substantial. Salmon carcasses not consumed decompose, enriching streamside plant communities and aiding in the decomposition of the autumn litter of leaves and woody debris. As the season progresses, elk and blacktail deer take shelter in these riparian forests, and the early leaf and ground-cover growth in spring provides an important part of their seasonal food. In fact, the riparian forests that border Olympic streams serve essential functions in the life histories of a number of wildlife species. The clear, cold waters, deep pools, and clean spawning gravels necessary for spawning salmon are to a large part dependent on riparian forests, as are many of the creatures that feed on spawned salmon. Some 87 percent of the birds, amphibians, reptiles, and mammals found in western Washington use these streamside zones during certain seasons or parts of their life cycles. In the maritime Olympics, where the landscape is laced with rivers and streams, the networks of riparian areas along streams, lakes, and wetlands are among our most critical and productive habitats.

THE INTERPLAY OF FOREST AND STREAM

Most river valley roads and trails in the Olympics skirt riparian forests. Shady bands of red alder, black cottonwood, and bigleaf maple mix with a lower growth of vine maple, Scouler's and Sitka willow, and cascara to form ribbonlike oases of leafy deciduous growth through the conifer forests. Western red cedar, western hemlock, and Sitka spruce also form an important part of mature riparian communities. As transition zones between aquatic and upland environments, riparian areas provide the three essentials of wildlife habitat: food, cover, and water. Varying degrees of moisture within these areas support a mixture of plant communities. Songbirds such as warblers, vireos, finches, tanagers, grosbeaks, and thrushes use riparian areas for nesting and foraging. Common and hooded mergansers nest in cavities here, and ospreys and bald eagles build nests in the broken tops of large streamside conifers. As we've seen in the

Large glacier-fed west-side rivers like the Hoh meander across wide floodplains, cutting banks, toppling trees, and building new river bars. Logs and rootwads left strewn by the river help regulate high flows, maintain floodplains, and create habitat for fish and aquatic invertebrates. PHOTO BY JANIS BURGER.

rain forest, riparian forests provide seasonal migratory routes, as well as calving and fawning areas and cover for Roosevelt elk and blacktail deer. They serve as travel corridors for a host of bird and mammal species and as critical habitat for a number of amphibians, including some endemic to the Olympic Peninsula.

Riparian forests are essential to watershed health in other important ways as well. The leafy limbs of deciduous trees and shrubs shade streams, keeping water temperatures cool enough for salmon and trout. Overhanging brush and roots provide havens where salmon fry and fingerling trout can hide from predators. Leaf-dwelling insects and their droppings provide food for aquatic invertebrates and fish, and fallen leaves and wood debris add important nutrients to streams, feeding aquatic invertebrates— the grazers, shredders, and collectors—that form the basis of stream ecology. Tree roots stabilize stream banks, and streamside plants filter runoff in wet seasons, further protecting water quality.

Historically, one of the most important functions of riparian forests within the Olympic ecosystem was to render the spare, scoured, post-Pleistocene landscape fit for salmon. In the millennia that followed the retreat of the Cordilleran ice sheet, the rivers that drained the Olympic Mountains were steep, raw torrents carrying large loads of sediments from deeply incised canyons to braided floodplains. Forests made inroads into these newly carved valleys during the climatic fluctuations that followed the Ice Age, reclaiming mineral soils and stabilizing young landscapes. But it wasn't until the climate approached that of today and forests matured and developed old-growth characteristics some 4,000 to 5,000 years ago that large numbers of salmon were able to spawn and rear in these quick mountain streams.

Geologically, the peninsula's rivers are still quite young. Fed by the heavy precipitation of the coast, they are subject to floods and mass landslides. As old-growth forests developed, large conifers fell across rivers and streams, slowing the water and adding structure and complexity to these mountain streams. Downed logs create pools, riffles, and glides. They also stabilize shorelines and create meanders with their deep eddies and gravel riffles. On larger rivers, logs stack up in logjams, creating deep pools as well as multiple side channels, hallmarks of a good salmon stream. Logjams also dissipate floodwaters onto floodplains, where the current is slowed by vegetation and drops much of its sediment load, conserving soils and nutrients in the watershed. Over time logjams shoulder rivers back and forth across their floodplains, cycling old forests and creating new habitats. Studies conducted on the Queets River suggest a 900-year cycle for this process.

The overall effect of the old-growth forest is to render streams and rivers less efficient conduits for flowing water but optimal habitats for salmon and trout. Each blockage creates places where salmon and trout can rest, feed, and hide; gravels trapped by downed logs or built up downstream from logjams serve as spawning areas for salmon as well as rearing areas for insect larvae that feed the fry. Downed wood retains salmon carcasses in the stream, and nutrients from spawned salmon feed the forest. The wild stocks of Pacific salmon could never have proliferated in Olympic streams without the development of old-growth forests across the landscape. Their continued health today remains utterly dependent on the health of their forested watersheds.

LIVES OF THE RIVER

Although fall and winter present a movable feast for wildlife along salmon streams, Olympic's rivers teem with life in all seasons. Spring brings its own rich assemblage of species to the swollen streams, often when the high country is still locked in winter. Nesting waterfowl are most notable, and singularly conspicuous among these are harlequin ducks.

Harlequins look as though they've been painted by tribal fetishists. Breeding males are blue-gray and russet, streaked with splashes of brilliant white edged in black. When they arrive in the forested reaches of Olympic rivers in March or early April to breed, it's as if the village minstrels had been let into the cathedral. For me, spring hasn't begun until I've encountered these elegant and tough little ducks in the steep, fast-moving rivers of the northern or eastern Olympics. Like salmon, they return to their native rivers at breeding time. Once there, they surf the rapids, plunging and diving among boulders and pools to scour the substrate for invertebrates, then climb atop midstream boulders to preen. The moss-capped rocks of snowmelt streams grow vibrant beneath them.

Harlequins seem drawn to rough water, whether the white water of their breeding streams or the dark currents and plunging surf along the rugged seacoast where they spend the rest of their year. They are the only duck in North America that breeds in steep mountain streams and they add their splashes of color to some of the grandest landscapes in the country. In the Olympics, harlequins nest in nooks and on knobs of streamside cliffs, in tree cavities, and down logs in riparian forests. Some birds are known to return to the same nest sites and repeat nesting over years. Soon after incubation begins, the drakes head back downstream to saltwater. Females and their hatched young remain in rivers through most of the summer. More than once I've held my breath along a riverbank as a startled female and her brood half flew, half surfed across a boiling rapid to arrive intact and unruffled in a far eddy.

You might think, with the white water of the Olympics for a nursery, there's no environment that would cause young harlequins concern. Yet as recently as the 1990s the harlequin duck was a candidate for the federal endangered species list. Harlequin populations on the east coast never recovered from earlier hunting for trophies and feathers, and some west coast areas have shown marked declines. But with a wintering population of some 3,000, harlequins are now doing well in Washington. And they have historically been plentiful in the Olympics. Surveys of harlequins in the Olympics found few on the lower meandering portions of large west-side rivers, but numbers increased as river gradients steepened. Highest harlequin counts were reported for the Elwha River, at more than two nesting pairs per river mile. A minimum of 352 breeding pairs are esti-mated for Olympic streams, which support 60 to 70 percent of the state's breeding population. About a third of available females have broods in any given year. In winter, harlequins from throughout the intermountain West converge on the outer coast and Strait of Juan de Fuca to winter by the thousands.

If harlequins have any competition in their specialized breeding habi-tat, it can only come from that most intrepid of songbirds, the dipper. Dippers also breed along quick mountain streams, but unlike harlequins, they live there year-round. They are easily recognized by their plump, slate gray plumage and constant bobbing motion while on boulders or on shore, and their mellifluous song carries above the noise of the loud-est rapids and ranks among the sweetest of mountain sounds. John Muir called dippers "the hummingbirds of blooming waters," and wrote that they love "rocky ripple-slopes and sheets of foam as a bee loves flowers." Alone among songbirds, dippers have forsaken foraging in forests and fields; instead they feed in the roiling waters of mountain streams. Diving under water, swimming and walking along the rocky substrate, they work the gravels for insect larvae—like trout. Upon emerging they fly upriver at spray height or briefly rest, "dipping" on a rock.

Ornithologists disagree over the function of this bobbing behavior; some suspect it's a camouflage mechanism effective in their quick-moving environment. In the damp shade of river canyons, I've often wondered if it might have more to do with keeping warm, but their thick plum-age and oversized preen glands for waterproofing their feathers seem to render them impervious to the icy waters. And their spring singing is undampened even when neighboring shorelines are still thick with snow.

The highest densities of dippers (more than four per mile) were found along the Duckabush River, one of the steepest in the Olympics. Nearly as

Commonly seen (and heard) along streams, lakeshores, and protected coastal areas on the peninsula, belted kingfishers are superb divers and expert fishers. They nest in tunnels on bluffs and river banks, and keep watch for fish on overhanging limbs. PHOTO BY JANIS BURGER.

many occur in the Elwha. Dippers' large mossy nests are built along cliffs, often behind waterfalls; in downstream reaches, bridge abutments suffice. Both adults tend the young. After their mating season, dippers follow the thawing drainages upstream. Later in summer, as invertebrate numbers thin in Olympic streams, dippers can be seen working the edges of high mountain lakes. In winter, dippers migrate downstream to lower rivers or large lowland lakes. Like their smaller (and equally melodic) cousins, the winter wrens, dippers lend spirit and warmth to river walks, even in deepest winter.

Another conspicuous bird common to Olympic streams is the belted kingfisher. The loud rattling calls of kingfishers are unmistakable and are usually heard well before the bird shows itself along the waterway. Large headed, with a long stout beak, a kingfisher's compact body seems expertly designed for diving and catching fish, a feat it accomplishes with unfaltering accuracy. Kingfishers visit virtually every Olympic stream as well as the shores of the strait and Puget Sound. They prefer to nest in burrows in high banks. In saltwater I've watched kingfishers dive from a hover, but on streams they seem to prefer to plunge from low-hanging limbs over pools. They are far from inconspicuous, with their blue and white plumage, belted breast, and punkish topknot. Still, they do well on unwary salmon fry and fingerling trout, supplementing their diet with insects, amphibians, and even small birds when necessary—a plentiful and varied fare that allows them to remain in the park year-round.

Other birds commonly seen along Olympic streams—mergansers, great blue herons, wood ducks, spotted sandpipers, and killdeers—are habitués of the lower rivers, well below the flash and fury of rapids. Common mergansers visit rivers during their March to August breeding season where river gradients flatten and rapids become scarce. They are found in river mouths and lower reaches, slightly higher on the larger west-side rivers such as the Hoh and Queets. Mergansers feed on coho and chinook salmon and steelhead smolt as the young fish swim downriver toward the ocean. With their hooked, serrated bills and excellent diving ability, they are effective fishers and can reduce a fish population in a given stretch of river by as much as half. As one fisheries biologist put it, "They're hell on coho." Mergansers nest in cavities in riparian snags as well as in banks and among boulders, brush, and roots. Brood sizes are large, up to fourteen, but eight to ten is more common. In winter, when salmon are scarce, they head out to saltwater and feed on herring.

Wood ducks and great blue herons, while sometimes seen in lower rivers and streams, are more often found in lakes, ponds, and tide flats. Wood ducks may well be the most striking nesting bird on the peninsula. Breeding males have deep green and purple heads with downswept crests, striped and speckled throats, chestnut breasts, and iridescent wings and backs punctuated by upswept tails. Even harlequins pale beside wood ducks, with which they are often confused. Wood ducks nest almost exclusively in riparian snags along slow streams, lakes, or ponds. They were hunted nearly to extinction in the late 1800s for their plumes, but populations have recovered since the turn of the last century, and now they are frequently seen on the peninsula. Wood ducks, harlequins, and other breeding birds may be the flashiest inhabitants of Olympic's riparian environs, but the distinction of most pervasive must go to an older and more secretive order, the amphibians.

THE DOUBLE LIVES OF AMPHIBIANS

The first vertebrates to venture onto terra firma, amphibians are the oldest land dwellers. Reptiles, birds, and mammals all came later. Amphibians still carry the signature of their watery origins; they keep a foot in each world (amphibian means "double life"). Although a few nest in cool, damp forests, most are hatched in ponds, lakes, and streams. In their legless, larval stage, most amphibians live in water and breathe through gills, like their ancestors of 360 million years ago, fish. Unlike reptiles and other true land dwellers, amphibians lack moisture barriers, either in their skin or their eggs, and so depend on moist environments to regulate body temperature. Adults of most species also return to water to breed. Few amphibians travel very far from water, and most venture out only at night. The wetlands, streams, lakes, and damp woods of the maritime Olympics provide an ideal habitat for a variety of amphibians. And because nearly all of the park remains in a pristine natural condition, a number of sensitive species flourish here.

Thirteen species of salamanders, frogs, and toads are known to occur in the Olympics, including one species endemic to the peninsula, the Olympic torrent salamander. The near-endemic Cope's giant is found primarily in the Olympics, but also in coastal hills to the south. Isolated populations of rare Van Dyke's salamander and tailed frogs are also found here; both are endemic to the Pacific Northwest. It's estimated that there may be up to 250 amphibians per acre in some areas of the Olympics; they may in fact be the major predators of invertebrates in many forest and stream communities. As is the case with many less-than-conspicuous species, scientists are just beginning to understand amphibians' importance to forest and aquatic ecosystems.

Cold, fast-flowing mountain streams in the Olympics are home to both the torrent salamander and the tailed frog. Torrent salamanders are small, about four inches, greenish brown above, with distinctive yellow undersides. They blend well with the icy creeks and wet, rocky stream margins they favor as habitat. Little is known about this small, unique salamander.

They appear to favor the west side of the peninsula, where they can be numerous in small seeps as well as streams, but their eggs have not been found. Tailed frogs are the only frog species in the Olympics that breed in fast-moving water; their tadpoles have large sucker mouths that allow them to cling to rocks. They are also small, about the size of a tree frog, but lack the latter's dark mask (and exquisite singing voice). Tailed frogs thrive in mountain torrents all the way up to headwaters, usually in stream reaches inaccessible to trout, but they are absent from rainshadow streams.

Both these species are considered quite primitive by herpetologists. Stream-dwelling salamanders like the torrent salamander have been proposed as the ancestral form from which modern terrestrial salamanders evolved. The tailed frog is the most ancient species of frog in the world. It is the only frog that reproduces through internal fertilization (its "tail" is a male copulatory organ). The tailed frog's closest relatives are found in the rainy forests of New Zealand. Though plentiful in the park, both these species are extremely susceptible to changes in their environment, and populations have been seriously reduced or eliminated in streams affected by logging.

Rarest of Olympic's amphibians, Van Dyke's salamanders are present in just a few locations besides the Olympics. Like the western red-backed and other woodland salamanders, Van Dyke's lays its eggs on land, usually beneath mossy stones and downed logs of the riparian area. The western red-back and the ensatina (a stouter salamander that lives in rotting logs and woody debris) favor divots and rodent burrows beneath the surface. In all three, the gilled larval stage is completed within the egg, and the young emerge as miniature adults.

Most secretive of Olympic's salamanders is the beautiful Cope's giant. This species remained unknown until 1970, and only a scattering of terrestrial adults have been observed since then. As of 2005, six have been found in Olympic National Park, all of them in west-side drainages. For unknown reasons, Cope's giants do not occur east of the Sol Duc and Skokomish river valleys. Most Cope's remain in streams and cold mountain lakes as larvae or in a subadult breeding form known as a neotene. Large enough to eat not only insects but fish and the eggs and larvae of other amphibians, Cope's are easily recognized. At maturity, adults reach eight inches and are strikingly marbled with hues of gold, copper, and slate.

Amphibians have become the focus of increasing attention over the past several years as indicators of ecosystem health. Because their habitats are highly specialized, amphibians appear to be acutely sensitive to changes in their environment. Keyed to distinct microhabitats, they are generally unable to cope with rapid environmental changes by leaving disturbed areas. Some populations and even some species are small and isolated, yet their importance as major consumers of invertebrates is significant—particularly in ecosystems that lack other kinds of insectivores.

Declines in amphibian populations worldwide have sparked concern among biologists, but disappearances from undisturbed and protected areas reported in the late 1980s are particularly troubling. Acid rain, increased levels of ultraviolet radiation, and global warming are among the possible causes for such losses. Studies conducted in high lakes in the Olympics suggest that ponds that experience less ultraviolet radiation were more likely to have breeding populations of Cascades frogs. Although these frogs are declining at the southern edge of their range in northern California, they remain common in the Olympics.

Efforts to restore damaged ecosystems—forests, streams, and wetlands—hold promise for a broad array of species across the Olympic ecosystem. For aquatic habitats this can mean replanting riparian areas or mechanically placing logs and rootwads in streams to create spawning and rearing habitat. In some cases, restoring stream meanders, floodplains, and estuaries is needed. Peninsula tribes, federal and state agencies, and local governments have undertaken major salmon habitat restoration projects on dozens of streams across the peninsula. Restoration work on the Dungeness River, Jimmycomelately Creek, Salmon Creek, Chimacum Creek estuary, and other streams has already yielded positive results. On a larger scale, the National Park Service, along with other federal and state agencies and the Elwha Klallam Tribe, are pursuing a salmon recovery effort for one Olympic river system that promises to be the most successful ecosystem restoration in the Pacific Northwest.

FREEING THE ELWHA

The Elwha River salmon runs were legendary. In his book *Mountain in the Clouds*, Bruce Brown notes that as early as 1790 the Spanish explorer

Manuel Quimper recorded purchasing a number of hundred-pound salmon from nearby Indians. Reports of large Elwha chinook remained common through the early years of this century as well, and it's estimated that at one time more than a quarter million pink salmon returned to the Elwha to spawn. Largest of Olympic National Park's watersheds, draining one-fifth of the park, the Elwha was undoubtedly one of the most productive. The river supported ten distinct runs of anadromous fish, including all five species of local Pacific salmon. It was one of the few rivers in the contiguous United States that harbored all the ocean-running fish species native to the Northwest.

The Elwha flows north out of the interior Olympics into the Strait of Juan de Fuca. In its lower reaches, where the river cuts through the resistant basalts of the Crescent formation, it narrows into a series of steep canyons and shoulders through a jagged notch called Goblin's Gate. Only the most vigorous wild salmon could ascend these canyons to spawn. Records suggest that Elwha chinook may have remained at sea longer to gain the size and strength needed to surmount the canyons. They were certainly the largest chinook in any Olympic river. An estimated 8,000 of them spawned in the Elwha each year. Equally impressive runs of coho, pink, sockeye, and chum salmon, as well as steelhead, sea-run cutthroat trout, char, and bull trout spawned in the Elwha's pristine mountain waters. Estimates of historic runs in the Elwha are just under 400,000 fish annually. For the Elwha Klallam people who lived at the river's mouth and for the wildlife populations who inhabited the 175,000 acres of the Elwha watershed, these runs were an incredible bounty as well as a dependable source of nourishment for much of the year.

But in 1913, all that changed. That was the year the Olympic Power Company began operations of its Elwha Dam.

Built to provide power for a local sawmill, this was the first of two dams constructed on the lower river. In 1926, a second, the Glines Canyon Dam, was constructed several miles upstream. In spite of an 1890 Washington State statute requiring fish passage facilities on all dams, both dams formed a complete barrier to all salmon moving upstream to spawn. As early as 1911, while the Elwha Dam was still under construction, Clallam County game warden James Pike wrote the state fish commissioner. He reported "thousands of Salmon at the foot of the Dam, where they are continually trying to get up the flume. I have watched them very close and I am satisfied now that they cannot get above the dam." Despite Pike's report and the protests of the Klallam people, whose very livelihood and culture was bound to the Elwha's salmon, state officials ignored the problem. Finally, the year the dam went into operation, its owners reluctantly agreed to fund construction of a hatchery to mitigate the loss of native fish. But hatcheries were an unproven technology at that time, rife with problems. Within a decade the hatchery failed and was abandoned.

Of more than seventy miles of available spawning habitat in the Elwha watershed, only the lower five miles remain accessible to salmon today. And with the dams holding back the gravel needed to replenish spawning beds and warming impounded waters to dangerous temperatures in summer, even this short reach has become degraded. The river's sockeye salmon are now considered to be extinct, and native chum and spring chinook are rapidly approaching extinction. The once-great runs of pink salmon have dwindled to a few dozen and are now listed as runs of critical concern. Summer steelhead and sea-run cutthroat trout are also in steep decline. Current wild fish returns to the Elwha total 3,000 to 4,000. The beneficiary of the power generated by the dams today is the Nippon U.S.A. paper mill in Port Angeles; the dams supply about a third of the mill's energy needs.

The Elwha dams were products of an era of unbridled resource exploitation in the West, a time when few considered the environmental costs of development. With the subsequent declines of Pacific salmon throughout the region, and the recent listing of several Northwest stocks under the Endangered Species Act, the true costs of such "free" sources of energy as hydropower have become apparent. As always, it is the generations that follow those early boosters who must bear the costs. Beginning in 1968 the Elwha Klallam Tribe requested that the Federal Energy Regulatory Commission (FERC) address the problem of fish passage on the Elwha during its relicensing proceedings. The fifty-year license for the Glines Canyon Dam expired in 1976; the Elwha Dam was never licensed. In the 1980s, as part of the relicensing process, the National Park Service and the U.S. Fish and Wildlife Service studied the feasibility of fitting both dams with fish passage facilities. The results showed little promise. Only five of the ten original fish stocks showed any chance of recovery with

The legendary Elwha River chinook attained weights of 100 pounds before its spawning habitat was blocked by two hydroelectric dams early in the twentieth century. Dam removal promises to restore all species of anadromous fish to the Elwha watershed and open 75 miles of pristine spawning habitat now inaccessible to salmon. PHOTO BY JANIS BURGER.

the retrofitting of the dams, and the prospects for even these were poor. By contrast, studies rated the chances of restoring nine of the ten original runs as good to excellent if both dams were removed.

In 1986, the Point-No-Point Treaty Council, which represents the Elwha Klallam and other area tribes, petitioned FERC, requesting the removal of both dams to restore the Elwha's fisheries. Later that year, a coalition of environmental groups, Olympic Park Associates, Seattle Audubon Society, Friends of the Earth, and Sierra Club, also intervened in the relicensing proceedings. The groups questioned FERC's jurisdiction to license dams in national parks and petitioned that the Glines Canyon Dam, which was located entirely in the park, be removed. In the intervening years, federal agencies became convinced of the wisdom of dam removal. In 1990, a consortium of federal and tribal agencies recommended both dams be removed to fully restore the fishery (fish restoration is a condition of dam relicensing). Two years later, with the support of a broad coalition of conservationists, sportsmen, public agencies, and tribes, Congress passed the Elwha River Ecosystem and Fisheries Restoration Act. To accomplish its goal of "full restoration" of the Elwha River ecosystem and native anadromous fish, the law authorized the Department of the Interior to acquire both dams and remove them if necessary to meet this objective. In 1995, the Department of the Interior and the National Park Service announced their intent to remove both dams, a visionary decision that would return one of the Northwest's premiere salmon-producing rivers to its natural state. In 2000, the government purchased the dams, reservoirs, and surrounding lands. In 2004, following years of negotiations, the park, Elwha Tribe, and the City of Port Angeles signed a final agreement insuring water quality and flood protection for downstream users. The actual removal of the dams, which may begin in 2012, is expected to take two to three years to accomplish. Full recovery of historic fish runs may take up to thirty years. That's a short time, really, to right a century-old wrong to a spectacular river system and the people who for thousands of years have made it their home.

The Elwha offers a rare opportunity to restore a major ecosystem to its unspoiled condition. Since the watershed lies almost entirely within Olympic National Park, the habitat degradation from industrial logging, chemical pollution, and irrigation that has stymied salmon restoration efforts elsewhere in the Northwest is not an issue. I can't imagine another river that holds more promise, and I can think of no finer investment than freeing this magnificent river system to simply do what it does best.

Part 3

THE COAST

CHAPTER 7

Life at the Edge of Land and Sea

F OR three days the winter storm lashed the coast. Dark skies leaned over mountainous waves, and gusts of wind whistled through the spruce limbs above my camp. From a perch well back in the trees I watched the waves crash against a rocky headland to the south. White water exploded nearly a hundred feet upward, flinging spray into wind-swept headland trees, then drained off the cliff face in torrents. A half-breath later a second explosion burst like a cannon shot as the same wave crashed through a tunnel in the headland. The two waves then chased each other as they fanned out across a protected cove, crested once more, and broke against the shore. It was seconds before the sound reached me—a muffled concussion I could feel in my chest.

For me, winter storms define the essence of this wild and rugged shore-line. The Olympic coast juts into the north Pacific like the prow of a ship, and the unbridled forces of winter seas have sculpted it into a magnificent landscape. Storms give shape to the thick-limbed coastal spruces; they rake the tops of offshore islands, rearrange river mouths, and cut away coastal bluffs, sending huge trees crashing into the waves and leaving others leaning awkwardly, like stunned giants. As with the glaciers and rivers inland, the erosive power of waves—and the drift logs, rock, sand, and trapped air they carry—batter and tear at the shoreline relentlessly. Storm-driven surf is a major force shaping both the character and ecology of the outer coast. Hammering at the edge of the continent, stripping away more than three feet of land each year in places, it quarries the coast into dramatic formations. The arches, tunnels, caves, and sea cliffs, as well as sea stacks and rugged offshore islands that typify the Olympic coast, are the work of winter seas. And the intertidal communities that flourish within this powerful environment carry the surf's signature.

The wildness wrought of winter seas helped protect the coast during the past century of development on the peninsula. Nowhere else in the contiguous United States has so generous a portion of wild coastline been preserved in its natural state, free of the roads, condominiums, resorts, and other trappings of commerce that pass these days for progress. The small Native American fishing villages at Neah Bay, La Push, Hoh, and Taholah remain largely unchanged. And the wild reaches of unbroken shoreline that stretch between them appear as they must have when the ancestors of today's coastal inhabitants guided their cedar canoes along the headlands, islands, and rocky coves.

THE SHAPE OF THE OLYMPIC COAST

The sixty-two-mile coastal area of Olympic National Park stands apart. Not only does it remain undeveloped, but its rugged nature lies in marked contrast to the low bluffs and long, smooth beaches that characterize the coastline to the south. There, millions of tons of sediments washed into the sea by the Columbia River and carried by coastal currents give rise to extensive sandy beaches. But like the mountains a short distance inland, the shape and structure of the north Olympic coast reflect an uneasy marriage between the geologic forces that gave birth to the Olympic Peninsula and the climatic forces that conspire to worry it away.

The signature landforms of the Olympic coast—its islands, sea stacks, and towering headlands—are hewn of tough, erosion-resistant rocks. Like most of the core rocks of the interior peninsula, coastal rocks are sedimentary; sequences of sandstones, siltstones, and conglomerates (rounded fragments of rock in a matrix of sand or silt) were laid down on the ocean floor by ancestral rivers 20 to 40 million years ago. As the ocean plates ground beneath the edge of the continent, these sediments were scraped off the seafloor and plastered onto the continent's edge. Though bent, twisted, and broken into the usual lithic smorgasbord of Olympic rock,

Tough sandstone is slower to yield to the erosive power of the surf than adjoining melange rocks. This leads to the creation of the headlands, sea stacks, islands, and interspersed pocket coves and beaches that typify the north Olympic coast. PHOTO BY JANIS BURGER.

these coastal rocks (known to geologists as the Hoh assemblage) are not nearly as deformed as the interior core rocks that abut the submarine basalts of the Crescent Formation. Most of the headlands, sea stacks, and islands that have held their own against the sea's onslaught are composed of tough sandstones and conglomerates deposited in undersea river channels and largely spared from severe folding and faulting during subduction and uplift.

The more worked-over sedimentary rocks, where the tectonic stresses of subduction caused extensive folding and thrust faulting, resulted in a jumbled formation of unconsolidated rock called a melange. Here fragments and blocks of sediments and basalts are embedded in a soft mix of sheared and broken siltstones, sandstones, and clays. Melange rocks are much more susceptible to erosion. Yielding to the cutting power of the surf, they tend to form inlets and beaches rather than headlands and islands. The popular Second and Third beaches near La Push, as well as the long beach north of Hoh Head, are carved into melange rocks. In contrast, James Island off La Push, Teahwhit Head between Second and Third beaches, Toleak Point, and Hoh Head are all composed of tougher sandstone conglomerate.

A notable exception to this story—indeed to the entire geologic history of the Olympics—is found at Point of the Arches, a spectacular array of sea stacks and arches on the northern coast. There, cliffs and sea stacks composed of basalts, sandstones, and gabbro (a dark, igneous rock formed at great depths) are about 144 million years old—twice the age of the oldest known rocks in the interior Olympics. This formation is the only exposure of its kind on the peninsula, and its origin remains a puzzle to geologists. Some theorize the rock arrived from the north by way of a massive submarine avalanche during the formation of the Olympics. Others suggest it was rafted here from the Klamath Mountains region in northern California as part of the crustal movement associated with the San Andreas Fault. That its origin remains a mystery is somehow in keeping with the haunting beauty of the northern coast.

The more recent 2-million-year history of the Pleistocene epoch is also written into the coastal text. During this time, when alpine glaciers were honing the peaks and carving the valleys of the interior, and great ice sheets advanced repeatedly from the north, the coastline was also in flux. Outwash from the meltwaters of alpine glaciers covered most of the coastal area, a fact evidenced by the unconsolidated glacial drift seen along much of the coast today. About 125,000 years ago, sea level stood about 100 feet higher than it stands today. Now covered by younger deposits of sand and gravel, the remnants of a flat, elevated, wave-cut terrace can easily be seen at the top of bedrock exposures along sea cliffs of the middle coast, as well as along the flattened tops of some offshore stacks and islands. Geologists have traced this Pleistocene terrace as far as a mile inland. It indicates the extent of an older coastline, much as today's wave-cut platforms surrounding headlands reflect present sea level. This same terrace cut into older glacial deposits as well. Deposits from more recent alpine glacier advances between 16,000 and 70,000 years ago lie atop the older terrace. This Ice Age story can easily be read along the coast south of the Quillayute River. North of there, the text has been revised by the more recent movements of the Cordilleran ice sheet bearing down on the peninsula from the north.

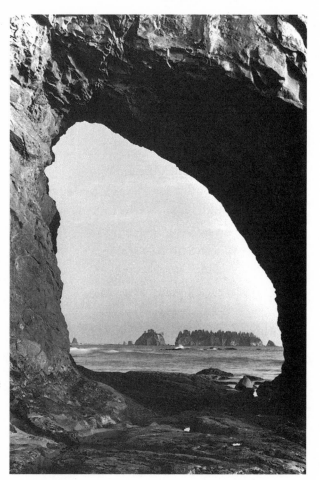

As winter seas work away at cracks and weaknesses in coastal rocks, headlands are quarried into caves, arches, and eventually free-standing seastacks and islands. The view is south, through Hole-in-the-Wall, toward James Island just off La Push. PHOTO BY JANIS BURGER.

During the maximum advance of the Cordilleran ice, around 15,000 years ago, sea level is estimated to have been as much as 400 feet lower than it is today, and a vast, ice-free plain stretched out along the coast. Dry westerly winds sweeping across the plain deposited between 3 and 15 feet of silt and sand along the coastal area. This fine, buff-colored layer is noticeable atop most coastal bluffs today. As the ice sheet retreated and the sea returned to its present level, wave action tore into the young glacial deposits with a vengeance. The islands and sea stacks trailing off from the coast today mark the past extent of the continent's domain, the flat tops of the larger islands the final, glacial-deposited remnants of the once-vast Pleistocene coastal plain.

Hikers along the coast sometimes notice wave-sculpted sea stacks and arches reemerging from their casts of glacial drift like half-finished sculptures; Quateata Point, north of Second Beach, is one example of this process. At the same time, new caves, tunnels, and (eventually) arches are being carved from joints or weaknesses in coastal bedrock. All along the Olympic coast, offshore rock gardens such as Quillayute Needles and Giants Graveyard, and larger islands such as Tatoosh, Ozette, Alexander, and Destruction, stand as testimony to that powerful dynamic by which the sea lays claim to the land. It is a process that pulses and ebbs through the ages like a tide, while in the relative stillness of the ocean's depths, riverborne grains of quartz, feldspar, mica, and clay deepen and compress into strata—laying foundations for mountains and coastlines yet to be born.

THE DIVERSITY OF COASTAL ENVIRONMENTS

Although rocky shores dominate the Olympic coastline, the coast is remarkably varied. River mouths, pocket coves, sand and gravel beaches, and protected reefs in the lee of sea stacks and islands create a complex array of intertidal environments, each teeming with life. The sheer diversity of coastal life-forms is comparable to the inland ecosystem. And the marine shoreline of Olympic National Park is the most biologically complex and diverse in all of the United States. This tremendous diversity is brought about by a number of factors. Some are products of the geologic forces that shaped the present coast; others find their origins in the wide and bountiful ocean from which the peninsula itself was drawn.

The Pacific is an old ocean—much older than its sister the Atlantic—and its rocky shores have served as a refuge for marine plants and animals for hundreds of millennia. This relatively stable marine environment has allowed, in Thoreau's words, "a liberal amount of time" for evolution to perform its magic. A continuous rain of organisms and nutrients sifts down from surface layers into cold, deep offshore waters. Plumes from the Columbia River south of the Olympic coast and the Strait of Juan de Fuca to the north add to these deep, nutrient-rich waters. In summer, north winds parallel to the shoreline push warm surface waters away from the coast. This causes cool, rich water from the depths to upwell to the surface. The surge of nutrients feeds an abundance of free-floating microscopic plants in sun-warmed surface waters. They and the microscopic animals that feed on them (which include the larval stages of many larger animals) are called plankton—phytoplankton for plants, protoplankton for animals. Plankton forms the base of the food chain in open-water ecosystems and also supplies important food for filter feeders on the shore. Some of the most productive fisheries in the world are located in areas of coastal upwelling. Twice each day the sea floods the lush intertidal areas of the North Pacific with this plankton-rich broth.

The Olympic coast's biological diversity is also enhanced by climate. Unlike many rocky shorelines elsewhere in the temperate zone, the Pacific Northwest coast enjoys a consistently mild maritime climate. Temperatures do not vary greatly from season to season. The same coastal fogs that nurture the Olympic rain forest in summer cloak the shoreline and temper the desiccating effects of the July sun. Hard freezes, which can wreak havoc on intertidal organisms exposed during low tides, are rare; sea ice, which can seriously abrade intertidal communities, is nonexistent. The Olympic coast's location midway between California and Alaska allows it to harbor species common to both boreal and temperate marine environments. All this combines with the variety of habitats and the relative absence of human-caused disturbances to create a realm of exceptional productivity and beauty.

In summer, low tides and calm seas grant us terrestrials passage among the tidal pools, surge channels, and seaweed-covered rocks to glimpse communities that stay hidden for much of the year. Researchers estimate that there are at least 150 plant and 200 animal species inhabiting the narrow zone between Olympic tides, along with more than 50 fish. These figures do not take into account the many birds, sea mammals, and land animals that also use the Olympic coast. This high level of biodiversity is reflected throughout the coast's environments, rocky shores, cobble benches, sandy beaches, and estuaries, but it reaches its fullest expression along exposed rocky shores. Rocky shores and reefs hold the greatest number and variety of marine organisms—from cormorants and turnstones to anemones and mussels—of any coastal environment. By observing the ways key intertidal plants and animals interact and respond to competition, predation, and disturbance, we can gain a better understanding of this dynamic environment and a keener appreciation of its place within the Olympic ecosystem and the larger Pacific world.

A RAMBLE THROUGH THE ROCKY INTERTIDAL

If winter storms punctuate one end of the coastal year, summer explorations of the low tide zone illuminate the other. I like to start early on summer mornings, well before the first rays of sunlight stir the fog from the tops of shoreline spruces. The cries of western and glaucous-winged gulls announce the turn of the tide as I clamber around the high rocks of the spray zone to see what I might scare up. Like the plants and animals of the interior mountains, marine organisms of the rocky coast arrange themselves in layers or zones in response to environmental conditions, including the biological conditions of competition and predation. On rocky shores, these zones are compressed into tens rather than thousands of vertical feet, all reachable in the lull of an outgoing tide.

The Spray Zone

The spray zone is moistened only by the highest tides and rain, and last night's quiet high didn't bring much action. Temperature and salinity vary greatly, and the few organisms that live here have learned to cope with extremes. A band of dark lichen grows along the upper end of the spray zone, and bright green sea hair algae mark the freshwater seeps. Below them, clusters of common acorn barnacles (*Balanus glandula*) crowd shoulder to shoulder with small acorn barnacles. Like many species, common acorns are found throughout the intertidal area. They would crowd the small acorns out completely if not for heavy surf and wave-tossed driftwood that clear patches of them, allowing small acorns to recruit. Barnacles, lichens, and other dwellers of the high shore can thrive higher up on the wave-exposed sides of rocks; they are found slightly lower on lee sides. An occasional rock louse darts across a rock; this small marine isopod shows a decided leaning toward dry land. I notice a few checkered and Sitka periwinkles huddled in a wet crevice along with some tiny finger limpets. Limpets are tough, conical mollusks that clamp themselves to rocks with a muscular foot. They can stick with a force equal to eighty pounds—a handy trait when winter seas pound the coast. By sealing themselves into their "home scars," which they wear into the rocks, some limpets can also stay wet during low tides. Farther down among the boulders, larger speckled limpets feed on algae growing on the undersides of rocks.

The High Tide Zone

As I climb down into the high tide zone, thick beds of common acorn barnacles cover the rocks—the small acorns of the splash zone are less apparent here. Larger limpets also appear; brown and white shield limpets are common, and flatter plate limpets sport tufts of algae that allow them to blend inconspicuously with their surroundings. Limpets make their living by scraping algae from the rocks with toothed feeding organs called radulas. Farther down in this zone, whelks use radulas to prey on acorn barnacles and mussels by boring holes through their shells. In fact the presence of predatory whelks inhibits the downward spread of acorn barnacles. Where the acorns become thin, I notice the dull gray husks of larger thatched barnacles, and dense clusters of black turban snails congregate among the cracks and crannies in areas protected from the waves. Turban snails can live for forty years, as measured by growth rings. When they die, their shells are commonly appropriated by hermit crabs. Lacking a shell of their own over their soft, vulnerable abdomen, hermit crabs must frequently trade old shells for new as they grow. They seem continually preoccupied with their search for new shells, and, as in certain desirable neighborhoods elsewhere, contests over available homes can become pitched. Hairy and glandular hermits inhabit the wetter parts of the high tide zone; both protect their newly acquired real estate with stout, oversized claws.

Like their alpine counterparts, organisms of the high tide zone must be able to cope with demanding conditions—not only heavy wave action but long periods of exposure to air, drying winds, and sunlight. Some, like the rockweeds, have become specialists. Thick beds of brown rockweed drape the substrate of the middle high tide zone, and the pale air bladders at the tips of their fronds pop wetly under my feet. When damp, rockweeds photosynthesize better in air than in seawater—one reason I find them this high on the shore. Rockweeds hold up under winter freezes and summer heat. And like oaks and a few other terrestrial plants, rockweeds contain tannins, which may inhibit grazing by periwinkles. Moving aside the fronds, I find congregations of limpets, snails, and isopods living beneath rockweeds, eluding predators as well as escaping drying heat. Thin, nearly transparent fronds of bright green sea lettuce wave lightly in the nearby current, and low-growing tufts of sea moss, looking like a forest moss, wedge among the rocks and cobbles. Purple shore crabs scuttle sideways from rock to rock. If I inadvertently corner one of these tiny creatures away from cover, I'm always a bit startled to see the fierceness with which it bares its small pincers. Inevitably, I'm the one who retreats.

The Middle Intertidal

By early morning, the lush seaweed gardens of the middle intertidal zone begin to emerge, and rivulets of seawater pulse back and forth at their fringe. This zone is bathed in seawater about half the time, and seaweeds here grow profusely. As algae, which lack the roots, leaves, flowers, and stems of herbaceous land plants, seaweeds are classed low on the evolutionary ladder. Their "roots" are really holdfasts that keep them attached to the bottom, their "leaves" blades that absorb minerals from seawater as well as photosynthesize sunlight. But in spite of their simple structure, these ocean plants embody a variety of shapes, textures, and colors, and they vary widely in reproductive strategies as well as habitats.

I find fewer rockweeds in the middle intertidal, but bright bundles of sea lettuce linger, sometimes in thick beds draping the rocks. Sea lettuce here is joined by other garden-variety seaweeds—sea cauliflower and sea cabbage among them. The cauliflower resembles a brownish version of its garden namesake, while sea cabbage spreads long, leathery split leaves over the rocks. In the calmer waters of Puget Sound it more resembles a cabbage. Sea sacs lift two- to three-inch clusters of water-filled, saclike tubes into the current, and black pine, which is actually brownish in the water, trails bristly needlelike branchlets in the outgoing tide.

On the steeper, more exposed, wave-swept shores, a true indicator plant of the open coast, the sea palm (*Postelsia palmaeformis*) occupies cleared patches in mussel beds. Its presence is a warning for hikers to proceed with caution. Growing on flexible stalks up to two feet tall and with long, shaggy blades at their tops, sea palms droop when out of the water, resembling miniature palm trees. Their tough holdfasts grow over barnacles and

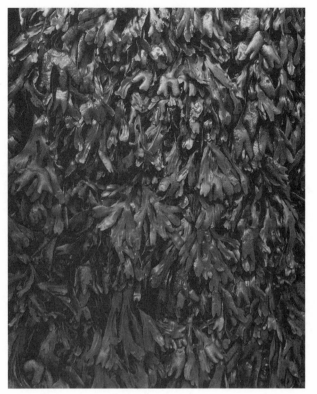

Among the most common seaweeds of the upper and middle intertidal zones, thick beds of a number of rockweed provide a wet protective cover for limpets, snails, and other intertidal species during low tide. PHOTO BY RUTH KIRK.

mussels, providing a firm anchor in battering surf. Sea palms are annuals, and fall storms strip them away, along with the plants and animals caught in their holdfasts, creating new attachment sites for their spores.

Such wave-cleared patches enhance community diversity in mussel beds by allowing new plants and animals to get a start. If patches are small, limpets and chitons may keep them free of algae, and barnacles can set. If patches are larger, islands of algae will form in their centers, and sea sac and other seaweeds soon follow. The plant communities of the middle intertidal harbor a greater number of animal species than are found in the high tide zone. But the most characteristic organism of this zone, the California mussel, creates its own microenvironment.

Mussels and Sea Stars

If there is a signature species of the coast's rocky intertidal zone, it's the California mussel (*Mytilus californianus*). As the tide recedes about halfway out, I find wide bands of these large bivalves cobbling the rocks;

Common organisms of the intertidal area. DRAWING BY DIANE GUSSET.

they seem to crowd out everything but scattered clumps of gooseneck barnacles. The mussels range from dark blue to brown and black in color, and the shells of the larger ones are often encrusted with acorn barnacles and limpets. These mussels can live up to twenty years. Quiet hissing and popping sounds permeate the bed as water drains away, and I try to step lightly over this crowded neighborhood. Though they appear a monoculture at first glance, these beds can be several layers deep, and they offer a rich, protected microclimate for as many as 300 other species. Tube and ribbon worms, small clams, snails, limpets, and crabs all find suitable habitat in the interstices of mussel beds and feed on the detritus, algae, and small animals that collect there.

Mussels attach themselves to rocks with tough elastic byssus threads that can be absorbed or respun, affording them a small degree of mobility. I notice a few smaller, smooth-shelled Pacific blue mussels (*Mytilus trossulus*) scattered among the beds, but they generally prefer more protected sites in the lee of sea stacks and islands or above California mussels on shore. Blue mussels are much more mobile than California mussels and are quick to colonize wave-cleared patches. Eventually, the larger Californians outcompete them on the open coast; they overgrow the smaller mussels and crush them out. Pacific blues find more favorable habitat in calm bays and the inland waters of the Strait of Juan de Fuca and Puget Sound.

The other contenders that wedge their way into mussel beds are gooseneck barnacles. The larvae of both goosenecks and California mussels prefer to settle among the byssus threads and stalks of their own kind. Like their thick-shelled neighbors, goosenecks are well adapted to life on the stormy coast. Their short, tough stalks, tipped with pearly, light gray segmented plates, give and bend with the surf. Unlike other barnacles that pull in their food with featherlike cirri, goosenecks simply strain runoff from wave-inundated rocks, making them well suited to the vertical walls and undersides of rocks the mussels force them to occupy. Although gulls, sea otters, and occasionally humans are known to feed on these barnacles, the major predator of both goosenecks and California mussels is the common ochre sea star.

Looking near the water line just below the mussel beds, I can easily find them. The purple or ochre sea star (*Pisaster ochraceus*) is the most common sea star on the open coast. A stout, five-rayed starfish, it can grow to more than a foot across. As its name implies, a Pisaster can range from ochre-orange to bright purple, with shades of tan and brown in between. Ochre is the color I see most often on the open coast; purple is more common in Puget Sound. Their bright colors make them stand out conspicuously at low tide, and I soon notice several more clumped beneath an overhanging ledge by a pool. Though ochre sea stars feed on barnacles, limpets, chitons, and snails, the prey they most prefer are mussels.

An exquisitely evolved predator, sea stars cover mussels and pull their shells open with powerful arms and strong tube feet. Once a mussel is open even a crack, the sea star can insert its stomach into the shell and digest it. Sea stars are equipped with light- and chemical-sensitive tentacles at the tips of their arms and have rough backs, rasplike to the touch. Their backs are covered with microscopic pincers that keep other organisms from settling on them. Pisasters' unusual dining habits limit their feeding to high tides, and they show a strong aversion to air and sunlight. This keeps them generally low in the intertidal zone—and keeps mussels growing higher on rocks and reefs generally safe from sea star predation.

Predation by purple or ochre sea stars creates openings in beds of California mussels and enhances intertidal diversity. Some 25 intertidal species benefit from ochre sea stars' predation on mussels. PHOTO BY JANIS BURGER.

The University of Washington's Robert Paine, studying sea star predation of mussels at Tatoosh Island on the northern Olympic coast, discovered that sea stars define the lower edge of California mussel beds. When they are removed, mussels rapidly extend their ranges deeper into the intertidal. Paine also found that by limiting the sizes of mussel beds and clearing patches of bare rock within them by predation, sea stars play a pivotal role in the ecology of the middle intertidal zone. Some twenty-five other species—including a number of barnacles and algae—depend upon ochre sea stars to create open patches in mussel beds.

Another interesting intertidal relationship Paine discovered is that between the sea stars and a seaweed, sea moss (*Endocladia muricata*). Among the first algae to colonize the clearings that sea stars carve in mussel beds, sea moss provides an ideal base for mussel larvae to settle. Limpets are the primary grazers of sea moss, and so limit attachment sites for mussels. Conveniently, ochre sea stars also prey on limpets and, by trimming their numbers, help insure a future supply of their preferred prey, California mussels.

Through his studies of Pisaster and California mussel interactions on Tatoosh Island, Dr. Paine developed the groundbreaking ecological concept of "keystone species." These are organisms, usually high on the food chain, that through their activities exert an influence on the composition of their communities disproportionate to their numbers. Pisaster is a quintessential keystone species. Paine and other scientists studying the rocky intertidal have found that the lower ranges of a number of species are set by predation as well. The distribution of acorn barnacles is limited by predatory whelks, and the lower limits of some seaweeds are probably set by the grazing of black chitons. In contrast, the upper limits of many species' ranges are most often determined by environmental factors—exposure to waves, air, and desiccating wind, and lethal warming by sunlight.

Poking around, I notice a few six-rayed sea stars occupying the same niche as ochre sea stars. They have the same feeding patterns as ochres but are much smaller (three to four inches) and feed only on smaller individuals—barnacles, limpets, snails. They are generally found under rocks and exert much less influence on the ecology of this zone. As one biologist told me, Pisaster drives the middle intertidal; remove it and diversity crashes. Unfortunately, the illegal collection of starfish in some heavily visited intertidal areas outside the park, such as Pillar Point on the Strait of Juan de Fuca, has led to that result.

Along the wet edges of mussel-cobbled rocks, I find clusters of aggregating sea anemones (*Anthopleura elegantissima*) hunched together like Easter eggs in a carton. Their small, pale green and pink-tipped "flowers" have closed as the tide has retreated, and they are covered with bits of gravel and shell. Able to withstand the pressures of wave action, sunlight, and wind, these tough, two-inch-high animals will wait for the returning tide to deliver zooplankton and other prey to their sticky tentacles. Though they frequently live next to mussel beds, most anemones aren't preyed upon by starfish. In fact, some benefit from starfish predation by picking up the table scraps from starfishes' meals. Aggregating anemones reproduce asexually by cloning; larger individuals divide as often as once a year. Interestingly, one cloned colony will keep another at "arm's length" with the stinging capsules at the tips of their tentacles.

I often find black chitons in association with anemone colonies. A tough mantle covering most of their shell allows these chitons to remain exposed to air and sunlight for long periods. Black chitons are easily identified by the eight overlapping plates along the spine of their shells as well as their medium size (three inches). A tough leathery foot keeps chitons fastened to rocks and allows them to move about and feed on diatoms (microscopic one-celled plants) and larger algae. They're also quite fond of sea cabbage. By clearing this fleshy seaweed from the rocks, chitons make room for coralline algae to grow. These are the lovely pink plants, both branching and crustlike, that lend to tide pools an almost otherworldly air.

The Low Tide Zone

By midmorning the tide has drawn well back from the shore, revealing a broad, low rocky platform glistening with dark seaweeds. Shallow ravines or surge channels bisect the rocks, and tide pools abound. These rocky depressions where seawater lingers at low tide are found throughout the intertidal area, but the tide pools of the low tide zone hold a special magic. The shapes and colors of low tide dwellers, particularly those revealed during the minus tides of spring and summer when water recedes more than ten feet below mean high tide, are most vivid. They suggest an even richer abundance and diversity of species that remains hidden in the subtidal zone. The sound of a subdued surf lapping nearby rocks and the brevity of each visit—dictated by the returning tide—heighten the sense of discovery.

Peering into a Tide Pool

By allowing marine creatures to stay active during low tides, tide pools act as lenses through which one can glimpse the dynamics of intertidal life. Barnacles and tube worms wave feathery feeding structures, and anemones open their flowerlike tentacles to the flow. Sheltered from the brunt of wave action, less resilient plants such as surfgrass and coralline algae flourish in these natural aquaria, and interactions between organisms can be easily observed. Limpets and chitons can be seen slowly scraping the rocks for food; a shrimp may nibble a bit of dead fish; a whelk may drill away at mussel. My first pool yields what many consider to be the most strikingly beautiful tide pool inhabitant, the painted, or red and green,

Sea urchins graze on kelp beds and other seaweeds in tide pools or offshore waters. The red sea urchin is the largest on the Olympic coast and prefers the shelter of tide pools and protected waters. Sea urchins are a favorite food for sea otters. PHOTO BY JANET LAMONT, OLYMPIC COAST NATIONAL MARINE SANCTUARY.

anemone. Algae living inside their tissues give most anemones their color, but the red streaks of this anemone's column and the pink to reddish stripes of its tentacles set it apart. The relationship between algae and their anemone hosts is symbiotic; anemones use carbohydrates fixed by the algae, and algae use carbon dioxide from anemones.

A relative, the giant green anemone, is larger in size (up to twelve inches in diameter), emerald green in color, and tends to favor more wave-swept environs. I often find them in surge channels, where food is carried to them by tidal flow, as well as alongside mussel beds, where, like aggregating anemones, they pick up meals loosed by starfish. Like all anemones, the giant green's tentacles close over its prey—crab, mussel, or limpet—and guide the prey into its gullet; the anemone then "swallows" it. Later the anemone expels undigested bits of shell. Green anemones enjoy long lives; some have lived more than thirty years in captivity. In habitats where waves are quieter, they are smaller and markedly fewer in number.

A tiny, almost iridescent anemone, the brooding anemone, also brightens some tide pools. They are only two to three inches in diameter. I find them hidden among blades of surfgrass, where, like the six-rayed sea star, they brood their young until offspring are large enough to survive on their own.

Spiny sea urchins add bright splashes of purple and green to some of the larger tide pools. The red sea urchin of the outer coast is the largest found here; it can grow to more than six inches across, with spines that jut out another three inches. Despite their formidable appearance, sea urchins feed primarily on algae. They also use their sharp teeth and spines to scour indentations in soft rock, where they are protected from tides and currents. Where wave action is severe, smaller purple sea urchins carve deep pockets.

Sea urchins are known to feed heavily on kelp across much of the low tide and subtidal zones. In southern California, an overabundance of sea urchins in past decades (brought about by the extirpation of their major predators, the sea otters) led to the destruction of large offshore kelp beds. The resulting "urchin barrens" eventually became bereft of anything but urchins. When the urchins were artificially controlled, or as in the case on the Olympic coast, when sea otters were successfully reintroduced, kelp beds recovered. For years, sea urchin row has been considered a delicacy in Japan, where it fetches a very high price. In areas where urchins were commercially harvested, kelps tend to dominate seaweed communities. Sea urchins, on the other hand, take years to reestablish. But urchins are prolific, even among marine animals; a female can produce 20 million eggs in a single season.

Crouching low and peering beneath tide pool ledges, I find the long white casings of calcareous tube worms twined over a crusty bed of coralline algae. I don't see their feathery fans out sweeping the water for plankton, but nearby, clusters of smaller feather duster worms open thick multicolored mops that look like—well, like miniature feather dusters. Multiple layers and tiers of life deepen tide pools with vivid colors and textures. Coralline algae range from bright pink to pale purple in delicately branched or platelike form. The segmented calcified tissue of branching corallines lets them sway gently in the current. More than ten species of coralline algae are found in Olympic tide pools. Graceful coral coralline spreads pink lacelike branches, while coral leaf coralline is almost skeletal in comparison. Many of these delicate algae depend on chitons and other grazers to prune back fleshy seaweeds that would otherwise choke them out. They, in turn, feed communities of specialized grazers: lined chitons eat encrusting corallines; black chitons feed on branched.

Multihued rock crust seaweeds, brilliant sponges, and chartreuse hydrocorals carpet tide pools with dazzling displays of color—much of it sheer biological extravagance. Unlike the coloration of most terrestrial animals, that of many marine organisms seems to serve no adaptive purpose. An exception to this may be the small nudibranchs that move among the seaweeds. Their extravagant colors may advertise bitter tastes or even toxicity. One, the opalescent nudibranch, is particularly stunning. With cerata tipped with burnished scarlet and electric blue stripes lining its sides, it could have just wriggled out of Disney's *Fantasia*. Other nudibranchs blend inconspicuously with their surroundings, much like the small, quick-moving shrimp or darting tide pool sculpins that shoot under rocks as I approach their pools and stay hidden no matter how long I try to search them out.

Tangled Mats of Seaweed

Beyond the tide pools, the rocky reefs of the low tide zone stretch out to the low waves in a tangled mat of seaweeds. Stalks and blades eddy and bob as wavelets break against the rocks. The plant associations of the low tide zone are commonly arranged in multistoried communities, not unlike the layers of an old-growth forest. Large kelps or sometimes surfgrass form the upper canopy. Kelps are tough brown seaweeds, often growing in dense colonies just offshore. Surfgrass is one of the two vascular plants of the intertidal, getting its nutrients through roots and reproducing by flower and seed like inland species do (seagrasses may have found their way back to the ocean by way of rivers and tidal estuaries). An understory of corallines and various red algae thrives in the shelter of the kelps, and a layer of red algae often encrusts the rock surface below. Many of the more than 120 species of algae that grow in Olympic's intertidal areas appear to require the cover of larger seaweeds for protection from wave shock as well as exposure during low tides.

Researchers have found that grazing by herbivores such as mollusks does not seem to significantly hamper plant growth on the Olympic coast. Limpets, which are among the most numerous grazers elsewhere, are abundant only in the middle and high tide zones here, and most chitons are generally too small and slow moving to have a significant impact on intertidal plants. The large black chitons, which scrape portions of the rocks bare in parts of Puget Sound, are less abundant on the outer coast; other grazing species may be fewer in number as well.

This relative paucity of herbivores may be partly explained by predation. Gulls, oystercatchers, and starfish are all known to feed on these species; oystercatchers in particular have been known to put serious dents in limpet populations within their territories. By keeping herbivorous species in check, the predators on the Olympic coast may be partly responsible for the lushness of these low tide gardens. Of course, a healthy flow of nutrient-rich water and the early morning timing of low tides during the warmest months (covering seaweed beds with seawater during the heat of the day) are also important factors.

Among the algae most often found in the lower reaches of the low tide zone are several species of kelps. Split kelp is fairly common, with its blades cut into wide ribbonlike strips. Alaria, or winged kelp, grows up to ten feet long and has rich brown blades with pronounced central ribs and furled edges. Ornate, fringed feather boas live up to their name, and wide blades of yellow-green sugar kelp drape the wet rocks. Just offshore, bull kelp and perennial kelp grow in dense "forests" that mirror the upland rain forest in species diversity and fecundity. These kelps can grow to a hundred feet long, adding more than five inches of growth per day. Their dense, tubelike stems, or "stipes," and flowing blades provide shelter and offer a range of complex habitats for a variety of fish, as well as sea otters and other marine organisms. Bull kelp (*Nereocystis luetkeana*) is an annual and is frequently found washed up on beaches after fall and winter storms. Perennial kelp (*Macrocystis integrifolia*) thrives year-round on the open coast and serves as critical habitat for sea otters, who feed among its stalks, raft together in its beds, and "tie into" it dur-

Like virtually all seaweeds growing off the coast, the common kelp, feather boa, is an alga. Algae absorb nutrients from seawater and photosynthesize sunlight through their blades. Only a few marine plants, such as surfgrass and eelgrass, have roots, stems, and flowers. PHOTO BY JANIS BURGER.

ing rough weather. When cast ashore as wrack, both kelps form huge, tangled drifts on the beach. Most kelp are more easily seen when washed up after storms. Their littered remains, strewn along the high tide line, harbor busy colonies of beach hoppers and other tiny scavengers. They, in turn, are an important food for a variety of shorebirds. Like downed logs in the rain forest, rotting kelp plays an important role in cycling nutrients back into the nearshore system.

One last seaweed, the rainbow, or iridescent, seaweed, deserves mention—not only for its abundance along rocky shores but for its sheer beauty. Its smooth, wide blades are coated with a lustrous cuticle, which imparts to this red alga a shimmering blue-green iridescence. Its rainbow colors shift with the angle of the viewer or as sunlight moves across the sky.

On the lowest of tides, kelp fronds drift on slack offshore waters, and creatures more common to the subtidal area sometimes make themselves known. On other explorations at very low tides I've been lucky enough to spot bright orange sunflower stars. Up to three feet in size and with as many as twenty-four rays, sunflower stars are the largest and fleetest of foot among the sea stars, and they inspire in their prey dramatic acts of escape. Scallops will clap their valves together frantically to swim away; large sea cucumbers have been known to "gallop," and the common cockle will kick its foot in a rapid retreat across the substrate.

The smaller sun stars are a striking orange to rose color with gray or blue stripes extending from the center of their backs down the lengths of their ten rays. I find neither of those on this visit, but the much smaller blood stars are out and about, their five slender rays a brilliant orange-red. Like brooding anemones, these sea stars share the unusual habit of brooding, or keeping their eggs with them, until they hatch.

I keep an eye over my shoulder, watching the two or three high rocks I used to skip across channels, making sure they're still there for my retreat. Like darkness on a forest trail, the change in tide can come suddenly, often when I've got my face in a tide pool and my hind end to a wave. As the tide turns and I begin to retrace my route to shore, I find a giant Pacific, or "gum boot," chiton—looking quite like the cast-off sole of an old rubber boot—clamped to the wall of a channel. Up to a foot or more in length (much larger and more leathery than the hairy and mossy chitons also found here), the gum boot is the largest chiton in the world and can live more than twenty years. As I hop and skip back to shore, I hear the clicking of crabs hidden beneath seaweeds—kelp crabs and other spider crabs no doubt, stealthily working their weedy worlds. Spider crabs such as the decorator crab adorn themselves with stuck-on bits of seaweed and shell. Hairy and helmet crabs sprout less elaborate growths of seaweed. No doubt all are grateful for the return of the tide and the departure of unwelcome visitors like me—turning over rocks, poking through seaweeds, and making a general nuisance of myself. It's probably for the best that these lowest tides come only every month or so in summer.

COBBLE, DRIFTWOOD, AND SAND

Toward the southern end of the Olympic coast, south of the Hoh River, sand and cobble beaches become more common. The forests that thatch the roofs of sea stacks and headlands to the north step down gently here, and spruce limbs bow to the tide line. Beneath them, a band of silvery driftwood marks the fluid and shifting edge between land and sea. At a few places along the coast, such as Rialto Beach, this dynamic edge is quite vivid as the forest retreats from the restless advance of the surf. Just past the parking area at Rialto, dead and dying spruce trees rise from a litter of wave-tossed cobbles. Mossy logs, tree roots, and brush of the forest floor poke out from beneath heaps of stones cast up by winter storms. Cobble, or shingle, beaches such as these are among the most actively shifting on this restless coast, and they provide the poorest habitats for organisms. Constantly shuffled and ground together by wave action, cobble on the open coast supports little of the marine life found on cobble beaches in the more protected waters of the strait and Puget Sound. Sandy beaches provide much more hospitable homes.

The smooth sandy beaches at Kalaloch, Ruby Beach, Second Beach, Sand Point, and Shi Shi are among the most beautiful stretches of the Olympic coast. Long breakers curl toward the shore, and gulls wheel above blowing spray. Like exposed cobble beaches, the sandy beaches that dimple pocket coves and line unbroken stretches of shoreline seem rather lifeless at first. But feeding gulls and flocks of western sandpipers, sanderlings, and plovers that skirt the water's edge hint at the life hidden beneath the tide-washed sand. Sandy beaches support less than a tenth of the number of life-forms found on rocky shores. A sand beach may host thirty-five species in its intertidal area. But life communities here supply other kinds of essential functions, such as filtering phytoplankton and contributing nitrogen, that benefit the entire coastal ecosystem.

Like the rocky headlands and cobble beaches that separate them, sandy shores receive the full force of stormy seas. The jumble of huge driftwood logs lining their upper reaches attests to the power of winter surf. Though logs help stabilize the upper reaches, most sandy beaches are pummeled, churned, and abraded relentlessly by the pounding surf. Even adjoining rocky areas are scoured by the action of sand- and pebble-laden waves. The only large organisms that can survive in this tumultuous environment are those that can burrow down into the sandy substrate—such as crustaceans and worms—or those able to move quickly up and down the beach with the tides. Most noticeable among the latter are the ubiquitous beach hoppers. Beach hoppers, or sand fleas as they're sometimes called, burrow into shallow sand or hide beneath tangles of seaweed and pieces of driftwood to stay moist by day. At night they turn sandy beaches into moonlit sock hops as they pop about scavenging for food. These small creatures actually rely on the moon to navigate back to their burrows on the upper beaches.

Opossum shrimps and waterline isopods drift in with the tides to feed in the shallows. They and other invertebrates loosed from the sand by waves serve as food for larger predators. Hundreds of thousands of surf perch inhabiting the waves feed on these small crustaceans. Higher on shore, snails leave wriggly trails across the wet sand as they scavenge for food. One of the most striking is the purple olive snail. An inch or so long, this snail has a smooth, shiny, purple-gray shell that may be the loveliest on the coast; it was used as money and ornament by Northwest coast people. Another favorite among beachcombers is the sand dollar. The small, flat hollow disk cast up on shore is the skeleton of this urchinlike animal. It plows the sandy offshore bottom, picking out bits of organic matter with tiny, hairlike cilia. The five-petal pattern inscribed on the sand dollar's shell resembles a sea star, a hint that these species are closely related.

Sandy intertidal areas provide no holds for seaweeds, and large seaweeds cannot grow here, but the incoming tide brings microscopic phytoplankton, which feeds many sand dwellers. The same tides also bring predators such as flatfish, crabs, even starfish to feed on the submerged life. Razor clams, which inhabit the lower end of the intertidal, cope with their turbulent environment by rapidly burying themselves. Thrusting downward with a powerful foot and inflating its tip with water, a razor contracts its foot muscles to pull itself deeper into the sand. As anyone who has dug razor clams can attest, these long slender bivalves can be amazingly fast, moving up to a foot in twenty seconds. Razors, which are prized by clam diggers, are found mostly along the broad sandy beaches of the Kalaloch area, at the lowest of low tides. Just over four miles of beach at Kalaloch supports an estimated 15 million razor clams, supplying tremendous filtering and nitrogen contributions to coastal waters.

Razor clam harvests in the park are managed by the Washington Department of Fish and Wildlife, but as the number of visitors to the coast increases, managers are reassessing long-standing recreational uses of clams and a variety of other intertidal organisms. Researchers and park managers are concerned that even recreational activities in the intertidal zone could pose a threat to diversity. Sport fishermen harvesting tube worms for bait have already put a serious dent in populations in the Kalaloch area; some species were beginning to disappear. Illegal collection of starfish and other organisms have altered intertidal communities and affected other species as well. Overgathering of mussels for food poses a threat to the many species that find habitats within mussel beds.

Park managers have stepped up research and management in heavily used areas. Sport fishermen are now prohibited from harvesting tube worms or any intertidal species for bait. Park rules also prohibit the collecting of gooseneck barnacles, starfish, and other creatures. Some scientists and conservationists feel that any harvesting of intertidal species, including clams, mussels, and nearshore fish, should be prohibited within Olympic National Park—just as hunting, cutting trees, and gathering wildflowers are prohibited in the park's interior. In 2008, the park service increased its protection of coastal areas by proposing a series of intertidal reserves. These would be designated areas along rocky reefs that are particularly rich in species diversity. They would be protected from harvest of any kind, and public use would be regulated to protect the areas' ecology.

The Olympic coast is a realm of transformation, an ecotone between a unique terrestrial ecosystem and the larger North Pacific of which it is a part. That a relatively intact forest ecosystem should be complemented by a protected marine area with the richness of the Olympic coast is the rarest of good fortunes. We owe it to future generations, as well as to the life-forms themselves—the numerous birds and mammals that share the coast and the myriad creatures that inhabit its intertidal edge—to keep this wonderfully complete ecosystem intact.

CHAPTER 8

Seabirds and Mammals of the Outer Coast

T HE soft winds and quiet tides of summer on the outer coast belie
the storm-swept coves and driftlog-pounded beaches that thunder
here for much of the year. Alaskan writer Richard Nelson compared walking a similar stretch of northern coast in summer with visiting a stadium where no game is being played. The sleeping summer sea
allows access, but the landscape tells a different story. The history of maritime tragedy here underscores the coast's tempestuous, sometimes violent,
nature.

South of Yellow Banks, a small granite monument stands half hidden by surrounding trees. The Norwegian Memorial marks the common
grave of the crew of three-masted schooner *Prince Arthur.* The ship ran
aground in the winter of 1903, killing eighteen of her twenty crew members. Farther south, a smaller stone marks the grave of eighteen sailors
who drowned when the Chilean schooner *W. J. Pirrie* struck an offshore
reef during a winter storm in 1920. This marker is not far from the site
of another Chilean ship that wrecked here in 1883. The calls of gulls and
slow lapping of waves are a quiet counterpoint to the image of ships cast
up on the rocky shore.

The sea cliffs, stacks, islands, and reefs of the Olympic coast have
troubled the dreams of generations of mariners. Storm winds on the outer
coast (as distinct from the more protected "inside waters" of Puget Sound
and the Strait of Juan de Fuca) can exceed 150 miles per hour. Waves can

tower fifty to ninety feet in height. Fog may blanket the coast for days, and safe anchorages are few to nonexistent. No one knows how many lives have been lost to this rugged coastline, but historical records list 180 ships that met their end here since 1810. Prior to that, a number of Asian boats are known to have washed up at various points along the Pacific coast. As recently as 1927, the Japanese fishing boat *Ryo Yei Maru* was found drifting toward the shore south of Cape Flattery bearing the skeletal remains of its crew.

Hikers sometimes find pieces of shipwreck debris scattered among driftwood on coves and beaches. I have vivid memories of my fist exploration of the coves north of Shi Shi Beach, where the wrecked World War II–era troopship *General M. C. Meigs* lies, its mast leaning sharply amid wave-pounded sea stacks and billowing spray. Thirty-five years later the image lingers, its juxtaposition of human industry and the wildness of this untamed coast still poignant. But humans made their home here for thousands of years before the ships of exploration and commerce came calling. And the jagged, rock-studded jaws of the coast so dreaded by mariners have provided a safe harbor for seabirds and sea mammals for many more millennia.

In the early years of the last century, little was known to science about the seabird colonies nesting on the offshore rocks and islands of the Olympic coast. That changed dramatically in 1906 when an intrepid ornithologist named William Dawson first explored the area. Traveling by cedar canoe with his family and two Quileute guides, Dawson encountered one of the most productive seabird nesting areas on the Pacific coast. He documented rookeries of auklets, puffins, and storm-petrels and listed numerous other species using these offshore islets. His writings in scientific journals and the popular press galvanized the support that led to President Theodore Roosevelt's executive order establishing sanctuaries on the coast the following year "as preserves and breeding ground[s] for native birds and animals."

Today, some 870 islands, sea stacks, rocks, and reefs are protected as part of the Flattery Rocks, Quillayute Needles, and Copalis Rock national wildlife refuges (collectively known as the Washington Islands National Wildlife Refuges). The steep, rocky shores and inaccessible uplands of forty named islands and hundreds of smaller rocks and reefs provide habitat for more than 70 percent of Washington State's nesting seabird population, harboring some of the largest seabird colonies in the United States. The islands also provide critical habitat for threatened bird species that nest on the coast, such as bald eagles and peregrine falcons. The islands' isolation offers protection from terrestrial predators, and their cliff faces, ledges, and glacier- and wind-deposited soils host a variety of nest sites. Some of the same factors that lead to the incredible productivity of Olympic's intertidal area—moderate climate, upwelling of deep-water nutrients, and undeveloped character—make this a prime area for seabirds.

Seabirds animate the rocky coast. Their bright spring plumage, their incessant calls, the vigorous trajectories of their flights charge the coastal atmosphere with life. They are the winged expression of the tremendous fecundity of the marine environment—feathered offspring of sunlight and sea. The sight of cormorants or oystercatchers skimming across the waves as I clamber over driftwood onto an open beach brings a special kind of gladness.

BIRD ROCKS OF THE OUTER COAST

At first light in early summer, birds are already leaving the rocks and islands to fish. Auklets, guillemots, cormorants, and murres fan out over the waves and head for open water. Other birds more familiar to beach walkers peruse the tide line and seaweed-covered rocks: oystercatchers utter chattering calls as they careen low over the rocky shore, and ubiquitous glaucous-winged gulls patrol the tide line like cops on a beat. Overhead, where spruces trace the ragged edge of the sky, two bald eagles circle on motionless wings while a gaggle of crows caw loudly and take turns diving at the eagles' broad white tails.

Along with bald eagles, other threatened and endangered species thrive along the coast. Marbled murrelets and peregrine falcons find refuge here. Since the 1980s brown pelicans have begun to visit the area in late summer and early fall. Sea mammals feed in productive coastal waters and haul out on rocky terraces and reefs. Sea otters continue to repopulate the coast, and Steller's sea lions, too, are increasing in number. Just offshore, the spring and fall migrations of California gray whales remind us of the long history humans share with sea mammals on the outer coast.

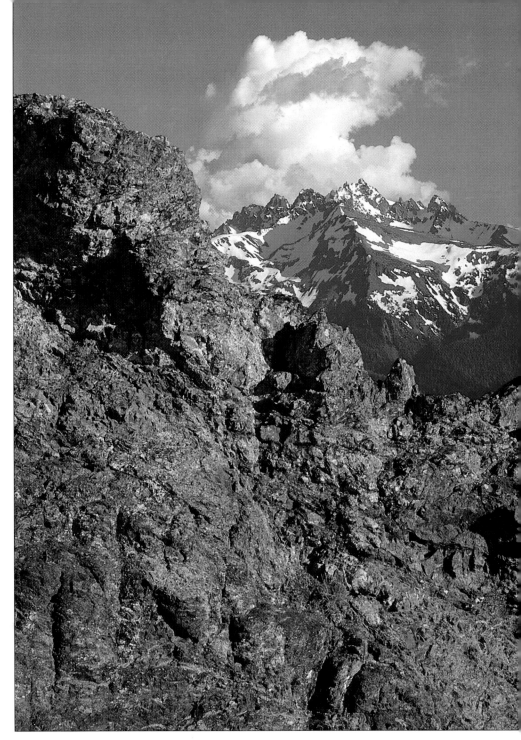

Lichens color a basalt outcrop on Blue Mountain. The jagged spires of the Needles, in the distance, are part of the Olympics' inner basalt ring, a section of submarine lava sheared off by faulting and folded in among mixed sedimentary rocks. PHOTO BY KEITH LAZELLE.

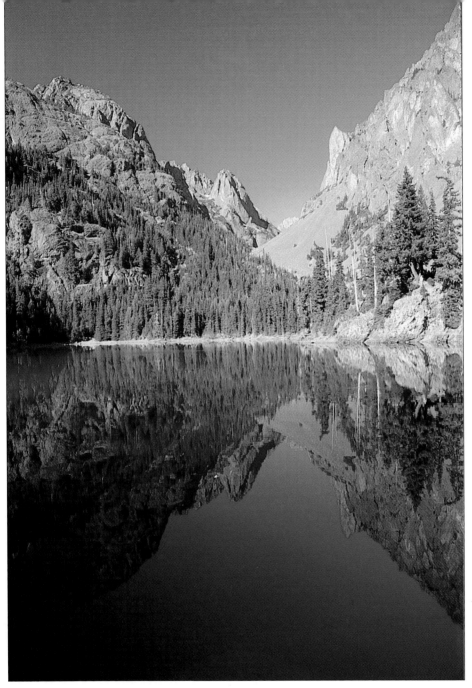

ABOVE Lake Constance and Avalanche Canyon below Mount Constance are carved into thick marine basalts of the Crescent Formation. The rugged character of the east Olympics is a product of its geological origins. PHOTO BY KEITH LAZELLE.

LEFT As winter snow melts back from High Divide in the central Olympics, fields of avalanche lilies flutter in the summer breeze. The glaciers of Mount Olympus in the background are still laden with winter snow. PHOTO BY KEITH LAZELLE.

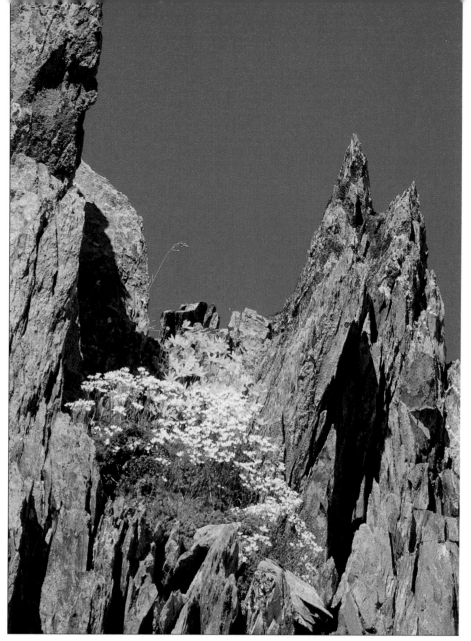

ABOVE As soon as snow melts from the high mountains, even rock faces and
ridgetops burst into bloom. Spotted saxifrage, arnica, and Davidson's penstemon
grow among splintered shale near Gray Wolf Pass. PHOTO BY KEITH LAZELLE

RIGHT TOP Dawn light on Mount Olympus. Collecting more than 100 feet of
snowfall each year, Mount Olympus supports the lowest-elevation system of glaciers
in the forty-eight contiguous states. PHOTO BY KEITH LAZELLE.

RIGHT BOTTOM The crevassed mouth or "snout" of Blue Glacier on Mount
Olympus. Like many large glaciers in the Olympics, Blue Glacier has been in fairly
steady retreat since the 1920s. PHOTO BY KEITH LAZELLE.

ABOVE Plants of the alpine and subalpine zones have adapted to cope with quickly changing conditions. An early summer snowfall melts back from the blossoms of spreading phlox. PHOTO BY KEITH LAZELLE.

LEFT TOP Lake Crescent after a rain. As winter clouds rise over the mountains, they bury the high country in snow, but in the lowlands precipitation falls mainly as rain. Lake Crescent, 17 miles west of Port Angeles, receives more than 80 inches of rain a year. PHOTO BY KEITH LAZELLE.

LEFT BOTTOM Sunset from Blue Mountain. The rounded foothills west of Blue Mountain reflect shaping by the Juan de Fuca lobe of the Vashon ice sheet 15,000 years ago. One lobe of ice flowed west over these low ridges and foothills toward the Pacific, carving the Strait of Juan de Fuca; another pushed south along the east Olympics to carve Puget Sound. PHOTO BY KEITH LAZELLE.

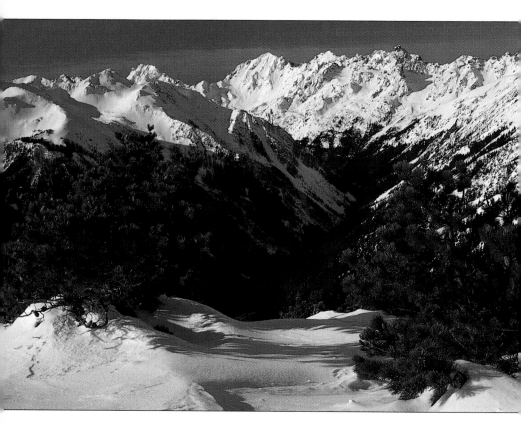

ABOVE Winter on Gray Wolf Ridge. In the heart of the northeast rainshadow, stunted lodgepole pines reach toward treeline on dry south-facing slopes. An adaptable tree, at home in stressful environments, lodgepoles also thrive in a few locations along the Pacific coast and Puget Sound. PHOTO BY KEITH LAZELLE.

RIGHT TOP One of the most beautiful of Olympic's endemic plants, Piper's bellflower, grows in cracks and crannies in the rocks of the high mountains. Biologists suspect it is a "paleoendemic," a plant whose former range was erased by the Cordilleran ice sheet. Its closest relative grows more than 600 miles to the north. PHOTO BY KEITH LAZELLE.

RIGHT BOTTOM Another Olympic endemic, Flett's violet, also prefers rocky crevices. Blossoming in early summer, it brings a special delight to alpine scramblers. PHOTO BY KEITH LAZELLE.

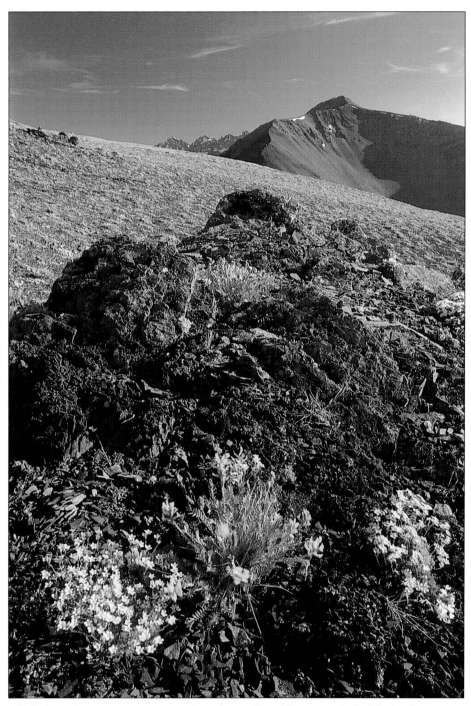

Tufted saxifrage, mountain oxytropis, and spreading phlox are typical of the hardy low-growing plants found in Olympic's alpine zone. Summers are short and conditions often severe in this realm above the trees. PHOTO BY KEITH LAZELLE.

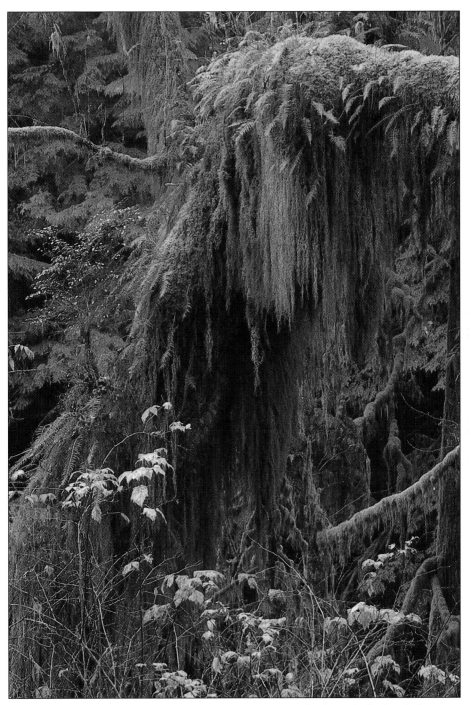

Moss, licorice fern, and the hanging clubmoss selaginella drape the limbs of a big-leaf maple in the Queets rain forest. Epiphytic growth on some rain forest trees can amount to as much as four times the weight of a tree's foliage. PHOTO BY KEITH LAZELLE.

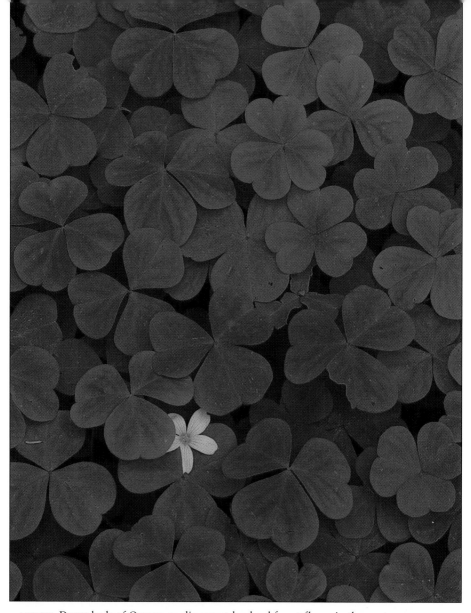

ABOVE Dense beds of Oregon oxalis carpet lowland forest floors in the western Olympics but virtually disappear in dryer east-side forests. The small inconspicuous flowers of oxalis bloom from early spring to late summer. PHOTO BY KEITH LAZELLE.

RIGHT TOP The sight of Roosevelt elk in valley forests always brings a thrill. It was to protect elk habitat that Theodore Roosevelt created Mount Olympus National Monument in 1909. Currently, an estimated population of 5,000 elk inhabit the park. PHOTO BY KEITH LAZELLE.

RIGHT BOTTOM The canopy lichen lobaria serves an important role in the forest ecosystem by absorbing valuable nitrogen from the atmosphere and making it available to the forest. When it falls to the forest floor, it also serves as an important seasonal food for elk. PHOTO BY JANIS BURGER.

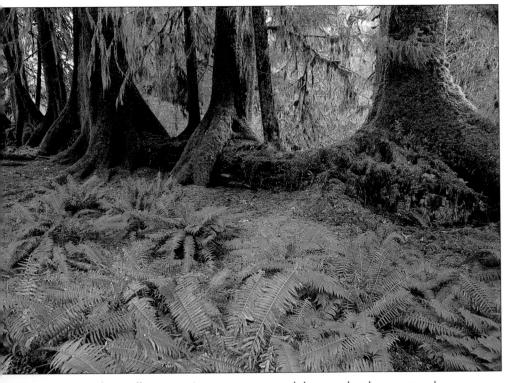

As nurse log seedlings grow into mature trees and the nurse log decomposes, the row of stilted trees that result is called a "colonnade." Colonnades are a common feature of Olympic's temperate rain forests. PHOTO BY KEITH LAZELLE.

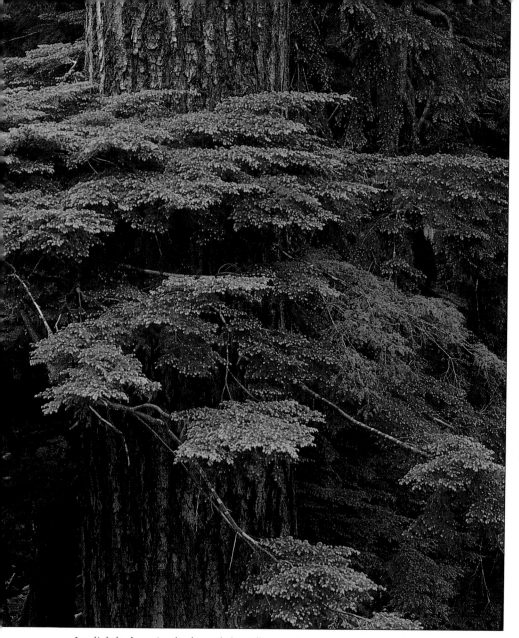

Its slightly drooping limbs and short flat needles make western hemlock easy to recognize. Hemlock's tolerance to shade makes it the major understory tree in Olympic forests, and it is common from coastal areas well into the mountains. PHOTO BY KEITH LAZELLE.

Young hemlocks, old Douglas fir. The thick corky bark of mature Douglas firs insulates them from most small wildfires and seedling Douglas firs do well in bare ashen ground. Barring fires and other disturbances, the young hemlocks that grow up in the shade of old Douglas firs will eventually dominate the stand. PHOTO BY JANIS BURGER.

Northern spotted owls have come to symbolize the old-growth forest ecosystem in the Northwest. Feeding on flying squirrels and woodrats and nesting in cavities in snags, spotted owls need large tracts of old-growth forest to successfully reproduce. In the Olympics, spotted owls are near the northern extent of their range. PHOTO BY KEITH LAZELLE.

ABOVE Pacific rhododendron flourishes in open Douglas fir forests of the eastern Olympics, where it blooms from April in the lowlands through June in montane forests. An indicator of the relatively dry forests of the east Olympics, its range is opposite that of Oregon oxalis. PHOTO BY KEITH LAZELLE.

RIGHT TOP East Olympic rivers have a character and flavor all their own. Streams like the Duckabush are marked by narrow valleys and steep gradients. Down logs play an important role in these rivers, regulating high flows and creating pools and hiding cover for young salmon and trout. PHOTO BY KEITH LAZELLE.

RIGHT BOTTOM The cool wet forests and shaded streams of the Olympics make ideal habitat for salamanders; eight species of salamanders and newts are found here. The western red-backed salamander is a small woodland species. Most woodland salamanders lay their eggs on dry land and the young hatch as miniature adults. PHOTO BY JANIS BURGER.

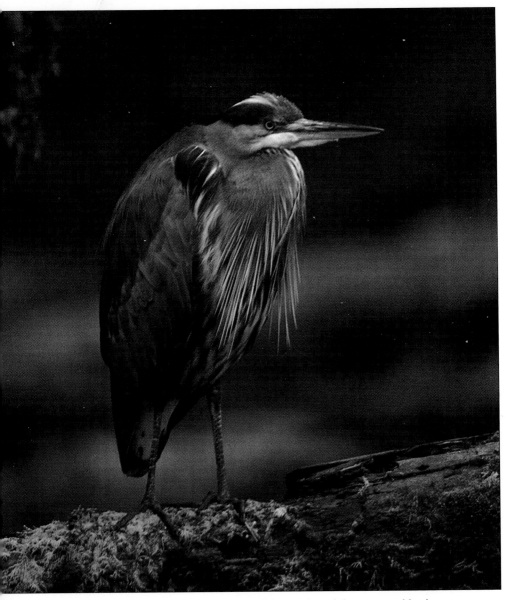

Most elegant of the birds that feed on small fish and amphibians, great blue herons nest in colonies in dense forests and feed along the Peninsula's streams, lakes, and coastal areas. PHOTO BY KEITH LAZELLE.

Spring brings brilliant flashes of color to swollen streams in the form of harlequin ducks. Harlequins leave coastal waters to mate and nest among snowmelt rapids of Peninsula rivers. PHOTO BY KEITH LAZELLE.

ABOVE One of the most spectacular parts of the outer coast is Point of the Arches. Sandstone strata at the south end of Shi Shi Beach fold into the complex assemblage of basalts, breccias, and conglomerates that form the Point. Rocks at Point of the Arches have been dated at more than twice the age of the oldest rocks in the interior. PHOTO BY KEITH LAZELLE.

LEFT Cape Flattery at the northeast tip of the Peninsula typifies the rugged, rocky shoreline of the northern coast. Short coastal streams bisect steep headlands, and intertidal organisms are subject to heavy pounding by winter seas. PHOTO BY KEITH LAZELLE.

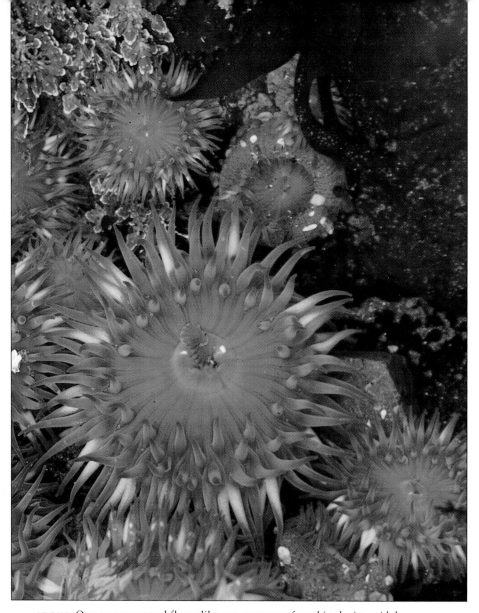

ABOVE One among several flowerlike sea anemones found in the intertidal area, aggregating sea anemones often form dense colonies. This species can reproduce sexually or asexually by cloning. Cloned colonies are known to maintain strict territorial boundaries. PHOTO BY KEITH LAZELLE.

RIGHT TOP Coralline algae and surfgrass. A common seaweed on the outer coast, surfgrass lines submerged tide pools and rocky shelves. Unlike almost every other seaweed (eelgrass is another exception) surfgrass is not an alga but a true grass with roots, flower heads, and seeds. PHOTO BY KEITH LAZELLE.

RIGHT BOTTOM Blood sea star on eelgrass. In more protected waters of the Strait of Juan de Fuca and Puget Sound, eelgrass provides important habitat for a variety of fish and invertebrates. The small blood star retains its young, an unusual behavior for intertidal species. PHOTO BY JANIS BURGER.

ABOVE Gulls and sea stacks near Cape Johnson. Olympic's offshore rocks and sea stacks, first protected as national wildlife refuges in 1907, provide nesting habitat for more than 100,000 pairs of breeding seabirds. PHOTO BY KEITH LAZELLE.

LEFT TOP The elevational ranges of many intertidal species are determined by predation. Here, the lower ends of gooseneck barnacle colonies are preyed upon by ochre and purple sea stars. Sea stars' aversion to drying sunlight limits their upward spread, allowing gooseneck and mussel beds above them to flourish. PHOTO BY JANIS BURGER.

LEFT BOTTOM Large numbers of red and purple sea urchins graze on kelp beds and other seaweeds. Sea otters are known to prey heavily on urchins. In the absence of such predation, urchins can turn kelp forests into "urchin barrens" devoid of plant life. PHOTO BY JANET LAMONT, OLYMPIC COAST NATIONAL MARINE SANCTUARY.

ABOVE Black oystercatcher nest. For many marine birds, a nest is a mere scrape on a ledge or amid the sod of offshore islands and sea stacks. Oystercatchers' eggs blend well with the rock substrate. The eggs of common murres are pear-shaped to prevent their rolling off rocky ledges. PHOTO BY KEITH LAZELLE.

RIGHT TOP Bald eagles are a frequent sight along the outer coast where dozens of nesting pairs find habitat. In winter, eagles from northern and inland regions migrate to the Olympic coast to feed in nearshore waters. By spring nesting season, they have returned to their breeding areas. PHOTO BY KEITH LAZELLE.

RIGHT BOTTOM Brown pelicans began appearing along the Olympic coast in the 1980s, as El Nino events shifted their prey populations northward. Once nearly destroyed by DDT, pelicans are now common visitors along the Washington coast in summer and fall. NATIONAL OCEANIC AND ATMOSPHERIC ADMINISTRATION.

Although sea otters were extirpated from the Northwest coast by the early 1900s, their successful reintroduction in 1970 has resulted in a healthy breeding population in the park's coastal waters. Sea otters' luxuriant fur insulates them from cold north Pacific waters, but also makes them highly vulnerable to oil spills. PHOTO BY FRED FELLEMAN.

Steller's sea lions visit Olympic Peninsula waters from northern breeding ranges. Larger and shaggier than California sea lions, the two mix amiably here, even sharing haulouts on offshore rocks. PHOTO BY FRED FELLEMAN.

California gray whales often swim close to Olympic beaches straining bottom sediments through their fringed baleen as they migrate to their northern ranges. Once hunted nearly to extinction, gray whale populations now approach their original numbers. PHOTO BY FRED FELLEMAN.

With federal protection, California gray whales have made a remarkable recovery. Centuries after humans first arrived on these shores, the whales, seals, sea otters, and sea lions that return to the coast continue to stir the hearts of visitors.

Other cetaceans also ply Olympic coastal waters: harbor and Dall's porpoises, orcas or killer whales, and several species of dolphins, but few of these are easily seen from the shore.

The eagles and peregrines, shorebirds, seabirds, and marine mammals of the Olympic coast are part of the warp and woof, the intricately woven fabric of the Olympic ecosystem. By exploring the natural histories of some key breeding birds and resident and migratory sea mammals of the coast, we get a fuller sense of the coast's unique place within the larger ecosystem.

RECOVERY ON THE COAST:
BALD EAGLES AND PEREGRINE FALCONS

The old Sitka spruces that cling tenaciously to the tops of headlands seem to stand in defiance of the elements. Roots woven firmly into cracks in bedrock and stout limbs jutting into the wind, these aging sentries of the forest's edge are holdouts against the incessant advance of the sea. When at last they succumb, we find them weathered and broken, angled against a sea cliff or cast back up on the beach by waves, their tangled roots ground to nubbins. But while they stand—and some lean over the sea's edge for centuries—they serve as fitting perches for that largest bird of prey that hunts the shore, the bald eagle.

Bald eagles (*Haliaeetus leucocephalus*) are strikingly noticeable along the coast all year. Their white heads and tail feathers stand out in the misty light, and the dark silhouettes of their eight-foot wingspans are unmistakable against the sky. Eagles spend so much of their time perching conspicuously in headland spruces or gliding on thermals in search of food, they've come to share an irrevocable identity with this rocky coastline—so much so that for some, a visit to the outer coast seems incomplete without sighting one. Bald eagles lack the distinctive white head and tail feathers for their first four years, but their shape is hard to miss. Golden eagles, with which they are sometimes confused, inhabit the interior

Olympics and are far fewer in number.

Bald eagles begin their courtship behavior as early as December in some years, and their displays can be quite spectacular. Territorial males will sometimes lock talons and plummet from great heights in a series of somersaults; pairs will spiral upward close together on soaring thermals. They usually nest in March or April, constructing or refurbishing bulky platforms of large sticks and lining them with finer material. Not all these nesting materials are gathered from the ground. One biologist observed a bald eagle descend as if to land on a stout limb that jutted from the dead top of a Douglas fir. But rather than slowing as it approached the tree, the bird maintained speed, stretched out its talons, and hit the limb hard, snapping it off with a riflelike crack. The eagle then flew off with the large limb grasped firmly in its claws.

Eagles seem to prefer rocky headlands, islands, even some sea stacks over beaches for nesting sites. Eagles nesting on the open coast seldom use the tops of trees, as they do in inland areas. Instead, the nests are usually found farther down in the canopy of tall Sitka spruces—a concession no doubt to Pacific storms. Nests are maintained and repaired each year, but only one nest in a given breeding territory is occupied. Eaglets are born in late April or May and usually fledge in mid-July. Their early weeks are spent close to the nest site, learning to hunt and scavenge. Dead and dying fish are generally the staples of the bald eagle's diet, but some biologists suspect that on the Olympic coast they may rely more heavily on birds. Having watched eagles casually pluck gulls from the waves and shoreline, I believe this.

A curious migration occurs throughout Washington's coastal waters in late summer. Newly fledged eagles and their parents disperse for a few months in the fall, returning again in December. Telemetry work has shown that some Washington birds fly north to British Columbia to feed on early returning salmon runs. It may be that this strategy allows home territories to recover from the intense feeding associated with nesting, or the birds may need the added nutrients of a salmon diet to store up energy for winter. In early winter, a much larger migration occurs. Bald eagles from as far away as Alaska, interior British Columbia, and the northern Rocky Mountains flock to Washington's coastal areas as inland waters freeze up. Large numbers of these overwintering eagles from far-flung territories mingle with Washington birds along coastal and inland waters, putting aside the territorial behavior they exhibit so robustly during the nesting season.

For the past several decades the remote forested coastlines of Washington, British Columbia, and southeast Alaska have served as a stronghold of North America's bald eagles. Here, feeding on plentiful fish from the Pacific and shorebirds and small mammals on the uplands, they were able to persist while bald eagle numbers elsewhere declined sharply. Pollutants in lakes, rivers, and coastal waters; widespread declines in fish runs; and destruction of nesting and roosting habitat all took a toll. Eagles were listed as federally threatened in 1973. But with protection under the Endangered Species Act and the banning of DDT and other harmful pesticides, bald eagles have made a strong comeback in recent decades. From a low of fewer than 400 pairs (outside Alaska) in 1963 to 10,000 pairs today, eagles were removed from the U.S. endangered species list in 2007. Bald eagle numbers in Washington have reached target figures established in the U.S. Fish and Wildlife Service's Pacific Bald Eagle Recovery Plan. Nesting success throughout Washington has shown a steady upturn during the 1980s, going from 86 young produced in 1975 to more than 400 in the early 1990s. By the mid-1990s, there were 450 occupied nesting sites in Washington State, more than 200 of them on the Olympic Peninsula.

Although some of this increase may be due to better observation, there is no doubt that bald eagles are doing well here. Surveys of bald eagles on the Olympic coast have identified some 52 nesting territories north of the Queets River. In 2002, 38 of these were occupied by nesting pairs, with 38 young counted in June. This high level of productivity on the coast follows an upward trend since monitoring began in 1980 and reflects the quality of the coastal habitat. Surveys of more developed areas in the Strait of Juan de Fuca and Puget Sound show that the number of nesting territories has increased there as well. Unfortunately, the small number of bald eagles that nest along Olympic Peninsula rivers and those nesting along Hood Canal on the eastern shore of the peninsula are often unsuccessful in raising young. Some biologists suspect this may be due to declining salmon runs and pollutants along the canal. On the Columbia River, where salmon numbers have been decimated by dams and pollution, very few chicks hatch. Although the overall picture here is good, some areas are clearly faring worse than others.

Another bird of prey that nests along the Olympic coast—though one seen far less frequently than bald eagles—is that living incarnation of flight, the peregrine falcon (*Falco peregrinus*). Renowned for their speed and mastery of the air as hunters, peregrines were revered in ancient Egypt and coveted by feudal lords. Many ornithologists today consider peregrines to be among the most highly evolved birds of prey. Inhabiting the wildest, least-disturbed places—desert ranges, canyons, uninhabited coasts—and nesting on steep, inaccessible cliffs, peregrines at one time enjoyed the widest distribution of any bird in the world. They feed exclusively on live birds and take their prey on the wing. Dropping into a stoop from a mile above the earth, peregrines can attain speeds of more than 200 miles per hour, yet control their flight with pinpoint accuracy. Hunting at sea, peregrines are known to cruise low in the troughs of rolling waves to surprise unsuspecting seabirds.

Historically, thousands of peregrines followed the migrations of other birds along the great flyways of North America. But by the mid-1960s, fewer than twenty known pairs of peregrine falcons remained in all of North America. The presence of DDT and other pesticides in the environment resulted in thin, brittle eggshells and pushed these magnificent birds to the edge of extinction. DDT was finally banned in the United States in 1972. Since then, an intensive captive breeding effort has allowed peregrines a remarkable recovery. Reared and released birds and their offspring now populate former ranges in the eastern United States, the Rocky Mountains, and throughout much of the West. Although no captive-bred falcons have been introduced on the Olympic coast, some twenty-five peregrine nesting territories have been identified here. By the late 1990s, seventeen of these were occupied (up from two a decade earlier), producing two young per breeding pair. The trend continues with occasional setbacks in nesting success during El Niño years.

El Niño or southern oscillation events occur regularly off the coast of South America, triggered by disturbances in the pattern of trade winds. As warm water flows up the coast toward north America, it alters the pattern of currents and hampers the upwelling of deep-water nutrients onto the continental shelf. This, in turn, limits the productivity of phytoplankton and other marine organisms that form the basis of the coastal food chain. El Niño events send a ripple effect through the entire marine ecosystem. Significant such events have occurred along the Pacific coast in 1982–83, 1987, and 1997–98. El Niño events and accompanying rising surface temperatures can result in widespread breeding failures among seabird colonies. Top-feeding predators such as peregrines are affected, as are salmon, sea mammals, and seabirds.

In 1999, with the recovery of peregrines in Washington State and elsewhere, peregrine falcons were removed from the federal endangered species list. With their rate of nesting success here, the year-round presence of falcons on the Olympic coast seems assured.

Two-thirds of Olympic's peregrines nest in scrapes on offshore sea stacks, and the remainder nest on steep sea cliffs. They feed primarily on smaller seabirds: storm-petrels, auklets, guillemots, and puffins; but, as with peregrines elsewhere, most any bird will do, including an occasional crow or robin. They also hunt Bonaparte's gulls and bufflehead ducks, taking on the average a bird a day. Falcon pairs roost together and hunt cooperatively. Since peregrines usually hunt offshore, and much of their time is spent roosting (where they blend in well with the dark canopies of trees), sightings are not common. Only a handful of other nests have been reported in Washington, on the Strait of Juan de Fuca, the San Juan Islands of Puget Sound, and the Columbia River gorge.

Nonresident peregrines can sometimes be seen migrating along the coast, particularly in spring. Migratory birds winter along the Gulf Coast, through Mexico and Central America and as far south as Chile and Uruguay. Since DDT is still in use in some of these countries, the fate of North American peregrines is still less than secure. As recently as the late 1980s falcons nesting along the Big Sur coast of California were still suffering nesting failures due to thin eggshells. Such instances should make us all the more protective of those remaining wild enclaves like the Olympic coast, which have allowed these resident masters of the wind to thrive.

BIRD LIFE ON THE ROCKY SHORE

If there is a single bird that embodies the wave-swept intertidal area of the Olympic coast, it is the black oystercatcher (*Haematopus bachmani*). Its sharp, whistled staccato notes are synonymous with the sound of waves

The black oystercatcher is easily recognized by its stout red beak. These shorebirds feed on shellfish and crustaceans on exposed rocks of the intertidal zone and utter sharp chattering calls as they fly above the surf. PHOTO BY JANIS BURGER.

rolling over rocky reefs. Its dark plumage, offset by bright red bill and ringed yellow-gold eyes, suggests the hidden colors of a coastal tide pool. Oystercatchers seem as adept and well suited to their tumultuous intertidal environment as dippers are to mountain streams. I've watched them feed on rocky reefs all but oblivious to the waves breaking around them. A last-minute hop or skip sets them effortlessly clear of harm's way. When seriously involved with a mussel or chiton, they often let small waves wash over them. As backwash streams off the rocks they reappear, still occupied with their meal, as if the surf were no more cause for alarm than a passing shower.

Oystercatchers are superbly adapted to their intertidal world. Their legs and feet are tawny and strong enough to grip the substrate, and their long beaks are stout and effective. In spite of their name, black oystercatchers eat very few oysters, but they have little trouble popping limpets from the rocks and working them free of their shells. Chitons, small crabs, even mussels offer little challenge. Working the surf line where mussels often remain at least partly open, oystercatchers cut their quarry's abductor muscles with quick stabs of their beaks. A few shakes then frees the mussel from its shell. Small crabs or tightly closed mussels require a bit more effort, but these are pummeled open with the chisel-like tip of the beak and consumed without further fuss. The effectiveness of these birds as feeders is apparent in the low numbers of limpets in feeding territories occupied by the large black birds. Few other birds besides gulls and occasional crows compete with oystercatchers for large intertidal mollusks. Even so, oystercatchers fiercely defend their rather large territories well beyond the nesting season.

Black oystercatchers locate their nests in depressions on rocky ledges, sometimes behind clumps of sod, and on sea cliffs or islands (Destruction Island off the mouth of the Hoh River hosts large numbers of them). Some nests are loosely lined with pebbles or shells. Both males and females incubate eggs and feed their young, often far beyond the fledging stage. Young oystercatchers, which are a lighter brown than their parents, must learn the tricks of foraging before striking out on their own. Ravens and gulls are the primary predators of eggs and chicks, but the parent birds are remarkably effective in fending them off. The old broken-wing ploy is often trotted out, and more inventive games resembling hide-and-seek have been reported.

Oystercatchers seem unafraid to nest in glaucous-winged gull colonies, and there may be some advantages to this. Gull nests may signal that a site is safe from predatory mammals, gulls may serve as an early warning system when danger is about, and intertidal invertebrates may be more plentiful as a result of nutrients from gull wastes.

Oystercatchers are a common sight on rocky coasts from California to Alaska. They inhabit the Olympic coast year-round and are probably joined in winter by migrants from the north. Some ninety nests were identified along this coast, producing more than 300 birds. Far fewer inhabit the shores of Puget Sound, and oystercatchers have disappeared entirely from its southern waters. But their rhythmic calls and bright good looks continue to animate the open rocky coast.

Wherever oystercatchers are foraging, off-season visitors are likely to see two smaller shorebirds feeding among them. Black turnstones and surfbirds are robin-sized shorebirds that migrate along the Olympic coast. Flocks of black turnstones, common in fall and winter, frequently join oystercatchers on reefs at low tide, searching among rockweeds and kelp for small limpets, barnacles, and other crustaceans (their cousins, the ruddy turnstones, are abundant in spring). A stately combination of black and white, their upper parts becoming striped in spring, turnstones can be seen probing cracks and fissures in the rocks and poking about beneath them for food. True to their names, they do turn rocks over—some of them quite sizable—with a quick flip of the bill. When the tide is in, turnstones also rummage through seaweed litter on the beach (sanderlings sometimes follow behind them, feeding in the freshly exposed sand and gravel). Gregariously social and keeping up a constant chatter as they feed, black turnstones are occasionally joined by smaller numbers of surfbirds.

These intertidal feeders closely resemble turnstones, but they are slightly larger and a lighter gray. In spring, surfbirds turn a beautiful pattern of brown, black, and white. Both are inland breeders (surfbirds migrate north in summer to nest in Arctic tundra). But in fall, winter, and early spring, they feed in flocks along the coast. A flock of 100 to 200 is known to winter on Destruction Island. I sometimes see them hopping from rock to rock in continual search for tiny shellfish, which they swallow in the shell. Like turnstones and most other shorebirds, surfbirds consume about a third of their body weight in food each day. Interestingly, though black oystercatchers rigorously protect their territories from others of their kind, including dispersing young, they show a marked tolerance for these migratory neighbors. The surfbird is one of the most appropriately named of shorebirds; its genus name, *Aphriza*, means "lives in the sea's foam."

CORMORANTS, PUFFINS, AND AUKLETS

Much like the intertidal habitats of the Olympic coast, the offshore rocks and islands are located at an interface between northern and southern seabird nesting ranges. As a result, the outer coast of Washington supports a greater diversity of species than do coastal areas to the south, but the total number of birds nesting here is lower than in either Oregon or British Columbia. Though the Washington Islands Refuges harbor some 110,000 pairs of nesting seabirds, the rocks and islands lie at the edge of both northern and southern ranges for many species, and a number of species do not breed here. The coastal islands do serve as important nesting habitat for some fourteen species of seabirds and are critical for a few species, such as the rhinoceros and Cassin's auklets. Seabirds spend much of their time feeding out on the open water. But among the species most distinctive and easily recognized by visitors on the shore are the cormorants.

Three species of cormorants nest on the outer coast. All are large, dark, long-necked seabirds that perch upright with graceful S-shaped curves of their necks and lifted beaks. In their trademark posture, they perch with wings held loosely out to their sides, rather like princes striking poses at court. Cormorants have serrated, hooked bills like those of mergansers (excellent for catching and holding fish), and they store food in pouches below their lower mandibles. Their wide webbed feet, like diving ducks', are designed to maximize underwater propulsion. They lack ducks' water-repellent plumage though and must frequently land and spread their wings to dry.

Pelagic cormorants (*Phalacrocorax pelagicus*) are the smallest of the three and by far the most common. They are distinguished from the others by their dull red faces and throat patches and by white patches on their flanks during the spring breeding season. Pelagics dive quickly without a splash and swim swiftly underwater in pursuit of herring, sand lance, sculpin, and other fish. Pelagic cormorants breed throughout Puget Sound as well as on the outer coast. The number of breeding pairs on the coast increased from around 700 in the mid-1980s to more than 2,000 by the early 1990s. But pelagic cormorant numbers are always in flux, responding to ocean conditions and food abundance. In El Niño years the number of breeding pairs can drop to 1,500 or 1,000, due to warm surface water and declining fish populations.

Double-crested cormorants (*P. auritus*) are also a frequent sight on the coast. They can be distinguished from the others by their orange throat pouches (the double head crest is usually not apparent). In spring their black plumage takes on an iridescent green sheen. Double-crested cormorants are a northern species, finding their southernmost breeding habitat on Washington's coastal islands. Some reside on the coast year-round, while others migrate to the more protected waters of the Strait of Juan de Fuca and Puget Sound in winter. On good breeding years in the past, the coastal islands hosted from 400 to 800 breeding pairs. But double-crested numbers never bounced back from the 1997–98 El Niño, either on the outer coast or in Puget Sound. The current coastal population is less than 300 pairs.

Brandt's cormorants (*P. penicillatus*) are the least numerous of the three. Brandt's is a southern species; the Olympic Peninsula and Vancouver Island are the northern extent of its range. During breeding season, Brandt's is distinguished by a blue throat pouch with a yellow patch behind. Brandt's favor the southern end of the coastal area, where between 50 and 600 nest on islands and sea stacks. They often nest in association with glaucous-winged gulls. Many also winter in Puget Sound. When disturbed, all three cormorants will fly away from their nests, leaving their young exposed to predators.

Three similar species nesting together and sharing the same food resources would be expected to have evolved some noncompetitive breeding strategies—and they have. The three nest at different times. Double-crested cormorants nest earliest, usually by early May. Brandt's cormorants begin nesting in late May, and pelagic cormorants nest and lay eggs between these two. Nesting locations are also somewhat stratified. Double-cresteds prefer to build their messy, guano-covered nests on the upper slopes of offshore islands; pelagic cormorants prefer steeper, rocky or sand cliff faces, usually below the double-cresteds. Brandt's cormorants prefer the tops of islands as well as south-facing slopes. By staggering their nesting times, cormorants minimize competition when feeding nestlings. It's possible that cormorants divide up some food resources as well.

Tufted puffins (*Fratercula cirrhata*) are among the most charismatic of Olympic's offshore breeding birds. They are seldom seen close to shore but are well known to boaters and fishermen—from whom they rob herring off baited lines quite effectively. In summer plumage, puffins' clownish faces sport oversized multicolored bills and long, straw-colored tufts that curl shaggily behind their eyes. The tufted puffin's face is white, the rest of its body jet black. Like other alcids of the coast—guillemots, murrelets, auklets, and murres—the puffin uses its short, powerful wings to "fly" underwater in pursuit of fish. Its large beak proves handy in carrying numbers of fish back to its nesting young, and it can hold captured fish securely in its beak with its tongue while continuing to catch more. Herring, smelt, sardines, and perch are among the puffin's preferred prey.

Tufted puffins are common from north of the Aleutians to British

Columbia, and localized residents from Washington to Baja. They nest on islands of the outer coast; a few small colonies also nest on islands in Puget Sound. Puffins nest in burrows in steep, turf-covered slopes or cliff tops; they seem to prefer high locations for easy takeoffs. Their burrows are commonly two to six feet long and five to six inches in diameter. A single egg is laid on bare ground in a cavity at the end.

About 23,000 tufted puffins are known to nest in twenty-five colonies along the Olympic coast. The largest colonies are on Jagged Rock and Alexander Island. As recently as the 1950s and 1960s, more than 1,000 tufted puffins also bred on islands in Puget Sound; Protection and Smith islands each harbored more than 300 birds. Fewer than fifteen pairs occupy those islands today. Breeding pairs elsewhere on inside waters have been wiped out by agriculture and residential development, predation by pets, and indiscriminate shooting. Puffins may be among the most disturbance-sensitive of all nesting seabirds. They seem exceptionally high-strung, leaving their nests frequently when trespassers are near, keeping an eye on them, flying over, or harrying them.

Fortunately, puffins' breeding habitat on the outer coast is safe from most such disturbances, and large breeding colonies in British Columbia and southeast Alaska number in the hundreds of thousands. Tufted puffins make occasional appearances on the Strait of Juan de Fuca and Puget Sound when they leave the outer coast in winter. Others head out to open sea or to slightly warmer waters to the south.

An alcid more commonly seen in Olympic's coastal waters is the rhinoceros auklet (*Cerorhinca monocerata*). Described by some as a "misnamed puffin," this auklet is dark like the puffin but with a lighter breast. Rhinos are named for the small, stout horns that sprout from their upper mandibles during breeding season; they also wear white "eyebrows" and understripes then. Like puffins they nest in burrows on offshore islands but leave to secure food and return to their nests in the predawn and after dark. The peninsula's offshore islands form a major part of the rhino's breeding territory. Colonies of about 13,000 birds nest on Destruction Island, their largest southernmost breeding colony. But rhino auklets on the inside waters have suffered a precipitous decline since the mid-1970s. The population on Protection Island has dropped from 17,000 pairs a decade ago to 12,000 today, possibly due to entanglement in fishing nets

The rhinoceros auklet, a common seabird along the coast, nests in burrows on off-shore islands. Destruction Island on the Pacific coast and Protection Island in Puget Sound are among its major breeding grounds. PHOTO BY JANIS BURGER.

and the increase in recreational boat traffic. If this rate of decline continues, these birds could be extirpated from Puget Sound by 2050. Rhinoceros auklets are excellent flyers; birds fledging from Protection Island fly to the outer coast to feed. Like puffins, most rhinos also spend their winters at sea.

STORM-PETRELS, MURRES, AND GULLS

Among the farther-ranging birds that nest on the outer rocks are the storm-petrels. These small, songbird-sized flyers range from the Arctic to the Galapagos Islands. Storm-petrels do not dive, but skim the ocean surface for fish, small squid, and crustaceans. Fork-tailed storm-petrels (*Oceanodroma furcata*), which are mostly gray, breed on offshore islets from Oregon to Alaska. The closely related Leach's storm-petrels (*O. leucorhoa*), which are black with white rump patches, find most of their home breeding range on rocks and islands off the Olympic coast. Both birds spend most of their time on the water, coming ashore only to breed. When

William Dawson explored the Olympic coast in the early years of the twentieth century, he found an island off La Push "honeycombed" with the shallow burrows of Leach's storm-petrels and estimated a Washington population of 100,000 birds. More recent estimates set the population at 50,000 for Leach's, and around 4,000 for fork-tailed storm-petrels.

During breeding season, storm-petrels are entirely nocturnal, leaving their nests and returning under cover of darkness. Ill-suited for getting around on land and small enough to be ideal prey for peregrine falcons as well as gulls, river otters, and other predators, storm-petrels are even reluctant to venture out on moonlit nights. The ornithologist E. A. Kitchen, who studied birds on the peninsula in the 1930s and 1940s, wondered how the fork-tailed storm-petrel, which he called "this mite of a bird," is able to survive the storms of the open ocean, where it spends the nonbreeding months. Fork-tails are more pelagic than Leach's storm-petrels; during nesting they feed much farther out at sea. Average feeding distance from shore for fork-tails is 185 miles. Consequently, their eggs and chicks are well adapted to being left for days at a time.

Leach's storm-petrels are known for their dense colonies; burrows on one islet in the Quillayute Needles average twelve holes per square yard. Ecologists have long proposed that herding behavior is in the best interests of individuals of many species because it lessens their chances of predation. The same may be true for nesting seabirds. It may be that the nesting behavior of the Leach's storm-petrels of the Olympic coast developed in the presence of a predator, though there is no major predatory threat there now.

Closer to shore, one of the most frequently seen of Olympic's nesting shorebirds is the common murre (*Uria aalge*). Murres are easily identified by their compact bodies, dark backs, white sides, and long, slender bills. They nest in crowded colonies on offshore rocks and islets, their "nests" mere scrapes on ledges and clefts of rock. During the spring breeding season, I've seen them from shore, sitting upright almost shoulder to shoulder, penguinlike, along a high, rocky ledge. Their single, pear-shaped eggs are well suited for staying put on narrow ledges. Murres are monogamous and live to be thirty years old. They are the largest and probably most commonly seen seabirds along the coast year-round. They nest strictly on the outer coast. In winter, they congregate in large flocks and are fre-

Common murres, the most abundant of Olympic's breeding seabirds, nest in dense colonies on step offshore rocks, often among colonies of double-crested and Brandt's cormorants. In winter, they flock together on open water. PHOTO BY MARY SUE BRANCATO, OLYMPIC COAST NATIONAL MARINE SANCTUARY.

quently seen in the waters of the strait and Puget Sound. At rest on water, they tilt their beaks up, a good identification point.

Like other alcids, murres are excellent divers and powerful underwater swimmers. They can typically dive 100 feet deep in pursuit of fish, and are capable of reaching depths of 500 feet. Alcids are as well adapted to underwater swimming as to flight, and murres take large numbers of sand lances, smelt, and herring, and some bottom fish. But unlike some other alcids, they can carry fish to their young only one at a time. Murres frequently locate their colonies adjacent to double-crested, pelagic, and Brandt's cormorant rookeries, an arrangement that, as with cormorants and gulls, may provide some advantages for murres.

Historically, common murres were quite numerous off the Olympic coast. Prior to 1982, the coastal population numbered from 20,000 to 30,000 nesting birds. In 1983 the population crashed to one-tenth of that, and it remained there for more than a decade. Research done at the University of Washington suggests that El Niño conditions triggered the population drop in 1983. Although El Niños have occurred several times in the past, murre numbers traditionally recovered following a return to normal conditions. This decline was particularly disturbing for its persistence. Studies conducted by the university's Julia Parrish on Tatoosh Island suggest that the recovery of bald eagles on the coast may be a contributing factor. Bald eagles flying over murre and cormorant colonies cause nesting birds to flee, thereby allowing gulls to prey on murre eggs and chicks. Even changes in wind patterns that prevent upwelling of deep, nutrient-rich waters at critical times can affect a population's numbers, as occurred as recently as 2005. Ulrich Wilson, a retired U.S. Fish and Wildlife Service biologist, points out that once a seabird population has been drastically reduced, disturbances that could normally be sustained by a larger population can be seriously detrimental to the remnant populations.

A study conducted by Wilson on the effects of El Niño events on common murres as well as double-crested and Brandt's cormorants on the Washington coast found that their numbers decreased markedly during El Niño occurrences in 1982–83 and 1987. But El Niño's effects on murres were complicated by several types of human-caused disturbance. Tens of thousands of murres and other seabirds were killed in each of several oil spills, and thousands more murres became entangled in commercial gill nets (about 2,500 were killed this way during the 1989 nesting season alone), events that may have conspired to keep murre populations depressed. Other human-caused activities—including the U.S. Navy's practice bombing of the wrong island—certainly took a toll as well. Murre numbers have recovered somewhat, to about 8,000 on the coast, but they have never reached their pre-1983 population. During the best years, they have reached about 40 percent of their earlier numbers.

In another study, Wilson and others looked at seabird population trends along the entire west coast of North America. They showed that encroachment of humans and their animals on breeding islands and overfishing of seabird prey species have had severe impacts on seabird populations along the west coast of North America. These are further compounded in areas affected by El Niño events. Along with understanding the environmental factors at work on seabird populations, we must, for the sake of the future conservation of seabirds, fully comprehend and manage our own impacts as well.

One group of seabirds that doesn't seem to be suffering declines on our account is the gulls. Both western and glaucous-winged gulls nest on the coastal islands, while a number of other species migrate through or winter here. With a breeding range that stretches from Oregon to Japan, glaucous-winged are the most commonly seen gulls along Olympic Peninsula shorelines at any time of year. They tend to favor the inside waters of the strait and Puget Sound; Protection Island alone harbors a breeding colony of more than 3,000 nesting pairs, though that population is beginning to show some decline. Western gulls are fewer in number and prefer the outer coast from Washington south to Baja California; Destruction Island is one of their northernmost nesting colonies. But their natural history becomes somewhat complicated on the outer coast because the two species interbreed. Their offspring are sometimes called "Olympic" gulls. The large, dark gray Olympics are common on the north Olympic coast. In general, glaucous-winged gulls are distinguished by their white heads and pale gray plumage; western gulls have dark gray mantles. All three gulls carry yellow bills with distinctive red spots.

Maybe it's their strident voices, or their propensity for feeding at garbage dumps and sewage treatment plants, but gulls rank low on most bird-lovers' appreciation lists, and that is unfortunate. As Kitchen has pointed out in his adulatory style: "Few birds are their equal in gliding through the air, either with or against the wind. They are wonderful swimmers and many varieties are expert divers. . . . Gulls are at home on land, walking or running on the sand or a hard surface. Few birds can do all these things well." Gulls do seem to enjoy loafing about the beach or holding court along rooflines in Neah Bay and La Push—maybe that's why I'm drawn to them.

Both glaucous-winged and western gulls are serious predators on other seabird eggs and chicks, going after auklets, puffins, murres, cormorants, guillemots, and others in season. They've learned to drop shellfish on rocks to crack them open (a trick they might have picked up from crows), pirate the catches of a number of diving birds, forage over all marine environments, and scavenge virtually everywhere. One does not encounter a high level of concern for gulls among most biologists. As one researcher put it, "Gulls are very smart and opportunistic; they'll take care of themselves. They may well be the last seabirds left." Call me a sentimentalist, but the sight of a flock of western gulls rising and circling on the oncoming edge of a Pacific storm is a piece of the coastal world that still brings a smile.

One bright spot on the coastal horizon has been the recovery of the brown pelican. Almost pterodactyl-like in appearance, this large, shovel-beaked, and somewhat ungainly bird flies with heavy wingbeats and dives with wings extended, more or less crashing into the water. Areolar tissue beneath the skin cushions the impact and pops the bird almost instantly back to the surface—usually with a fish in its beak. As with the peregrine falcon, brown pelican numbers were drastically reduced by pesticides and habitat loss. The only viable populations in North America remained in Florida. The ban on DDT allowed them to recover in California and Mexico as well as along the southeast U.S. and Gulf coasts, and populations there seem to have stabilized. As El Niño events shifted the pelicans' prey populations northward, they have been showing up along the Washington coast in summer, arriving as early as May in El Niño years, and staying through fall. The first sightings were associated with the 1982–83 El Niño, but annual visits persist. A fall survey off the Olympic coast identified between 1,100 and 1,200 birds. Grays Harbor and Willapa Bay in southwest Washington reported 10,000 to 15,000.

Pelicans are only occasionally seen from shore; they are among the many species that dive and fish in offshore waters. But another family of migratory animals feeds close in to the Olympic shoreline; some even haul out on nearshore rocks and islands. Visible from beaches, headlands, and bluffs, sea mammals tie this rocky coast to offshore waters for thousands of miles north and south.

MAMMALS OF THE COASTAL WATERS

The warm days of early spring bring the first blooms to coastal forests. Crimson salmonberry blossoms brighten trailsides, and pioneer violets and slender bittercress flowers wink among mosses and newly greening leaves. The large yellow bracts of skunk cabbage fairly shout from marshy spots along streams and seeps, and swelling knots of coltsfoot erupt through roadside gravel. Spring brings an equally dramatic bloom of marine plants and animals to nearshore waters, and a succession of migratory sea mammals is drawn to the Olympic coast in response. By late spring, foraging sea lions can be seen (or heard) hauled out on off-shore rocks and islands. Northern fur seals and elephant seals fish the offshore waters, along with the large resident population of harbor seals. Sea otters surface and bob lazily among kelp beds, meticulously grooming their handsome fur. And in March and April, one of the greatest migrations on the planet skirts the Olympic coast as California gray whales cruise close to shore on their 6,000-mile annual migration between their summer feeding and winter calving grounds.

MIGRATIONS OF THE GRAYS

Gray whales are true harbingers of the turn of seasons on the coast, and each spring I make a pilgrimage with family and friends out to greet them. From an overlook on a favorite headland, we watch for the spouting plumes that lift briefly into the wind and vanish as these gentle, thirty-to forty-ton mammals sound and dive in the offshore swells. From their calving grounds in Baja's coastal lagoons to summer feeding grounds far north in the Chukchi and Bering seas, migratory grays form a season-long procession on the outer coast. Pregnant females and adult males are the first to arrive here, their knobby, finless backs cresting above the waves. They are followed by juveniles of both sexes. Toward late spring and summer, mothers and their calves can be seen close to shore, feeding among the kelp beds. Gray whales (*Eschrichtius robustus*) follow the contours of the continental shelf over the course of the spring, feeding on plankton, small schooling fish, and shrimplike organisms called krill.

Grays, like other baleen whales (humpback, minke, sei, fin, and right whales), strain their food through the fringed baleen that hangs from their upper jaws. Grays are primarily bottom feeders, straining tons of sediments as they feed. Some grays enter the Strait of Juan de Fuca, staying and feeding for a few days or weeks; some even reside year-round. Many more stop to feed in shallow bottom sediments off the coastal mouths of rivers such as the Quillayute and Hoh. This is the best chance for coastal visitors to catch something of the whales' immense grace as they dive and surface, their great fluted tails flashing balletlike in the churning water.

Decimated by commercial hunting in the nineteenth century, gray whales were eliminated from the Atlantic; Pacific populations were reduced to a few thousand. But California gray whales have made an astounding recovery since they were listed under the Endangered Species Act and protected by the International Whaling Commission in the 1970s. Today the Pacific coast population exceeds 23,000, and most biologists consider gray whale numbers to have returned nearly to their original level. Grays were removed from the endangered list in 1994. Unfortunately, this isn't true for other small-toothed cetaceans that ply Washington's coastal waters. Minke, humpback, fin, and other whale populations remain small by comparison; less than 1,000 humpbacks are estimated for the Washington, Oregon, and California coast. Perhaps most threatened are right whales; their population may be down to no more than 50 to 200 animals.

Gray whales and other sea mammals were important sources of food and materials for Native American hunters who lived along the Olympic coast. The archaeological record, along with a large body of myths and stories, reflects the importance of these creatures to the material and spiritual fabric of early coastal life. The Makah and Quileute were whaling people, and much of these tribes' social structure centered on this demanding and highly skilled way of life. This type of subsistence hunting, even as practiced by the Makahs, who excelled at taking sea mammals, probably had little effect on the abundance of sea mammals at the time. But human impacts on the marine mammals of the North Pacific accelerated rapidly with the arrival of Europeans.

Following the visits of Vitus Bering in 1741 and James Cook in 1778, reports of the wealth of fur-bearing sea mammals spawned an aggressive trade in furs. Over the next century, the killing of countless numbers of seals, sea lions, sea otters, and whales for fur, baleen, oil, and meat drove many species to the brink of extinction. By the late nineteenth century, most of the species commercially hunted had reached "economic extinction," a point at which their numbers had plummeted so low as to make hunting them unprofitable. International treaties in the first years of the twentieth century, as well as federal statutes and the removal of bounties in more recent decades, allowed most species to recover somewhat. A few, such as California gray whales and sea otters, now approach pre-exploitation numbers. Others, like the blue and right whales, continue to hang on by a thread.

From the distant plumes of gray whales sounding past the breakers to the simple grace of a harbor seal surfacing in a nearshore swell, the Olympic coast offers a rare opportunity to encounter a variety of marine mammals in their natural environment. The story of how these animals interact with this coastal world helps make the offshore rocks and tangled kelp beds come to life.

HARBOR SEALS AND ELEPHANT SEALS

In spite of the tremendous bounty of the Olympic coast, few marine mammal species breed and reside here year-round; winter seas are prohibitive. But located at the interface of northern and southern breeding ranges for a number of species, these productive coastal waters support a wealth of seasonally foraging sea mammals. Among the few year-round residents, harbor seals are by far the most plentiful, as well as the easiest to observe. I often notice a dark, round, earless shape bobbing low among the kelp beds, large eyes turned to the beach. When I look again, it has dropped out of sight, only to reappear—and look back—a little farther out.

Harbor seals (*Phoca vitulina*) will often forage quite close to shore at high tide. At low tide, groups haul out on low rocks or reefs, never far from the edge of water. Viewed from a nearby headland, their sleek, silvery or dark gray pelage is usually covered with whitish spots or rings. Like other pinnipeds ("fin-footed" mammals), seals evolved paddlelike hind flippers, which make them swift and graceful swimmers underwater. They can dive to depths of 600 feet and remain submerged for twenty minutes—though three to five minutes is more common. On dry land, however, seals are awkward and clumsy. Pinnipeds took to the sea about 20 million years ago, much later than the cetaceans—the whales, dolphins, and porpoises—and must come ashore to rest, breed, and give birth to their young.

Harbor seals pup in May and June on the outer coast, a bit earlier than the seals of Puget Sound and Hood Canal. Females nurse and tend to their pups continuously for a month to six weeks, then teach them to fish. Females occasionally leave their young on the beach during this time; most of these pups are not abandoned, as visitors sometimes think, and they should always be left undisturbed.

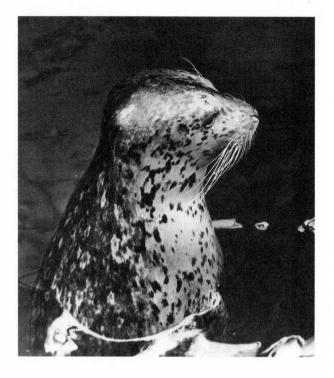

Among the few sea mammals that breed in Olympic waters, harbor seals can be seen year-round along most Olympic coastal areas. Although they were formerly hunted for bounty in Washington, they are now protected. PHOTO BY RUTH KIRK.

Harbor seals are fairly opportunistic feeders, taking whatever is available, usually bottom and middle fish: herring, pollock, hake, and such. For years it was mistakenly believed that harbor seals fed primarily on salmon. From the 1920s through the early 1960s, the Washington Department of Fisheries offered a bounty on seals. In the years from 1947 to 1960, the state paid bounties on more than 17,000 animals without apparent benefit to commercial fisheries. In fact, harbor seals take relatively few salmon; salmonids are generally faster swimmers than seals, and most mature salmon pass through seal habitat only on their return to their rivers to spawn.

The Marine Mammals Protection Act in 1973 has allowed the number of harbor seals to increase considerably in Washington. Seal numbers on the outer coast increased at about 5 percent each year until recently, when they began to level off. In 1977 there were an estimated 1,800 on the Olympic Coast. A decade later there were between 4,000 and 5,000. By 1999, the population for all of Washington was estimated at 16,000, with about a third of these breeding along the Olympic coast, utilizing some fifty haul-out sites and producing about 800 pups per year. The more protected estuaries of Grays Harbor and Willapa Bay to the south support considerably larger numbers. Harbor seals have few predators on the coast, though orcas and sharks take a few pups. And since they feed on whatever is abundant, it is expected that the coastal population will remain stable.

Warm weather also brings much larger elephant seals up from their California and Mexico breeding ranges to forage in Olympic's coastal waters. Northern elephant seals (*Mirounga angustirostris*) are large; males weigh up to 8,000 pounds. Females are much smaller but can still reach 1,000 pounds. The males, which are our usual migrants, have bulbous protruding snouts (thus their name), and are known to float lazily on the surface, resembling nothing so much as large sunken logs. They come ashore rarely, to breed in their southern ranges and occasionally on the Olympic coast in summer to molt—a unique trait among seals.

Elephant seals are phenomenal divers and can pursue their prey of rockfish, squid, rays, and other deep-water fish to depths of more than 2,500 feet. They actually spend more time underwater than on the surface—behavior more often associated with cetaceans such as sperm whales than pinnipeds. Even so, elephant seals must have proven easy targets for commercial sealers when they came to the surface to nap, for by the mid-1880s they had nearly become extinct. In less than a century, a breeding population numbering in the hundreds of thousands was reduced to fewer than a hundred animals isolated on a group of islands off Baja. Since then their numbers have recovered somewhat, and for the past few decades elephant seals have been expanding their range to the north, reoccupying former breeding sites. They recolonized a breeding site off the central Oregon coast, and elephant seal breeding has been documented on Destruction Island. Several sightings of adults with pups off the Washington coast and in the Strait of Juan de Fuca hold promise for the Olympic coast. Unfortunately, the recovery of northern fur seals has been less dramatic.

FUR SEALS AND SEA LIONS

Most pelagic of the seals, northern fur seals (*Callorhinus ursinus*) spend the greatest part of their lives in open water, where they sleep curled on the surface. They tend to favor the outer edge of the continental shelf to feed. At the peninsula's northwest tip, the Juan de Fuca canyon brings the shelf edge close to Cape Flattery, and fur seals figured prominently in the lives of the Makah people who still inhabit the cape. Not nearly as large as elephant seals, male fur seals can reach 600 pounds; females are considerably smaller. It's the females that usually show up off the Olympic coast. Champion swimmers, they migrate from their breeding grounds in Alaska's Bering Sea as far south as Baja, California. An estimated 80,000 to 90,000 fur seals migrate past the Olympic coast in spring, feeding on Pacific hake, squid, ratfish, and small sharks in the outer waters. Impressive as these numbers may seem, they are not what they once were.

Fur seals were decimated by a century and a half of unrestricted commercial hunting, during which sealers took breeding females as well as males. A 1911 treaty among the United States, Russia, England, and Japan put an end to wasteful open-water commercial hunting (in which half the animals sank out of sight when shot), and regulated commercial hunting on land. The population rebounded, reaching an all-time high in the 1950s. Then managers mistakenly allowed the commercial hunting of females to resume, which led to a second slide in population. Though the practice was discontinued in the early 1960s, fur seal numbers continued to decline for another two decades. The Fur Seal Act was passed in 1966, and the population stabilized in the mid-1980s but has never quite recovered. A combination of disease, competition for prey from human fishing, and entanglement in drift nets cast off from commercial fishing vessels at sea may be responsible.

Fur seals breed primarily on two islands in the Pribalofs; a much smaller population has colonized San Miguel Island in California's Channel Islands. We should count ourselves lucky that fur seals continue to migrate and feed along the Northwest coast today, passing close to Cape Flattery and Cape Alava as they have for centuries.

Sea lions are regular visitors to the Olympic coast. They haul out in great numbers on offshore rocks, and their large, dark shapes are sometimes seen from the shore. Tatoosh Island off Cape Flattery, the Bodelteh Islands off Cape Alava, and Carroll Island (visible only by boat) are all favored haul-outs. Two species forage and rest together here. The northern or Steller's sea lion (*Eumetopias jubatus*) is the larger of the two,

California sea lions migrate north in late summer and fall to feed in Olympic's coastal waters and haul out on offshore rocks (sea lions are excellent climbers). Most return to southern breeding grounds in spring. OLYMPIC NATIQNAL PARK.

with males weighing about 2,000 pounds. Steller's sea lions are tawny in color, and adult males wear shaggy blond manes over broad necks and shoulders. The California sea lion (*Zalophus californianus*) is smaller; males are about half the size of Steller's, with dark brown to black pelage. Adult male California sea lions also have prominent crests on their foreheads. Both species possess large, powerful hind flippers that can rotate forward. These and their well-developed front flippers allow them to walk and climb around comfortably on land. As a result, sea lions can climb much higher on rocks than seals can. There, they sit up on their flippers or lounge about in the sun blissfully regardless of tides. Though it may be difficult to tell the two species apart without binoculars, one identification is nearly foolproof: California sea lions often bark like circus seals (most performing "seals" are actually sea lions), while their northern cousins remain regally quiet. Both differ from seals by their curled external ears, long front flippers, and their ability to walk on "all fours."

A distinct population of Steller's sea lions numbering between 10,000 and 20,000 breeds from northern Japan out into the Aleutian Islands. A southern population of about 20,000 breeds from southeast Alaska as far south as Santa Cruz, California. About 1,000 male and female Steller's sea lions that visit the coastal waters of the Olympic Peninsula disperse from these southern breeding territories, though some nonbreeders reside here year-round.

California sea lions breed in May and June, mostly among California's Channel Islands but as far south as Baja. Neither California nor Steller's sea lions breed along the Washington coast. This may be due in part to the steep and exposed nature of this coast's rocks and islands. Many haul-outs here are intertidal, and larger rocks and islands have steep slopes. Few are protected from the fifteen- to twenty-foot waves that often pound the coast during breeding season. Large numbers of both sea lion species arrive to feed here in late summer and fall, however, and many stay through spring. Between 2,500 to 5,000 California sea lions pass along the Olympic coast in late August and September en route to foraging areas in the Strait of Juan de Fuca and the inland waters of British Columbia and Puget Sound. Another 500 or so remain on the outer coast, frequenting haul-outs on Carroll and the Bodelteh islands and Sea Lion Rock, just south of Carroll Island. The coastal population swells again in May as sea lions wintering in inland waters head back to their southern breeding grounds.

Steller's and California sea lions share haul-out and feeding sites rather amiably on the coast. During peak migrations in fall and spring, their numbers are about evenly divided; during the rest of the year Steller's hold sway. Codfish, smelt, squid, rockfish—almost any available middle and bottom fish—serve as prey for sea lions. Steller's take mostly pollock in Alaska; Californians concentrate on hake.

California sea lion numbers have been increasing in recent years, and large numbers of males range north as far as British Columbia (only a handful of females have been identified in this area over the past thirty years). A small band of California sea lions became infamous in Puget Sound by persistently feeding on a recovering steelhead run that returns through Ballard locks to Seattle's Lake Washington to spawn. Efforts by state and federal agencies to harass the feeding sea lions away from the site were remarkably unsuccessful. Even capturing and removing the culprits to California proved futile; the same individuals returned to the Ballard locks in little more than a month. "Hershel," as the group collectively became known, made few friends among sport fishermen. More recently, sea lions have been feeding heavily on threatened salmon and steelhead ascending the fish ladder at the base of Bonneville Dam on the Columbia River. Hazing efforts have been renewed, and more lethal controls proposed.

Obviously, California sea lions are doing well; Steller's are less fortunate. Although the southern population (the one that visits peninsula waters) is fairly stable, the northern population has declined precipitously. Their numbers dropped from an estimated 100,000 in the mid-1980s to 10,000 to 20,000 a decade later, and more than 90 percent of their rookeries have been abandoned. This dramatic decrease caused this population to be listed as threatened under the Endangered Species Act in 1990.

The problem may have to do with the animals' food base. Disease and natural environmental changes, possibly triggered by El Niño-related events, may be a factor, but more likely are human impacts on their food sources. Pollock, their major food, is fished heavily by huge factory processors operating in the Bering Sea. Entanglement in fishing nets and illegal shooting may also be compounding the problem. Interestingly, the southern Steller's sea lion population—indistinguishable from the northern population and sharing the same natural history, except for a dependence on pollock—is doing fine, even increasing in numbers slightly. Research on this problem continues in northern waters. Meanwhile, another threatened marine mammal, the sea otter, has become a success story on the Olympic coast.

THE SEA OTTERS' RETURN

A highlight of any trip to the outer coast is to look down from a headland or bluff and spot a sea otter playing among the kelp. Small, animated, and incredibly agile, sea otters (*Enhydra lutris*) differ from other marine mammals in that they lack a thick layer of blubber. Instead, a thick, luxuriant coat of fur keeps them well insulated—so well, in fact, that sea otters seem loath to haul out on anything but cool, wet, kelp-covered rocks. As a result, sea otters along the Olympic coast haul out only at the lowest tides when suitable rocks are exposed. Sea otter populations to the north are much less discriminating about their haul-outs, while otters in California rarely haul out at all.

Sea otters here are often confused with river otters. The latter are smaller animals that inhabit streams and coastal areas all around the peninsula. River otters forage along intertidal areas close to shore and are by far the most common otter seen on the outer coast. They are small (three to four feet, around thirty pounds) and weasel-shaped, with brown faces and long slender tails. Sea otters are larger (up to five feet and a hundred pounds). They are also brown but have buff-gray heads and faces, and short, stout tails. River otters spend much of their time out of the water and never swim or float on their backs; sea otters rarely leave the water and spend most of their time on their backs, feeding and resting. They float high in the water, held up by their buoyant fur, which they aerate and groom incessantly. Their grooming sessions are a delight to watch. The animals twist, turn, and tumble in the water, scouring and puffing up every part of themselves, making their sleek, wet fur—considered to be the finest of any mammal—glisten.

Sea otters have a special relationship with the kelp forests that grow off Olympic's rocky shores—in fact the two are almost as inseparable as spotted owls and old-growth forests. Along with clams, crabs, and snails, a favorite food of sea otters is sea urchins, the larger red urchins in particular—and urchins feed on kelp. Nibbling at the stipes and holdfasts of giant and perennial kelp, sea urchins left unchecked can do serious damage to kelp forests, even to the point of eliminating them. When otters were extirpated from most of the California coast by the turn of the century, many of the kelp forests soon disappeared. Research conducted in the Aleutian Islands, southeast Alaska, and Vancouver Island has shown that predation by sea otters dramatically reduces the abundance of sea urchins, which in turn favors the development of kelp forests.

These dense, tangled habitats are home to a super-abundance of marine organisms, fish, and the birds and mammals that feed on them. Though they feed both in perennial and bull kelp, sea otters here are particularly fond of perennial, or giant, kelp (*Macrocystus integrifolia*), which grows in the more sheltered areas of the outer coast. This preference may have to do with the year-round protection and stability perennial kelp forests offer from waves. When the first storms hit the coast in fall, neighboring bull kelp—an annual—ends up in heaps on the beach. But otters and their pups wrap their webbed hind feet in perennial kelp to ride out swells and currents. Large numbers of otters are often seen rafted together in kelp beds off Cape Johnson and Makah Bay. Otters also seem to favor perennial kelp for diving, feeding, and pupping. Sea otters (and kelp) congregate north of Kalaloch around Destruction Island, Teahwhit Head, Cape Johnson, Jagged Island, Yellow Banks, Sand Point, Cape Alava, and Cape Flattery. I have also spotted them rafted up in the nearshore waters of western Juan de Fuca Strait.

Sea otters forage early in the morning and again later in the afternoon, resting, grooming, and playing in midday (which is the best time to watch for them) and rafting up toward evening. They are voracious feeders, consuming up to a third of their body weight each day. Since shellfish are a major part of their diet, sea otters have developed the ingenious habit of cradling a flat rock on their chests as they float and using it to break open shellfish too large to crack with their teeth. In captivity, otters are known to keep their favorite rocks, tucking them under their arms as they dive. In California, otters' taste for abalone and crab has drawn the ire of some commercial fishermen, but biologists point out that many of these species reached artificially high numbers in the absence of sea otters, and sustainable harvest levels must be recalculated with the otters' recovery in mind.

In retrospect, the sea otter's recovery was remarkable. During the late eighteenth and nineteenth centuries, between 100,000 and 200,000 sea otters were slaughtered by Russian, English, French, Portuguese, and American fur traders. Coveted both for its beauty as well as its warmth, the sea otter's luxuriant fur was almost the animal's undoing. Hunts were unregulated, and traders moved quickly from one area to the next as populations disappeared. The last sea otter was shot on the Washington coast in 1910; the last professional sea otter hunters in Washington had quit the trade a few years earlier. By the time an international treaty was signed, too late, in 1911, sea otters were extirpated from most of their range, from Baja to the northern islands of Japan. Fortunately, remnant populations survived in remote locations in Alaska, and in 1938, a small band was discovered off the Big Sur coast of California.

Under the treaty's protection, surviving populations began to recover. In the late 1960s and early 1970s, a concerted effort was made by wildlife agencies to restore sea otters to their former ranges in southeast Alaska, British Columbia, Washington, and Oregon. Fifty-nine sea otters from a healthy population on Amchitca Island in the Aleutians were introduced to the Olympic coast in 1969 and 1970. The animals released at Point Grenville in 1969 were not given an opportunity to acclimate or to clean their fur, and most are believed to have died. But the 30 animals released at James Island the following year were allowed to acclimate in floating pens, and the introduction proved successful. Seven years later, 19 otters were counted; by 1981, the number had increased to 36. The population continued to grow, reaching the biological equivalent of "critical mass" in the late 1980s; then numbers shot up. A 1994 survey placed the population for the Olympic coast at 360. By 2007 there were more than 1,000. Because of their limited range and vulnerability to oil spills, Olympic's sea otters have been classified as endangered by the State of Washington. But since they came from a healthy parent stock in Alaska, they have avoided federal listing.

Ironically, just as the sea otter's uniquely rich fur nearly brought about its demise a century ago, its fur puts it most at risk today. When coated or even spotted with oil, a sea otter's dense fur loses its remarkable insulating properties, and cold seawater soaks through the coat. With no blubber layer to act as backup insulation, an otter quickly becomes hypothermic and dies. Otters also sicken by ingesting oil while trying to "groom" it out of their fur. Today, the greatest threat to the interconnected community that exists on the outer coast—sea mammals, birds, and intertidal species—is the singular risk of spilled oil.

OIL AND WATER

Though the long progression of shipwrecks noted earlier in this chapter proved fatal to most of the ships' crews, these wrecks were fairly benign with respect to coastal marine life. Sailing ships had no need of fuel, and early steamers carried little that would damage fragile coastal environments. The period of grace ended in January 1972, when the *General M. C. Meigs* ran aground in a winter storm at Portage Head and spilled 2,300,000 gallons of fuel oil onto the rocky northern coast. The spill did tremendous damage to birds and intertidal organisms. It also alerted managers of natural resource agencies to the dangers posed by ships and tankers operating off this rugged coast.

But it wasn't until December 1985, when the single-hulled oil tanker *Arco Anchorage* ran aground in Port Angeles harbor and spilled 239,000 gallons of crude oil into the Strait of Juan de Fuca that both national park and national wildlife refuge managers snapped to attention. While it occurred well outside the boundaries of Olympic National Park, the grounding was just ten miles east of Dungeness National Wildlife Refuge, home to some 15,000 wintering waterfowl. Even though the ship struck in a harbor adjacent to a Coast Guard station, it was more than three hours before containment booms were available to surround the spilled oil, and many thousands of birds became coated as the oil spread on the incoming tide. The vast majority sank beneath the sheen, but thousands were picked up along area beaches and taken to an improvised cleaning and rehabilitation facility in Port Angeles.

I remember Christmas of that year well, as my wife and I joined thousands of volunteers streaming into Port Angeles to help clean and care for the oiled seabirds. Washing the sick and listless grebes and murres made vivid the cost of our national addiction to oil and the risk that shipping oil poses to this fragile coastal ecosystem. Of the thousands of injured birds collected and treated (a small percentage of those affected), less than 10 percent survived.

Interagency coordination in dealing with the *Arco Anchorage* spill was virtually nonexistent. A few years later, when a lumber barge broke up off the outer coast and millions of board feet of lumber washed up on park beaches, biologists breathed a worried sigh. What if the barge had been one of the countless oil tankers plying coastal waters?

In December 1988, their fear became a reality. The barge *Nestucca* was rammed by its own tug after it had broken free in rough waters just south of the Olympic coast. Nearly a quarter-million gallons of fuel oil spilled into the open ocean. Within days, tar balls and sheets of oil began to wash ashore. Then came the dead and dying birds: murres, auklets, scoters, grebes. Again, a rescue effort was mounted, but many birds were missed on the winter shoreline and oil reentered the food web through scavengers. Of the 10,000 birds collected on the peninsula, more than 7,000 of them were dead; a little over 1,000 were rehabilitated. The total estimated number of birds killed exceeded 55,000. Common murres suffered the greatest losses, making up 72 percent of all birds affected—11 percent of the total murre population for the area.

Because most of the oil from the *Nestucca* came ashore in stormy conditions at high tide, it was the upper intertidal areas, driftwood logs, and kelp mats on the beaches that received the brunt of the oil. By sheer luck, the spill did not seriously affect the park's intertidal communities. Even so, coordination of cleanup efforts through a maze of state and federal agencies resulted in confusion, frustration, and crossed efforts. This led Olympic National Park officials to insist that the U.S. Coast Guard adopt a system to coordinate multiagency response to future spills similar to the one used by the U.S. Forest Service to respond to large wildfires that sweep across jurisdictional boundaries.

The effectiveness of the system was tested three years later when another spill hit the Olympic coast. The Japanese fish-processing ship *Tanya Maru* was struck midship by a Chinese freighter in Canadian waters twenty-five miles off Cape Flattery. The processor sank in a matter of minutes, releasing more than 350,000 gallons of diesel and other fuel oils into south-flowing currents that carried it onto the Makah Indian Reservation and the north Olympic coast. Again, the oil laid waste to seabirds: common murres, murrelets, auklets, and puffins. This time, the cleanup effort was well coordinated: oil-absorbent pom-poms were strung across beaches on incoming tides; rocks were scrubbed, and oiled driftwood logs and seaweed mats were removed by helicopter to keep oil from reentering the coastal ecosystem. Still, it became painfully clear that even with extensive planning and expert coordination, as soon as oil enters water, much of the battle is lost.

Although ships and tankers continue to pose the greatest immediate threat to the coastal resources of the Olympic Peninsula, another threat began to surface in the 1980s. The same year as the *Nestucca* spill, the U.S. Department of the Interior's Minerals Management Service under the Reagan administration proposed oil and gas leasing on the continental shelf off the Washington coast. The proposal brought strong opposition from tribes, fisherman, coastal residents, and conservationists nationwide. Their arguments were underscored a few months after the *Nestucca* spill when the *Exxon Valdez* released nearly 11 million gallons of crude oil into the pristine waters of Alaska's Prince William Sound. Clearly, greater protection was needed for the Olympic coast and its off-

An oil-killed scoter washed up on Third beach after the *Nestucca* spill in December of 1988. More than 55,000 birds were killed as a result of that single spill. Offshore oil spills continue to pose the greatest threat to the coastal ecosystem. PHOTO BY JANIS BURGER.

shore waters. Responding to pressure from constituents in Washington and across the country, Congress directed the National Oceanic and Atmospheric Administration that year to create a national marine sanctuary along the Olympic coast.

The Olympic Coast National Marine Sanctuary was dedicated in 1994. Congress had designated an area from Cape Flattery south to Copalis Rock and thirty to forty miles out to the break of the continental shelf, encompassing 3,300 square miles. Offshore oil and gas drilling is prohibited within the sanctuary, and vessels carrying hazardous cargo are requested to avoid sensitive areas adjacent to the coast. The area was later expanded. Soon after designation, the Department of the Interior rescinded the Navy's permit for practice bombing of Sea Lion Rock just south of Olympic National Park, restoring peace to nearby nesting and haul-out sites.

In an effort to prevent shipping accidents off the coast, a rescue tug was stationed at the entrance to the Strait of Juan de Fuca at Neah Bay during the winter storm season. Sponsored by federal and state governments and aided by a tax on oil revenue, rescue tugs have come to the aid of more than thirty disabled vessels since the program was put in place in 1999. With more than 6,000 cargo ships and tankers entering the strait each year, conservationists, tribes, and agencies agree that there is an overriding need for a rescue tug to be stationed year-round. Currently, state and federal lawmakers are working toward that end.

By extending much-needed protection to offshore and nearshore marine areas, the Olympic Coast National Marine Sanctuary is an important addition to the Washington Islands National Wildlife Refuges and the magnificent coastal wilderness of Olympic National Park. These agencies, which represent some of our government's best aspirations toward the natural world, join Native Americans of the Makah, Quileute, Hoh, and Quinault tribes in a long tradition of stewardship for this splendid merging of land and sea.

Part 4

HUMANS AND THE LANDSCAPE

CHAPTER 9

Footprints on the Land

AFTERNOON clouds were settling over the mountains and foothills above the Dungeness River on the northeast Olympic Peninsula, but valley fields were still bright with spring sunlight. The high shoulders of Blue Mountain and Deer Ridge were edged in winter snow, and the silhouette of Mount Angeles rose over the green slopes of Lost Mountain to the west. I crossed a field of wet spring grass where the foothills met the valley floor and stopped by a small marsh. Dry cattails rustled in the cool north wind, and a pair of mallards dabbled in the shallows of a winter pond.

It wasn't hard to imagine this low, rolling landscape in late Pleistocene time. The same ice-rounded foothills and hummocky piedmont plain stretched north to the Strait of Juan de Fuca. Just as now, the snowpack would be melting back from the mountains. The small marsh and pond was larger then, and bordered then as now by a thick growth of cattails. Instead of the grassy fields of the valley and second-growth Douglas firs and cedars covering the foothills, there were shrubby patches of willow and alder interspersed with sedges, grasses, trailing blackberry, and wild rose. And in place of houses, lately sprung up in the old farmlands of the Dungeness Valley, were slowly melting blocks of ice, stranded remnants of the last advance of the Cordilleran ice sheet that pressed against the northern Olympics like a wedge.

This was the landscape the earliest known inhabitants of the Olympic

Peninsula encountered more than 12,000 years ago. We know this because it was here in the late 1970s that a valley resident turned up one of the most significant archaeological finds in the Pacific Northwest. Emanuel Manis was deepening a pond for wintering waterfowl when he uncovered what he recognized as the tusks of a prehistoric mammal. Archaeologists from Washington State University examined the site and confirmed it was a mastodon, a large elephantlike mammal that inhabited Pleistocene landscapes. Within hours of beginning work, archaeologist Carl Gustafson made a remarkable discovery. Embedded in one of the mammal's ribs was a broken piece of antler or bone resembling a spear point. The fragment was lodged more than three-quarters of an inch deep, suggesting a blow delivered with great force. Further examination under a microscope revealed that the outer covering of the fragment was worn away, typically the result of human workmanship. The rib had partly grown over the spear point; this was not a fatal wound.

Other evidence indicated human involvement as well. A number of bones showed telltale signs of butchering, and the skull, which had been turned 180 degrees out of its natural position, was smashed into thousands of pieces. Several bones from the upper side of the skeleton were moved a short distance, presumably out of the pond in which the carcass lay; these also showed signs of butchering. The skeleton was buried in stream-deposited sand and gravel, which lay directly atop the rocky rubble of glacial drift. Seeds and bits of wood recovered from the strata that contained the bones were radiocarbon dated at more than 13,000 years. The Manis discovery was not only the earliest evidence of human presence in Washington, but the earliest association of Paleolithic hunters with mastodons anywhere in North America.

Not far from the pond is a small grassy rise alongside the road. It was the only high ground close to the watering hole, and researchers thought it might be the hunters' campsite. A cross-section excavation of the rise revealed the charred remains of six to seven fire pits, all in different-aged strata. Bones of bison were found in strata more than 9,000 years old. A fire pit dating back 7,500 years contained the butchered bones of very large black bears. There was also evidence of caribou, muskrats, and ducks in soil strata showing eight or nine layers of occupation by hunting people at this site between 6,000 and 13,000 years ago.

Early prehistoric hunters and gatherers probably followed the large Pleistocene herbivores to the northern peninsula from the south after the ice had retreated and vegetation began to reclaim the scraped and rocky landscape. As the climate warmed and became drier, human populations in the Great Basin and Columbia Plateau gravitated to rivers and lakes. Population pressures might have prompted some groups to explore the recently deglaciated landscapes to the north. Their dwellings must have been temporary, sewn hides or woven mats over post frames; none has survived the passage of time. The people carried a few simple tools of bone and stone (a flaked cobblestone and a flensing tool and bone and antler spear points were found at the Manis site), but little else is known of them. Who were these earliest wayfarers on the peninsula, these small nomadic bands who hunted the raw glacial landscapes for mastodon, caribou, bison? What brought them to this remote and rugged corner of land, and what was their relation to the people who followed them thousands of years later?

Archaeological investigations in Olympic National Park have been fairly limited in the past. The park's rugged topography and thick forests proved daunting, and the mistaken belief that Native Americans were loath to venture into the interior mountains dissuaded early investigators. But archaeologists have taken a closer look at the mountains and river valleys of the park in recent years, and the picture of early human presence here is becoming much more complete. Early hunters left traces in the Olympics that lead from this small marsh at the edge of the northern foothills, up through the facing mountains and deep into the interior ranges. The cultural artifacts that reappear on the coast thousands of years later offer a stunningly clear window into the sophisticated ways of sea mammal hunters whose descendants still live in the area. Though much of the archaeological record is missing—only fragments and a few simple stone tools remain from great sweeps of millennia—the story of how the earliest inhabitants of the peninsula learned to adapt and thrive within this dynamic ecosystem unfolds like a blossom in a newly greening landscape.

THE MOUNTAIN HUNTERS

From the Manis site, Blue Mountain dominates the southwestern horizon. A gentle, broad-shouldered peak with fingers of forest reaching nearly to its summit, Blue Mountain opens on its south side into the subalpine meadow lands of Deer Park, named for the creatures drawn to its warm, south-facing slopes in spring. Deer Ridge swings east from Deer Park in a long, green undulating line before plunging south into the valley of the Gray Wolf River. The ridge drops abruptly at a low pass called Slab Camp, where a tongue of Cordilleran ice pushed through into the steep, rugged canyon of the Gray Wolf. From the flat, glacier-carved gap that remains, it's a few hours' walk to the subalpine meadows of Deer Park, an even shorter walk down to the Gray Wolf. Sheltered from prevailing storms and watered by a perennial stream and wetland, Slab Camp was once the site of an old U.S. Forest Service ranger station and primitive campground.

Archaeological work done at Slab Camp in the 1980s uncovered extensive evidence of early human use of the area. The evidence suggests a large hunting camp, possibly a staging area for high-country travel. The site yielded no hearths or animal remains, but more than sixty-four stone tools were discovered—points, flakes, hammer stones, and cobble tools— as well as thousands of worked chips. The artifacts were located below a layer of volcanic ash from Mount Mazama, a volcano that erupted in the southern Cascades about 7,600 years ago (the clear waters of Oregon's Crater Lake now rest in its caldera). Mazama's ash plume spread north and east as far as British Columbia and Montana, and the deposit it left behind provides a handy benchmark for archaeologists. This date and the nature of the artifacts recovered show the Slab Camp occupants practiced a way of life archaeologists describe as the coastal Olcott pattern, named for the family farm in the Stillaguamish River east of Puget Sound where the pattern was first identified.

Olcott people were "generalists"; they hunted land animals, gathered plants and berries, and probably fished, though no fish or shellfish remains show up in their deposits. Little is known of these early inhabitants other than the scant evidence gleaned from the stone tools they left behind. They chipped basalt into simple, expedient tools, including a wide variety of scrapers and choppers; many of these tools appear to have been quickly made, probably on site. They also fashioned more elaborate blades and spear points of varying sizes. These were worked into the distinctive shape of a willow leaf, an indicator of the coastal Olcott pattern.

Creators of the Olcott pattern enjoyed a widespread subsistence life-style on the Northwest coast that remained stable for several thousand years, from as long as 12,000 to 6,000 years ago. Their way of life is well represented on the peninsula. Olcott sites near Lake Cushman in the southeastern Olympics, Quilcene, Port Angeles, Ozette Lake, and a large site near Sequim yielded distinctive "willow leaf" spear points (an Olcott point was also found just above Mazama ash at the Manis site). A number of other Olcott pattern tools turned up in these sites as well. Choppers and scrapers indicate that people were working animal hides; abrading stones suggest the manufacture of bone awls or needles, probably used for clothing or basketry, and gravers point to working with wood or bone. This hunting and gathering way of life raises an intriguing question: Does this land-based pattern indicate that people had not yet learned to use nearby marine resources? Or were these hunting camps merely the inland component of a seasonal round that included coastal sites now lost to erosion and changing sea levels?

At this point no one can say. During much of Olcott pattern life on the peninsula, sea levels were considerably lower than today. The "rebounding" of the land surface, after the weight of the ice sheet had been lifted, and resulting fluctuations in sea levels would have placed most coastal sites of those days below current sea level. Further seismic activity may have elevated parts of the coast somewhat above current sea level as well. This, combined with the dense, junglelike growth along the coast and the erosive power of the waves, may have conspired to hide or eliminate an important component of Olcott pattern life here. But evidence of early human use of Olympic National Park's high country abounds.

From Slab Camp, the subalpine meadows of Deer Park are easily reached by following open slopes along Deer Ridge. A large archaeological site at Deer Park yielded artifacts similar to those found at Slab Camp: points, flakes, a cobble tool, unfinished points and blades, an abrading slab. There was no organic material by which to date the site, but the tools match the Olcott pattern. Interestingly, the basalt from which they were fashioned is different from native Crescent basalt. In fact, the rock is dacite, a glassy, fine-grained, extrusive rock similar to andesite. Dacite weathers slate gray and fractures into smooth, shiny black faces; it feels lighter in the hand than Crescent basalt, and it flakes to a finely honed edge. Cobbles and boulders of dacite are believed to have been rafted to the Olympic Peninsula by the Cordilleran ice sheet from parent rock in the Howe Sound area of British Columbia. The rocks are still commonly found in streams and along shorelines that lay in the path of the continental ice sheet, largely below 3,500 feet (the Slab Camp site is at about 2,500 feet). The presence of dacite in the interior mountains or above the height of the last ice sheet is an invaluable reference point for archeologists; it means that humans brought it there.

If you trace the interconnecting ridges on a topographic map from Deer Park and Blue Mountain west along Grand Ridge to Obstruction Point, then farther on to Hurricane Ridge or south around the Gray Wolf and Dosewallips headwaters, you'll notice vast stretches of open subalpine country joined by ridges and watered by lakes and snowmelt streams. The high country here is mantled with lush meadows, pocketed with marmot burrows, and crisscrossed with the meandering trails of deer and elk. Nearly everywhere they have looked, archaeologists have found ample evidence of human use of these areas in the form of dacite flakes, points, and worked cobbles. Investigations by park archaeologists have shown that early hunters and gatherers left traces even farther into the interior, along the open ridges of High Divide and the remote Bailey Range. The Olympics show a far greater density of high-country archeological sites than either the North Cascades or Mount Rainier in Washington. The places where the early people camped, perched on a scenic overlook, or stopped to rest in the shelter of a rock outcrop are often the same places backcountry hikers stop, rest, or camp today.

I find a deep satisfaction in thinking of the old ones—"the People," as early Native Americans everywhere referred to themselves—ranging over these mountains with a few simple, honed tools. Their knowledge of plants and their uses and the behavior of animals was refined and sophisticated. I think they must have shared something of the delight we feel in the rugged splendor of this mountain landscape. Their stone whittlings scattered across upland ridges and basins are words spoken across a changing landscape of 12,000 years. They add a familiar element to the haunting beauty of these coastal mountains. And they cast our wilderness wanderings today in a different light.

Only a few sites have yielded positive dates for early human use of the Olympic high country. One is by a tarn in Seven Lakes Basin in the north central Olympics. Charred ash from a fire pit buried beneath a foot of organic litter was dated at more than 5,000 years before the present. Chipped dacite and charred bones suggest the site was used as a hunting camp. By that time the period of postglacial warming had ended and the climate had cooled in the Olympics. Sea level was beginning to stabilize, and vegetation had come to resemble that of today. The elk and deer that summer in this scenic, north-facing basin today may be descendants of the animals that drew small hunting bands from nearby lowlands in summer and fall long ago. Perhaps those distant travelers were gathering berries and meat to dry for winter use, or simply enjoying the largess of a fall high-country hunt. Either way, the Seven Lakes site suggests a seasonal use of high-country resources at a time when seasonal adaptations to marine resources were also beginning to appear on the Northwest coast.

EARLY COASTAL CULTURES

To trace the path of early maritime culture in the Pacific Northwest— from hunting of land mammals to use of nearshore resources—it's necessary to venture slightly north, to the lower Fraser River in mainland British Columbia. There, the Glenrose site discovered on the grounds of an old cannery near the river mouth shows evidence of stable, long-term human occupation from about 8,000 to 2,000 years ago. Stone hunting artifacts of the Olcott pattern dominate the lower archaeological strata, but about 4,500 years ago, increasing numbers of bone and antler tools began to appear. Chopping cobbles became rare around that time and abrading stones for wood and bone work much more common. Chipped stone points became smaller, and ground slate points appeared. New tools also made their first appearance: carving tools made with rodent teeth for detailed woodworking, mussel shell adze blades, and antler wedges.

But the most significant difference from earlier time was a marked increase in the use of marine resources. Remains of salmon, sturgeon, and other fish as well as mussels and seabirds were added to the earlier remains of land and sea mammals. Antler wedges suggest large-scale woodworking, and it is very likely that seagoing canoes had been developed by this time. Shellfish became a winter staple, marking the beginnings of a

A Makah fishing camp on Tatoosh Island, showing cedar canoes and halibut drying racks. The photograph was taken by Samuel Morse, an agent at Neah Bay from 1890 to 1903. OLYMPIC NATIONAL PARK.

seasonal adaptation that would soon unfold into the later maritime and Northwest Coast Culture.

A similar evolution of hunting and gathering strategies was doubt-less unfolding on the Olympic Peninsula as well—particularly as the climate cooled and the forest canopy began to close. A glimpse into one of these early maritime sites on the peninsula was recently uncovered on a high coastal terrace above the Wa'atch River a mile south and inland of the Makah Reservation town of Neah Bay. The Wa'atch today is a slow coastal stream that drains a low valley to the Pacific. In 2005, archaeologists found evidence of long-term habitation of the site that could date back possibly as far as 3,800 years. At that time, possibly due to seismic subsidence, the terrace was much closer to sea level, and the Wa'atch Valley was a saltwater bay or channel. A test excavation produced hundreds of stone artifacts, including points, cutting blades, hammer stones, whetstones, and flakes. Numerous bone points, which may have been used in hooks for fishing, were discovered, and an antler wedge suggested working with wood. The deep shell midden at the site indicates a maritime way of life that took advantage of an abundance clams, mussels, chitons, limpets, and crabs. Similarly, fish bones testify to a nearshore marine fishery that included herring and salmon. Sea mammal and bird bones also give credence to a rich and diversified maritime way of life. Only a small section of the site was analyzed, but it points to a much earlier adaptation to maritime culture on the peninsula than was previously assumed.

A more recent, but much more extensive, site was discovered at the mouth of the Hoko River, fifteen miles east of Cape Flattery on the Strait of Juan de Fuca. The Hoko drains wet coastal lowlands in the northwest corner of the peninsula. Running brown and muddy during winter storms, the river deposits tons of silt along its lower floodplain and on its delta on the Strait of Juan de Fuca. Here, a rich assemblage of wooden artifacts preserved in the wet mud of the river mouth shows that the site has served as an important seasonal fishing camp for more than 3,000 years. Radiocarbon dates from Hoko indicate regular occupation of the site from 1,700 to 3,200 years ago. The mouth of the Hoko remains a favorite fishing spot for Makah people in whose traditional territory it lies.

Sealed from oxygen and organic decay in the wet mud of the river mouth, well-preserved wood and fiber artifacts and abundant animal remains paint a vivid picture of an early coastal and riverine fishing culture. By carefully excavating artifacts with spray from hoses pumped from the river, archaeologists uncovered bent-wood halibut hooks used in offshore fishing, bone or antler harpoon heads for hunting sea mammals, a fragment of a weighted split-spruce fishing net, and a possible fish weir. Also washed from the mud were wooden wedges, carved points, and a piece of adze-hewn cedar plank.

One fascinating find at Hoko included six intact knives made by lashing flakes broken from quartzite beach pebbles into split-cedar handles. Replicas of these knives proved excellent for cleaning and filleting fish. The number of knives and blades recovered from the site, along with fragments of burden baskets, suggests that the people who camped here caught and processed large numbers of fish, most likely for storage and later use. Hooks and net fragments indicate they fished the offshore bank. In fact, remains of fish from offshore waters were twice as plentiful as salmon, which were most likely speared in the river. Canoes were almost certainly used to take so many offshore fish, though no canoe fragments were found at the site. Nor was evidence of plank houses, though tools for splitting large cedar boards found elsewhere make archaeologists suspect that such dwellings were part of early maritime culture. Remains of seals, porpoises, and dolphins show that these sea mammals were hunted regularly, probably using the barbed spear points found at the site. Though the bones of a gray whale were found, no whaling tools accompanied them, suggesting the whale was scavenged from the beach.

A presage of the flowering of the Northwest Coast Culture to come was also washed from the mud of the Hoko River. A red cedar tool identified as a mat creaser, used to soften cattail or rush fibers to be woven into mats, was carved into the likeness of a pair of kingfishers joined at the tips of their beaks. At the time, this stylized design, simple and elegant, represented the oldest wood artwork found anywhere on the Northwest coast.

Other early maritime sites, like Wa'atch, have been discovered on the peninsula, along the outer coast and the strait. All are shell middens containing bone artifacts and antler woodworking tools, along with plentiful remains of sea mammals, birds, and shellfish. Their location on uplands and terraces above today's coastline points to a higher sea level at that time. As with the lower strata at the cannery site in British Columbia, test excavations show widespread use of worked stone tools at lower levels. But this earliest of technologies, by which humans lived here for the last 13,000 years, all but disappears from northern coastal sites on the peninsula about 1,000 years ago. Instead, Native Americans developed highly refined skills for detailed working of wood, shell, and bone. This mastery of the resources of forest and sea led to the development of the elaborate cultures that followed.

TSE-WHIT-ZEN AND OZETTE: TWO EARLY NATIVE AMERICAN VILLAGES

Contact with European seafarers in the later part of the eighteenth century changed the lives of the indigenous people of the Northwest coast. New technologies and a different kind of material wealth introduced by fur traders disrupted long-standing social traditions and alliances. The introduction of exotic diseases wiped out entire villages and devastated Native American society. It is estimated that more than one-half of the native populations of the Olympic Peninsula were felled by European diseases. In some areas the toll approached 90 percent. Treaty policies of the 1850s and the government schools that followed often outlawed Indian cultural practices and beliefs, and generations of Native people became for a time exiled from their past.

Early observers writing in the wake of these social upheavals often reflect a skewed and somewhat limited view of indigenous life on the coast. Many details of the ways in which Native Americans interacted with each other and with the ecosystem were lost. Archaeological knowledge of early Northwest lifeways was also limited by the perishable nature of the wood, bone, and fiber materials that supported coastal culture over the past 1,000 years. To see how native cultures here evolved with the natural systems of the Olympic Peninsula, it's necessary to look to the time prior to their first contact with Europeans. Fortunately, on the northern shores of the Olympic Peninsula, two of the most important archaeological sites in North America reach back to that time and offer a detailed look at daily life in two prosperous coastal villages.

A major discovery on the shore of Port Angeles harbor has recently shed light on a large native fishing village, the largest ever excavated in Washington. It spans the time of European contact and reveals evidence of human occupation dating back almost three millennia.

In 2003, archeologists working in advance of a large dry dock for a bridge construction project uncovered the site of an early Klallam village and burial ground. The Elwha Klallam people of today, whose ancestors lived there and whose oral traditions tell of the former settlement, know the village as "Tse-whit-zen." The archeological excavation was extensive, and the site showed evidence of continuous occupation from 1,700 years ago until about 200 years ago. Radiocarbon dates from a cooking hearth at the inland edge of the beach date to 2,700 years, roughly equivalent to Hoko.

Working against an impossibly tight deadline and in less than ideal conditions, more than a hundred members of the Elwha Klallam tribe and fifty professional archaeologists unearthed more than 13,000 artifacts, the remains of several structures, hearths, and cooking preparation areas, and more than 300 ancestral burials. No other archaeological site in the Northwest has yielded such a diversity of artifacts over so long a period of time. Nonetheless, due to the large number of burials discovered—and the likelihood of many more to be disturbed—the Elwha tribe requested the project be halted late in 2004. Cataloging and analysis will be ongoing for many years, but the picture that emerges from Tse-whit-zen is one of a highly skilled and resourceful people successfully developing a sophisticated marine-based way of life.

Tse-whit-zen village is located on a deep harbor protected by the three-mile-long sand spit of Ediz Hook. Evidence suggests that as soon as the spit began to form and the beach stabilized, people began to use the area. It's no wonder. The beach was cobbled with shellfish: clams, oysters, mussels. Salmon ascended nearby streams and rivers; halibut and herring swam just offshore. Sea mammals—fur and harbor seal, sea lion, and sea otter—were plentiful, and flocks of ducks and seabirds were close at hand. Elk, deer, and other animals inhabited the upland forest, and a profusion of roots and berries was available in season. Amid this bounty, perhaps 400 or 500 years ago, Tse-whit-zen evolved from a seasonal encampment to a permanent year-round village.

Due to the size of the planned construction project, a large area was excavated. Archaeologists found evidence of houses and outbuildings with posts, planks, hearths, and fish-drying racks. Land and sea mammal hunting was evident in faunal remains, along with numerous stone and bone arrow, spear, and harpoon points used to hunt them. Artifacts for fishing included carved bone halibut hooks, herring rakes, and weights.

Large shell middens form a basic environment that preserves a wealth of bone and antler artifacts (they would be dissolved by acids in groundwater elsewhere). Split bones of elk and deer were shaped and honed into blades and points. Some of the artifacts exhibited a sophisticated artistry. Delicate blanket pins were carved in the likeness of deer and seal. A beautifully carved ornamental comb was shaped in the likeness of two birds poised over a human figure. An amazing find at the site was more than 300 etched beach stones similar to stones still used by Klallam people on Vancouver Island today. Some were decorated with ochre pigment, some almost hieroglyphic in their designs. All hold significant sacred and ceremonial implications for the Elwha tribe.

Archaeologist Dennis Lewarch, who coordinated the excavation, described the site as containing one of everything—as well as some artifacts that have never been found before. He speculates that when cataloging and analysis are complete, the bone and antler artifact collection will represent the largest in the Northwest, possibly in the United States. It also confirms a long and illustrious history of the Elwha Klallam people on the north Olympic Peninsula. The tribe hopes to house its collection in a curation facility, with a museum and educational center, at the village site, a process that came a step closer in 2006 when a settlement agreement was reached between the tribe and state, federal, and local governments. When the Elwha people's dream is realized, there is little doubt Tse-whit-zen will become as world famous as another precontact Native American coastal village on the peninsula, Ozette.

Ozette Village is situated in the lee of Cape Alava, just south of the Makah Indian Reservation on the northern Pacific coast. A photograph taken of the village in the late 1800s shows a cluster of a dozen or so houses. Most are built of split cedar planks, and a few are in the old shed roof longhouse style. One of five permanent Makah villages located around Cape Flattery on the northwest tip of the peninsula, Ozette remained occupied into the twentieth century. Beginning in 1896, families leaving the village to be with children attending mandatory boarding school in Neah Bay eventually led to Ozette's demise. Some returned to hunt and fish in summer, but by the time Washington State University archaeologist Richard Daugherty surveyed the village site in 1947, the houses were tumbled down and the hillside grown over with trees and brush.

Daugherty was keenly interested in Ozette. The site contained an extensive undisturbed shell midden, and it was known to have been a principal whaling village for the Makah. Its location was ideal for sea mammal hunting. Situated on the westernmost point of land in the contiguous United States, the village lay close to the migratory routes of whales, fur seals, and other sea mammals. Large offshore reefs and islands offered protection from pounding Pacific swells and provided easy passage for canoes.

A fairly detailed picture of Makah whaling culture had been pieced together from ethnographic reports and accounts from tribal elders. According to tribal traditions, whale hunting defined Makah society. The endeavor was undertaken by hereditary whaling chiefs and only with a great deal of prescribed ritual and religious observance. Pursuing

Ozette Village at the end of the nineteenth century. The remains of the ship *Austria*, shipwrecked in 1887, litter the beach in the foreground. CLALLAM COUNTY HISTORICAL SOCIETY.

gray or humpback whales at sea—eight men to a thirty-five-foot cedar whaling canoe, armed with mussel shell-tipped harpoons and sealskin floats—was a difficult and dangerous undertaking. Whalers fasted, purified themselves, and prayed to their spirit guides well in advance of the spring hunts, and they and their family members adhered to strict taboos. A whale could sustain a whole village for weeks, with plenty of oil and blubber left for trade.

Whalers were afforded tremendous prestige, and whaling families formed an aristocracy. Like most indigenous societies on the Northwest coast, Makah society was stratified. The noble class consisted mostly of whaling chiefs and their families; if successful at hunting they enjoyed a high degree of wealth and status. The broad class of commoners possessed a variety of learned skills, from basketry and canoe carving to seal hunting, and enjoyed a good deal of social mobility. The underclass of slaves (probably about 5 percent of the population at the time of European contact) had been captured in battle, traded from other villages, or born into slavery. By and large, they led lives of drudgery.

Nobles enjoyed privileged access to prime hunting, fishing, and gathering sites throughout the Northwest coast; these rights were inherited or acquired through marriage. Members of noble families were expected to marry within their class, either among different villages or different tribal groups. Despite this strict social order, all classes enjoyed a good deal of social mobility. Commoners could better their standing and increase their wealth through marriage, by acquiring any of a number of specialized skills, or through warfare. They could also shift allegiances among chiefs. All classes, nobles, commoners, and slaves, lived together in the longhouses at Ozette.

In the late 1960s Daugherty returned with a team of archaeologists to investigate the site. As they excavated a test trench in the large shell midden, working from the beach up through successive layers of coastal terrace, their shovels turned up more than 2,000 objects. Some—buttons, coins, rifle parts—were obviously from the historic period. But layers beneath them predated European contact. Bone fish hooks, stone sinkers, bone and shell blades, and carved combs dated back an estimated 2,000 years. The abundance of fish and sea mammal bones throughout the midden showed that a stable and highly organized hunting and fishing society had inhabited the site almost continually during that time. Nearly all of the bones found were from sea mammals, predominantly fur seals, but the discovery of whale bones confirmed what had long been known by Makahs: Ozette was indeed a whaling village, possibly one of the largest south of Alaska.

During the second year of initial excavation at Ozette, archaeologists sunk a test pit in a wet area back from the beach. Deep in the mud, they unearthed a coiled rope made of cedar boughs. Further excavation revealed fragments of woven cedar bark mats and basketry, along with a section of hewn cedar house plank—all perfectly preserved in the wet clay. Makah oral traditions told of landslides that buried Ozette Village in the distant past; here was evidence. Like the alluvial deposits that preserved highly perishable artifacts at Hoko, clay had apparently preserved similarly perishable artifacts at Ozette. If the oral traditions were accurate, here, beneath the shrubs and young trees, may lie a virtually intact whaling village—complete with wood, fiber, and bone artifacts—sealed since the day it was buried. A find of this magnitude required major excavation, and Daugherty and the Makah Tribal Council began to plan for one. As it turned out, the Pacific Ocean had plans of its own.

A severe storm early in 1970 battered the upper beach with waves and began to erode the sea bank in which the collapsed longhouses were buried. The midden slumped, and house planks and artifacts were exposed: an inlaid box, a canoe paddle, a woven rain hat. Daugherty and the Makah Tribal Council secured emergency funding so that excavation could begin that spring. Forgoing shovels and trowels for seawater pumps and hoses, spray nozzles, and fine-bristled brushes, teams of archaeologists, Makahs, and students from around the country began the work of unearthing the first houses. Artifacts sealed in clay for three centuries or more were coaxed once more into coastal sunlight: delicately wrought combs, whale bone clubs used for seal hunting, dozens of finely woven baskets, and elaborately carved wooden bowls. Not only finished pieces but artifacts in various stages of manufacture and repair were also recovered, offering a rare cross section of a functioning coastal culture. Piece by carefully excavated piece, the story of early everyday life on this coast—and something of the people who lived it—was revealed.

A burden basket was washed free of the clay filled with rolls of cedar bark, newly stripped from a tree and not yet processed into fibers for mats, baskets, or clothing. Spindles and pieces of looms emerged, along with an intricately woven plaid blanket in a pattern previously unknown on the coast. Other items emerged from the clay: carved bent-corner cedar boxes used for cooking with heated stones, larger decorated storage chests, rain hats, halibut hooks, wedges, and woodworking tools. Some chisels were fitted with steel blades, possibly salvaged from shipwrecked Japanese fishing boats. Woodworking technologies evident in earlier archaeological finds had obviously been carried to a high level on the coast by this time. The level of detail and distinctive style of the decorative artwork suggested a highly developed aesthetic.

The lay of the houses and artifacts recovered also gave clues to the structure of Makah society. Whaling equipment was often found at the rear of the houses, places occupied by whaling chiefs and their families. Sleeping platforms covered with cedar mats lined the walls, and each household maintained its own hearth, sometimes separated from the others by screens.

The mudslide that buried and preserved Ozette Village, possibly triggered by the great subduction earthquake of 1700, came so suddenly that

"Wedding rocks." It is impossible to date these petroglyphs south of Cape Alava on the coast, but their style closely matches designs carved into some of the artifacts dated at close to 500 years old found at Ozette Village. PHOTO BY JANIS BURGER.

there was no time to retrieve valuables. Inside a cedar bark sheath lay a finely honed harpoon head of mussel shell with carved elk bone barbs and fitted with woven fiber rope (similar points were found broken off in whale bones). A long cedar plank was carved with the likeness of a whale that matched the petroglyphs at "Wedding Rocks" a short distance down the coast. Wood and bone handles of everyday tools were carved in the stylized likeness of people, owls, wolves.

Some objects seem to have been made for ceremonial or purely artistic purposes. A bone carving of a small human figure crouched within a mussel shell echoes a Makah creation story, and a beautifully carved cedar whale fin was inlaid with 700 sea otter teeth in the motif of the mythical Thunderbird. The striking beauty of these designs reflects not only the

Ozette people's reverence for the natural world that sustained them, but their close ties to a spirit realm that permeated that world and insured their well-being and prosperity.

The archaeological dig at Ozette lasted eleven years. Three of five known longhouses were fully excavated and more than 50,000 artifacts recovered. All remain with the tribe. Many of the finest pieces from this collection can be seen at the Makah Cultural Museum in Neah Bay. For the Makah people of today, Ozette is a gift from the past offering a deeper perspective on their own rich heritage, a fuller sense of who they are. For all of us, Ozette is a window on a stage of the human journey on this coast, from nomadic hunters following game across the spare, postglacial landscape to sophisticated village dwellers living amid plenty and sharing such "contemporary" pursuits as trade, status, and the cultivation of artistic expression.

NORTHWEST COAST ADAPTATIONS

The way of life enjoyed by the Makahs reflected their unique position at the peninsula's northwest tip. Access to migratory fur seals at Umatilla Reef and halibut banks off Cape Flattery as well as Ozette's proximity to the migratory routes of whales influenced many of their cultural practices. The location of other Native American villages at the mouths of peninsula salmon streams similarly influenced their cultures. The Makah shared many of their cultural practices with other Wakashan-speaking whaling people of Vancouver Island (the Nitinat and Nootka), but they also shared important cultural traits with their peninsula neighbors. All tribal groups on the peninsula shared in a broad cultural pattern practiced from Yakutat Bay in Alaska to Cape Mendocino in California. This "Northwest Coast Culture" is one of the most elaborate and sophisticated indigenous cultural patterns north of Mexico.

Generally speaking, Northwest Coast people are distinguished by an orientation toward marine resources, communal winter villages, extensive use of canoes for water transport, and a strong reliance on salmon. Northwest Coast Cultures are also known for their specialized adaptations to particular environments and the skilled use of a number of widely scattered seasonal resources. Both traits are well illustrated among the tribal groups of the peninsula. Though peninsula peoples shared a number of traits, the wide cultural diversity found among these groups—their languages, beliefs, ceremonials, artistic expressions, and subsistence strategies—reflect the natural diversity of the Olympic ecosystem itself.

With the peninsula's heavy rains and long hours of darkness, winter villages here consisted of groups of up to twenty longhouses, though most villages had only a few. The houses were usually about thirty feet wide and sixty feet long, constructed of split or adze-hewn red cedar planks lashed to post-and-beam frames with cedar withes; they were usually aligned along a river or shoreline. Two to six related families shared each house, each family maintaining its separate household. Wide cedar planks lined the walls, serving as beds and seating areas, and cedar baskets or bent-corner cedar boxes held family possessions.

Villages were occupied throughout the winter months, some year-round. In spring, summer, and fall, smaller family groups usually traveled to hunting, fishing, and gathering sites: shellfish beaches, salmon streams, inland lakes, prairies. Surpluses were gathered, processed, and stored at these seasonal settlements, supporting winter village life and affording the leisure time to develop the traditions of elaborate winter ceremonials that were a central part of Northwest Coast life.

"Tribes," as we've come to think of them today, were actually loose associations of villages at the time of European contact, sharing languages, kinship ties, and common food-gathering locations. Formal tribal structure was imposed by the United States government with implementation of the treaties of the 1850s. Villages as well as "tribes" traded and intermarried, establishing important alliances and renewing intertribal relations. Central to this social order was the "potlatch." Every momentous event in village life, every claim to hereditary privilege, whether an inherited name or song or a prized fishing site passed on to a new generation, required a potlatch.

Preparations for these elaborate gift-giving ceremonies sometimes took years. Guests traveled from distant villages, and the feasting, dancing, and singing that preceded gift-giving often went on for days. A village headman or host family gained great prestige by giving away amassed wealth. The songs and dances affirmed the heritage and position of the host family, and the value and order of gifts distributed acknowledged the status of the guests. By accepting the gifts, guests acknowledged the hereditary claims, prosperity, and social status of their hosts, thus reaffirming a family's place in the strict social order.

Potlatches also served another important function in Northwest society. Though the region is blessed with unusual abundance, it is also subject to unpredictable seasonal shortages. Individual salmon runs can fail because of flooding or drought; changes in weather patterns and currents can cause shifts in sea mammal migrations; occasional "red tides" may contaminate shellfish; a berry or camas crop may fail. Along with its other functions, the institution of the potlatch served to redistribute resources and "share the wealth." Since well-to-do families were expected to reciprocate in kind, a mutual sharing was assured. In spite of this kind of cooperation, warfare among tribal groups and even among villages was not uncommon. Some crimes and social improprieties were deemed so egregious they could be resolved in no other way. Raiding was also an accepted way to obtain slaves or increase one's status.

Whether for raiding or visiting, hunting or fishing, all transportation along the peninsula's coastlines, rivers, and lowland lakes was by carved western red cedar canoe. The technology of canoe manufacture, from felling the giant red cedars to carving or painting the bow designs, was attended by a great deal of ceremony. Cedars were felled using a combination of chopping and controlled burning, then were split and hollowed out with adzes and burning coals.

Most tribal groups are known to have employed at least six sizes of these versatile craft. Small "shovelnose" canoes were popular on inland rivers and along parts of Hood Canal; larger sealing and whaling canoes of the open coast were extremely seaworthy under a variety of conditions, and huge sixty-foot seagoing canoes were used for long-distance transport. Canoes were also an important trade item among tribal groups, with most of the larger seagoing canoes originating on the northern coast.

One tree, the western red cedar, formed the foundation of Native American culture on the Northwest coast. "If mankind in his infancy had prayed for the perfect substance for all material and esthetic needs," wrote Northwest carver Bill Reid, "an indulgent god could have provided nothing better." Lightweight, decay resistant, and easily split into boards and huge house planks, red cedar was both versatile and lasting. Houses, canoes, and clothing; baskets, boxes, and cooking containers; masks, headdresses, and rattles; ropes, mats, and spear and arrow shafts; cradles, dolls, and even diapers—all were fashioned from its dark aromatic wood or reddish brown bark. Western red cedar and the salmon that spawned in its shade along the peninsula's rivers and streams were the heart and soul of Northwest culture. Human life here without them—whether in the distant past or the near future—is hard to imagine.

Indigenous people on the peninsula were masters of woodworking and knew the distinctive qualities and appropriate uses of a wide variety of woods. Hard, resilient yew was best for bows and harpoon shafts; light, straight-grained cedar for boxes and boards. The hardwoods, maple and alder (which wouldn't flavor foods), were used for bowls; tough, flexible spruce root and limbs for burden baskets and rope; young Douglas fir for dip net handles and spears.

Foods were plentiful nearly everywhere on the peninsula in season, and tools made of wood, shell, fiber, and bone allowed people to harvest and preserve it in quantities. Saltwater fish were taken with hooks and lines, gill nets, and seines; anadromous and freshwater fish with weirs, dip nets, and spears. Shellfish of many varieties were gathered in large numbers from intertidal areas all around the peninsula; surpluses were smoked, dried, and stored. During times of seasonal shortages of other foods, shellfish beds could prove sound village bank accounts. More than fifty species were identified in a single midden in La Push, and records show that large quantities of dried shellfish were sold to white settlers on the peninsula.

All tribal groups on the peninsula hunted land mammals as well as sea mammals. Elk and deer supplied meat, hides, antlers, and bone (land mammal bones are a much harder and denser medium for tools and weapons). For tribal groups that maintained upriver villages, such as the Quinault, Quileute, Elwha Klallam, and Skokomish, land mammals formed an important part of their diet.

Inhabitants of the Olympic Peninsula were incredibly imaginative and resourceful in making good use of the abundant resources that surrounded them. Berries were gathered throughout the summer and fall, from early ripening salmonberries along streams to late-blooming blueberries in the mountain meadows. Eaten fresh or dried (often mixed with seal fat), berries, along with bracken fern roots and camas bulbs gathered from open prairies, were among the principal plants used for food. Anthropologist Erna Gunther lists more than 150 plants used by Native Americans in western Washington, for foods, medicines, and materials.

OTHER PENINSULA CULTURES: THE QUILEUTE AND THE HOH

South of the Makah villages on the Olympic coast lies the territory of the Quileute and Hoh people. Their traditional territory included the Quillayute River and its tributaries, the Dickey, Sol Duc, Calawah, Sitkum, and Bogachiel, as well as the Hoh River. The Quileute and Hoh are Chemakuan speakers, a language group unique to the Olympic Peninsula. At the time of European contact they occupied three principal winter villages at the mouths of the Quillayute River (the site of the present Quileute Reservation at La Push), the Hoh River (site of the present Hoh Reservation), and Goodman Creek, as well as smaller settlements upriver and at other locations. They also maintained some forty seasonal settlements scattered along the coast and inland river valleys. For countless generations, Quileute people enjoyed what may have been the most varied way of life on the peninsula. Though tremendous runs of salmon and steelhead filled the Quillayute and Hoh rivers, Quileutes also excelled at hunting sea mammals, taking seals and whales on occasion. They fished offshore and gathered shellfish, mounted elk hunts up the inland valleys, and gathered bracken fern roots and camas bulbs from Quillayute and other prairies. Camas was an important trade item with the Quinault to the south, who traded sockeye salmon in return. Like many tribal groups on the peninsula, the Quileute kept their prairies productive and held back the encroaching forest by burning (today's town of Forks was settled on Forks Prairie).

Like the Makah to the north and Quinault to the south, the Quileute fashioned highly decorative artwork. Quileute women were known for their watertight cooking baskets and for blankets woven from the hair of "wool dogs" kept for the purpose and from mountain goat wool imported from the mainland. Their art also reflected strong ties to the spirit world: to K'wati, the Changer, who made the rivers and headlands and created the first people from wolves, and to Hayak, the Raven, who

A Native whaler prepares to harpoon a surfacing gray whale. Sealskin floats attached to the harpoon head will drag as the whale tries to dive, eventually exhausting it. PHOTO BY ASAHEL CURTIS; UNIVERSITY OF WASHINGTON LIBRARIES SPECIAL COLLECTIONS NO. 56519.

stole back the sun from the powers of darkness. The spirit world was also celebrated by five secret societies, which initiated participants into the ritual lore of the tribe. Initiates into the "wolf society" gained warrior spirit power; another society harbored fishermen. One small secret society was the exclusive domain of whale hunters, members of the "weathermen society" were said to exercise power over weather and the migrations of whales, and elk hunters followed the dictates of the hunters' society. Only the latter is believed to be entirely Quileute in origin; the other societies had counterparts among the Quinault and Makah. Unfortunately, little remains of the precontact religious life of the Quileute. A fire set in 1889 by Dan Pullen, a scofflaw white claimant to tribal land, destroyed all twenty-six houses at La Push, along with nearly every tool, mask, basket, and hunting or ceremonial artifact.

Contact came early for the Quileute, and the record suggests they wanted no part of it. In 1775, the Spanish schooner *Sonora* lost a landing party and longboat to Quileute warriors, as did the British ship *Imperial*

Eagle a dozen years later. Shipwrecked crew members of the Russian-American Company ship *Sviatoi Nikolai* were captured as slaves in 1808, though most were later ransomed. Quileute warriors had a reputation for fierceness, and they conducted raiding and retribution parties along the coast from Vancouver Island to the mouth of the Columbia. James Island just off La Push, a burial place for Quileute chiefs, also served as a nearly impenetrable fortress when the village was under attack.

Besides the Quileute and the Hoh, the only other members of the Chemakuan language group were the Chemakum people of the Port Townsend area at the northeast corner of the peninsula. Quileute legend tells of a great flood that separated them from the Chemakum. The Chemakum people were a small, isolated band who fended off hostile neighbors on all sides, until they were finally destroyed by Chief Seattle's Suquamish in the 1850s. Surviving Chemakum speakers intermarried into the S'Klallam and Skokomish tribes. The last died in the 1940s.

Treaties were signed with the Quileutes in 1885 and 1886. Western civilization gained a firm foothold in Quileute country in 1882 with the establishment of a government school. Today a rebirth of cultural awareness among all the tribes on the peninsula has led to the teaching of native languages and tribal traditions to young tribal members, keeping ancient legacies alive as the last native speakers approach the end of their days.

THE QUINAULT AND THE QUEETS

South of the Quileute are the Quinault and Queets people. Like the S'Klallam along the strait, and the Twana of Hood Canal, the Quinault are Salish-speaking people. Salish speakers probably spread south from the Fraser River delta and now inhabit much of Puget Sound and British Columbia's Georgia Strait, as well as the south Olympic Coast. The Quinault lived in five large winter villages near the mouth of the Quinault River; the closely related but less numerous Queets people lived in one or two villages on the nearby Queets River. Both occupied nearly fifty smaller settlements scattered along the two river systems—some a good ways inland of Quinault Lake.

Their territory was particularly productive; the Queets and Quinault rivers supported all five species of Pacific salmon, including large runs of sockeye in Quinault Lake, as well as anadromous steelhead. Sockeye or "blueback" were particularly important to the Quinault. They are rich in oil and flavor, and since they do not spawn in large quantities elsewhere on the peninsula, they were a cherished trade commodity. The numbers of sockeye and other salmon running in the Quinault River system may account for the large number of villages (and the large population) recorded there around the time of contact.

Like Coast Salish people elsewhere in the Northwest, the Quinault maintained numerous fish weirs and traps on their rivers. Each village had at least one weir, a V of sticks planted in the riverbed and woven with a mesh of other sticks or a net to trap or concentrate salmon or steelhead on their upstream migration. The fish could then be taken with dip nets or spears. A large run of sockeye that spawn in Quinault Lake in late winter and early spring provided a surplus that was dried for later use as well as traded. Early runs of smelt on the coast were taken for trade; the oil they yielded was highly valued throughout the peninsula. Halibut, rock cod, herring, sea bass, sole, and other ocean fish filled out the Quinault's seasonal fishery.

Like most Northwest Coast people, the Quinault practiced a First Salmon ceremony. Its intent was to honor and give thanks to the salmon, supernatural humans who lived in longhouses beneath the sea. If the salmon people were shown proper respect and gratitude when they visited a village in salmon form, they would return in great numbers, bequeathing the gift of their flesh to the villagers, thus insuring the people's survival. Ethnographer Ronald Olson recorded such a ceremony among the Quinault in the 1930s. The first salmon caught by the village headman in late winter or early spring was laid carefully on the river bank, its head pointing upstream. The fish was cut in a prescribed manner, using a mussel shell knife. The salmon's heart was carefully removed and ceremonially burned in a fire; its head, bones, and entrails were kept intact. After it was cooked, pieces of the first salmon were shared with each member of the village, and its bones were carefully returned to the river.

Salmon were central to all Quinault villages, though inland settlements are believed to have also relied on elk, deer, and bear. Upriver Quinault are reported to have dressed in hides, furs, and moccasins and hunted with bows. Log "deadfall" traps were set for bears, and snares were used for smaller animals. There is little doubt that seasonal hunting forays took many coastal people into the high country of the interior. The Quinault maintained extensive trail systems, and traditions tell of inland skirmishes between Quinault and Klallam people who entered the mountains from the north. The notion that prehistoric Native American people avoided the mountains was laid to rest by the Olcott findings of the 1980s and 1990s. Accounts from tribal elders from around the peninsula, including a Klallam's memory of family members traveling overland from Elwha to Quinault every summer to visit relatives, indicate that this was just as untrue in recent times.

THE KLALLAM

The historical territory of the Klallam people comprised the northern Olympic ridges, the forested streams and rivers that drain them, and the eighty-mile stretch of bays, points, and shoreline that form the peninsula's northern shore. At the time of European contact, about 1,500 Klallam occupied thirteen winter villages and as many as thirty seasonal settlements along the Strait of Juan de Fuca from the Hoko River east to Discovery Bay. Small clusters of gable-roofed longhouses lined the shores of protected coves, bays, and river mouths. Large settlements were located at the mouths of the Clallam, Elwha, and Dungeness rivers, Sequim Bay, and Port Angeles Harbor, and at least one permanent village was located up the Elwha at a site later flooded behind Elwha Dam. With salmon spawning in the northern streams and all the Puget Sound runs passing through the strait, the Klallam enjoyed a readily available and nearly year-round source of protein. From late winter through spring they trolled and netted chinook and coho in the strait. Halibut were plentiful in late spring, and sockeye and pink salmon arrived in summer. The Klallam shared the use of salmon camps of woven mat huts with their eastern neighbors, the Twana, along Hood Canal as well as with other Klallam-speaking groups across the strait on Vancouver Island. Later in the season, as fall chum and winter steelhead runs headed up their rivers, the Klallam rounded out the year fishing their own streams with weirs and spears. Typically, village headmen controlled the first weir on each stream. Great quantities of salmon—as many as several thousand a day at the height of the runs—

were dried on racks or smoked and stored.

Klallam people netted seabirds and ducks with large nets stretched over sand spits, or hunted waterfowl at night from canoes using long-handled dip nets. Each village had a deer and elk hunter and a sea mammal hunter. Furs, bones, and antlers were always in demand, and hunters and their families sometimes spent whole seasons in the mountains hunting and dressing hides. A 3,000-year-old basket fragment recently discovered at Obstruction Point provides evidence of seasonal high-country use. Seals were hunted for meat and oil; whales were taken only occasionally, when one was sighted in the strait. Camas, bracken fern root, and other plant foods were gathered at Sequim, Port Townsend, and other prairies.

Like their coastal neighbors to the west, the Klallam were fierce warriors. They warred with the Makah as well as with tribal groups inhabiting Puget Sound. They in turn were raided by northern tribes, and many of their villages were well stockaded. Nonetheless, they frequently intermarried with Makah and Twana people and enjoyed extended social relations with other tribal groups, trading, gambling, and potlatching well up the coast. By the mid-nineteenth century the Klallam had expanded their territory to the east, occupying the land formerly held by the Chemakum.

THE TWANA

Hood Canal, which bounds the eastern shore of the peninsula, was misnamed by cartographers. The "canal" is actually a glacial fjord carved into the base of the mountains. Fed by the rivers pouring off the steep eastern front of the mountains, and regulated by a glacial sill at its mouth, Hood Canal provides a rich marine environment hosting salmon, sea mammals, and exceptionally productive shellfish beds. Before the coming of Europeans, its shorelines, bays, and upland valleys were home for the Twana people.

Nine Twana villages and nearly two dozen settlements have been identified along the shores and river valleys abutting Hood Canal. Villages were located at the mouths of the Dosewallips, Duckabush, Hamma Hamma, and Skokomish rivers, as well as along the shores of Dabob and Quilcene bays and many smaller creek mouths. Most populous among the Twana were the Skokomish people who lived in five villages along the lower Skokomish River and maintained a permanent village on the inland tributary, Vance Creek. The Twana villages along the canal shared a salmon-oriented culture quite similar to that of their Klallam neighbors, with perhaps a greater reliance on shellfish. Littleneck, butter, and horse clams, as well as cockles, geoducks, mussels, and native oysters were gathered in quantities (Quilcene Bay today remains one of the most important oyster-producing areas in the country). Like the Klallam, most Twana villages had land mammal and sea mammal hunters, as well as those specializing in waterfowl. But the Skokomish villagers evolved some unique cultural patterns. Anthropologist William Elmendorf reported that the inland villages of the Skokomish were apparently more cohesive and closely allied than those of the coastal Twana. And while they relied heavily on salmon, land mammals were a key part of their local economy. In fall the villages would band together for organized elk hunts in the upper valley of the South Fork Skokomish. The headman of the most highly ranked village led the hunt, assisted by specialists whose spirit power gave them influence over the movements or behavior of elk. Like other activities that involved the taking of animals, elk hunting was carried out with elaborate ritual and preparation. The Skokomish practiced a First Elk ceremony as well as a First Salmon ceremony. Families of hunters dressed the hides and processed and cured the meat over low fires. The meat was temporarily stored in raised cedar caches and later moved to winter villages. Vital food-procuring and tool-making skills among the Skokomish—as among other tribal groups on the peninsula—were often believed to have come from a spirit power. From an early age, young people were encouraged to make a spirit quest into the forest, to fast and bathe in hope of being visited by a spirit power who would assist and guide them later in life.

Coast people believed in a mythic time when creatures shared both human and animal characteristics. To prepare the world for humans, the Changer transformed many of these creatures into the animals we know today. Some frightful beings were changed into rocks or landforms; others were banished to the mountains or the depths of the ocean. People were given their human shape then and instructed in the fundamentals of culture. During a spirit quest, a youth or adolescent might be approached by an animal or spirit being and given a song. The seeker might then fall into a trance, enter myth time, and be taken to his or her spirit animal's human village, where the youth would be given special powers. Among the Twana, it wasn't until years later in an individual's life, usually during an illness, that a shaman would recognize the return of a spirit power and assist in a ritual in which the spirit song would be sung, danced, and acknowledged among the village, perhaps to be melded into the cycle of winter ceremonies.

These strong ritualized ties with the world of spirit permeated every aspect of native life. Every skill, every success in hunting, fishing, or gathering was accomplished only with the help of guardian spirits. By aligning themselves with the spirit powers that governed the abundance and availability of plants, fish, birds, and other animals, and by following the mores prescribed for taking them for their use, indigenous peoples lived as equals within their larger natural communities. The means of sustaining a human population through times of scarcity and abundance, disturbance and environmental change, were woven into the fabric of native cultures over millennia and reinforced through a strict set of beliefs and ritual practices. The fit between these primary cultures and the changing dynamics of the Olympic ecosystem was seamless.

TREATIES AND TREATY RIGHTS

By the mid-nineteenth century, when Isaac Stevens was appointed governor of the newly created Washington Territory, the fabric of Native American culture had been deeply torn, and remaining populations were ravaged by disease and alcohol. The Donation Land Act of 1850 had allowed settlers to stake claim to Indian lands well in advance of negotiated treaties. The years 1851 and 1852 saw the first registered homestead claims in the Port Townsend and Sequim areas. Gold was discovered in eastern Washington Territory a few years later, and the floodgates opened. Liquidating native land claims to make way for settlers was high on Governor Stevens's agenda, and he accomplished it through a series of hastily drawn treaties. Stevens signed treaties with peninsula tribal people in 1855 and 1856, negotiating with designated "tribes" and appointed "chiefs" in Chinook jargon, a trading medium of limited vocabulary wholly inadequate for complex treaty issues. Nonetheless, Stevens persuaded Native Americans to cede ownership of their lands (a concept foreign to native cultures) in exchange for reservations, certain specified goods and services, and the guarantee that native people would retain the right to hunt and gather on open and unclaimed land and to fish "in all their usual and accustomed grounds and stations" in common with whites. This last part of the agreement proved critical over the next century and a half as tribes challenged a relentless array of state-imposed assaults on their fishing rights.

In 1905 and again in 1908, Northwest tribes won important Supreme Court contests affirming their right to fish in accustomed areas. Nonetheless, by the 1960s, Washington State agents were arresting native fishermen on the grounds that traditional net fishing was "incompatible" with modern fisheries management. Although the tribal portion of the statewide catch amounted to only about 6 percent at the time, native fishermen were blamed for the overfishing that was depleting the runs.

Following a 1964 attempt by Washington State to nullify tribal fishing rights on the Nisqually River, the federal government again stepped in. In a landmark 1974 decision, U.S. District Court judge George Boldt upheld treaty fishing rights and changed more than a century of fisheries management in Washington. Judge Boldt interpreted the 1855 treaties to mean that Indians were legally entitled to half of the harvestable salmon and steelhead in Washington State. A later decision granted tribes the right to protect the habitats of salmon and steelhead. That decision led to the 1987 Timber, Fish, and Wildlife Agreement, which provided an opportunity for tribes, state agencies, private timber companies, and environmental groups to work together to find solutions to environmental threats to salmon habitat. In 1999 the TFW Agreement, as it's known, was incorporated into the government-sanctioned Forest and Fish Agreement. Both place Native Americans' traditions and ethics once more in the forefront of habitat protection on the peninsula, a role tribal peoples have implicitly assumed for hundreds if not thousands of years.

A CULTURAL REAWAKENING

Native Americans have been remarkably resilient in maintaining cultural traditions in the midst of profound economic, social, and religious change. Largely through oral traditions, elders have managed to keep tribal iden-

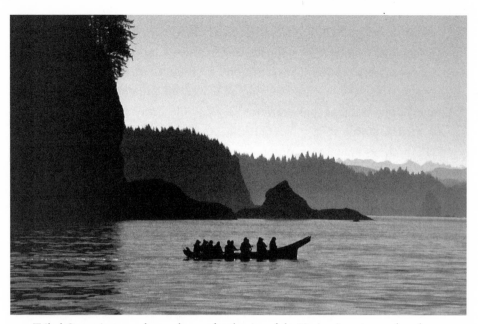

Tribal Canoe journeys have a been a focal point of the Native American cultural resurgence on the Northwest coast. Here, Suquamish tribal canoe *Raven Spirit* paddles past Teawhit Head south of La Push. PHOTO BY ROBERT STEELQUIST, OLYMPIC COAST NATIONAL MARINE SANCTUARY.

tities and values intact despite intensive government efforts to "assimilate" native peoples into nineteenth- and twentieth-century American culture. This amazing resilience, combined with federal acknowledgment of long-suppressed treaty rights, and the rediscovery of a rich and proud heritage, has led to a cultural reawakening among Native Americans on the peninsula and throughout the Northwest coast. Programs to preserve native languages and teach them to tribal members, begun as early as the 1960s and 1970s among the Quileute and Makah, are now well under way among other peninsula tribes. And potlatches and tribal gatherings remain vibrant with traditional songs and dances.

The most visible expression of this rebirth of Native American culture on the peninsula has been the resurgence of the red cedar canoe. To commemorate the centennial of Washington's statehood in 1989, sixteen Washington tribes took part in a celebratory "Paddle to Seattle." A number of tribes carved traditional canoes from red cedar logs for the occasion. At a welcome celebration hosted by the Suquamish Tribe, the paddlers were invited to participate in a much more ambitious international effort, a Paddle to Bella Bella on British Columbia's northern coast.

Four years of planning, carving, and training led up to the event, and in the summer of 1993, six Washington tribes and an international group pointed their cedar canoes north for the 650-mile journey and began singing their paddling songs. The Quinault, Quileute, Makah, and all three Klallam tribes mounted traditional canoes, crews, and additional support boats. The enthusiasm and dedication of the paddlers and the spirit of intertribal cooperation proved infectious. Whole families of supporters, from elders to small children, went along in cars, trucks, and vans. At each stop along the way, paddlers and guests were ceremonially welcomed and hosted by local tribes. Singing, dancing, and feasting filled traditional longhouses along the northern coast as nations celebrated their diversity as well as their common cultural bonds.

Many Native Americans on the peninsula see the Paddle to Bella Bella as a turning point in cultural awareness for tribal members of all ages. Elwha S'Klallam carver and head paddler Al Charles Jr. was twenty-one at the time of the paddle. "To be able to see our culture and beliefs put into practice on a daily basis really brought the culture alive for young people," he said. "The farther we paddled toward Bella Bella, the more people came out of their shells, joining in the singing and drumming. By the north end of Vancouver Island, we were singing our tribal songs for crowds of 300 to 400 people as we pulled into the beaches."

From cedar, native songs, discipline, and communal effort, a defining characteristic of Northwest Coast Culture was reborn. In 1997 the Quileute Tribe hosted an international paddle to their coastal village at La Push. Eighteen canoes representing tribes from the northwestern U.S. Canada and Alaska participated, celebrating diverse cultures and common heritage.

Two years later, the Makah Tribe reasserted its treaty-guaranteed right to hunt whales, reviving a tribal tradition that goes back thousands of years. Removed from the federal endangered species list in 1994, California gray whale populations had recovered to more than 25,000. In May 1999, following months of training, fasting, and prayer, a crew of eight Makahs in the cedar canoe Hummingbird harpooned a thirty-ton gray whale. The whale was then quickly killed by shots from a .50-caliber rifle delivered from an assist boat and hauled to shore. The hunt made history. It was the first whale taken by the Makah in more than seventy years, a culmination of years of planning, permitting, and court challenges, and a confirmation of the Makah Tribe's celebrated history as whale hunters. A potlatch was held in Neah Bay a few days after the hunt. The high school gym echoed with chanting, drums, and speeches by Makah hosts and visiting tribes as tribal hunters shared the meat of their whale with some 800 supporters and native groups from across the country.

Reclaiming their right to hunt whales marked a cultural watershed for the tribe and its supporters. The hunt was covered by media around the world, but it was seen by some as a high crime against nature. Court challenges and legal roadblocks have persisted. (When some tribal members took part in an unsanctioned whale hunt in 2007, legal action was taken by tribal and federal governments.) A decade after the initial hunt, the tribe has not repeated it. In the interim, the cultural reawakening has continued to flourish among the peninsula's tribal people. The largest celebration of native cultural diversity in the peninsula's recent history took place in August 2005.

The excavation of Tse-whit-zen village on Port Angeles's industrial waterfront was a bittersweet event for the Elwha Klallam people. Among the wealth of artifacts uncovered were hundreds of native graves. Most of the deceased had been buried with attention to ritual and tradition but many graves reflected the hurried burials that resulted from European-borne smallpox epidemics that devastated Tse-whit-zen and other native villages. The discovery also opened old wounds dating from the tribe's turn-of-the-century eviction from their ancestral home and the desecration of their village site and cemetery by mill construction and later expansion.

In the winter of 2004, the Elwha Tribe called a halt to the archaeological dig and the industrial dock facility that was to follow. The loss of the $17-million facility was met with anger and resentment from city and port officials, business groups and labor leaders, much of it aimed at the small, 900-member tribe. Despite broad support from around the country, immense local pressure was brought on the tribe to reverse its decision. For the Elwha people, there was no question; their loyalty remained with their ancestors and their heritage.

The following summer, the Elwha Klallam hosted a paddle journey to Elwha to celebrate the rediscovery of their ancient village and help heal tribal wounds. The response was overwhelming. On the afternoon of August 1, a crowd of 3,000 gathered on the beach in Port Angeles to welcome fifty-four canoes carrying representatives from thirty-five tribes and nations. The canoeists paddled the open waterways of the Pacific coast, Canada's Georgia Strait, Hood Canal, and Puget Sound to arrive that warm sunny afternoon. Paddlers from as far away as Alaska sang their traditional songs, requested permission to land, and beached their colorful cedar canoes on the Elwha's traditional homeland. It was a spectacular sight. What followed was a week-long celebration of feasting, singing, traditional dancing, and games. A highlight for everyone, native and non-native, was a healing ceremony at the site of Tse-whit-zen village.

All told, the Paddle Journey to Elwha was the largest gathering of Native Americans on the peninsula's shores in more than a century. As such, it marked the rebirth of the peninsula's original cultures, two and a half centuries after Europeans first reached these shores. Elwha Klallam elder Bea Charles spoke for all native people present when she said of the event: "It stirs up something inside me of how it must have been long ago. It brings back our culture, our way of life. It's making us whole again."

CHAPTER 10

Protection for Olympic's Wildlands

I N 1890, the same year the U.S. census pronounced the American
frontier closed, a "rush" of exploration hit the Olympic Mountains.
Two of the Olympics' most noteworthy explorers met in July of that
year at a forest camp in the Skokomish Valley. Judge James Wickersham
was an inveterate explorer and mountaineer who had traveled widely in
the Northwest. A year earlier he and a companion explored the upper
reaches of the Skokomish Valley; he returned this year with a larger party
to pioneer a route north across the mountains to Port Angeles.

Sharing a campfire with Wickersham was Lieutenant Joseph P. O'Neil.
Also a seasoned wilderness traveler, O'Neil had led an exploratory expedition into the northern Olympic high country five years earlier, eventually
reaching the Dosewallips headwaters and the northern flanks of Mount
Anderson. "The travel was difficult," he confessed in his report, "but the
adventures, the beauty of the scenery, and the magnificent hunting and
fishing amply repaid all hardships." Now he returned with a large party
of enlisted men and members of the Oregon Alpine Club, a pack train,
and mountains of supplies. The explorers built trail as they advanced up
the Skokomish River and progress was slow.

Though members of O'Neil's party would explore sections of the
Duckabush and Dosewallips rivers to Hood Canal and descend the East
Fork Quinault River to the Pacific that summer, O'Neil's men were not
the first to cross the range. A small party led by Melbourne Watkinson

Mount Carrie and Cat Basin. Though the interior mountains had been traversed by Native Americans for millennia, they were *terra incognita* to Euroamericans until the latter part of the nineteenth century. PHOTO BY JANIS BURGER.

crossed by a route similar to O'Neil's in 1878. Dining on abundant fish, game, and berries, and following Indian and elk trails (and traveling by Indian canoe as they neared the coast), they made the round trip in an astonishing eighteen days. The glory of "first Olympic crossing," however, went to a well-publicized expedition sponsored by the *Seattle Press*. Its ragtag members emerged from the rain forests of the Quinault, battered, footsore, and hungry, only weeks before Wickersham and O'Neil's meeting. The *Press* party had started across the Olympics by way of the Elwha River the previous December, largely in an effort to scoop Wickersham and O'Neil (few were aware of the Watkinson expedition at the time) and ran headlong into one of the worst Olympic winters on record. The travels and travails of the *Press* party's ill-timed adventure are delightfully told in Robert L. Wood's *Across the Olympic Mountains*.

No record remains of the conversation Wickersham and O'Neil shared around the fire that July afternoon. They undoubtedly discussed their previous routes and the nature of the country they had crossed. It's also quite likely that there, as afternoon breezes wafted their smoke through the valley forest, the seed for the creation of Olympic National Park was planted.

By the late 1800s, the wholesale destruction of the virgin pine forests of the Great Lakes states by large timber companies sparked a nationwide movement to protect American forest lands. In 1864, a federal grant allowed the state of California to designate Yosemite as a park. In 1872, President Grant signed the act creating Yellowstone National Park, and by 1885, nearly three-quarters of a million acres were set aside as a forest preserve in the Adirondacks in New York. The popular writings of John Muir extolled the majesty of western mountains and forests and demanded government protection for them. "Every other civilized nation in the world has been compelled to care for its forests," he wrote, "and so must we." In 1891, Congress responded to growing popular sentiment and granted the president power to create forest preserves by proclamation. The reserves withdrew land from the public domain and closed it to homesteading and private speculation. Judge Wickersham knew that Major John Wesley Powell, intrepid explorer of the Grand Canyon and head of the U.S. Geological Survey, was preparing a list of forest reserve recommendations for the president's signature. Wickersham sent Powell his unpublished report and urged that Olympic be recommended as a national park:

In all the great commonwealths of Idaho, Montana, Nevada, Oregon, Washington and Alaska, there is not a national park. The forests are being felled, and destroyed, the game slaughtered, and the very mountains washed away, and the beauties of nature destroyed or fenced for private gain . . . The heaviest growth in North America lies within the limits of [the Olympic] region, untouched by fire or axe, and far enough from tidewater that its reservation by the government could not possibly cripple private enterprise in the new state, and by all means it should be reserved for future use. The reservation of this area as a national park will thus serve the twofold purpose of a great pleasure ground for the Nation, and a means of securing and protecting the finest forests in America.

Lieutenant O'Neil was equally struck by the beauty of the peninsula's mountains, forests, and streams, and the abundance of wildlife he found there. He concluded his report, written in 1890 and published six years later, by noting that while the area was unfit for settlement, it would "serve admirably as a national park."

But the commercial wealth of the Olympics' forests did not go unrecognized by powerful timber interests. It would take nearly a half-century—and one of the most bitterly fought conservation battles in American history—before Wickersham and O'Neil's vision of a national park in the Olympics would be realized.

EARLY PROTECTION FOR THE OLYMPICS

Following the passage of the 1891 Forest Reserve Act, President Cleveland appointed a committee to make recommendations regarding proper management of the forest reserves. Two key figures in American conservation were involved in the committee's deliberations: John Muir, the eloquent and impassioned advocate of forest and wildland preservation and founder of the Sierra Club, and a young millionaire named Gifford Pinchot, a leading proponent for sound commercial utilization of public forests. Muir envisioned a system of reserves protected from logging, grazing, mining, and dams, in the manner of Yosemite and Yellowstone. Pinchot, with his background in European forest management, saw the reserves quite differently. Thus began a national debate over the use of public forest lands that still rages in the Pacific Northwest more than a century later, a debate in which the Olympic Peninsula has served as center stage.

Though Pinchot's influence held sway over the committee's recommendations, its final report recommended the establishment of Mount Rainier and Grand Canyon national parks. The committee also recommended a large forest reserve for the Olympics. Established by President Cleveland on February 22, 1897, the 2,188,800-acre Olympic Forest Reserve encompassed all of the mountains, foothills, and lowland valleys of the peninsula, along with the rich, productive forests of the western slope out to the Pacific coast. It was by far the largest as well as the most valuable forest reserve in the nation, and timber interests in Washington State lost no time mounting a campaign to wrest it from public hands.

Arthur Dodwell and Theodore Rixon were assigned the considerable task of surveying the new reserve and assessing its forest resources. It took three years, working year-round, but that was all the time commercial interests needed. Thomas Aldwell, a Port Angeles real estate speculator who would later become the developer of the Elwha Dam, petitioned Congress to eliminate the most valuable timber lands from the reserve. He predicted economic ruin for the peninsula, going so far as to invoke the indebtedness of "many widows and orphans in the East who had been persuaded to buy securities" in Clallam County. Congressman William Jones fanned the flames with rhetoric, crowing that the reserve's establishment was "the most despotic act that has ever marred our history." Local officials maintained that the peninsula's rain-drenched coastal plain, remote from population centers and crowded with some of the largest trees in the world, was too valuable as agricultural land to be locked up in a forest reserve. They pointed to the public law stating that parts of any reserves "better adapted for mining or agricultural purposes than for forest usage may be restored to the public domain." Demands by local politicians, chambers of commerce, and industrialists were well received in Washington, D.C., particularly after a timber company executive was installed by the Washington State legislature in the United States Senate.

In 1900, a proclamation by President William McKinley reduced the reserve by more than a quarter million acres; the following year he cut it by nearly a half million more. By the time Dodwell and Rixon published their report on the Olympic Forest Reserve in 1902—a report specifying that soils, rainfall, and the size of the forest made the area completely unsuitable for agriculture—over 700,000 acres of the richest forest lands in the reserve had been opened to claims by settlers.

Chris Morgenroth homesteaded in the Bogachiel Valley a decade earlier and developed many of the first trails on the western Peninsula. After McKinley's deletions he watched in dismay as "not serious homesteaders" made fraudulent claims to the best tracts of forest, "then sold out to eastern timber speculators [for] $200 to $500," as he later noted in his memoir, "a tidy profit for the claimholder, and scandalously cheap timber land for the speculator." Contrary to the claims of Tom Aldwell and company, this mass transfer of public forest land into the hands of a few private timber companies dashed the hopes of Morgenroth and other early settlers for rural development of the area. The new "settlers" in the Olympic rain forest valleys eventually included the Milwaukee Land Company, Weyerhaeuser, Simpson Timber Company, Merrill and Ring, and others. Nearly three-quarters of a million acres of some of the nation's finest forest lands passed, in the words of Gifford Pinchot, "promptly and fraudulently into the hands of lumbermen." A national forest inspector who toured the area a few years later observed "scarcely a cabin on the lands in question." He concluded that "elimination from the Olympic was perhaps the biggest robbery of a National Forest ever pulled off."

While this unprecedented land grab was under way, another sort of trade was devastating the peninsula's elk herds. Elk carcasses were found scattered across the western valleys stripped of hides and incisor teeth. The teeth were popular among members of the Benevolent and Protective Order of the Elks as watch fobs, and commercial hunters killed elk indiscriminately. By the turn of the century, the peninsula's elk population had been reduced to fewer than 2,000 animals. The Seattle Mail and Herald published a lengthy exposé on the situation, and conservationists around the state clamored for protection. In 1905, the Washington state legislature passed a stopgap ten-year moratorium on elk hunting on the peninsula, a measure legislators hoped was a "first step in what will ultimately be Olympic National Park."

In 1906 Congress passed the Antiquities Act, giving the president the power to preserve objects of historic or scientific interest by designating national monuments by proclamation. Conservationists saw this as an opportunity to bypass a Congress heavily influenced by timber and mining interests and gain stronger federal protection for the Olympics. The following year, The Mountaineers, a Seattle hiking and climbing club, organized a large outing into the heart of the reserve. Its members, moved by the beauty of the forests and glacier-clad peaks, enthusiastically took up the cause of a national park. During the last days of his administration, President Theodore Roosevelt, an early champion of conservation causes, was asked by Congressman W. E. Humphrey of Tacoma to create a national monument in the Olympics. Roosevelt (for whom the Olympics' elk were later named) was agreeable, and on March 3, 1909, he designated the 600,000-acre Mount Olympus National Monument.

Though intended to protect habitat for elk, the monument protected

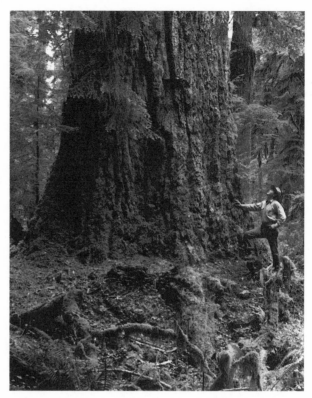

The Queets Fir in Olympic National Park. More than three-quarters of a million acres of some of the most productive low-elevation forests on the Olympic Peninsula were fraudulently removed from the Olympic Forest Reserve in 1900 and 1901. Nearly all of it has since been logged.
OLYMPIC NATIONAL PARK.

only the upper portions of the rain forest valleys remaining in the forest reserve and little to none of the winter habitat critical to elk. But it was a start. Together with the coastal wildlife refuges Roosevelt had established two years earlier, the groundwork for the protection of the Olympic ecosystem had begun.

THE BATTLE FOR A NATIONAL PARK

In his excellent book *Olympic Battleground*, Carsten Lien traces the long campaign for a national park in the Olympics. In one sense, it was a classic competition between two youthful land management agencies—the forest service and the park service—for control of the same land. Gifford Pinchot had been appointed to head the Department of Agriculture's Division of Forestry. After the timber giveaways and other abuses of the forest reserves in the early 1900s, he succeeded in having the reserves transferred from the Department of the Interior to the Department of

Agriculture. And so in 1905, the Olympic Forest Reserve became Olympic National Forest.

Pinchot imbued his agency with an ethic of commercial utilization and responsiveness to the needs of local resource industries. John Muir and the growing number of preservationists of the day had no illusions that the reserves would be managed for anything but timber under Pinchot's new agency; they pressed even harder for the creation of new national parks. Since many of these parks were carved out of existing national forests, the fundamental dichotomy within the American conservation movement was cast in stone. The National Park Service, created at the urging of preservationists in 1916, was directed to manage its lands "to conserve the scenery and the natural and historic objects and the wild life (sic) therein and to provide for the enjoyment... of future generations." In order to build a constituency for national parks by increasing their popularity, the park service's first director, Stephen Mather, emphasized the "enjoyment" clause in his mandate. The roads, resorts, golf courses, and entertainments he brought to Mount Rainier and other newly designated parks increased their popularity but lost critical preservationist support in the Northwest at a time when Olympic needed it most. Taking advantage of this, Olympic Forest Supervisor Rudo Fromme joined the outdoor clubs on their Olympic outings and succeeded in gaining The Mountaineers' and the local Klahhane Club's support for continued forest service management of the area. This was in spite of Fromme's advocacy for roads up the Elwha Valley and into Seven Lakes Basin in the headwaters of the Sol Duc.

By 1912, a coalition of Washington timber and business interests recommended removing all stands of commercially valuable timber from Mount Olympus National Monument, then designating the remaining high country a national park—albeit one that would allow logging, mining, and dams. This strategy of excluding any lands with commercial potential from preservation was scrupulously followed by timber companies as well as the U.S. Forest Service throughout the ensuing quarter-century-long battle for a national park.

With the election of President Woodrow Wilson, the timber companies got their wish. In 1915, Wilson slashed 170,000 acres of forest from the monument, eliminating all that was left of the rain forest valleys and

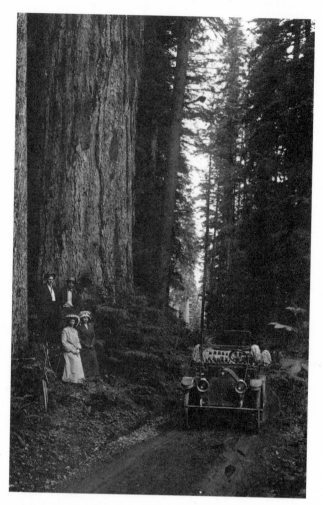

As roads were opened into the Peninsula's lowland forests and visitors encountered Olympic's magnificent old-growth trees, sentiment for preserving a part of this heritage as a national park began to grow. BERT KELLOGG COLLECTION, NORTH OLYMPIC LIBRARY SYSTEM.

virtually all of the heavily timbered southern Olympics. Park bills in 1911 and 1916 were also defeated in Congress. But local and regional sentiment for a national park continued to build in light of these reductions, and conservation and outdoor groups renewed their press for a park.

During World War I, the army mounted a major effort to harvest the dense stands of Sitka spruce on the west side of the peninsula; the strong, durable, lightweight wood was needed for the construction of warplanes. The army's Spruce Production Division assisted private contractors in the massive undertaking of building a thirty-six-mile railroad to deliver spruce logs from the peninsula's West End to a mill Port Angeles. The railroad was the fastest (and at more than $30,000 per mile, most expensive) ever constructed in the United States. But the armistice ending the war was signed a few weeks before the last rail was laid. The railway did provide a means for timber companies to log the western rain forests. Lumbering on the peninsula now began in earnest.

By the late 1920s, much of the forests removed from the original Olympic Forest Reserve were gone, and mill owners turned their gaze to the trees in the national forest. The forest service was happy to accommodate. A 1915 timber management plan for the forest announced the "chief function of the national forest is the furnishing of a continuous supply of timber." Cutting levels on Olympic that year were around 12 million board feet. They shot up to 175 million by 1928. In its 1926 timber harvest plan, the forest service went so far as to include forests inside the national monument in its cutting circles. Around this time, citizen efforts for a national park took on a nationwide scope.

Herb Crisler's well-publicized 1930 trek across the Olympic Mountains without food or supplies captured public interest in the Olympics, and his film documenting his adventure, *America's Last Wilderness*, made the beauty and wildness of the range come alive for West Coast audiences. The Olympic Highway, completed in 1931, further opened the door to general tourism on the peninsula.

Continuing concern over the fate of Roosevelt elk in the Olympics prompted the Izaak Walton League to become involved in the park issue. And in New York, an associate curator of the American Museum of Natural History named Willard Van Name emerged as a key player. Respected among the scientific and conservation communities, Van Name was a sharp and widely published critic of both forest service and park service management of public lands. His 1929 book, *Vanishing Forest Reserves*, focused national attention on the growing crisis in our public forests. In 1930, Van Name joined forces with Irving Brant, an influential St. Louis newspaper editor, and Rosalie Edge, an outspoken New York conservationist active with the Audubon Society. They formed the Emergency Conservation Committee (ECC), and protection of the Olympics' magnificent old-growth forests was high on their list of priorities. In 1932, Van Name traveled to the Olympic Peninsula to investigate the situation. He reported that none of the lands within Olympic National Forest offered secure protection for either forests or wildlife, nor were roads or summer homes prohibited in the national monument. He also learned that the recently completed Olympic Highway would allow the forest service to intensify its cutting of the national forest. Van Name was particularly struck by the grandeur—and vulnerability—of the western rain forests, and he returned to the East determined to fight for their protection. Van Name and the ECC proposed a large park, which would include portions of the forested valleys of the Sol Duc, Bogachiel, Hoh, Queets, and Quinault, as well as Lake Crescent and the north shore of Quinault Lake.

Through its publication and wide distribution of pamphlets and papers, the ECC was successful in galvanizing members of national conservation organizations, scientific societies, universities, and natural history museums into an informed and effective broad-based coalition. Through letters to newspapers, agencies, Congress, and the White House, citizens expressed overwhelming support for an Olympic National Park. With the election of Franklin Delano Roosevelt in 1933, the campaign for a park hit high gear.

In a widely distributed pamphlet "The Proposed Olympic National Park," Van Name stated the case for a park forcefully.

The Peninsula affords the last opportunity for preserving any adequate large remnants of the wonderful primeval forests of Douglas fir, hemlock, cedar, and spruce which were not so many years ago one of the grandest and the most unique features of our two northwestern-most States, but which everywhere have been or are being logged off to the very last stick.

With the movement for a park reaching a boiling point, the park service now conducted its own study into the feasibility of making Olympic a national park. Cowed by the forest service and timber interests, the park service rejected the ECC's proposal, claiming it included "much available timber on lands that are not of national park caliber" in the proposed park. The agency recommended instead a much smaller park devoid of commercially valuable trees.

When the park service distributed an early draft report to a timber industry lobbying group, Van Name went directly to Roosevelt's secretary of the interior, Harold Ickes. At Ickes's direction, the park service revised its recommendations to agree with the conservationists' proposal. The resulting bill, introduced by Congressman Mon Wallgren in 1935, was opposed by the forest service and the timber industry, of course, and failed to pass. Pressure ran high and both sides were deadlocked. It was then that President Roosevelt entered the discussion. Determined to resolve the issue, he traveled to the Olympic Peninsula to look into the matter for himself.

When Roosevelt arrived in Port Angeles on a drizzly day in September 1937, he was met by more than 3,000 schoolchildren from around the peninsula, who turned out in front of the Clallam County Courthouse beneath a banner that read, "Please Mr. President, we children need your help. Give us our Olympic National Park." Popular support for a park was at its peak on the peninsula at that time, and Roosevelt told the children and an assembled crowd of about 10,000 adults that they could count on his help in getting a park for the Olympics.

That evening, in his cabin at Singer's Tavern (now Lake Crescent Lodge), Roosevelt made it clear to representatives of the park service, the forest service, and the congressional delegation that he wanted a large park, with "more large timber" than either agency had proposed. Roosevelt concluded his visit with an auto tour of the western peninsula, stopping at Forks and Lake Quinault Lodge. In a comically futile gesture, the forest service—clearly the loser in the president's visit—had moved the sign marking the southern boundary of the forest two miles north in an attempt to disown a large fire-blackened clearcut.

FDR's trip crystallized national attention on the park, defeated forest service opposition, and at least temporarily silenced the timber industry. On June 29, 1938, Roosevelt signed the bill creating Olympic National Park. The park encompassed 638,280 acres, with the provision that the president could expand it by proclamation up to 898,292 acres. In order to insure protection for the peninsula's coastal strip, the Bogachiel rain forest, and a corridor along the Queets River within the allowed acreage (all were high priorities for FDR), conservationists reluctantly agreed to eliminate the middle Dosewallips Valley and much of the upper Dungeness watershed in the northeast Olympics. These areas were administratively protected at the time as part of the forest service's Olympic Primitive Area. The forest service dropped its primitive area status the following year.

At long last, the battle to create Olympic National Park was won. Some of the finest examples of old-growth forest and wildlife populations in the Pacific Northwest were preserved for future generations. It had been a long and contentious struggle. A powerful industry, one that had controlled the political life of the region for nearly a century, and a timber-oriented government agency had been overcome by widespread citizen activism and the vision of a handful of dedicated leaders. At the celebratory banquet in Seattle, Secretary Ickes reaffirmed that Olympic would remain a wilderness park. But any savoring of the victory on the part of conservationists would prove short lived. Though the park was established, the battle to preserve its irreplaceable old-growth forests was far from finished.

ATTACKS ON THE WEST-SIDE FOREST

With the onset of World War II, the timber industry redoubled its efforts to remove valuable west-side forests from the park. In 1944, to the shock of the environmental community, the park service recommended deleting from the park much of the lower Bogachiel as well as lowland rain forests in the Quinault Valley. When these recommendations were introduced as a bill in 1947, the same environmental coalition that brought about the creation of the park rose to its defense. Irving Clark Sr. of The Mountaineers addressed a national audience in "The Living Wilderness" that year. In defense of the Olympic forest he wrote, "[It] fills lowland valleys, and covers ridges and mountainsides in unmarred splendor." Letters poured in to congressional offices and to the park service condemning the bill, and a public hearing held at Rosemary Inn on Lake Crescent overwhelmingly denounced the measure. The public won this battle, but conservationists realized that protection of Olympic's forests would require continued vigilance. Clark, Leo Gallagher, John Osseward, and other Northwest conservationists organized the Olympic Park Associates (OPA) as a watchdog group dedicated to preserving the wilderness integrity of the park. OPA and other conservation organizations had their work cut out for them as assaults on the newly created park continued.

In the meantime, lumbering interests on the peninsula found a way to quietly move old-growth trees out of the park and into local mills by means of "salvage" contracts. The 1916 Organic Act creating the National Park Service allowed for the removal of insect-damaged trees to preserve forest health. At Olympic, this directive was broadened to include the salvage logging of downed and damaged trees as well as any *potential* insect trees. Beginning in 1941 and continuing until it was stopped by a national outcry from environmental organizations in 1958, more than 100 million board feet of timber, both standing and down, were removed from the park and trucked to area mills. Noted environmental writer Paul Shepard and Olympic historian Carsten Lien were among the seasonal naturalists at the time who blew the whistle on park logging.

Another threat to the wilderness integrity of Olympic surfaced in the 1950s with a proposal to construct a scenic highway along the length of the park coastal strip. This attempt was also met head-on by conservation activists. In 1958, United States Supreme Court Justice William O. Douglas led a hike along the coast from Lake Ozette to Rialto Beach to dramatize the issue. A second hike led by Douglas in 1964, from the mouth of the Hoh River north to Third Beach laid the road proposal permanently to rest. That same year saw road proposals up Tshletshy Creek in the Queets area and along spectacular Skyline Divide between the Queets and Quinault rivers, as well as the alpine meadowlands between Deer Park and Hurricane Ridge. All were soundly defeated.

A final effort to delete the Bogachiel River Valley from the park was mounted in 1966 as part of a "boundary adjustment" bill. Ingeniously, it was packaged with legislation that would create the North Cascades National Park complex in Washington. Again it was defeated by citizen conservationists. The history of preservation in the Olympics has been one of concerned citizens making their voices heard.

It wasn't long after these episodes that I unwittingly joined this citizens' campaign. On a hike along Shi Shi Beach in the early 1970s, I followed the sound of chainsaws up a creek and stumbled into a clearcut that seemed to extend for hundreds of acres. Climbing past stumps and logging slash to the top of a rise, I looked down on timber fallers working a stand of spruce in a shallow draw. Trees dropped like matchsticks. This northern reach of coastline was not included in the park's coastal strip at that time. But what stunned me the most was that the logging occurring was no more than a twenty-minute walk from one of the most startlingly

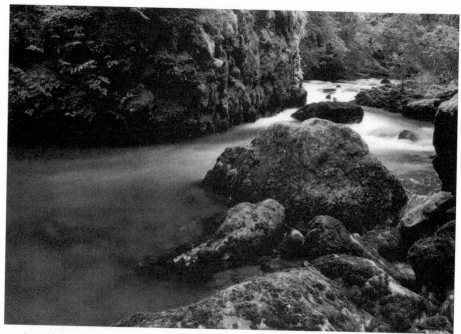

One of the last unprotected treasures of the Olympics, the lower Gray Wolf River canyon was among some 90,000 acres of national forest lands surrounding the park that Congress added to the National Wilderness Preservation System in 1984. PHOTO BY JANIS BURGER.

beautiful beaches I had ever seen.

Not long after that I found myself working with Olympic Park Associates and other environmental groups to secure protection for the splendid northern coast. Protection came in 1976 when Congress added Shi Shi, Point of the Arches, and the east shore of Lake Ozette to Olympic National Park. By that time, virtually all of the Ozette basin had been logged, and forest service and Washington Department of Natural Resources clearcuts were chewing back the old-growth forests flush with the park boundary. The damage to aquatic habitats, spawning areas for salmon, and lowland old-growth forest habitat affected park resources. It became clear to me and other conservationists that if Olympic National Park was to remain ecologically viable, some means of protecting critical ecosystem functions on lands outside the park would be needed.

PROTECTION FOR THE OLYMPIC ECOSYSTEM

During the 1970s and '80s, the inadequacies of Olympic National Park's boundaries were particularly apparent in the high rugged country of the east Olympics. Here the park boundary cut randomly across alpine areas, migration routes, and the upper portions of six river drainages. Calving and wintering areas for east-side elk herds were unprotected, and critical habitat for salmon and steelhead had been lost to logging and development. As clear-cutting accelerated on the national forest in the 1960s and '70s, roads were punched into upper watersheds, and steep mountainsides wholly unsuitable for timber management were clear-cut, often with disastrous results.

Following passage of the 1970 National Environmental Policy Act, national forest personnel were directed to inventory remaining roadless lands and make recommendations for wilderness designation. Local conservationists rallied to the cause, and much of the high scenic country adjoining the east side of the park was recommended by the agency, including most of the botanically rich uplands of the Dungeness rainshadow. But few of the lower forested valleys were recommended, and very little of the heavily timbered west side of the national forest was included. Of some 53,000 acres of roadless lands inventoried on the two west-side districts of Olympic National Forest at that time, only part of one area, the 12,000-acre Colonel Bob area above Quinault Lake, was recommended for wilderness.

In the mid-1970s, local conservationists began a grassroots campaign to rally support for protection of ecologically important forest service lands surrounding the park. Their proposal was embraced by regional and national environmental groups, and a decade-long effort culminated in the passage of the 1984 Washington Wilderness Act. The Buckhorn, Brothers, Mount Skokomish, Wonder Mountain, and Colonel Bob wilderness areas were designated by Congress, protecting nearly 90,000 acres of outstanding national forest wildlands. Important migratory and calving areas for east-side elk and critical salmon habitat along the lower Gray Wolf and the middle Dosewallips and Duckabush river valleys were included, as well as low-elevation east-side valley forests not represented in the park. In 2001, the Clinton administration's Roadless Area Conservation Rule curtailed road building and commercial activities and granted additional protections to undeveloped lands in Olympic National Forest. Seventeen areas comprising more than 85,000 acres were protected under the new rule, which survived a final court challenge in 2006.

Congressional designation of forest service wilderness areas and later roadless area protection were important steps in establishing an interagency network of safeguarded habitats on the peninsula. But as overcutting on federal, state, and private lands accelerated during the 1980s and '90s throughout the region—leading eventually to legal action mandating protection for the spotted owl—scientists and conservationists sought new ways to address habitat needs on an ecosystem scale.

A central issue facing protected areas worldwide is their long-term viability. Ecosystem management entails managing large areas to insure that all plants and animals are maintained at viable levels in their natural habitats and that basic ecosystem processes are perpetuated over time. The dynamics of natural change in a system are compounded by the effects of human activities, including human-caused global warming. The ecological history of the peninsula since the retreat of the Vashon ice shows that this isolated, "islandlike" landform was not only adequate to provide viable habitat for a range of plant and animal species over time, but it supported an exceptionally high level of biological diversity for an area its size. But the last hundred years of intensive human use of the peninsula has effectively shrunk that habitat island for many species to the confines of the park and protected areas within the national forest.

Wolves and fishers were extirpated from the peninsula, and pine martins have become extremely rare. Wild salmon stocks are at risk in a number of Olympic rivers and streams, with Puget Sound chinook, Hood Canal chum, Ozette Lake sockeye, Puget Sound steelhead, and bull trout all listed as threatened under the Endangered Species Act. Northern spotted owl numbers are in steep decline, and marbled murrelet populations have failed to recover fifteen years after being listed. Four Olympic wildlife species are candidates for listing, including the endemic Mazama pocket gopher. Currently, there are eighteen species of Olympic wildlife—from the northern goshawk to the endemic Olympic torrent salamander— and five plants that are federally classified as "species of concern." Washington state lists nine Olympic species on its threatened and endangered list, with twenty-two more as candidates. Thirty-five plants in Olympic are on state threatened or sensitive lists, and 313 nonnative plants have found their way into the park. Among the ten or so nonnative fish and mammals in Olympic, feral hogs, opossum, and bullfrogs are recent arrivals. Nonnative species can outcompete and displace natives and degrade sensitive habitats. Though the peninsula's forest and aquatic communities are incredibly resilient, the pressures now facing them are without ecological precedent.

A major effort to address ecosystem issues on the peninsula came with the Northwest Forest Plan. Released by federal agencies in 1994, the plan aims to provide critical habitat for old-growth-dependent species such as northern spotted owls and marbled murrelets and to offer protection to streams and salmon. The plan established a series of late successional forest reserves (old-growth and near-old-growth forest areas) and a network of riparian reserves and identified key watersheds on national forest lands for special management. It reduced timber cutting on federal lands by about a third from existing plans (though considerably less than congressionally mandated cut levels of the late 1980s and early '90s), and encouraged restoration measures for degraded habitats. But in spite of its strong conservation emphasis, the plan fails to insure the survival of the region's old-growth associated wildlife. More than a third of these species are given less than an 80 percent probability of long-term survival under the plan.

In 1998 Congress passed the groundbreaking National Parks Omnibus Management Act, the first law authorizing the park service to monitor the health of park ecosystems in perpetuity. The goal is to take the pulse of park ecosystems and assess critical "vital signs." At Olympic these include glaciers, subalpine areas, lowland and alpine lakes, rivers and streams, forest landscapes, elk, and intertidal communities, among others. Research protocols have been put in place, and monitoring is now under way. As data accrue over the coming years, a detailed report card for the health of the Olympic ecosystem will emerge.

In 2008, Olympic National Park released its long-awaited general management plan, the document that sets management direction for the next fifteen to twenty years. The plan takes some important steps toward long-term ecosystem protection. It establishes "no-take" intertidal reserves along critical portions of the Olympic coast, covering about a third of the park's coastal strip. It recommends expanding the park's boundaries to better protect riparian and lowland forest areas and foster fisheries restoration in the Ozette Lake and Lake Crescent areas and along the Queets River corridor, which also harbors the highest densities of Roosevelt elk. It recommends a wilderness eligibility study for Ozette Lake. And it proposes to relocate Kalaloch Lodge and the coast highway away from the coastal erosion zone. Other recommendations encourage mass transit for heavily visited areas and expansion of educational programs.

Even so, conservationists criticized the plan for not going far enough. Proposed park boundary changes fail to conform to watershed boundaries or offer protection to headwater streams. No wild and scenic river recommendations are made for park rivers, and no special management status is afforded rivers to protect critical salmon habitats. River protection zones were discussed but are not part of the plan. Developed areas are expanded, often in low-elevation forests and floodplains, and all existing park roads are to be maintained or relocated. No recommendation is made to reintroduce wolves into the park, and scant mention is given to nonnative mountain goats. Alternatively, conservation organizations are promoting an Olympic ecosystem protection initiative that is commensurate with the planetary resource of this irreplaceable natural preserve.

Ultimately, the diverse natural systems of the Olympic Peninsula are parts of a single whole, sharing the same rich genetic reserves and biological processes, and subject to the same threats from population pressures, land use, and a changing climate. We are fortunate in the Olympics that many of the most sensitive and crucial parts of the ecosystem have been protected, and that important restoration activities, such as the Elwha dam removal and fisher reintroduction are under way. The peninsula faces an uncertain future with nearly every "cog and wheel" intact, as Aldo Leopold counseled. Generations of Americans touched by the beauty and power of the Olympic Peninsula have spoken up for its protection. But protection for the Olympic ecosystem is far from complete.

Continued deforestation of the peninsula's lowlands, degradation of salmon streams, conversion of forest and farm lands to residential development, overfishing at sea, and increasing hunting pressure (both legal and illegal) along park boundaries call for new approaches to conservation. The scientific certainty of human-caused global warming and the magnitude and suddenness of its effects on glacier and river dynamics, alpine plant and animal communities, wildfire frequency and intensity, forest health, and wildlife habitats are matters of pressing concern. In the face of this, the island ecology that gave rise to much of the uniqueness of the Olympic ecosystem becomes its biggest liability. Genetic isolation places threatened species such as the northern spotted owl in a particularly vulnerable position. Alpine and subalpine species, such as the Olympic marmot, could face significant loss of habitats. More frequent winter floods and dwindling summer snowpacks will take heavy tolls on salmon and steelhead. And extirpated species will be even less likely to naturally recolonize the area.

If Americans are to complete the more than century-long process of protecting the Olympic wilderness for future generations, a number of tasks remain. Key lands should be added to park in the Ozette and Crescent lake basins, as well as the Hoh, Queets, and Quinault watersheds. Forest service wilderness should be shored up with mid- and low-elevation forest additions in the Dungeness, Dosewallips, Hamma Hamma, Skokomish, Quinault, Queets, Bogachiel, and Elwha watersheds. But such additions alone will not secure ecosystem protection. Rivers, streams, coastal areas, and wetlands must be sensitively managed to protect habitat values across the peninsula. The long process of removing two dams from the Elwha River and restoring native salmon runs to this largest of the peninsula's watersheds will be a flagship for salmon and ecosystem restoration nationwide. But it is also essential that protection be extended to portions of existing free-flowing rivers that lie outside the park's boundaries. Currently, none of the peninsula's many wild rivers are included in the National Wild and Scenic Rivers system, a program that prohibits in-stream development and requires multiagency management plans for protecting resource values. The forest service has recommended portions of three rivers for designation; conservationists have proposed several more. It remains for Congress to take the necessary action to complete this vital link in ecosystem conservation. In the meantime, private sector land conservation efforts are coming to the aid of peninsula rivers and other critical habitat areas. Area tribes, local land trusts, and collaborative groups are protecting and restoring a network of aquatic lands across the peninsula. On the West End, the Hoh River Trust, with the help

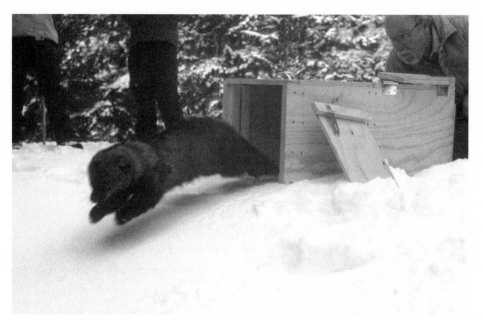

A milestone in ecosystem restoration was reached in 2008 when the first fishers were reintroduced to Olympic National Park. Eliminated from Olympic forests by trapping during the first half of the 20th century, these lithe, cat-size predators are resuming their role in Olympic's forests. OLYMPIC NATIONAL PARK.

of federal grants and private donations, has purchased nearly 5,000 acres of former timber industry lands along Hoh River from the park boundary to the Pacific with the intent of restoring habitat and protecting this last great river.

A critical step in ecosystem protection for the Olympics is restoring extirpated species. A significant start has been made by returning the first fishers to Olympic's rain forest valleys. And a first, important step has been taken to bring back the Olympic's top predator, the wolf, to its former range. A 1999 U.S. Fish and Wildlife study determined that wolf reintroduction was biologically feasible in the Olympics, and that elk and deer populations were adequate to support it. Wolf reintroductions in Yellowstone and the northern Rocky Mountains have revitalized ecosystems from riparian songbirds to major prey populations. Returning wolves to Olympic would rekindle this predator's evolutionary relationship with Roosevelt elk and deer. It would restore the predator-prey balance throughout the park's ecosystems. And it would return the wolves' haunting music to valley forests now empty of their songs.

The world scientific community has twice recognized the importance of Olympic National Park on a planetary scale. In 1976 the United Nations Educational, Scientific, and Cultural Organization (UNESCO) designated Olympic as part of its system of International Biosphere Reserves. The Man in the Biosphere program, of which the reserves are a part, identified representative examples of the world's major ecosystems in seventy-two countries. The reserves are intended to safeguard genetic diversity worldwide. They also serve as research centers and global benchmarks against which to measure human impacts on surrounding areas.

In 1981, Olympic National Park was selected by UNESCO as a World Heritage Site. As such, Olympic takes its place among some of our planet's most treasured natural and cultural sites: the Grand Canyon, the redwoods, the pyramids of Egypt, the cathedral at Chartres. Such places are part of our common human heritage. UNESCO recognizes that these and other irreplaceable World Heritage sites are older than the nations where they happen to be located. They belong to the entire world.

In its evaluation of Olympic for world heritage distinction, UNESCO concluded that "Olympic National Park is the best natural area in the entire Pacific Northwest, with a spectacular coastline, scenic lakes, majestic mountains and glaciers, and magnificent temperate rain forest; these are outstanding examples of on-going evolution and superlative natural phenomena. It is unmatched in the world."

THE ESTUARY

Winter fog hugged the shoreline and spilled over the road as I wound my way south along Hood Canal in early predawn light. As I dropped into the Dosewallips River floodplain and approached the narrow two-lane bridge, dark shapes rose through the fog, danced across the roadway, and slipped off into the mist. I killed the engine and rolled to a stop on the gravel shoulder. Stepping out of the car, I watched a herd of thirty or forty elk bound off through stiff winter marsh grass, then spread over the estuary and begin to feed.

A few weeks earlier my wife, Mary, and I had wandered across this estuary and found side channels of the river full of spawning chum salmon.

Their dark, iridescent shapes rippled beneath the surface. Now, as the morning lightened and the fog began to lift, the blond rump patches of elk ranged out toward the slack blue-gray waters of the canal—mountain gods come to drink at the sea's edge. The summer before, I had watched what may have been these same elk browsing the high meadowlands below Hayden Pass in the long shadows of evening. The shrill calls of the bulls echoed off surrounding peaks. The rut now over, they had followed their old trails down the steep mountain valley, through open bottom lands and dense patches of second growth, fenced pastures, and scattered farms, to slip past the small sleeping town and cross the highway into the deep growth of the estuary. It must have been an ancient route for them, carved when winter herds dappled the shores of these inland waters, and salmon swelled the streams. We've left few valleys wild enough for these grand migrations. Still, the elk manage to return, their large hooves clacking across the blacktop.

An empty log truck rumbling by brought me back to myself. The lowlands had cleared, and clouds were rising against the steep forested ridges upvalley. Mount Constance, one of my favorite winter views, stayed hidden. Snows deepened over the summer ranges of elk and deer, heather vole and marmot. Icy water churned over the deep redds of salmon and carried a plume of nutrients into the saltwater bay, where grebes and mergansers wintered.

It occurred to me that the seasonal pulse at the heart of these mountains was not unlike the beat of our own hearts. It infuses the land with vitality, beauty, and grace. Maybe that is why human hearts have responded so passionately to this place. Maybe its future and our own are deeply joined.

Visitor's Information

GENERAL INFORMATION

Visitor Centers

The Olympic National Park Visitor Center is located at 3002 Mt. Angeles Road in Port Angeles. It offers interpretive exhibits, along with a small theater/auditorium, a children's activity room, wilderness information center, and interpretive trails. The Hoh Visitor Center is located in the heart of the Hoh Rain Forest. It has exhibits and three short nature trails. Both offer a wide selection of publications as well as maps and information. Both are open all year, although the Hoh Visitor Center is staffed only on weekends from October through May.

The information center in Forks, which provides visitor information for the west side, is open year-round but staffed only on weekends from October to May. Summer information centers are located at Storm King on Lake Crescent and at Kalaloch on the ocean coast. The Hurricane Ridge Visitor Center is located in scenic subalpine meadowlands seventeen miles south of Port Angeles. It is open from early May into October, as well as on weekends and holidays from late December through March, and features an information desk, exhibits, and publications. Call (360) 565-3130 for off-season road conditions for Hurricane Ridge Road.

A free park newspaper, *The Bugler,* is distributed at visitor centers and entrance stations; it lists services, seasonal schedules, campfire talks, and guided nature walks. There is also a Junior Ranger program for young people. Schedules for interpretive programs are also posted at visitor centers and campgrounds.

For information, write to Superintendent, Olympic National Park, 600 Park Avenue, Port Angeles, WA 98362; phone (360) 565-3130; or visit the park's Web site at www.nps.gov/olym/. For information on Olympic National Forest, call (360) 956-2402 or visit the forest's Web site at www.fs.fed.us/r6/olympic.

For information on the Olympic Coast National Marine Sanctuary, call (360) 457-6622 or visit the sanctuary's Web site at www.ocnms.nos.noaa.gov/. The sanctuary's visitor center, the Olympic Coast Discovery Center, is located at 115 East Railroad Avenue in downtown Port Angeles. It is open daily during the summer months, Thursdays through Sundays the rest of the year.

Information on the peninsula's national wildlife refuges is available by calling the Washington Maritime Wildlife Refuge Complex at (360) 457-8451.

Seasons and Fees

Olympic National Park is open all year. Some roads and facilities are closed in winter. The summer season begins around Memorial Day and extends through Labor Day. Entrance fees are collected from May through September and year-round at some locations. Campground fees and wilderness use fees are also required. Call the park at (360) 565-3130 for current fee information.

Transportation

Ferries operate regularly across Puget Sound from Seattle, Edmonds, and Keystone. Schedules are available from Washington State Ferries at (888) 808-7977 or on the Web at www.wsdot.wa.gov/ferries/. Ferry service is also available between Victoria, British Columbia, Canada, and Port Angeles. Schedules are available from Black Ball Transport, Inc., (360) 457-4491.

Sightseeing by Car

U.S. 101 is the main scenic route around the peninsula, with numerous spur roads providing access into interior and coastal areas of the park. No roads pass through the rugged heart of the Olympics. Temperate rain forests may be seen along the Hoh, Queets, and Quinault valley roads, and old-growth Douglas fir forests along the Sol Duc and Elwha roads. The road to Hurricane Ridge offers splendid views from lowland forest to subalpine meadows. Hurricane Ridge offers stunning views into the wilderness heart of the Olympics. Forest roads also access the Deer Park, Dosewallips, and Staircase areas of the park during the summer. The Pacific coastal strip is accessible from U.S. 101 at Kalaloch, or by spur roads to Oil City at the mouth of Hoh, La Push, and Rialto Beach.

Camping and Lodges

The park has sixteen established campgrounds. Most consist of individual sites with tables and fireplaces. Water and toilet facilities are nearby. No showers, laundry, or utility connections are provided in park campgrounds; a few have dump stations. Additional campgrounds are located in Olympic National Forest. Overnight accommodations in the park are available at Kalaloch Lodge, (360) 962-2271; Lake Crescent Lodge, (360) 928-3211; Log Cabin Resort, (360) 928-3325; and Sol Duc Hot Springs Resort, (360) 327-3583. Kalaloch Lodge is open year-round; the others operate only in summer. Lake Quinault Lodge in Olympic National Forest, (360) 288-2900, is also open year-round. Meals and accommodations are also available at numerous locations outside the park.

The Olympic Park Institute, an environmental education facility, is housed at historic Rosemary Inn on Lake Crescent. It offers a variety of field seminars and Elderhostel programs for adults, as well as environmental education programs for youth and mixed-generation programs. The institute can be reached at (360) 928-3720, or on the Web at www. olympicparkinstitute.org.

Hiking

Olympic is a wilderness park, best experienced by leaving roads and cars behind and venturing out on park trails. Short, easy loop trails are located close to most campgrounds and visitor centers. The lower Hurricane Hill trail and Meadow Loop trail at Hurricane Ridge, and the first one-half mile of the Marymere Falls trail at Lake Crescent are wheelchair accessible with assistance. The Madison Falls trail on the Elwha, the Hoh Visitor Center loop trail, the Moments in Time nature trial on Lake Crescent, and the Maple Glades nature trail at Quinault are fully accessible.

More than 500 miles of backcountry trails provide access to the interior mountains of the park. Backcountry rangers are stationed throughout the park in summer months. Some trails are suitable for horseback riding as well as hiking, but pets, bikes, and weapons are prohibited on all park trails. Hikers should be prepared for inclement weather at any time of year; stoves, tents, and warm clothing are advised. Permits are required for all overnight backpackers and climbing parties. Quotas and reservations are in effect for some heavily used wilderness areas. Wilderness use fees are required for overnight trips. Hikers should contact the Wilderness Information Center at (360) 565-3100 or on the Web at www.nps.gov/olym/wic/.

WHERE TO SEE WILDFLOWERS

With its abundant precipitation and mild maritime climate, the Olympic Peninsula harbors a wide variety of wildflowers. Diverse habitats support more than 1,400 species of vascular plants. After the peninsula's heavy winter rains, the first warm days of spring bring coastal areas and lowland valleys into bloom, and the lowland trails of the park become lined with blossoms. The wildflower season extends into late summer as cool, north-facing slopes of the high mountains melt free of winter snow. Charles Stewart's *Wildflowers of the Olympics and Cascades* is a handy and easy-to-use trailside identification guide tailored to Northwest flora.

Lowland Forest Wildflower Walks

The Peabody Creek trail, beginning at the Olympic National Park visitor center in Port Angeles, is an excellent place to sample the spring bloom. From mid-April through May, trailsides are dotted with pioneer violet, trillium, false Solomon's seal, twisted stalk, twinflower, fringe cup, and wild ginger. The Marymere Falls trail at Lake Crescent hosts similar wildflower gardens, and the nearby Spruce Railroad trail, with its gravel slopes and rocky outcrops, adds paintbrush, sedum, and spotted saxifrage, as well spirea and chocolate lilies to the lowland display.

In the western rain forest, the Hall of Mosses trail at the Hoh Visitor Center meanders through pale sprays of white foamflower and slender boykina and thick beds of oxalis, as well as pioneer violet, beadruby, springbeauty, and trillium.

Mountain Forest Wildflower Walks

In late May and June, the wildflowers of the mountain forests are at their peak. The Hurricane Ridge and Deer Park roads pass through this zone, and trails at Heart of the Hills, Elwha, Staircase, Dosewallips, Sol Duc, and other locations provide access to the montane forest. Pipsissewa, pyrola, bunchberry, and delicate fairy slippers bloom in this shady realm. These mid-elevation forests are also home to shade-loving plants that lack green chlorophyll: pinedrops, pinesaps, and ghostly Indian-pipes.

Subalpine Meadow Wildflower Walks

Beginning in June, the subalpine meadows begin to melt free of snow. The Hurricane Hill and Deer Ridge trails take hikers through carpets of mountain wildflowers. Smooth douglasia and spreading phlox are among the first to bloom on south-facing rocky slopes, and glacier lilies follow the melting edges of snowbanks. Colorful gardens of subalpine buttercup, Sitka valerian, pale larkspur, arnica, hook violet, paintbrush, and cow parsnip cover the hillsides. In the Hurricane Ridge area and along the Hurricane Ridge Road, monkey-flowers and marsh marigolds crowd snowmelt streams, and purplish pink Jeffrey's shooting stars add splashes of color to moist swales. Other trails from which to sample the subalpine gardens in early summer include the Royal Basin and Boulder Lake trails in the park, as well as the Mount Townsend and Marmot Pass trails in Olympic National Forest.

Alpine Wildflower Walks

The Elk Mountain and Lillian Ridge trails from Obstruction Point venture past tree line into the Arctic-alpine zone. The windswept ridges and shallow soils of this zone limit plant growth to low-growing and "cushion" plants. Here phlox and douglasia are joined by western and rock-loving anemone, sweet vetch, phacelia, and Webster's senecio (an Olympic endemic). Pale agoseris, woolly pussytoes, small-flowered penstemon, and several saxifrages also inhabit this airy realm.

Park naturalists lead nature walks at several locations throughout the summer season. Check for scheduled walks at park visitor centers.

WHERE TO SEE OLD-GROWTH FORESTS

Olympic National Park harbors some of the finest examples of temperate old-growth forests remaining in the Pacific Northwest. Lowland forests can be visited any time of year, and several short, easy loop trails provide access to some of the park's most magnificent forest stands. Robert L. Wood's *Olympic Mountains Trail Guide* provides detailed descriptions of these short forest walks.

Ancient Forests of the Northern and Eastern Olympics

An excellent introduction to the old-growth Douglas fir and western hemlock forests of Olympic National Park is the Ancient Groves nature trail just off the Sol Duc River Road. This half-mile loop trail meanders through an ancient stand of fir and hemlock. The largest trees, with thick, deeply furrowed, reddish brown bark, are Douglas fir; smaller trees, with ridged, somewhat scaly, gray-brown bark, are western hemlock. Douglas fir requires a disturbance such as a wildfire or windstorm to create openings in the forest before its seeds can germinate; this stand may have seeded in following wildfires that burned this area 300 to 500 years ago. Western hemlock can thrive in the shade of the older fir forest, and if left undisturbed, hemlock will eventually dominate the stand. Old-growth features such as standing dead trees, downed logs, and an open, multi-storied canopy can be seen throughout the forest. Because the Sol Duc swings west and drains to the Pacific, the valley draws moist coastal air. This results in a rain forest influence that is evident in the presence of Sitka spruce and nurse logs.

The Sol Duc River trail at the end of the Sol Duc Road explores miles of this valley forest. For an intimate glimpse of one of the Northwest's finest ancient forests, walk the first mile to Sol Duc Falls, or make a loop using the Lovers Lane trail.

The Marymere Falls and Moments in Time nature trails at Lake Crescent explore a stunning grove of ancient grand fir, Douglas fir, and western red cedar. Most of the peninsula's lowland stands containing old-growth grand fir were logged long ago. Less than 600 feet above sea level, the Barnes Point forest is among the few of its kind remaining. The bark of grand fir is grayer and less deeply textured than Douglas fir. Western red cedar's thin reddish bark is fibrous and somewhat stringy. The trails join and continue to picturesque Marymere Falls or extend into montane forests up Barnes Creek. In the vicinity of the Storm King Ranger Station, U.S. 101 passes through this forest, one of the few old-growth stands visible from the highway.

Farther east, the West Elwha trail follows the Elwha River downstream from Altaire campground through a mixed old-growth forest of Douglas fir and western hemlock. The Humes Ranch loop on the Elwha River trail passes beneath stately old Douglas firs and hemlocks. Some of the larger trees still bear signature blazes cut in 1889–90 by the Press party.

At Heart o' the Hills on the Hurricane Ridge Road, the Heart of the Forest trail passes through second growth and enters an old-growth forest a short distance in from the trailhead. The largest of the Douglas firs and red cedars here approach eight feet in diameter.

The first mile of the Dungeness River trail in Olympic National Forest traverses a handsome stand of old-growth Douglas fir growing on the narrow floodplain along the river. The bark of many of the trees growing in this rainshadow valley has been charred by frequent wildfires; growth beneath them is spare and the ground covered with moss.

At Staircase, in the far southeast corner of the park, rainfall is much more plentiful. The mile-long Shady Lane trail follows the Skokomish River beneath groves of bigleaf maples and through stunning stands of Douglas fir, western hemlock, and western red cedar. Many of the larger trees approach diameters of eight feet and exceed 250 feet in height. The nearby Staircase Rapids trail leads upriver through an equally impressive mixed forest of hemlock, cedar, and Douglas fir.

Rain Forests of the West-side Valleys

One of the loveliest walks through Olympic's temperate rain forest is along the Hall of Mosses nature trail at the Hoh visitor center. Starting in a lush riparian area alongside a spring-fed stream, the loop trail ascends a river terrace beneath massive, mossy Douglas firs, then meanders through a forest of large Sitka spruces and western hemlocks. The spruces have wide-spreading, buttressed, cylindrical trunks and gray scaly bark; some approach 300 feet in height. The forest floor is carpeted with oxalis, mosses, and ferns. The "Hall of Mosses" itself is an enchanting grove of bigleaf maples draped with hanging mats of selaginella clubmoss, mosses, and licorice ferns. Nurse logs, colonnades, and other signature characteristics of the temperate rain forest can be found along this gentle, three-quarter-mile-long trail.

The Quinault Loop trail, located on forest service land on the south shore of Quinault Lake, is a network of three trails. The loop trail traverses a grove of huge western red cedars as well as impressive Sitka spruces and western hemlocks. The Rain Forest nature trail that joins it ascends through the Big Tree Grove, a magnificent stand of six- to eight-foot-diameter Douglas firs that tower more than 275 feet in height. This stand may have seeded in on the ashes of massive fires that burned through the area around 1508.

Park roads up the Hoh and Quinault river valleys, and the main trails up the Bogachiel, Hoh, Queets, North Fork, and East Fork Quinault valleys also provide access to outstanding examples of temperate rain forest; they remain open year-round.

The Olympic Peninsula hosts several world record or near record-sized trees. Some are easy to see; some require extended hikes. The trips are always worthwhile. Outstanding specimens include the fourteen-foot-diameter and 212-foot-high "Queets Fir," located about two and a half miles up the Queets River trail. A record-sized Sitka spruce, eighteen feet in diameter and just under 200 feet in height, is found on the south shore of Quinault Lake in Olympic National Forest; an equally impressive giant is found on the South Fork Hoh trail. A champion western hemlock, measuring nine feet in diameter and 174 feet in height, is found up the East Fork Quinault trail, two miles past the Enchanted Valley chalet in the heart of the mountains. The record western red cedar, measuring more than twenty feet in diameter and 159 feet in height, stands on the north shore of Lake Quinault; a slightly smaller red cedar stands in the park near Kalaloch. The record subalpine fir and Alaska cedar are found in the interior mountains. Check with nearby ranger stations for locations, but bear in mind, large trees fall or lose their tops, and records often flit from state to state. It is the wholeness and complexity of the community that make Olympic's ancient forests so special, and that can be savored in any grove of old-growth forest on the peninsula.

WHERE TO SEE WILDLIFE

Mammals

Mammals thrive in every corner of Olympic National Park, from rocky shorelines to mountain meadows. Most are small, and some are active only at night. Even large mammals are often difficult to spot in the dense forests of the park. The best times for catching glimpses of Olympic's larger mammals are during the early hours of daylight and at dusk. Many animals retreat to forest shade and rest during the heat of the day.

Columbia blacktail deer are the most commonly encountered large mammals in the park, and visitors staying any length of time are almost sure to see them. Deer are often seen feeding along park roadsides and at the edges of forest clearings. Typically, does are seen with one or two young. Many deer summer in Big Meadow at Hurricane Ridge. Because of the large number of visitors to the ridge, these deer seem to have lost their fear of humans and sometimes approach quite closely. Remember it is unlawful, and ultimately harmful, to feed any wildlife in the park. Deer are also common at Deer Park and at most park campgrounds.

Roosevelt elk are a bit more elusive. They are frequently spotted in valley forests along the Hoh, Queets, or Quinault roads. Look for their blond rump patches among the trees. Bunch Field, just below the forks of the Quinault River, is an excellent spot for morning or evening viewing; and elk are often seen around the Hoh campground. All rain forest trails pass through prime elk habitat. Look for their large split tracks in wet spots, and watch for browsed ferns and shrubs.

Elk are also seen along the lower Elwha River in the park, especially at Anderson field and Humes Ranch along the Elwha trail. Roughly half of the park's elk migrate to the high meadows of the interior mountains in summer. Good places to watch for them are Heart Lake and High Divide above the Sol Duc valley, and Low Divide and Skyline Divide in the Quinault area. When rutting season begins in September, listen for the shrill calls of the bulls throughout the high country and in valley forests.

In summer, when mountain berries ripen, black bears also head to the high meadows to put on fat for their winter hibernations. Bears appear around Hurricane Hill in early summer some years, nibbling new plants and sampling the bark of subalpine firs. Later in the summer, look for them in the meadow country around Hayden and Anderson passes, the Marmot Lake area, Enchanted Valley, and Low Divide, as well as the high country around Seven Lakes Basin and Heart Lake.

Marmots also wake early in the season and can be seen from the Hurricane Hill trail. Look for them also at Obstruction Point. Subalpine meadows at Hurricane Ridge and Deer Park also support healthy populations of snowshoe hares and the endemic short-tailed weasels that hunt them. Another endemic subspecies, the Olympic chipmunk keeps busy around the forested edges of these meadows, and lots of smaller mammals scurry around beneath the brush.

Though cougar, bobcat, and coyote are known to hunt the high meadows as well as the lower forests, all are fairly reclusive and are seldom seen by visitors. River otters and raccoons, however, are quite common, especially along valley streams. Look for their five-toed tracks in the soft mud of stream banks, particularly along the coastal strip.

Sea Mammals

California gray whales often feed close to shore on their northern migrations in spring. Beginning in March and April, Cape Flattery, Cape Alava, La Push, Ruby Beach, and Kalaloch are good places to watch for them. A few whales sometimes linger in coastal waters or in the Strait of Juan de Fuca for the summer.

Harbor seals are abundant along the park's coastal strip any time of year. Look for them hauled out on offshore rocks at low tide or surfacing in offshore kelp beds. Harbor seals also haul out on the Dosewallips, Ducka-bush, and Hamma Hamma estuaries along Hood Canal, and at the end of Dungeness Spit in the strait. Seal pups—or any sea mammals—found along park beaches should be left alone; report such sightings to the near-est ranger station, or call the Olympic Coast National Marine Sanctuary at (360) 457-6622.

California and Steller's sea lions are a bit harder to see from shore. Look for them in early summer and fall on their haul-outs on Tatoosh Island off Cape Flattery and the Bodelteh Islands off Cape Alava. Sea otters love to float among kelp beds through much of the day, feeding actively in morn-ings and late afternoons. They are best seen from atop coastal headlands where nearby kelp beds are visible. Good viewing spots are at Cape Flat-tery, Cape Alava, Sand Point, and Cape Johnson. River otters are often confused with sea otters, especially when they are swimming in the surf. River otters are smaller than sea otters; unlike sea otters, they are quite agile on land, and they never float on their backs.

Birds

Marine birds and shorebirds can be seen anywhere along the park's coastal strip, as well as the Strait of Juan de Fuca and parts of Hood Canal. Shorebirds such as sandpipers, snipes, dunlins, and semipalmated plovers frequent sandy beaches at Shi Shi, Yellow Banks, Rialto Beach, and the beaches from Ruby Beach south to Kalaloch. Dungeness Spit National Wildlife Refuge near Sequim is also an excellent place for viewing shore-birds. Seabirds of the rocky shore, such as oystercatchers, cormorants, scoters, surfbirds, and murres can be seen by taking short hikes to Cape Flattery, Cape Alava, Cape Johnson, Second and Third beaches near La Push, and Hoh Head. Bald eagles and ospreys are seen almost anywhere along the park's coastal strip.

Beginning in late March and extending through April, one of the largest raptor migrations in North America occurs along the Olympic coast. Thousands of hawks—red-tailed, sharp-shinned, Cooper's, and goshawks, as well as kestrels, eagles, ospreys, turkey vultures, and other raptors—stream north on their spring migrations. At the northern tip of the peninsula, they ride the thermals above Cape Flattery, gaining the altitude needed to cross the strait to Vancouver Island. The summit of Bahokus Peak just west of Neah Bay on the Makah Indian Reservation is an excellent place to view this spectacle. On warm days during the peak of the migration, as many as 600 or more raptors may make the crossing.

More than 200 species of resident and migratory birds are found in Olympic National Park. Many inhabit a range of habitats over different seasons, and songbirds may be encountered anywhere in the park. In the forests of low and middle elevations birds are more often heard than seen, and many birders rely on songs for identification. During the breeding season, which begins in mid-April, most lowland forest trails and roadsides ring with bird songs.

Visitors to the Hoh, Queets, or Quinault rain forest can expect to encounter yellow warblers, chestnut-backed chickadees, and Vaux's swifts, among other birds. Winter wrens sing among the ferns and brush, and golden-crowned kinglets sweep through the canopy. Look for warblers, chickadees, and thrushes in the deciduous growth along rivers and streams.

In the drier Douglas fir and hemlock forests of the northern and eastern Olympics—the Elwha, Dungeness, Dosewallips, Duckabush, and Skokomish valleys—watch and listen for Townsend's warblers, evening grosbeaks, olive-sided flycatchers, and varied and Swainson's thrushes, as well as chickadees, warblers, northern flickers, and brown creepers.

Birds are less abundant in the cooler montane forests of higher elevations. In the silver fir and hemlock forests of the western slopes, look for varied thrushes, winter wrens, dark-eyed juncos, and both Steller's and gray jays. Subalpine fir forests of the eastern high country support breeding populations of olive-sided flycatchers, ruby-crowned kinglets, pine grosbeaks, and Townsend's solitaires as well as blue grouse.

The open alpine areas of the park are accessible along the road to Obstruction Point and by trails leaving from the Obstruction Point parking area as well as the Hurricane Hill trail. Alpine areas are breeding territories for horned larks, American pipits, and dark-eyed juncos. Rosy finches and occasional golden eagles may also be seen here. In late summer and fall, south-migrating raptors hunt the high meadows and ridges.

A final avian feast takes place in the high meadows each fall as huckleberries and mountain ash berries ripen. Band-tailed pigeons, robins, thrushes, and sparrows come in flocks to feed. As the first fall snows dust the high country and heavy rains dampen the lower forests, many of the park's songbirds begin their migrations south.

Plants and Animals of Olympic National Park

SELECTED WILDFLOWERS

❏ Common Yarrow	*Achillea millifolium*
❏ California Vanillaleaf	*Achlys californica*
❏ Trail Plant	*Adenocaulon bicolor*
❏ Pale Agoseris	*Agoseris glauca*
❏ Scalloped Onion	*Allium crenulatum*
❏ Nodding Onion	*Allium cernuum*
❏ Pearly-everlasting	*Anaphalis margaritacea*
❏ Pacific Anemone	*Anemone multifida*
❏ Western Pasqueflower	*Anemone occidentalis*
❏ Sitka Columbine	*Aquilegia formosa*
❏ Broad-leaf Arnica	*Arnica latifolia*
❏ Wild Ginger	*Asarum caudatum*
❏ Olympic Mountain Aster	*Aster paucicapitatus*
❏ Elkslip MarshMarigold	*Caltha leptosepala*
❏ Fairy Slipper	*Calypso bulbosa*
❏ Piper's Bellflower	*Campanula piperi*
❏ Bluebells-of-Scotland	*Campanula rotundifolia*
❏ Merten's Mountain-heather	*Cassiope mertensiana*
❏ Harsh Paintbrush	*Castilleja hispida*
❏ Magenta Paintbrush	*Castilleja parviflora*
❏ Common Pipsissewa	*Chimaphila umbellata*
❏ Indian Thistle	*Cirsium edule*

❏ Lance-leaved Springbeauty	*Claytonia lanceolata*
❏ Siberian Springbeauty	*Claytonia sibirica*
❏ Queen's Cup	*Clintonia uniflora*
❏ Unalaska Bunchberry	*Cornus unalaschkensis*
❏ Rockslide Larkspur	*Delphinium glareosum*
❏ Pale Larkspur	*Delphinium glaucum*
❏ Pacific Bleeding Heart	*Dicentra formosa*
❏ Jeffrey's Shooting Star	*Dodecatheon jeffreyi*
❏ Smooth Douglasia	*Douglasia laevigata*
❏ Elmera	*Elmera racemosa*
❏ Alpine Willow-herb	*Epilobium alpinum*
❏ Fireweed	*Epilobium angustifolium*
❏ Wandering Fleabane	*Erigeron peregrinus*
❏ Woolly Sunflower	*Eriophyllum lanatum*
❏ Western Wallflower	*Erysimum capitatum*
❏ Glacier Lily	*Erythronium grandiflorum*
❏ Avalanche Lily	*Erythronium montanum*
❏ Mission Bells	*Fritillaria lanceolata*
❏ Fragrant Bedstraw	*Galium triflorum*
❏ Old Man's Whiskers	*Geum triflorum*
❏ Cow Parsnip	*Heracleum lanatum*
❏ Columbia Lily	*Lilium columbianum*
❏ Twinflower	*Linnaea borealis*
❏ Fern-leaved Lomatium	*Lomatium dissectum*
❏ Martindale's Lomatium	*Lomatium martindalei*
❏ Orange Honeysuckle	*Lonicera ciliosa*
❏ Partridgefoot	*Luetkea pectinata*
❏ Broadleaf Lupine	*Lupinus latifolius*
❏ Lyall's Lupine	*Lupinus lyallii*
❏ Yellow Skunk Cabbage	*Lysichiton americanum*
❏ Beadruby	*Maianthemum dilatatum*
❏ Large False Solomon's Seal	*Maianthemum racemosum*
❏ Great Purple Monkey-flower	*Mimulus lewisii*
❏ Large Mountain Monkey-flower	*Mimulus tilingi*
❏ Woodnymph	*Moneses uniflora*
❏ Pinesap	*Monotropa hypopithys*
❏ Indian-pipe	*Monotropa uniflora*
❏ Mountain Owl-clover	*Orthocarpus imbricatus*
❏ Oregon Oxalis	*Oxalis oregana*

❏ Elephant's Head	*Pedicularis groenlandica*
❏ Sickletop Lousewort	*Pedicularis racemosa*
❏ Davidson's Penstemon	*Penstemon davidsonii*
❏ Small-flowered Penstemon	*Penstemon procerus*
❏ Olympic Rockmat	*Petrophytum hendersonii*
❏ Silky Phacelia	*Phacelia sericea*
❏ Spreading Phlox	*Phlox diffusa*
❏ Red Mountain-heather	*Phyllodoce empetriformis*
❏ Greater Butterwort	*Pinguicula macroceras*
❏ Dilated Bog Orchid	*Platanthera dilatata*
❏ Showy Polemonium	*Polemonium pulcherrimum*
❏ American Bistort	*Polygonum bistortoides*
❏ Fan-leaf Cinquefoil	*Potentilla flabellifolia*
❏ Self-heal	*Prunella vulgaris*
❏ Pinedrops	*Pterospora andromedea*
❏ Common Pink Pyrola	*Pyrola asarifolia*
❏ Eshscholtz's Buttercup	*Ranunculus eschscholtzii*
❏ Dwarf Bramble	*Rubus lasiococcus*
❏ Spotted Saxifrage	*Saxifraga bronchialis*
❏ Tufted Saxifrage	*Saxifraga cespitosa*
❏ Tisch's Saxifage	*Saxifraga tischii*
❏ Broad-leaved Sedum	*Sedum spathulifolium*
❏ Olympic Mountain Groundsel	*Senecio neowebsteri*
❏ Parry's Silene	*Silene parryi*
❏ Subalpine Spirea	*Spiraea densiflora*
❏ Clasping-leaved Twisted-stalk	*Streptopus amplexifolius*
❏ Fringecup	*Tellima grandiflora*
❏ Trefoil Foamflower	*Tiarella trifoliata*
❏ Youth-on-age	*Tolmiea memziesii*
❏ American Starflower	*Trientalis borealis*
❏ Large White Trillium	*Trillium ovatum*
❏ Sitka Valerian	*Valeriana sitchensis*
❏ Green False Hellebore	*Veratrum viride*
❏ Cusick's Speedwell	*Veronica cusickii*
❏ American Vetch	*Vicia americana*
❏ Hook Violet	*Viola adunca*
❏ Flett's Violet	*Viola flettii*
❏ Pioneer Violet	*Viola glabella*
❏ Beargrass	*Xerophyllum tenax*

SELECTED TREES

❏ Pacific Silver Fir	*Abies amabilis*
❏ Grand Fir	*Abies grandis*
❏ Subalpine Fir	*Abies lasiocarpa*
❏ Vine Maple	*Acer circinatum*
❏ Douglas Maple	*Acer glabrum douglasii*
❏ Bigleaf Maple	*Acer macrophyllum*
❏ Speckled Alder	*Alnus incana*
❏ Red Alder	*Alnus ruba*
❏ Sitka Alder	*Alnus sinuata*
❏ Pacific Madrona	*Arbutus memziesii*
❏ Alaska Yellow Cedar	*Chamaecyparis nootkatensis*
❏ Pacific Dogwood	*Cornus nuttallii*
❏ Douglas' Hawthorn	*Crataegus douglasii*
❏ Oregon Ash	*Fraxinus latifolia*
❏ Common Juniper	*Juniperus communis*
❏ Rocky Mountain Juniper	*Juniperus scopulorum*
❏ Western Crabapple	*Malus fusca*
❏ Engelmann Spruce	*Picea engelmanni*
❏ Sitka Spruce	*Picea sitchensis*
❏ Whitebark Pine	*Pinus albicaulis*
❏ Lodgepole Pine	*Pinus contorta*
❏ Quaking Aspen	*Populus tremuloides*
❏ Black Cottonwood	*Populus trichocarpa*
❏ Bitter Cherry	*Prunus emarginata*
❏ Common Chokecherry	*Prunus virginiana*
❏ Douglas Fir	*Pseudotsuga menziesii*
❏ Western Crabapple	*Pyrus fusca*
❏ Garry Oak	*Quercus garryana*
❏ Cascara Buckthorn	*Rhamnus purshiana*
❏ Pacific Willow	*Salix lasiandra*
❏ Pacific Yew	*Taxus brevifolia*
❏ Western Redcedar	*Thuja plicata*
❏ Western Hemlock	*Tsuga heterophylla*
❏ Mountain Hemlock	*Tsuga mertensiana*

SELECTED SHRUBS

❏ Western Serviceberry	*Amelanchier alnifolia*
❏ Bristly Manzanita	*Arctostaphylos columbiana*
❏ Kinnikinnick	*Arctostaphylos uva-ursi*
❏ Goatsbeard	*Aruncus dioicus*
❏ Oregon Grape	*Berberis nervosa*
❏ Redstem Ceanothus	*Ceanothus sanguineus*
❏ Creek Dogwood	*Cornus sericea*
❏ Salal	*Gaultheria shallon*
❏ Ocean-spray	*Holodiscus discolor*
❏ Black Twinberry	*Lonicera involucrata*
❏ Fool's Huckleberry	*Menziesia ferruginea*
❏ Indian Plum	*Oemleria cerasiformis*
❏ Devil's Club	*Opliopanax horridus*
❏ Pacific Ninebark	*Physocarpus capitatus*
❏ White Rhododendron	*Rhododendron albiflorum*
❏ Pacific Rhododendron	*Rhododendron macrophyllum*
❏ Swamp Gooseberry	*Ribes lacustre*
❏ Red-flowering Currant	*Ribes sanguineum*
❏ Baldhip Rose	*Rosa gymnocarpa*
❏ Nootka Rose	*Rosa nutkana*
❏ Western Blackcap	*Rubus leucodermis*
❏ Western Thimbleberry	*Rubus parviflorus*
❏ Salmonberry	*Rubus spectabilis*
❏ Hooker Willow	*Salix hookeriana*
❏ Scouler Willow	*Salix scouleriana*
❏ Sitka Willow	*Salix sitchensis*
❏ Blue Elderberry	*Sambucus cerulea*
❏ Coast Red Elderberry	*Sambucus racemosa*
❏ Sitka Mountain-ash	*Sorbus sitchensis*
❏ Douglas' Spirea	*Spiraea douglasii*
❏ Dwarf Huckleberry	*Vaccinium cespitosum*
❏ Blue-leaf Huckleberry	*Vaccinium deliciosum*
❏ Oval-leaf Huckleberry	*Vaccinium ovalifolium*
❏ Evergreen Huckleberry	*Vaccinium ovatum*
❏ Red Huckleberry	*Vaccinium parvifolium*

SELECTED FERNS

❏ Maidenhair Fern	*Adiantum pedatum*
❏ Lady Fern	*Athyrium filix-femina*
❏ Deer Fern	*Blechnum spicant*
❏ Spreading Wood Fern	*Dryopteris expansa*
❏ Western Oak Fern	*Gymnocarpium disjunctum*
❏ Licorice Fern	*Polypodium glycyrrhiza*
❏ Sword Fern	*Polystichum munitum*
❏ Bracken Fern	*Pteridium aquilinum*

MAMMALS

❏ Masked Shrew	*Sorex cinereus*
❏ Trowbridge Shrew	*Sorex trowbridgei*
❏ Vagrant Shrew	*Sorex vagrans*
❏ Montane Shrew	*Sorex monticolus*
❏ Pacific Marsh Shrew	*Sorex bendirii*
❏ Northern Water Shrew	*Sorex palustris*
❏ Shrew-mole	*Neurotrichus gibbsii*
❏ Townsend's Mole	*Scapanus townsendii*
❏ Olympic Snow Mole	*Scapanus townsendii olympicus*
❏ Coast Mole	*Scapanus orarius*
❏ Little Brown Myotis	*Myotis lucifugus*
❏ Yuma Myotis	*Myotis yumanensis*
❏ Keen's Myotis	*Myotis keenii*
❏ Long-eared Myotis	*Myotis evotis*
❏ California Myotis	*Myotis californicus*
❏ Long-legged Myotis	*Myotis volans*
❏ Fringed Myotis	*Myotis thysanodes*
❏ Big Brown Bat	*Eptesicus fuscus*
❏ Silver-haired Bat	*Lasionycteris noctivagans*
❏ Hoary Bat	*Lasirus cinereus*
❏ Townsend's Big-eared Bat	*Corynorhinus townsendi*
❏ Showshoe Hare	*Lepus americanus*
❏ Mountain Beaver	*Aplodontia rufa*
❏ Douglas Squirrel	*Tamiasciurus douglasii*
❏ Northern Flying Squirrel	*Glaucomys sabrinus*
❏ Townsend's Chipmunk	*Tamias townsendii*
❏ Olympic Chipmunk	*Tamias amoenus caurinus*

❏ Beaver	*Castor canadensis*
❏ Muskrat	*Ondatra zibethicus*
❏ Olympic Marmot	*Marmota olympus*
❏ Mazama Pocket Gopher	*Thomomys mazama melanops*
❏ Keen's Mouse	*Peromyscus keeni*
❏ Deer Mouse	*Peromyscus maniculatus*
❏ Bushy-tailed Woodrat	*Neotoma cinerea*
❏ Heather Vole	*Phenacomys intermedius*
❏ Southern Redback Vole	*Clethrionomys gapperi*
❏ Townsend Vole	*Microtus townsendii*
❏ Long-tailed Vole	*Microtus longicaudus*
❏ Oregon Vole	*Microtus oregoni*
❏ Pacific Jumping Mouse	*Zapus trinotatus*
❏ Coyote	*Canis latrans*
❏ Wolf	*Canis lupus*
❏ Red Fox	*Vulpes fulva*
❏ Black Bear	*Ursus americanus*
❏ Raccoon	*Procyon lotor*
❏ Marten	*Martes americana*
❏ Fisher	*Martes pennanti*
❏ Short-tailed Weasel	*Mustela erminea olympica*
❏ Long-tailed Weasel	*Mustela frenata*
❏ Mink	*Mustela vison*
❏ River Otter	*Lutra canadensis*
❏ Spotted Skunk	*Spilogale putorius*
❏ Striped Skunk	*Mephitis mephitis*
❏ Cougar	*Puma concolor*
❏ Bobcat	*Lynx rufus*
❏ Roosevelt Elk	*Cervus elaphus roosevelti*
❏ Columbia Blacktail Deer	*Odocoileus hemionus columbianus*
❏ Mountain Goat	*Oreamnos americanus*

SELECTED MARINE MAMMALS (NEARSHORE)

❏ Sea Otter	*Enhydra lutris*
❏ Harbor Seal	*Phoca vitulina*
❏ Steller's Sea Lion	*Eumetopias jubatus*
❏ California Sea Lion	*Zaiophus californianus*
❏ Northern Elephant Seal	*Mirounga angustirostris*

❏ Northern Fur Seal	*Callorhinus ursinus*
❏ Gray Whale	*Eschrichtius robustus*
❏ Minke Whale	*Balaenoptera acutorostrata*
❏ Humpback Whale	*Megaptera novaeangliae*
❏ Harbor Porpoise	*Phocoena phocoena*
❏ Orca or Killer Whale	*Orcinus orca*
❏ Dall's Porpoise	*Phocoenoides dalli*
❏ Pacific White-sided Dolphin	*Lagenorhynchus obliquidens*

SELECTED BIRDS

❏ Red-throated Loon
❏ Pacific Loon
❏ Common Loon
❏ Pied-billed Grebe
❏ Horned Grebe
❏ Red-necked Grebe
❏ Eared Grebe
❏ Western Grebe
❏ Brown Pelican
❏ Double-crested Cormorant
❏ Brandt's Cormorant
❏ Pelagic Cormorant
❏ Black-footed Albatross
❏ Northern Fulmar
❏ Pink-footed Shearwater
❏ Flesh-footed Shearwater
❏ Sooty Shearwater
❏ Fork-tailed Storm-petrel
❏ Leach's Storm-petrel
❏ American Bittern
❏ Great Blue Heron
❏ Great Egret
❏ Tundra Swan
❏ Trumpeter Swan
❏ Greater White-fronted Goose
❏ Brant
❏ Canada Goose
❏ Wood Duck
❏ Green-winged Teal

❏ Mallard
❏ Northern Pintail
❏ Blue-winged Teal
❏ Cinnamon Teal
❏ Northern Shoveler
❏ Gadwall
❏ American Wigeon
❏ Eurasian Wigeon
❏ Canvasback
❏ Ring-necked Duck
❏ Greater Scaup
❏ Lesser Scaup
❏ Harlequin Duck
❏ Oldsquaw
❏ Black Scoter
❏ Surf Scoter
❏ White-winged Scoter
❏ Common Goldeneye
❏ Barrow's Goldeneye
❏ Bufflehead
❏ Hooded Merganser
❏ Common Merganser
❏ Red-breasted Merganser
❏ Ruddy Duck
❏ Turkey Vulture
❏ Osprey
❏ Northern Harrier
❏ Sharp-shinned Hawk
❏ Cooper's Hawk

❏ Northern Goshawk
❏ Red-tailed Hawk
❏ Golden Eagle
❏ Bald Eagle
❏ American Kestrel
❏ Merlin
❏ Peregrine Falcon
❏ Gyrfalcon
❏ Ring-necked Pheasant
❏ Blue Grouse
❏ Ruffed Grouse
❏ California Quail
❏ Virginia Rail
❏ Sora
❏ American Coot
❏ Black-bellied Plover
❏ American Golden-Plover
❏ Pacific Golden-Plover
❏ Semipalmated Plover
❏ Killdeer
❏ Black Oystercatcher
❏ Greater Yellowlegs
❏ Lesser Yellowlegs
❏ Willet
❏ Spotted Sandpiper
❏ Whimbrel
❏ Long-billed Curlew
❏ Marbled Godwit
❏ Ruddy Turnstone
❏ Black Turnstone
❏ Surfbird
❏ Red Knot
❏ Sanderling
❏ Western Sandpiper
❏ Least Sandpiper
❏ Rock Sandpiper
❏ Dunlin
❏ Short-billed Dowitcher
❏ Long-billed Dowitcher
❏ Common Snipe

❏ Red-necked Phalarope
❏ Red Phalarope
❏ Bonaparte's Gull
❏ Heermann's Gull
❏ Mew Gull
❏ Ring-billed Gull
❏ California Gull
❏ Thayer's Gull
❏ Western Gull
❏ Glaucous-winged Gull
❏ Black-legged Kittiwake
❏ Caspian Tern
❏ Common Murre
❏ Pigeon Guillemot
❏ Marbled Murrelet
❏ Ancient Murrelet
❏ Cassin's Auklet
❏ Rhinoceros Auklet
❏ Tufted Puffin
❏ Band-tailed Pigeon
❏ Mourning Dove
❏ Rock Dove
❏ Common Barn Owl
❏ Western Screech-Owl
❏ Great Horned Owl
❏ Snowy Owl
❏ Northern Pygmy-Owl
❏ Spotted Owl
❏ Barred Owl
❏ Short-eared Owl
❏ Northern Saw-whet Owl
❏ Common Nighthawk
❏ Black Swift
❏ Vaux's Swift
❏ Anna's Hummingbird
❏ Rufous Hummingbird
❏ Belted Kingfisher
❏ Red-breasted Sapsucker
❏ Downy Woodpecker
❏ Hairy Woodpecker

❏ Northern Flicker
❏ Pileated Woodpecker
❏ Olive-sided Flycatcher
❏ Western Wood-Pewee
❏ Willow Flycatcher
❏ Hammond's Flycatcher
❏ Pacific-slope Flycatcher
❏ Horned Lark
❏ Purple Martin
❏ Tree Swallow
❏ Violet-green Swallow
❏ Cliff Swallow
❏ Barn Swallow
❏ Gray Jay
❏ Steller's Jay
❏ Clark's Nutcracker
❏ American Crow
❏ Common Raven
❏ Black-capped Chickadee
❏ Chestnut-backed Chickadee
❏ Bushtit
❏ Red-breasted Nuthatch
❏ Brown Creeper
❏ Bewick's Wren
❏ House Wren
❏ Winter Wren
❏ Marsh Wren
❏ American Dipper
❏ Golden-crowned Kinglet
❏ Ruby-crowned Kinglet
❏ Townsend's Solitaire
❏ Swainson's Thrush
❏ Hermit Thrush
❏ American Robin
❏ Varied Thrush
❏ American Pipit
❏ Cedar Waxwing

❏ Northern Shrike
❏ European Starling
❏ Hutton's Vireo
❏ Warbling Vireo
❏ Orange-crowned Warbler
❏ Yellow Warbler
❏ Yellow-rumped Warbler
❏ Black-throated Gray Warbler
❏ Townsend's Warbler
❏ Hermit Warbler
❏ MacGillivray's Warbler
❏ Common Yellowthroat
❏ Wilson's Warbler
❏ Western Tanager
❏ Black-headed Grosbeak
❏ Spottted Towhee
❏ Savannah Sparrow
❏ Fox Sparrow
❏ Song Sparrow
❏ Lincoln's Sparrow
❏ Golden-crowned Sparrow
❏ White-crowned Sparrow
❏ Dark-eyed Junco
❏ Red-winged Blackbird
❏ Western Meadowlark
❏ Brewer's Blackbird
❏ Brown-headed Cowbird
❏ Gray-crowned Rosy Finch
❏ Pine Grosbeak
❏ Purple Finch
❏ House Finch
❏ Red Crossbill
❏ White-winged Crossbill
❏ Pine Siskin
❏ American Goldfinch
❏ Evening Grosbeak
❏ House Sparrow

AMPHIBIANS AND REPTILES

- Northwestern Salamander — *Ambystoma gracile*
- Long-toed Salamander — *Ambystoma macrodactylum*
- Olympic Torrent Salamander — *Rhyacotriton olympicus*
- Cope's Giant Salamander — *Dicamptodon copei*
- Rough-skinned Newt — *Taricha granulosa*
- Ensatina Salamander — *Ensatina eschscholtzi*
- Western Red-backed Salamander — *Plethodon vehiculum*
- Van Dyke's Salamander — *Plethodon vandykei*
- Western Toad — *Bufo boreas*
- Tailed Frog — *Ascaphus truei*
- Red-legged Frog — *Rana aurora*
- Pacific Tree Frog — *Pseudacris regilla*
- Bullfrog — *Rana catesbeiana*
- Cascades Frog — *Rana cascadae*
- Northern Alligator Lizard — *Elgaria coerulea*
- Rubber Boa — *Charina bottae*
- Common Garter Snake — *Thamnophis sirtalis*
- Northwestern Garter Snake — *Thamnophis ordinoides*

SELECTED FISH

- Chinook Salmon — *Oncorynchus tshawytscha*
- Coho Salmon — *Oncorynchus kisutch*
- Sockeye Salmon — *Oncorynchus nerka*
- Chum Salmon — *Oncorynchus keta*
- Pink Salmon — *Oncorynchus gorbuscha*
- Rainbow Trout or Steelhead — *Oncorynchus mykiss*
- Cutthroat Trout — *Oncorynchus clarki*
- Dolly Varden — *Salvelinus malma*
- Bull Trout — *Salvelinus confluentus*
- Brook Trout — *Salvelinus fontinalis*
- Pacific Lamprey — *Entosphenus tridentatus*
- River Lamprey — *Lampetra ayresi*
- Mountain Whitefish — *Prosopium williamsoni*
- Pygmy Whitefish — *Prosopium coulteri*
- Longfin Smelt — *Spirinchus thaleichthys*
- Surf Smelt — *Hypomesus pretiosus*
- Olympic Mudminnow — *Novumbra hubbsi*

❏ Northern Pikeminnow	*Ptychocheilus oregonensis*
❏ Pacific Staghorn Sculpin	*Leptocottus armatus*
❏ Torrent Sculpin	*Cottus rhotheus*
❏ Prickly Sculpin	*Cottus asper*
❏ Threespine Stickleback	*Gasterosteus aculeatus*
❏ Starry Flounder	*Platichthys stellatus*
❏ Pacific Sand Lance	*Ammodytes hexapterus*

SELECTED INTERTIDAL PLANTS

❏ Winged Kelp	*Alaria marginata*
❏ Coral Leaf & Branching Coralline Algae	*Bossiella & Callarthron* sp.
❏ Graceful Coral Coralline	*Corallina vancouveriensis*
❏ Flat Kelp	*Desmarestia ligulata*
❏ Feather Boa Kelp	*Egregia menziesii*
❏ Sea Moss	*Endocladia muricata*
❏ Rockweed	*Fucus gardneri*
❏ Rough Strap	*Gigartina harveyana*
❏ Sea Sac	*Halosaccion glandiforme*
❏ Sea Cabbage	*Hedophyllum sessile*
❏ Split Kelp	*Laminaria setchellii*
❏ Sugar Kelp	*Laminaria saccharina*
❏ Sea Cauliflower	*Leathesia difformis*
❏ Encrusting Coralline Algae	*Lithothamniun* sp.
❏ Perennial Kelp	*Macrocystis integrifolia*
❏ Iridescent seaweed	*Mazzaella splendens*
❏ Bull Kelp	*Nereocystis luetkeana*
❏ Surfgrass	*Phyllospadix scouleri*
❏ Red Laver (Dulse)	*Porphyra* sp.
❏ Sea Palm	*Postelsia palmaeformis*
❏ Broad Iodine Seaweed	*Prionitis lyallii*
❏ Black Pine Seaweed	*Rhodomela larix*
❏ Sea Lettuce	*Ulva* sp.
❏ Eelgrass	*Zostera marina*

SELECTED INTERTIDAL ANIMALS

❏ White Cap Limpets	*Acmaea mitra*
❏ Ostrich Plume Hydroid	*Aglaophenia* sp.

❏ Black and White Brittle Sea Star	*Amphipholis pugetana*
❏ Dwarf Brittle Sea Star	*Amphipholis squamata*
❏ Aggregating Sea Anemone	*Anthopleura elegantissima*
❏ Giant Green Sea Anemone	*Anthopleura xanthogrammica*
❏ Opossum Shrimp	*Archaeomysis grebnitzkii*
❏ Cup Coral	*Balanophyllia elegans*
❏ Thatched Barnacle	*Semibalanus cariosus*
❏ Common Acorn Barnacle	*Balanus glandula*
❏ Giant Acorn Barnacles	*Balanus nubilis*
❏ Yellow-edged Nudibranch	*Cadlina luteomarginata*
❏ Ghost Shrimp	*Callianassa californiensis*
❏ Blue Topsnail	*Calliostoma ligatum*
❏ Dungeness Crab	*Cancer magister*
❏ Red Rock Crab	*Cancer productus*
❏ Small Acorn Barnacle	*Chthamalus dalli*
❏ Water-line Isopod	*Cirolana kincaidi*
❏ Nuttall's Cockle Clam	*Clinocardium nuttallii*
❏ Ribbed Limpet	*Collisella digitalis*
❏ Shield Limpet	*Collisella pelta*
❏ Gum Boot Chiton	*Cryptochiton stelleri*
❏ Sand Dollar	*Dendraster excentricus*
❏ Keyhole Limpet	*Diodora aspera*
❏ Brooding Sea Anemone	*Epiactis prolifera*
❏ Feather Duster Worm	*Eudistylia vancouveri*
❏ White Sea Cucumber	*Eupentacta quinquesemita*
❏ Mottled Sea Star	*Evasterias troschelli*
❏ Hairy Crab	*Hapalogaster mertensii*
❏ Purple Shore Crab	*Hemigrapsus nudus*
❏ Green Shore Crab	*Hemigrapsus oregonensis*
❏ Blood Sea Star	*Henricia leviuscula*
❏ Opalescent Nudibranch	*Hermissenda crassicornis*
❏ Black Chiton	*Katharina tunicata*
❏ Pelagic Goose Barnacle	*Lepas anatifera*
❏ Six-rayed Sea Star	*Leptasterias hexactis*
❏ Pearly Topsnail	*Lirularia lirulata*
❏ Checkered Periwinkle	*Littorina scutulata*
❏ Sitka Periwinkle	*Littorina sitkana*
❏ Vermilion Sea Star	*Mediaster aequalis*
❏ California Beach Hopper	*Megalorchestia californiana*
❏ Hairy Chiton	*Mopalia lignosa*

❑ Mossy Chiton	*Mopalia muscosa*
❑ California Mussel	*Mytilus californianus*
❑ Pacific Blue Mussel	*Mytilus trossulus*
❑ Speckled Limpet	*Notoacmea persona*
❑ Purple Olive Snail	*Olivella biplicata*
❑ Daisy Brittle Sea Star	*Ophiopholis aculeata*
❑ Small Beach Hopper	*Orchestia traskiana*
❑ Decorator Crab	*Oregonia gracilis*
❑ Granular Hermit Crab	*Pagurus granosimanus*
❑ Hairy Hermit Crab	*Pagurus hirsutiusculus*
❑ California Sea Cucumber	*Parastichopus californicus*
❑ Piddock Clam	*Penitella penita*
❑ Green Sea Slug	*Phyllaplysia taylori*
❑ Encrusting Sponge	Phylum *Porifera*
❑ Purple or Ochre Sea Star	*Pisaster ochraceus*
❑ Lewis's Moon Snail	*Polinices lewisii*
❑ Gooseneck Barnacle	*Pollicipes polymerus*
❑ Pacific Littleneck Clam	*Protothaca staminea*
❑ Armored Sea Cucumber	*Psolus chitonoides*
❑ Graceful Kelp Crab	*Pugettia gracilis*
❑ Kelp Crab	*Pugettia producta*
❑ Sunflower Sea Star	*Pycnopodia helianthoides*
❑ Butter Clam	*Saxidomus gigantea*
❑ Spindle Whelk	*Searlesia dira*
❑ Calcareous Tube Worm	*Serpula vermicularis*
❑ Pacific Razor Clam	*Siliqua patula*
❑ Sun Sea Star	*Solaster stimpsoni*
❑ Green Sea Urchin	*Strongylocentrotus droebachiensis*
❑ Red Sea Urchin	*Strongylocentrotus franciscanus*
❑ Purple Sea Urchin	*Strongylocentrotus purpuratus*
❑ Brown Turban Snail	*Tegula brunnea*
❑ Black Turban Snail	*Tegula funebralis*
❑ Helmet Crab	*Telmessus cheiragonus*
❑ Channeled Whelk	*Thais canaliculata*
❑ Wrinkled Whelk	*Thais lamellosa*
❑ Lined Chiton	*Tonicella lineata*
❑ Horse Clam	*Tresus capax*
❑ Orange-spotted Nudibranch	*Triopha carpenteri*
❑ Painted or Red & Green Sea Anemone	*Urticina crassiocornis*

Notes

1 SHUFFLED TEXTS OF STONE

The best guide to the geology of the Olympic Mountains is Rowland Tabor's
Guide to the Geology of Olympic National Park (1988). A good overall
guide to Pacific Northwest geology is Hill Williams's *The Restless Northwest*
(2002). Bates McKee's *Cascadia* (1972) is also useful. A detailed geological
map of the Olympics is available from the U.S. Geological Survey (1978).

History of the geological exploration of the Olympics: C. E. Weaver, *Tertiary
Stratigraphy of Western Washington and Northwestern Oregon*, vol. 4
of Publications in Geology (Seattle: University of Washington, 1937); and
Tabor, *Guide to the Geology*, 1987.

Deposition of sedimentary rocks and geological processes: John S. Shelton,
Geology Illustrated, 1966.

Origin of Olympic rocks: Paul Heller et al., "Isotopic Provenance of Paleogene
Sandstones from the Accretionary Core of the Olympic Mountains, Washington," *Geological Society of America Bulletin* 104 (1992).

Deposition by a single river: William S. Lingly, "Preliminary Observations on
Marine Stratigraphic Sequences, Central and Western Olympic Peninsula,
Washington," *Washington Geology* 23, no. 2 (1995).

Plate tectonics revolution: McPhee, *Basin and Range*, 1981.

Basalt formation, basin and range expansion, and subduction: Mark Bran-
don and A. Calderwood, "High-Pressure Metamorphism and Uplift of the
Olympic Subduction Complex," *Geology* 18 (1990); also Mark Brandon and
J. Vance, "Tectonic Evolution of the Cenozoic Olympic Subduction Complex,

Washington State, as Deducted from Fission Track Ages for Detrital Zircons," *American Journal of Science* 292 (1992).

Farallon and Kula plates: R. S. Babcock, C. A. Suczek, and D. C. Engebretson, "The Crescent 'Terrane,' Olympic Peninsula, and Southern Vancouver Island," in *Regional Geology of Washington State*, ed. R. Lasmani and E. Cheny (Olympia: Washington State Department of Natural Resources, 1994).

Accretion of Northwest terranes: Yorath, *Where Terranes Collide*, 1990.

New dates for core rocks: Brandon and Vance, "Tectonic Evolution," 1992.

Pre–Ice Age erosion: Tabor, *Guide to the Geology*, 1988, and Shelton, *Geology Illustrated*, 1966.

Geologic structure of the Olympics: Tabor and Cady, *Geological Map*, 1978.

Rate of subduction: Williams, *The Restless Northwest*, 2002.

Continued uplift: Brandon and Calderwood, "High-Pressure Metamorphism," 1990.

Subduction earthquakes: Atwater and Hemphill-Haley, "Recurrence Intervals," 1997.

Geology along the Hurricane Ridge Road: R. W. Tabor, "A Tertiary Accreted Terrane: Oceanic Basalt and Sedimentary Rocks in the Olympic Mountains, Washington," in *Geological Society of America Centennial Field Guide*, vol. 1 (Boulder, Colo.: Geological Society of America, 1987).

2 LEGACIES OF ICE

Formation of glaciers: Shelton, *Geology Illustrated*, 1966.

Dynamics of glaciers: Sharp, *Glaciers*, 1960.

Origins of ice ages: Skinner and Porter, *The Dynamic Earth*, 1989.

Statistics on Olympic Glaciers: Richard C. Spicer, "Glaciers in the Olympic Mountains, Washington: Present Distribution and Recent Variations" (master's thesis, University of Washington, 1986).

Glacier carving of the Olympics: Tabor, *Guide to the Geology*, 1987, and Burns, *The Shape of Puget Sound*, 1985.

Glacier evidence in sea cliffs: Linda Florer, "Quaternary Paleoecology and Stratigraphy of the Sea Cliffs, Western Olympic Peninsula, Washington," *Quaternary Research* 2 (1972).

Continental glaciers in Puget Sound and the Strait of Juan de Fuca: Kruckeberg, *Natural History*, 1991; Williams, *The Restless Northwest*, 2002; Easterbrook, "Chronology of Pre-Late Wisconsin Pleistocene Sediments,"

1994; also Don J. Easterbrook, "Stratigraphy and Chronology of Quaternary Deposits of the Puget Lowland and Olympic Mountains of Washington and Cascade Mountains of Washington and Oregon," *Quaternary Science Reviews* 5 (1986).

Manis Mastodon site: Bergland and Marr, *Prehistoric Life*, 1988.

Paleobotany of the Olympics: Whitlock, "Vegetational and Climatic History," 1992; also Cathy W. Baronsky, P. M. Anderson, and P. J. Bartlein, "The Northwestern U.S. during Deglaciation: Vegetational History and Paleoclimatic Implications," in *The Geology of North America*, vol. K-3, *North America and Adjacent Oceans during the Last Glaciation* (Boulder, Colo.: Geological Society of America, 1987).

Olympics as Ice Age refuge for plants: Nelsa Buckingham, "The Uniqueness of the Olympics" (unpublished manuscript, Olympic National Park); Buckingham et al., *Flora of the Olympic Peninsula*, 1995; also Nelsa Buckingham and Ed Schreiner, personal communications, 1994.

Forests and return of salmon to Olympic Rivers: Lichatowich, *Salmon Without Rivers*, 1999.

Ice Age effects on Olympic fauna: Houston, Moorhead, and Schreiner, *Mountain Goats*, 1994.

Global warming projections: Alley et al., *Intergovernmental Panel Summary Report*, 2007.

Little Ice Age: Henderson et al., *Forested Plant Associations*, 1989; also Fagan, *The Little Ice Age*, 2000.

History of Blue Glacier: Calvin Heusser, "Variations of Blue, Hoh, and White Glaciers during Recent Centuries," *Arctic* 10 (1957); also Calvin Heusser, "Quaternary Vegetation, Climate, and Glaciation of the Hoh River Valley, Washington," *Geological Society of America Bulletin* 85 (1974).

Recent behavior of Blue Glacier: Richard Spicer, "Recent Variations of Blue Glacier, Olympic Mountains, Washington, U.S.A.," *Arctic and Alpine Research* 21, no. 1 (1989) ; and "University of Washington Research on Blue Glacier, Olympic National Park, Washington, U.S.A.," www.geophys.washington.edu/Surface/Glaciology/projects/blue_glac/blue.htm, 2005.

Current mass wasting studies on Blue Glacier: Howard Conway, University of Washington, personal communication, 2005.

Mass wasting of South Cascade Glacier: *Seattle Post-Intelligencer*, "Our Warming World," November 13, 2003

Impacts of global warming: Alley et al., United Nations Intergovernmental Panel, 2007.

Impacts of global warming in the Northwest: University of Washington Climate
    Impacts Group, "Northwest Climate Study," 2005 (*Seattle Times*, October
    18, 2005); also Philip Mote, University of Washington, personal communica-
    tion, 2005.
"This isn't an ideological debate . . .": Gore, *An Inconvenient Truth*, 2006.
Endemic species list: U.S. Department of the Interior, National Park Service,
    Draft General Management Plan, 2006; Houston et al., *Mountain Goats
    in Olympic National Park*, 1994; also Steve Acker, Olympic National Park,
    personal communication, 2007.

3 THE HIGH COUNTRY YEAR

An excellent and informative field guide to the Olympic's subalpine areas as well
    as its lowland forest communities is Daniel Matthews's *Cascade-Olympic
    Natural History* (1999). A fascinating comparison of Olympic's alpine areas
    with others in North America is Ann Zwinger and Beatrice Willard's *Land
    Above the Trees* (1972).
Ecology of subalpine forests: Arno and Hammerly, *Northwest Trees*, 1977;
    Henderson et al., *Forested Plant Associations*, 1989; Fonda and Bliss, "For-
    est Vegetation," 1969; and R. W. Fonda, "Ecology of Alpine Timberline in
    Olympic National Park," Proceedings, Conference on Scientific Research in
    National Parks, vol. 1, National Park Service, 1976.
Subalpine tree advancement into meadows: Andrea Woodward, University of
    Washington, personal communications, 1994, 2005.
Climate change as indicated by subalpine forests: Andrea Woodward, Michael
    Gracz, and Edward Schreiner, "Climatic Effects on Establishment of Subal-
    pine Firs (*Abies lasiocarpa*) in Meadows of the Olympic Mountains," *North-
    west Environmental Journal* 7, no. 2 (1991).
Alpine and subalpine wildflowers: Charles Stewart, *Wildflowers of the Olym-
    pics and Cascades*, 1988.
Subalpine plant communities: Kuramoto and Bliss, "Ecology of Subalpine
    Meadows," 1970.
Alpine meadow communities: Zwinger and Willard, *Land Above the Trees*,
    1972; and L. Bliss, "Alpine Community Patterns in Relation to Environmen-
    tal Parameters," in *Essays in Plant Geography and Ecology*, ed. K Green-
    ridge (Halifax: Nova Scotia Museum, 1969).
Cryptobiotic crusts: W. G. Gold, K. A. Glew, and L. G. Dickson, "Functional
    Influences of Cryptobiotic Surface Crusts in an Alpine Tundra Basin of the

Olympic Mountains, Washington, U.S.A.," forthcoming, *Northwest Science.*

Ecology and behavior of the Olympic marmot: David Barash, "The Behavior of the Olympic Marmot" (master's thesis, University of Wisconsin, Madison, 1967); David Barash, "The Social Biology of the Olympic Marmot" (PhD diss., University of Wisconsin, Madison, 1970); Roger del Moral, "The Impact of the Olympic Marmot," 1984; and William Wood, "Habitat Selection and Energetics of the Olympic Marmot" (master's thesis, Western Washington State College, 1973).

Current status of the Olympic Marmot: "Demography and Movement of Olympic Marmots," U.S. Department of the Interior, National Park Service, Investigator's Annual Report(s), 2004–2006; also Suzanne Cox Griffin, University of Montana, personal communications, 2005, 2006, 2008; and Bruce Moorhead, "The Status and Conservation Biology of the Olympic Marmot," part 1, *Voice of the Wild Olympics* 14, no. 2 (Summer 2006).

Small mammals of alpine and subalpine areas: James Kenagy, Burke Museum, University of Washington, personal communication, 2007; also James Reichel, "Ecology of Pacific Northwest Alpine Mammals" (PhD diss., Washington State University, 1984); and Larrison and Fisher, *Mammals of the Northwest*, 1976.

Mammals common in the Cascades but historically missing from the Olympics: Scheffer, *Mammals of the Olympic Peninsula*, 1995; and Dalquest, *Mammals of Washington*, 1948.

Mountain goats: U.S. Department of the Interior, National Park Service, *Goats in Olympic National Park: Draft Environmental Impact Statement for Mountain Goat Management within Olympic National Park*, Port Angeles, Wash., 1995.

Mountain goat effects on Olympic plant communities: U.S. Department of the Interior, National Park Service, *Mountain Goat Management*, 1995.

Review of mountain goat research by independent scientific panel: Noss et al., "Review of Scientific Material," 2000.

Mountain goat census 2004: P. J. Happe et al., "Mountain Goat Census in the Olympic Mountain Range, July 2004," Report to the Superintendent of Olympic National Park (unpublished report, October 2004).

Mountain goat status in Washington: Jim Downing, "Survey Assesses Elusive Goats," *Seattle Times*, July 24, 2004.

Black bears: Kim Sager, U.S. Geological Service, Olympic Field Station, personal communication, 2007; also Maser, *Mammals of the Pacific Northwest*, 1998.

4 THE RAIN FOREST

An extensive treatment of the ecology of the Olympic rain forest is Ruth Kirk
    and Jerry Franklin's *Olympic Rain Forest* (1992). A handy field guide to
    rain forest trees and shrubs is C. P. Lyons and Bill Merilees's *Trees, Shrubs
    and Flowers* (1995). An essential companion in the rain forest is Martin and
    Karen Hutten and Andrea Woodward's pocket guide *101 Common Mosses,
    Liverworts and Lichens of the Olympic Peninsula.*

Factors leading to the rain forest's development: Kirk and Franklin, *Olympic
    Rain Forest,* 1992.

Sitka spruce–western hemlock forest type: Franklin and Dyrness, *Natural Veg-
    etation of Oregon and Washington,* 1973.

Natural history of rain forest trees: Arno and Hammerly, *Northwest Trees,*
    1977; also Matthews, *Cascade-Olympic Natural History,* 1999.

River geomorphology in the rain forest: Lynda Mapes, "A River Reigns through
    It," *Seattle Times,* January 30, 2005; also Jim O'Connor, M. Jones, and T.
    Haluska, "Flood Plain and Channel Dynamics of the Quinault and Queets
    Rivers, Washington, USA," *Geomorphology* 51 (2003).

River terrace communities: Fonda, "Forest Succession," 1974.

Ecological function of downed logs in forests: Maser et al., *From the Forest to
    the Sea,* 1988.

Nurse logs: Kirk and Franklin, *Olympic Rain Forest,* 1992.

Nitrogen in rain forest soils: "200-Year Experiment Changes Face of Forest
    Management," Oregon State University *Science Daily,* August 21, 2005.

Rain forest mosses: Hutten, Hutten, and Woodward, *101 Common Mosses,
    Liverworts and Lichens.*

Canopy ecology: Bruce McCune, "Eradiants in Epiphyte Biomass in Three
    Pseudotsuga-Tsuga Forests of Different Ages in Oregon and Washington,"
    Brycologist 96, no. 3 (1993); also Osborne and Davis, *Rainforest,* 1998.

Rain forest trees rooting into epiphyte mats: Nadkarni, "Roots That Go Out on
    a Limb," 1985.

Elk in the Olympics: Patti Happe, Olympic National Park, and Kurt Jenkins,
    U.S. Geological Survey, personal communications, 2006; Moorhead, *The
    Forest Elk,* 1994; also Houston, Schreiner, and Moorhead, "Elk in Olympic
    National Park," 1990.

Elk–rain forest interactions: Jenkins and Starkey, "Habitat Use by Roosevelt
    Elk," 1984; also A. Woodward, E. G. Schreiner, D. B. Houston, and B. B.
    Moorhead, "Ungulate-Forest Relationships in Olympic National Park: Retro-
    spective Exclosure Studies," *Northwest Science* 68, no. 2 (1994).

History of elk management in the Olympics: Jenkins and Starkey, "Habitat Use by Roosevelt Elk," 1984.

Elk in the east side valleys: Gregory L. Schroer, "Seasonal Movements and Distribution of Migratory Roosevelt Elk in the Olympic Mountains" (masters thesis, Oregon State University, Corvallis, 1986).

Elk status outside Olympic National Park: M. E. Ferry, T. S. Peterson, and J. C. Calhoun, "Status of Elk Populations on the Olympic Peninsula," Olympic Natural Resources Center Conference Proceedings, University of Washington, Forks, 2001.

Cougars: Hornocker, "Learning to Live with Mountain Lions," 1992; also Ewing, *Shadow Cat*, 1998.

Cougar attacks on humans: "Mountain Lion Attacks on People in the U.S. and Canada Statistics from Others," http://tchester.org/sgm/lists/lion_attacks_statistics.html, 2003.

Other mammals: Scheffer, *Mammals of the Olympic Peninsula*, 1995.

Wolves in the Olympics: Peter Dratch et al., "A Case Study for Species Reintroduction: The Wolf in Olympic National Park" (unpublished report for The Evergreen State College, Olympia, Washington, 1975); also L. David Mech, "The Challenge and Opportunity of Recovering Wolf Populations," *Conservation Biology* 9, no. 2 (April 1995).

Wolf restoration and ecosystem recovery in Yellowstone: McNamee, *The Return of the Wolf*, 1997; also Smith and Ferguson, *Decade of the Wolf*, 2005.

Wolf recovery in Olympic: U.S. Fish and Wildlife Service, *Feasibility Study on the Reintroduction of Gray Wolves*, 1999; also McNulty, "Olympic Park's Missing Predator," 1997.

5 THE OLD-GROWTH FOREST COMMUNITY

The most comprehensive book for the general reader on the ecology of old-growth forests in the Northwest is Elliot Norse's *Ancient Forests of the Pacific Northwest* (1990). An excellent overview of ancient forests of the Northwest is Ruth Kirk's *The Enduring Forests*, 1996.

Spotted owls and old-growth forests: Norse, *Ancient Forests*, 1990.

Current status of spotted owls on the Olympic Peninsula: Scott Gremel, Olympic National Park, personal communication, 2005.

Wildlife species of the peninsula: Sharpe, *Olympic Wildlife Checklist*, 1992.

"Scuzz": Kirk and Franklin, *The Olympic Rain Forest*, 1992.

Spotted owls and flying squirrels: Norse, *Ancient Forests*, 1990.

Rodents and fungi in the forest ecosystem: Maser, *Forest Primeval*, 1989.

Barred owls: Sibley, *Sibley Guide to Bird Life*, 2001.

Barred owl–spotted owl interactions in the Olympics: Scott Gremel, Olympic National Park, personal communication, 2005.

Structure and ecological function of old-growth forests: Franklin et al., *Ecological Characteristics of Old-Growth Douglas-Fir Forests*, 1981.

Wildlife use of old-growth forests: Norse, *Ancient Forests*, 1990; Harris, *The Fragmented Forest*, 1984; also Bruce B. Moorhead, "A Summary of the U.S. Forest Service Symposium of Wildlife in Old-growth Douglas-fir Forests of the Pacific Northwest, March 1989, Portland, OR" (unpublished report, Olympic National Park).

Marbled murrelets: Ralph et al., *Ecology and Conservation of the Marbled Murrelet*, 1995; Tim McNulty, "The Northwest's Mystery Seabird," *Defenders Magazine*, Spring 2000, and "Marbled Murrelet," *Forest Magazine*, Fall 2002; also Susan McCarthy, "A Seabird's Secret Life Is Revealed—50 Miles Inland," *Smithsonian* 2, no. 9 (1993).

Murrelets declines: Michael Milstein, "Scientists Predict Gloomy Future for Coastal Marbled Murrelets," *The Oregonian*, May 5, 2004.

Birds of the old-growth forest: Norse, *Ancient Forests*, 1990; also Sharpe, *Olympic Peninsula Birds*.

Snags and other old-growth habitats: Brown, *Management of Wildlife*, 1985; also Norse, *Ancient Forests*, 1990.

Martins and fishers: Larrison and Fisher, *Mammals of the Northwest*, 1976; also Keith B. Aubrey and D. B. Houston, "Distribution and Status of the Fisher (*Martes pennanti*) in Washington," *Northwestern Naturalist*, Winter 1992; also D. B. Houston and D. E. Seaman, "Fisher in Olympic National Park," Research Note no. 2, Olympic National Park, 1983.

Reintroducing fishers: U.S. Department of the Interior, National Park Service, *Olympic National Park Fisher Reintroduction Plan/Environmental Impact Statement*, 2007; Jeffrey C. Lewis and Gerald E. Hayes, *Feasibility Assessment for Reintroducing Fishers to Washington*, Washington Department of Fish and Wildlife, Olympia, 2004; Tim McNulty, "Fishers are Returning to Olympic National Park," *Voice of the Wild Olympics*, Winter 2008; and McNulty, "Return of the Fisher," *Forest Magazine*, November/December 2001.

Forest vegetation types: Henderson et al., *Forested Plant Associations*, 1989; also Franklin and Dyrness, *Natural Vegetation of Oregon and Washington*, 1973.

Plants of the lowland forests: Arno and Hammerly, *Northwest Trees*, 1977; also

Matthews, *Cascade-Olympic Natural History*, 1999.

Montane forests: Fonda and Bliss, "Forest Vegetation," 1969.

Rainshadow vegetation/Sequim prairie: Jerry Gorsline, "The Cultural Transformation of the Sequim Prairie," in Gorsline, *Shadows of Our Ancestors*, 1992.

Early wildlife of the Sequim Prairie: James G. Swan, "Sequim Prairie, Washington Territory," *Washington Standard* 1, no. 15, February 23, 1861

Fire history of Olympic forests: Henderson et al., *Forested Plant Associations*, 1989; also James Agee, *Fire Ecology of Pacific Northwest Forests*, 1993.

Little Ice Age forest fluctuations: Jan Henderson, U.S. Forest Service, personal communication, 1995.

Current old-growth on the Olympic Peninsula: Morrison, *Ancient Forests of the Olympic National Forest*, 1989.

6 THE LIVES OF OLYMPIC RIVERS

A landmark book explaining the plight of wild salmon on the Olympic Peninsula is Bruce Brown's *Mountain in the Clouds: A Search for the Wild Salmon* (Seattle: University of Washington Press, 1995). Two comprehensive books about salmon and salmon habitats are Jim Lichatowich's *Salmon Without Rivers* (1999) and David R. Montgomery's *King of Fish* (2003); both are written by scientists for the general reader. Material on the natural history and biology of salmon is drawn from these texts and: Croot and Margolis, *Pacific Salmon Life Histories*, 1991; Wydoski and Whitney, *Inland Fishes of Washington*, 1979; and Steelquist, *Adopt-a-Stream Foundation Field Guide to the Pacific Salmon*, 1992.

Marine-derived nutrients delivered to inland streams by salmon: C. Jeff Cederholm et al., "Pacific Salmon Carcasses: Essential Contributions of Nutrients and Energy for Aquatic and Terrestrial Ecosystems," *Fisheries* 24, no. 10 (1999).

Percentage of nutrients from spawned salmon: U.S. Department of the Interior, *Olympic National Park*, 2006.

Salmon stocks in Olympic National Park: D. B. Houston, "Anadromous Fish in Olympic National Park: A Status Report," Olympic National Park, 1983, as well as "Fish of Olympic National Park," National Park Service brochure, 2001; also McNulty, "Salmon," 2002; and Sam Brenkman, Olympic National Park, personal communications, 2005, 2006, 2007.

Salmon stocks at risk in peninsula rivers: Nehlsen, Williams, and Lichatowich, "Pacific Salmon at the Crossroads," 1991; also Washington Department of

Fisheries, *Washington State Salmon*, 1993; also Lichatowich, "The Status of Anadromous Fish Stocks," 1993.

Salmon stocks in the Dungeness River: Tim McNulty, "The Dungeness: A River Unraveled," *Sequim Gazette/Port Townsend Leader*, September 20, 2000, and "Salmon in the Dungeness River: From Abundance to Emptiness," *Sequim Gazette/Port Townsend Leader*, September 13, 2000.

Bull trout peregrinations: Samuel Brenkman and S. C. Corbett, "Extent of Anadromy in Bull Trout and Implications for Conservation of a Threatened Species," *North American Journal of Fisheries Management* 25 (2005); also Sam Brenkman, fisheries biologist, personal communication, 2006.

Historic salmon canneries on the peninsula: Jeff Cederholm, Washington Department of Natural Resources, personal communication, 1995.

Spawned salmon as important seasonal food for wildlife, Olympic study: Cederholm, Houston, and Scarlett, "Fate of Coho Salmon," 1989.

Spawned salmon as important seasonal food for wildlife, Washington and Oregon Study: Cederholm et al., "Pacific Salmon and Wildlife," 2000.

Salmon cycling nutrients to streams and forests: Robert E. Bilby, B. Fransen, and P. Bisson, "Incorporation of Nitrogen and Carbon from Spawning Coho Salmon into the Trophic System of Small Streams: Evidence from Stable Isotopes," *Canadian Journal of Fisheries and Aquatic Sciences* 53 (1996).

Ecology of riparian areas: Art Oakley et al., "Riparian Zones and Freshwater Wetlands," in *Management of Wildlife and Fish Habitat*, ed. Brown, 1985; also McNulty, *Washington's Wild Rivers*, 1990.

Role of riparian forests in optimizing salmon habitat in post–Ice Age streams: Lichatowich, Salmon Without Rivers, 1999.

Downed logs provide structure for streams: Montgomery, *King of Fish*, 2003; also Maser et al., *From the Forest to the Sea*, 1988.

Dynamics of Olympic forests and streams: Joshua J. Latterell et al., "Dynamic Patch Mosaics and Channel Movement in an Unconfined River Valley of the Olympic Mountains," *Freshwater Biology*, 51 (2006); also Jim E. O'Connor, M. A. Jones, and T. L. Haluska, "Flood Plain and Channel Dynamics of the Quinault and Queets Rivers, Washington, USA," *Geomorphology*, 51 (2003).

Riparian-associated wildlife: Maser et al., *From the Forest to the Sea*, 1988.

Harlequin ducks: Greg Shirato, Washington Department of Fish and Wildlife, personal communications, 1994, 2005; and Barbara Blackie, Olympic Coast National Marine Sanctuary, personal communication, 2006; also Chadwick, "Bird of White Waters," 1993, and "Cavity Nesting Harlequin Ducks in the

Pacific Northwest," *Wilson Bulletin* 105, no. 4 (1993).

Dippers, kingfishers, and other river-associated birds: Ehrlich, Dobkin, and Wheye, *The Birder's Handbook*, 1988; Kitchin, *Birds of the Olympic Peninsula*, 1949; Peterson, *A Field Guide to Western Birds*, 1990; Sharpe, *Olympic Peninsula Birds*, 1993; and Barbara Blackie, personal communication, 2006.

Amphibians of the Olympics: Leonard et al., *Amphibians of Washington and Oregon*, 1993; Bruce B. Bury, "Amphibians and Reptiles of the Olympic National Park, Washington," Preliminary Report for Olympic National Park, 1982; Bruce B. Moorhead, "Report on Northwest Amphibians Symposium, Astoria, Oregon, March 1993," Olympic National Park science files; "Amphibians of Olympic National Park," U.S.G.S. Fact Sheet 098-000, U.S. Geological Survey, June 2000; and Pat Loafman, Olympic National Park, personal communication, 2002.

Worldwide amphibian declines: David B. Wake, "Declining Amphibian Populations," *Science* 253 (1991).

Stream and wetland restoration: Dave Shreffler, Shreffler Environmental, personal communication, 2007.

History of the Elwha dams issue: Richard Rutz and Shawn Cantrell, "Congress Passes Elwha Legislation," *Voice of the Wild Olympics*, October 1992; and David Ortman, "Free the Elwha," in *Coastal Zone '93*, vol. 1 (New York: American Society of Civil Engineers, 1993).

Restoration of the Elwha River: Cat H. Hoffman, "The Elwha Issue: A Fish Problem That Just Won't Die," *George Wright Forum* 9, no. 2 (1992); U.S. Department of the Interior, *Elwha Report*, 1994, and *Elwha River Ecosystem Restoration*, 1995; Wunderlich, Winter, and Meyer, "Restoration of the Elwha River Ecosystem," 1994; and Brian Winter, Olympic National Park, personal communications, 1995, 2006.

7 LIFE AT THE EDGE OF LAND AND SEA

The chapter on the ecology of Olympic's intertidal zones was assembled from the work of Megan Dethier of the University of Washington, interviews with Steve Fradkin of Olympic National Park, and a number of published sources. Gloria Snively's *Exploring the Seashore in British Columbia, Washington and Oregon* (1978) is probably the best introduction to intertidal zones and organisms; she provides illustrations and common as well as scientific names for each species and arranges subject matter by life zones. J. Duane Sept's

The Beachcombers Guide to Seashore Life in the Pacific Northwest (2004), is the most up-to-date popular guide. Snively and Sept were my sources for common names of intertidal species. Eugene N. Kozloff's *Seashore Life of the Northern Pacific Coast* (1983) presents a more detailed look at intertidal organisms; and Edward Ricketts, J. Calvin, and J. Hedgpeth's *Between Pacific Tides* (1992) is the classic in the field. Anne Wertheim's *The Intertidal Wilderness* (1984) offers exquisite underwater photography as well as keen ecological insight. Muriel L. Guberlet's *Seaweeds at Ebb Tide* (1956) and *Animals of the Seashore* (1962 revised edition), though somewhat dated, are both excellent introductions to marine organisms. Ruth Kirk's *The Olympic Seashore* (1962) and David Hooper's *Exploring Washington's Wild Olympic Coast* (1993) are popular hiking guides to the coast that contain some useful natural history as well.

Factors leading to the diversity of coastal environments: Dethier, "A Survey of Intertidal Communities," 1988; and Wertheim, *Intertidal Wilderness*, 1984.

Coastal geology: Rau, *Geology of the Washington Coast*, 1980; and Tabor, *Guide to the Geology*, 1987.

Shape of the Olympic coast: Thomas Terich and M. L. Schwartz, "A Geomorphic Classification of Washington State's Pacific Coast," *Shore and Beach* 49 (1981).

Origin of Point of Arches rocks: McNulty and O'Hara, *Olympic National Park*, 1984.

Currents and coastal upwelling: Steve Fradkin, Olympic National Park, personal communication, 2006; Julia Parrish, University of Washington, personal communication, 2004; also Carefoot, *Pacific Seashores*, 1977.

Species succession in the intertidal: R. T. Paine, and S. A. Levin, "Intertidal Landscapes: Disturbance and the Dynamics of Pattern," *Ecological Monographs* 51, no. 2 (1981).

Mussel bed communities and sea star–mussel predation: R. T. Paine, "Intertidal Community Structure: Experimental Studies on the Relationship between a Dominant Competitor and Its Principal Predator," *Oecologia* 15 (1974); also Wertheim, *Intertidal Wilderness*, 1984.

Interactions among sea anemones: Kenneth Sebens, "Population Dynamics and Habitat Suitability of the Intertidal Sea Anemones *Anthopleura elegantissima* and *A. Xanthogrammica*," *Ecological Monographs* 53 (1983).

Herbivores and seaweed community structure: Dethier, *A Survey of Intertidal Communities*, 1988.

Sea urchin and kelp interactions: Pat Iampietro, California State University,

Monterey Bay, personal communication, 1998.

Ecology of sandy beaches: Steve Fradkin, Olympic National Park, personal communication, 2006; and Snively, *Exploring the Seashore*, 1978.

8 SEABIRDS AND MAMMALS OF THE OUTER COAST

The natural history of seabirds and mammals on the coast was drawn from a number of published sources as well as interviews with several biologists conducting surveys and research in this area. Among books available on Washington's avifauna, Stanley Hewett, W. Taylor, W. Shaw, and J. Aldrich's *Birds of Washington State* (Seattle: University of Washington Press, 1953) was essential reading for its site-specific detail and historical perspective. E. A. Kitchin's *Birds of the Olympic Peninsula* (1949) was also extremely useful. Paul Ehrlich, D. Dobkin, and D. Wheye's *The Birder's Handbook* (1988) filled in biological and natural history details as well as conservation status for several species, as did C. J. Guiguet's *The Birds of British Columbia* (1971). I relied primarily on David Allen Sibley, *The Sibley Guide to Birds* (2000), for identification and descriptions.

For marine mammals, Tony Angell and K. Balcomb's *Marine Birds and Mammals of Puget Sound* (1982) is an excellent introduction to Northwest marine life. Richard Osborne, J. Calambokidis, and E. Dorsey's *A Guide to Marine Mammals of Greater Puget Sound* (1988) is a clear and insightful introduction to the area's marine mammals, and Delphine Haley's compilation, *Marine Mammals of Eastern North Pacific and Arctic Waters* (1986), contains excellent articles on the region's sea mammals by leading researchers. A pioneering paper on sea mammals in Washington is Victor Scheffer and J. Slipp's monograph, "The Whales and Dolphins of Washington State," in *The American Midland Naturalist* 39 (1948). A good overview of Washington's coastal areas is Steelquist's *Washington's Coast* (1987).

History of shipwrecks on the Olympic coast: Gibbs, *Shipwrecks of the Pacific Coast*, 1989; and Robert Steelquist, Olympic Coast National Marine Sanctuary, personal communication, 2006.

William Dawson's early work on coastal seabird colonies: Steelquist, *Washington's Coast*, 1987.

Establishment of Washington Islands National Wildlife Refuges: U.S. Fish and Wildlife Service, *Draft Comprehensive Conservation Plan*, 2005.

"Quileute": There are different spellings for the Native American tribe (Quileute) and the river (Quillayute).

Status of bald eagles: Gretchen Blatz and Shelly Ament, Washington Department of Fish and Wildlife, personal communication, 2007; also Patti Happe and Shelly Hall, "2002 Annual Wildlife Report" (unpublished report, Olympic National Park); and Kelly McAllister, T. Owens, L. Leschner, and Eric Cummins, "Distribution and Productivity of Nesting Bald Eagles in Washington, 1981–1985," *The Murrelet* 67 (1986).

Status of peregrine falcons: Ulrich Wilson, Anita McMillan, and Frederick Dobler, "Nesting, Population Trends and Breeding Success of Peregrine Falcons on the Washington Outer Coast, 1980–98," *J. Raptor Research* 34, no. 2 (2000).

El Niño: Ulrich Wilson, "Responses of Three Seabird Species to El Niño Events and Other Warm Episodes on the Washington Coast, 1979–1990," *Condor* 93 (1991).

Current status of Pacific seabirds: U.S. Fish and Wildlife Service, *Draft Comprehensive Conservation Plan*, 2005; Vermeer et al., *Status, Ecology, and Conservation*, 1993; also David G. Ainley, W. Sydeman, S. Hatch, and U. Wilson, "Seabird Population Trends Along the West Coast of North America: Causes and the Extent of Regional Concordance," *Studies in Avian Biology* 15 (1994); and Ulrich Wilson, U.S. Fish and Wildlife Service (ret.), personal communication, 2007.

Impacts of El Niño on seabird colonies: Wilson, "Responses of Three Seabird Species," 1991.

Status of marine mammals: Pat Gearin, "Marine Mammals of the Olympic Coast," in *Olympic Coast Marine Research, Proceedings of a Workshop, Forks, Washington, January 1996*, Olympic Coast National Marine Sanctuary, Port Angeles, 1996.

Natural history and recovery of gray whales: National Marine Fisheries Service, "Gray Whale (*Eschrichtius robustus*): Eastern North Pacific Stock, Stock Assessment Report," 2002; and Jones and Swartz, *The Gray Whale*, 1984; also Bennet, *The Oceanic Society Field Guide*, 1989.

Status of humpback whales: John Calambokidis, Gretchen Steiger, Barry Troutman, and Ed Bowlby, "Distribution and Abundance of Humpback Whales (*Megaptera novaeangliae*) off the Northern Washington Coast," *Fishery Bulletin* 104 (2004).

Overview of marine mammal research: Bruce Moorhead, "Notes on Marine Mammals from British Columbia/Washington Wildlife Society Conference, 1993" (unpublished notes, Olympic National Park).

Status of harbor seals: Harriet Huber, S. Jeffries, R. Brown, and R. DeLong,

"Abundance of Harbor Seals in Washington and Oregon," National Marine Mammal Laboratory, Seattle, 1992.

Recent harbor seal populations: Patrick J. Gearin and Harriet Huber, "Trends in Pinniped Populations in the Olympic Coast National Marine Sanctuary," in *Olympic Coast National Marine Sanctuary*, ed. Bowlby, Blackie, and Parrish, 2001; also U.S. Fish and Wildlife Service, *Draft Comprehensive Conservation Plan*, 2005.

Elephant seal, fur seal, and sea lion status in Washington: U.S. Fish and Wildlife Service, *Draft Comprehensive Conservation Plan*, 2005.

Sea lion populations on the Olympic Coast: Gearin and Huber, "Trends in Pinniped Populations," 2001.

Overview of sea otters: Nickerson, *Sea Otters*, 1989.

Sea otter recovery on the Olympic coast: C. Edward Bowlby, B. Troutman, and S. Jeffries, "Sea Otters in Washington: Distribution, Abundance, and Activity Patterns," Washington Department of Wildlife Report, Olympia, 1988; also R. Jameson, "Olympic Coast Sea Otter Study: 1994 Progress Report," U.S. Department of the Interior National Biological Service, Corvallis, Oregon; and McNulty, "Washington's Otter Comeback," 1998.

Reasons for limited sea mammal breeding on Olympic coast: Steve Jeffries, Washington Department of Fish and Wildlife, personal communication, 1995.

Effects of oil on seabirds: R. Glenn Ford et al., "Seabird Mortality Resulting from the Nestucca Oil Spill Incident," Washington Department of Wildlife Report, Olympia, 1991.

Impacts of oil on intertidal species: Megan Dethier, "The Effects of an Oil Spill and Freeze Event on Intertidal Community Structure in Washington," U.S. Department of the Interior, Minerals Management Service Report, Camarillo, California, 1991.

9 FOOTPRINTS ON THE LAND

An excellent overview of early archaeological findings on the peninsula is Eric Bergland and J. Marr's *Prehistoric Life on the Olympic Peninsula* (1988). The most up-to-date book on Washington archaeology is Ruth Kirk and Richard D. Daugherty's *Archaeology in Washington* (2007). Ethnographic information on peninsula tribal peoples is drawn largely from the Smithsonian Institution's excellent series *Handbook of North American Indians*, vol. 7, *Northwest Coast*, edited by Wayne Suttles (1990). *Native Peoples of* the Olympic Peninsula: Who We Are, edited by Jacilee Wray, 2002, is an excellent introduction to Olympic Peninsula tribal cultures written by tribal members. Olympic National Park Ethnographic Overview and Assessment, by park anthropologist Jacilee Wray (1997), is well documented and has a very helpful annotated bibliography.

Radiocarbon dates have been corrected to calendar years: Kirk and Daugherty, Archaeology in Washington, 2007.

Manis mastodon discovery: Carl Gustafson, D. Gilbrow, and R. Daugherty, "The Manis Mastodon Site: Early Man on the Olympic Peninsula," Canadian Journal of Archaeology 3 (1979).

Investigation of the Manis site hunting camp: Delbert Gilbrow, personal communication, 1995.

Prehistoric migrations to the peninsula: Eric Bergland, "Summary Prehistory and Ethnography of Olympic National Park, Washington" (unpublished report, U.S. Department of the Interior, National Park Service, Pacific Northwest Region, Seattle, 1983).

Slab Camp site: James Gallison, "Slab Camp: An Early to Middle Holocene Olcott Complex in the Eastern Olympic Mountains of Washington" (PhD diss., Washington State University, Department of Anthropology, Pullman, 1994).

Coastal Olcott pattern: Ruth Kirk and D. Daugherty, Archaeology in Washington (Seattle: University of Washington Press, 2007); Roy L. Carson, "Cultural Antecedents," in Handbook: Northwest Coast, ed. Suttles, 1990; and David Conca, Olympic National Park, personal communication, 2006.

Deer Park site: Gary C. Wessen, "Archaeological Survey and Testing Activities at and near Deer Park (45CA257), Olympic National Park, Washington" (unpublished report, USDI National Park Service, Pacific Northwest Region, 1992).

Seven Lakes Basin site: David Conca, "Soleduck Watershed High Country Archaeology Synopsis" (unpublished report, Olympic National Park, 1995).

Glenrose Cannery and Hoko River sites: Kirk and Daugherty, Exploring Washington Archaeology, 1978; Bergland and Marr, Prehistoric Life on the Peninsula, 1988; and Suttles, Handbook: Northwest Coast, 1990.

Wa'atch River site: Wessen, "Archaeological Site Testing Activities," 2006; and Bob Steelquist, Olympic Coast National Marine Sanctuary, personal communication, 2006.

Other early maritime sites: Gary Wessen, "Prehistory of the Ocean Coast of Washington," in Handbook: Northwest Coast, ed. Suttles, 1990.

Tse-whit-zen village: Lynda Mapes, "The Unearthing of Tse-whit-zen," *Seattle Times*, May 22–25, 2005; Tim McNulty, "Elwha Elegy," *Seattle Weekly*, March 2–8, 2005; also Carmen Charles, Elwha Klallam Tribe, personal communication, 2005; Darryl Barkley, Elwha Klallam Tribe, personal communication, 2005; Lynn Larson and Dennis Lewarch, Larson Archaeological, personal communications, 2005.

Discovery and early excavation of Ozette site: Kirk, *Hunters of the Whale*, 1974.

Ozette archaeological findings: Kirk and Daugherty, *Exploring Washington Archaeology*, 1978; Samuels, *Ozette Archaeological Project Research Reports*, 1991; also Paul Gleeson, Olympic National Park, personal communication, 1995.

Precontact Makah village life: Pascua, "Ozette," 1991.

Makah ethnography: Ann M. Renker and E. Gunther, "Makah," in *Handbook: Northwest Coast*, ed. Suttles, 1990; Swan, *The Indians of Cape Flattery*, 1974; and Wray, *Native Peoples*, 2002.

Northwest Coast cultural adaptations: Wayne Suttles, "Introduction to the Northwest Coast," in *Handbook: Northwest Coast*, ed. Suttles, 1990; Suttles, *Coast Salish Essays*, 1987; and Drucker, *Indians of the Northwest Coast*, 1955.

The potlatch: Kirk, *Tradition and Change on the Northwest Coast*, 1986; Suttles, *Handbook: Northwest Coast*, 1990; and Suttles, *Coast Salish Essays*, 1987.

Cedar technology: Hillary Stewart, *Cedar: Tree of Life to the Northwest Coast Indians* (Vancouver, B.C.: Douglas and McIntyre, 1984).

"If mankind in his infancy . . .": Reid and De Menil, *Out of the Silence*, 1972.

Traditional use of native plants: Gunther, *Ethnobotany of Western Washington*, 1973.

Quileute ethnography: James V. Powell, "Quileute," in *Handbook: Northwest Coast*, ed. Suttles, 1990; Powell and Jensen, *Quileute: An Introduction*, 1976; and Wray, *Native Peoples*, 2002.

Quinault and Queets ethnography: Yvonne Hajda, "Southwestern Coast Salish," in *Handbook: Northwest Coast*, ed. Suttles, 1990; and Wray, *Native Peoples*, 2002.

Klallam ethnography: Wayne Suttles, "Central Coast Salish," in *Handbook: Northwest Coast*, ed. Suttles, 1990; and Wray, *Native Peoples*, 2002.

Twana/Skokomish ethnography: Wayne Suttles and B. Lane, "Southern Coast Salish," in *Handbook: Northwest Coast*, ed. Suttles, 1990; Elmendorf,

Twana Narratives, 1993; and Wray, *Native Peoples*, 2002.

Treaties and fishing rights: Cohen, *Treaties on Trial*, 1986.

Cedar canoe revival: Al Charles Jr., Elwha Klallam Tribe, personal communication, 1995; and Wray, *Native Peoples*, 2002.

Makah whaling: Sam Howe Verhovek, "Joy and Anger as Tribe Kills a Gray Whale," *New York Times*, May 18, 1999; also Sullivan, *A Whale Hunt*, 2000.

Tse-whit-zen village controversy: McNulty, "Elwha Elegy," 2005.

Canoe journey to Elwha: "Paddle to Elwha, 2005 Canoe Journey," *Peninsula Daily News*, September 4, 2005.

10 PROTECTION FOR OLYMPIC'S WILDLANDS

The story of the long and contentious struggle to create Olympic National Park, as well as the ongoing effort to protect the park's valuable old-growth forests, is told in Carsten Lien's excellent study *Olympic Battleground: The Power Politics of Timber Preservation* (2000). A wonderful book on the early exploration of the Olympics is Robert Wood's *The Land That Slept Late: The Olympic Mountains in Legend and History* (1995). Original records of early European explorations of the Olympics are available in Carsten Lien's compilation *Exploring the Olympic Mountains: Accounts of the Earliest Expeditions, 1878–1890* (2001). A useful anthology that excerpts a number of primary texts on the park's history is Nancy Beres, M. Chandler, and R. Dalton's *Island of Rivers* (1988). And a record of citizen conservation efforts in Olympic National Park over the past half-century is *Voice of the Wild Olympics*, 50th Anniversary Edition, edited by Sally Soest (1998).

Wickersham and O'Neil on the Skokomish River: Wood, *Men, Mules and Mountains*, 1976.

Melbourne Watkinson's romp across the Olympics: Lien, *Exploring the Olympic Mountains*, 2001.

Account of the Press expedition: Wood, *Across the Olympic Mountains*, 1967.

Early expeditions into the Olympics: Evans, *Historic Resource Study*, 1983; and Lien, *Exploring the Olympic Mountains*, 2001.

Wickersham's park proposal, including letter to Powell: Wickersham, "A National Park in the Olympics," 1961.

Early conservation efforts in the United States: Nash, *Wilderness and the American Mind*, 1969.

"Every other civilized nation . . .": Muir, *Our National Parks*, 1991.

Creation and reduction of the Olympic Forest Reserve: Lien, *Olympic Battleground*, 2000.

Local efforts to reduce the reserve: Aldwell, *Conquering the Last Frontier*, 1950.

Quotes by Aldwell and Jones: Lien, *Olympic Battleground*, 2000.

McKinley Forest Reserve deletions: Evans, *Historic Resource Study*, 1983.

Chris Morgenroth and the homesteaders' perspective on forest reserve reductions, including Morgenroth quotes: Morgenroth, *Footprints in the Olympics*, 1991.

Pinchot, "promptly and fraudulently . . .": Pinchot, *Breaking New Ground*, 1945.

Dodwell and Rixon survey and report: Evans, *Historic Resource Study*, 1983, and Rooney, *Frontier Legacy*, 1997.

"That elimination from the Olympic . . .": Forest inspector W. T. Cox, quoted in Rooney, *Frontier Legacy*, 1997.

Theodore Roosevelt's creation of the Mount Olympus National Monument: Evans, *Historic Resource Study*, 1983.

Campaign for a national park: Lien, *Olympic Battleground*, 2000.

Gifford Pinchot and the formative years of the U.S. Forest Service: Pinchot, *Breaking New Ground*, 1945.

Power struggle between the park service and forest service: Twight, *Organizational Values and Political Power*, 1983.

Army Spruce Division and World War I: Tim McNulty, "The Spruce Railroad Trail, Olympic National Park," *Peninsula Magazine*, Winter 1989; and Rooney, *Frontier Legacy*, 1997.

Rudo Fromme's role in forest service retention of Olympic Mountains: Rooney, *Frontier Legacy*, 1997.

Early management of national parks: Runte, *National Parks*, 1979.

Early cutting on Olympic National Forest: Evans, *Historic Resource Study*, 1983.

Emergency Conservation Committee and the national campaign for a park: Lien, *Olympic Battleground*, 2000.

"The peninsula affords the last opportunity . . .": Willard Van Name, "The Proposed Olympic National Park," Emergency Conservation Committee pamphlet, 1934.

FDR and the creation of the park: Lien, *Olympic Battleground*, 2000.

Founding of Olympic Park Associates: Phil Zalesky, "Olympic Park Associates Emerges, 1948," in *Voice of the Wild Olympics*, ed. Soest, 1998.

Salvage logging in Olympic National Park: Lien, *Olympic Battleground*, 2000.

William O. Douglas protest hikes on Olympic Coast: Polly Dyer, "Keeping the Olympic Coast Roadless," in *Voice of the Wild Olympics*, ed. Soest, 1998.

Campaign for Forest Service Wilderness: Tim McNulty, "1974–1984: The Campaign for the Olympic National Forest Wilderness," in *Voice of the Wild Olympics*, ed. Soest, 1998.

Olympic Park reductions and North Cascades Park bill: Manning, *Wilderness Alps*, 2007.

Definition of ecosystem management: T. Clark and D. Zaunbrecher, "The Greater Yellowstone Ecosystem: The Ecosystem Concept in Natural Resource Policy and Management," *Renewable Resources Journal* 11 (1987).

Perspectives on ecosystem management: Grumbine, *Ghost Bears*, 1992; Agee and Johnson, *Ecosystem Management*, 1988; also Ed Grumbine, Prescott College, personal communication, 2005.

Components of the Olympic ecosystem: Smithson and O'Hara, *Olympic: Ecosystems of the Peninsula*, 1993.

Strategies for ecosystem management in the Olympics: Tim McNulty, "The Olympic Ecosystem," *Voice of the Wild Olympics*, October 1988; and Donna Osseward, olympicparkassociates.org, OPA scoping letter to Olympic National Park general management plan, October 10, 2001.

Federally listed and candidate threatened and endangered species in Olympic: U.S. Department of the Interior, *General Management Plan*, 2008.

Vital signs monitoring program at Olympic: Jerry Freilich, "Taking the Pulse of the Olympic Ecosystem," *Voice of the Wild Olympics*, Fall 2003; and Jerry Freilich, Olympic National Park, personal communication, 2007.

General management plan preferred alternative: U.S. Department of the Interior, *Olympic National Park*, 2008.

Critique of NPS preferred alternative: Tim McNulty, "Olympic National Park Management Plan Needs Your Help," *Voice of the Wild Olympics*, Summer 2006.

Island ecology: MacArthur and Wilson, *The Theory of Island Biogeography*, 1969; and Quammen, *Song of the Dodo*, 1996.

UNESCO's Biosphere Reserve and World Heritage programs: Michel Batisse, "Development and Implementation of the Biosphere Reserve Concept and Its Applicability to Coastal Regions," *Environmental Conservation* 17, no. 2 (1990); and "Comments of Dr. Michel Batisse, June 29, 1982," in Beres, Chandler, and Dalton, *Island of Rivers*, 1988.

UNESCO world heritage quote: U.S. Department of the Interior, *Olympic National Park*, 2008.

Bibliography

Agee, James, and D. Johnson. 1988. *Ecosystem Management for Parks and Wilderness.* Seattle: National Park Service, Pacific Northwest Region.

———. 1993. Fire Ecology of Pacific Northwest Forests. Washington, D.C.: Island Press.

Aldwell, Thomas T. 1950. *Conquering the Last Frontier.* Seattle: Superior Publishing.

Alley, Richard, et al. 2007. *Intergovernmental Panel on Climate Change of the United Nations Summary Report: The Physical Science Basis.* Summary for Policy Makers. Paris: United Nations Intergovernmental Panel on Climate Change.

Alt, David, and Donald Hyndman. 1995. *Northwest Exposures: A Geologic Story of the Northwest.* Missoula: Mountain Press.

Angell, Tony, and Kenneth C. Balcomb. 1982. *Marine Birds and Mammals of Puget Sound.* Seattle: Washington Sea Grant/Puget Sound Books.

Arno, Stephen, and Ramona Hammerly. 1977. *Northwest Trees.* Seattle: The Mountaineers Books.

Atwater, Brian F., and E. Hemphill-Haley. 1997. "Recurrence Intervals for Great Earthquakes of the Past 3,500 Years at Northern Willapa Bay, Washington." U.S. Geological Survey Professional Paper 1576. Washington, D.C.: U.S. Government Printing Office.

Barash, David. 1989. *Marmots: Social Behavior and Ecology.* Stanford, Calif.: Stanford University Press.

Bennet, Ben. 1989. *The Oceanic Society Field Guide to the Gray Whale.* Seattle: Sasquatch Books.

Beres, Nancy, Mitzi Chandler, and Russ Dalton, eds. 1988. *Island of Rivers: An Anthology Celebrating 50 Years of Olympic National Park.* Seattle: Pacific

Northwest National Parks and Forests Association.

Bergland, Eric O., and Jerry Marr. 1988. *Prehistoric Life on the Olympic Peninsula*. Seattle: Pacific Northwest National Parks and Forests Association.

Bowlby, Edward, Barbara Blackie, and Julia Parrish, eds. 2001. *Olympic Coast National Marine Sanctuary: Proceedings of the 1998 Research Workshop, Seattle, Washington*. Seattle: U.S. Department of Commerce, National Oceanic and Atmospheric Administration.

Brown, Bruce. 1995. *Mountain in the Clouds: A Search for the Wild Salmon*. Seattle: University of Washington Press.

Brown, E. Reade, ed. 1985. *Management of Wildlife and Fish Habitat in Forests of Western Washington and Oregon*. Washington, D.C.: USDA Forest Service.

Buckingham, Nelsa M., Edward Schreiner, Thomas Kaye, Janis Burger, and Edward Tisch. 1995. *Flora of the Olympic Peninsula, Washington*. Seattle: Northwest Interpretive Association.

Burns, Robert. 1985. *The Shape of Puget Sound*. Seattle: Washington Sea Grant/ Puget Sound Books.

Burt, William, and R. Grossenheider. 1976. *A Field Guide to the Mammals*. Boston: Houghton Mifflin.

Carefoot, Thomas. 1977. *Pacific Seashores*. Seattle: University of Washington Press.

Cederholm, C. J., D. Houston, and W. Scarlett. 1989. "Fate of Coho Salmon (*Oncorhynchus kisutch*) Carcasses in Spawning Streams." *Canadian Journal of Fisheries and Aquatic Sciences* 46.

Cederholm, Jeff, et al. 2000. "Pacific Salmon and Wildlife: Ecological Contexts, Relationships, and Implications for Management." Olympia: Washington Department of Fish and Wildlife.

Chadwick, Douglas H. 1993. "Bird of White Waters." *National Geographic*, November.

Cohen, Fay G. 1986. *Treaties on Trial*. Seattle: University of Washington Press.

Cowan, Ian M., and C. J. Guiguet. 1965. *The Mammals of British Columbia*. Victoria: British Columbia Provincial Museum.

Croot, C., and L. Margolis. 1991. *Pacific Salmon Life Histories*. Vancouver: University of British Columbia Press.

Dalquest, W. W. 1948. *Mammals of Washington*. Lawrence: University of Kansas Press.

del Moral, Roger. 1984. "The Impact of the Olympic Marmot on Subalpine Vegetation Structure." *American Journal of Botany* 71, no. 9:1228–36.

Dethier, Megan N. 1988. "A Survey of Intertidal Communities of the Pacific Coast Area of Olympic National Park, Washington." Unpublished report, Olympic National Park.

Dietrich, William. 1992. *The Final Forest: The Battle for the Last Great Trees of the Pacific Northwest*. New York: Simon and Schuster.

———. 2003. *Natural Grace: The Charm, Wonder, and Lessons of Pacific Northwest Animals and Plants*. Seattle: University of Washington Press.

Dodwell, Arthur, and Theodore F. Rixon. 1902. *Forest Conditions in the Olympic Forest Reserve, Washington*. U.S. Geological Survey Professional Paper No. 7. Washington, D.C.: U.S. Government Printing Office.

Drucker, Philip. 1955. *Indians of the Northwest Coast*. New York: McGraw-Hill.

Easterbrook, Don J. 1994. "Chronology of Pre-Late Wisconsin Pleistocene Sediments in the Puget Lowlands, Washington State." Bulletin No. 80. Olympia: Washington Division of Geology and Earth Resources.

Ehrlich, Paul, D. Dobkin, and D. Wheye. 1988. *The Birders Handbook: A Field Guide to the Natural History of North American Birds*. New York: Simon and Schuster.

Elmendorf, William W. 1993. *Twana Narratives: Native Historical Accounts of a Coast Salish Culture*. Seattle: University of Washington Press.

Evans, Gail. 1983. *Historic Resource Study: Olympic National Park*. Seattle: National Park Service, Pacific Northwest Region.

Ewing, Susan. 1998. *Shadow Cat*. Seattle: Sasquatch Books.

Fagan, Brian. 2000. *The Little Ice Age: How Climate Made History, 1300–1850*. New York: Basic Books.

Fonda, R. W. 1974. "Forest Succession in Relation to River Terrace Development in Olympic National Park, Washington." *Ecology* 55, no. 5.

Fonda, R. W., and L. Bliss. 1969. "Forest Vegetation of the Montane and Subalpine Zones, Olympic Mountains, Washington." *Ecological Monographs*, 39.

Franklin, Jerry F., and C. T. Dyrness, 1973. *Natural Vegetation of Oregon and Washington*. General Technical Report PNW-8. Portland, Ore.: USDA Forest Service Pacific Northwest Range and Experiment Station.

Franklin, Jerry F., et al. 1981. *Ecological Characteristics of Old-Growth Douglas-Fir Forests*. General Technical Report PNW-118. Portland, Ore.: USDA Forest Service Pacific Northwest Range and Experiment Station.

Gibbs, James. 1989. *Shipwrecks of the Pacific Coast*. Portland, Ore.: Binfords and Mort.

Gilkey, Helen M., and L. J. Dennis. 1975. *Handbook of Northwestern Plants*. Corvallis: Oregon State University Press.

Gore, Al. 2006. *An Inconvenient Truth: The Planetary Emergency of Global Warming and What We Can Do about It*. New York: Rodale Books.

Gorsline, Jerry. 1992. *Rainshadow: Archibald Menzies and the Botanical Exploration of the Olympic Peninsula*. Port Townsend, Wash.: Jefferson County Historical Society.

———, ed. 1992. *Shadows of Our Ancestors: Readings in the History of Klallam-White Relations*. Port Townsend, Wash.: Empty Bowl.

Grumbine, R. Edward. 1992. *Ghost Bears: Exploring the Biodiversity Crisis*.

Washington, D.C.: Island Press.

Guberlet, Muriel L. 1956. *Seaweeds at Ebb Tide*. Seattle: University of Washington Press.

———. 1962. *Animals of the Seashore*. Rev. ed. Portland, Ore.: Binfords and Mort.

Guiguet, C. J. 1971. *The Birds of British Columbia: Diving Birds and Tube-Nosed Swimmers*. Victoria: British Columbia Provincial Museum.

Gunther, Erna. 1973. *Ethnobotany of Western Washington*. Seattle: University of Washington Press.

Haley, Delphine, ed. 1986. *Marine Mammals of Eastern North Pacific and Arctic Waters*. Seattle: Pacific Search Press.

Harris, Larry D. 1994. *The Fragmented Forest: Island Biogeography Theory and the Preservation of Biotic Diversity*. Chicago: University of Chicago Press.

Henderson, Jan A., David Peter, Robin Lesher, and David Shaw. 1989. *Forested Plant Associations of the Olympic National Forest*. R6 Ecological Technical Paper 001-88. Portland, Ore.: USDA Forest Service, Pacific Northwest Region.

Hitchcock, C. Leo, and A. Cronquist. 1973. *Flora of the Pacific Northwest*. Seattle: University of Washington Press.

Hooper, David. 1993. *Exploring Washington's Wild Olympic Coast*. Seattle: The Mountaineers Books.

Hornocker, Maurice G. 1992. "Learning to Live with Mountain Lions." *National Geographic*, July.

Houston, D. B., E. G. Schreiner, and B. B. Moorhead. 1990. "Elk in Olympic National Park: Will They Persist Over Time?" *Natural Areas Journal* 10, no. 1.

———. 1994. *Mountain Goats in Olympic National Park: Biology and Management of an Introduced Species*. Scientific Monograph NPS/NROLYM/NSRM-94/25. Denver: U.S. Department of the Interior National Park Service.

Hult, Ruby El. 1954. *The Untamed Olympics: The Story of the Olympic Peninsula*. Portland, Ore.: Binfords and Mort.

Hutten, Martin, Karen Hutten, and Andrea Woodward. N.d. *101 Common Mosses, Liverworts, and Lichens of the Olympic Peninsula*. Seattle: Northwest Interpretive Association.

Jenkins, K., and E. Starkey. 1984. "Habitat Use by Roosevelt Elk in Unmanaged Forests of the Hoh Valley, Washington." *Journal of Wildlife Management*, 48.

Jewett, Stanley, W. Taylor, W. Shaw, and J. Aldrich. 1953. *Birds of Washington State*. Seattle: University of Washington Press.

Jones, Mary Lou, and S. Swartz. 1984. *The Gray Whale: Eschrichtius Robustus*. Orlando, Fla.: Academic Press.

Kozloff, Eugene N. 1976. *Plants and Animals of the Pacific Northwest*. Seattle: University of Washington Press.

———. 1983. *Seashore Life of the Northern Pacific Coast*. Seattle: University of Washington Press.

Kirk, Ruth. 1962. *The Olympic Seashore*. Seattle: Pacific Northwest National Parks Association.

———. 1974. *Hunters of the Whale*. New York: Morrow.

———. 1986. *Tradition and Change on the Northwest Coast*. Seattle: University of Washington Press.

———, ed. 1996. *The Enduring Forests: Northern California, Oregon, Washington, British Columbia, and Southeast Alaska*. Seattle: The Mountaineers Books.

Kirk, Ruth, and Richard D. Daugherty. 2007. *Archaeology in Washington*. Seattle: University of Washington Press.

Kirk, Ruth, and J. Franklin. 1992. *The Olympic Rain Forest: An Ecological Web*. Seattle: University of Washington Press.

Kitchin, E. A. 1949. *Birds of the Olympic Peninsula*. Port Angeles, Wash.: Olympic Stationers.

Kruckeberg, Arthur R. 1991. *The Natural History of Puget Sound Country*. Seattle: University of Washington Press.

Kuramoto, Richard, and L. Bliss. 1970. "Ecology of Subalpine Meadows in the Olympic Mountains." *Ecological Monographs* 40.Larrison, Earl J., and Amy Fisher. 1976. *Mammals of the Northwest*. Seattle: Seattle Audubon Society.

———. 1981. *Birds of the Pacific Northwest*. Moscow: University of Idaho Press.

Laskin, David. 1997. *Rains All the Time: A Connoisseur's History of Weather in the Pacific Northwest*. Seattle: Sasquatch Books.

Leonard, William P., H. Brown, L. Jones, K. McAllister, and R. Storm. 1993. *Amphibians of Washington and Oregon*. Seattle: Seattle Audubon Society.

Lewis, Jeffrey C., and Gerald E. Hayes. 2004. *Feasibility Assessment for Reintroducing Fishers to Washington*. Olympia: Washington Department of Fish and Wildlife.

Lichatowich, Jim. 1993. "The Status of Anadromous Fish Stocks in the Streams of Eastern Jefferson County, Washington." Report to Jamestown S'Klallam Tribe. Sequim, Wash.: Jamestown S'Klallam Tribe.

———. 1999. *Salmon Without Rivers: A History of the Pacific Salmon Crisis*. Washington D.C.: Island Press.

Lien, Carsten. 2000. *Olympic Battleground: The Power Politics of Timber Preservation*. 2d ed. Seattle: The Mountaineers Books.

———. 2001. *Exploring the Olympic Mountains: Accounts of the Earliest Expeditions, 1878–1890*. Seattle: The Mountaineers Books.

Little, Elbert L. 1980. *The Audubon Society Field Guide to North American Trees: Western Edition*. New York: Knopf.

Lyons, C. P., and B. Merilees. 1995. *Trees, Shrubs and Flowers to Know in Washington and British Columbia*. Vancouver, B.C.: Lone Pine Publishing.

MacArthur, Robert H., and Edward O. Wilson. 1969. *The Theory of Island Biogeography*. Princeton, N.J.: Princeton University Press.

Manning, Harvey. 2007. *Wilderness Alps, Conservation, and Conflict in Washington's North Cascades*. Bellingham, Wash.: Northwest Wild Books.

Maser, Chris. 1989. *Forest Primeval: The Natural History of an Ancient Forest*. San Francisco: Sierra Club Books.

———. 1998. *Mammals of the Pacific Northwest: From the Coast to the High Cascades*. Corvallis: Oregon State University Press.

Maser, Chris, R. F. Tarrant, J. M. Trappe, and J. F. Franklin. 1988. *From the Forest to the Sea: A Story of Fallen Trees*. Portland: USDA Forest Service, Pacific Northwest Research Station.

Maser, Chris, and James M. Trappe, eds. 1984. *The Seen and Unseen World of the Fallen Tree*. General Technical Report PNW-164. Portland, Ore.: USDA Forest Service and USDI Bureau of Land Management.

Matthews, Daniel. 1999. *Cascade-Olympic Natural History: A Trailside Reference*. Portland, Ore.: Raven Editions/Portland Audubon Society.

McKee, Bates. 1972. *Cascadia: The Geologic Evolution of the Pacific Northwest*. New York: McGraw-Hill.

McNamee, Thomas. 1997. *The Return of the Wolf to Yellowstone*. New York: Henry Holt.

McNulty, Tim. 1990. *Washington's Wild Rivers: The Unfinished Work*. Seattle: The Mountaineers Books.

———. 1997. "Olympic Park's Missing Predator." *Defenders Magazine*, Summer.

———. 1998. "Washington's Otter Comeback." *Defenders Magazine*, Summer.

———. 2001. "Return of the Fisher." *Forest Magazine*, November/December.

———. 2002. "Salmon: Swimmers in the Forest." Seattle: Northwest Natural History Association.

———. 2002. "Marbled Murrelet." *Forest Magazine*, Fall.

McNulty, Tim, and Pat O'Hara. 1984. *Olympic National Park: Where the Mountain Meets the Sea*. Del Mar, Calif.: Woodlands Press.

McPhee, John. 1981. *Basin and Range*. New York: Farrar, Straus, Giroux.

Meyers, Elizabeth. 2004. *State of the Parks: Olympic National Park, a Resource Assessment*. Fort Collins, Colo.: National Parks Conservation Association.

Montgomery, David R. 2003. *King of Fish: The Thousand-Year Run of Salmon*. Boulder, Colo.: Westview.

Moorhead, Bruce B. 1994. *The Forest Elk: Roosevelt Elk in Olympic National Park*. Seattle: Northwest Interpretive Association.

Morgan, Murray. 1955. *The Last Wilderness*. New York: Viking.

Morgenroth, Chris. 1991. *Footprints in the Olympics: An Autobiography*. Fairfield, Wash.: Ye Galleon Press.

Morrison, Peter. 1989. *Ancient Forests of the Olympic National Forest: Analysis from a Historical and Landscape Perspective*. Washington, D.C.: The Wilderness Society.

Muir, John. 1991. *Our National Parks*. San Francisco: Sierra Club Books.

Nadkarni, Nalini M. 1985. "Roots That Go Out on a Limb." *Natural History* 94.

Nash, Roderick. 1969. *Wilderness and the American Mind*. New Haven, Conn.: Yale University Press.

Nehlsen, Willa, J. Williams, and J. Lichatowich. 1991. "Pacific Salmon at the Crossroads: Stocks at Risk from California, Oregon, Idaho, and Washington." *Fisheries* 16, no. 2.

Nickerson, Roy. 1989. *Sea Otters: A Natural History Guide*. San Francisco: Chronicle Books.

Norse, Elliot A. 1990. *Ancient Forests of the Pacific Northwest*. Washington, D.C.: The Wilderness Society/Island Press.

Noss, Reed, et al. 2000. "Review of Scientific Material Relevant to the Occurrence, Ecosystem Role, and Tested Management Options for Mountain Goats in Olympic National Park." Corvallis, Ore.: Conservation Biology Institute.

Ortman, David. 1993. "Free the Elwha." In *Coastal Zone '93*, vol. 1. New York: American Society of Civil Engineers.

Osborne, Graham, and Wade Davis. 1998. *Rainforest: Ancient Realm of the Pacific Northwest*. Vancouver, B.C.: Greystone Books.

Osborne, Richard, J. Calambokidis, and E. Dorsey. 1988. *A Guide to Marine Mammals of Greater Puget Sound*. Anacortes, Wash.: Island Publishers.

Pascua, Mary Parker. 1991. "Ozette: A Makah Village in 1491." *National Geographic*, October.

Peterson, Roger Tory. 1990. *A Field Guide to Western Birds*. Boston: Houghton Mifflin.

Pinchot, Gifford. 1945. *Breaking New Ground*. New York: Harcourt Brace Jovanovich.

Pojar, Jim, and Andy MacKinnon. 1994. *Plants of the Pacific Northwest Coast*. Vancouver, B.C.: British Columbia Ministry of Forests / Lone Pine Publishing.

Powell, Jay, and Vickie Jensen. 1976. *Quileute: An Introduction to the Indians of La Push*. Seattle: University of Washington Press.

Quammen, David. 1996. *Song of the Dodo: Island Biogeography in an Age of Extinctions*. New York: Scribner.

Ralph, C. John, et al. 1995. *Ecology and Conservation of the Marbled Murrelet*. General Technical Report PSW-GTR-152. Berkeley: USDA Forest Service, Pacific Southwest Research Station.

Rau, Weldon W. 1980. *Geology of the Washington Coast Between the Hoh and Quillayute Rivers*. Bulletin No. 72. Olympia: Washington Department of Natural Resources.

Reid, William, and Adelaide De Menil. 1972. *Out of the Silence*. New York: Harper & Row.

Ricketts, Edward, J. Calvin, and J. Hedgpeth. 1968. *Between Pacific Tides*. 4th ed.

Stanford, Calif.: Stanford University Press.

Robbins, Chandler S., B. Bruun, H. Zim, and A. Singer. 1983. *Birds of North America*. New York: Golden Press.

Rooney, J. R. 1997. *Frontier Legacy: History of the Olympic National Forest, 1897 to 1960*. Seattle: Northwest Interpretive Association.

Runte, Alfred. 1979. *National Parks: The American Experience*. Lincoln: University of Nebraska Press.

Samuels, Stephen. 1991. *Ozette Archaeological Project Research Reports*, vol. 1. U.S. Department of Anthropology Reports of Investigations 63. Seattle: National Park Service, Pacific Northwest Region.

Scheffer, Victor B. 1995. *Mammals of the Olympic Peninsula*. Olympia, Wash.: Society for Northwestern Vertebrate Biology.

Sept, J. Duane. 2004. *The Beachcomber's Guide to Seashore Life in the Pacific Northwest*. Madeira Park, B.C.: Harbour Publishing.

Sharp, Robert P. 1960. *Glaciers*. Eugene: University of Oregon Press.

Sharpe, Fred. 1992. *Olympic Wildlife Checklist*. Seattle: Northwest Interpretive Association.

———. 1993. *Olympic Peninsula Birds: The Songbirds*. Unpublished manuscript, Olympic National Park.

Shelton, John S. 1966. *Geology Illustrated*. New York: W. H. Freeman.

Sibley, David. 2000. *The Sibley Guide to Bird Life and Behavior*. New York: Alfred A. Knopf.

Skinner, Brian, and Stephen Porter. 1989. *The Dynamic Earth: An Introduction to Physical Geology*. New York: John Wiley and Sons.

Smith, Douglas W., and Gary Ferguson. 2005. *Decade of the Wolf: Returning the Wild to Yellowstone*. Guilford, Conn.: Lyons Press.

Smithson, Michael, and Pat O'Hara. 1993. *Olympic: Ecosystems of the Peninsula*. Helena, Mont.: America and World Geographic Publishing.

Snively, Gloria. 1978. *Exploring the Seashore in British Columbia, Washington and Oregon*. Vancouver, B.C., and Seattle: Gordon Soules / Pacific Search Press.

Soest, Sally, ed. 1998. *Voice of the Wild Olympics*, 50th Anniversary Edition. Seattle: Olympic Park Associates.

Steelquist, Robert. 1987. *Washington's Coast*. Helena, Mont.: American Geographic Publishing.

———. 1992. *Adopt-a-Stream Foundation Field Guide to the Pacific Salmon*. Seattle: Sasquatch Books.

Stewart, Charles. 1988. *Wildflowers of the Olympics and Cascades*. Port Angeles, Wash.: Nature Education Enterprises.

Stewart, Hillary. 1984. *Cedar: Tree of Life to the Northwest Coast Indians*. Vancouver, B.C.: Douglas and McIntyre.

Sullivan, Robert. 2000. *A Whale Hunt: Two Years on the Olympic Peninsula with the Makah and Their Canoe.* New York: Scribner.

Suttles, Wayne. 1987. *Coast Salish Essays.* Vancouver, B.C.: Talonbooks.

——, ed. 1990. *Handbook of North American Indians,* vol. 7, *Northwest Coast.* Washington, D.C.: Smithsonian Institution.

Swan, James. 1857. *The Northwest Coast.* New York: Harper and Brothers.

——. 1974. *The Indians of Cape Flattery.* Washington, D.C.: Smithsonian Institution; facsimile reproduction, Seattle: Shorey Book Store.

Tabor, Rowland W. 1988. *Guide to the Geology of Olympic National Park.* Seattle: Pacific Northwest Parks and Forests Association.

Tabor, R. W., and W. M. Cady. 1987. *Geological Map of the Olympic Peninsula.* Denver, Colo.: U.S. Geological Survey.

Twight, Ben W. 1983. *Organizational Values and Political Power: The Forest Service Versus the Olympic National Park.* University Park: Pennsylvania State University Press.

Udvardy, Miklos. 1977. *The Audubon Society Field Guide to North American Birds: Western Region.* New York: Knopf.

U.S. Department of the Interior, Department of Commerce, and Elwha S'Klallam Tribe. 1994. *The Elwha Report.*

U.S. Department of the Interior, National Park Service. 1995. *Elwha River Ecosystem Restoration, Final Environmental Impact Statement.*

——. 1995. *Mountain Goat Management within Olympic National Park, Washington, Draft Environmental Impact Statement.*

——. 2007. U.S. Department of the Interior, National Park Service. *Olympic National Park, Washington, Fisher Reintroduction Plan/Environmental Impact Statement.*

——. 2008. *Olympic National Park, Washington, General Management Plan/ Environmental Impact Statement.*

U.S. Fish and Wildlife Service. 2005. *Washington Islands National Wildlife Refuges Draft Comprehensive Conservation Plan and Environmental Assessment.*

U.S. Fish and Wildlife Service, Western Washington Office. 1999. *Feasibility Study on the Reintroduction of Gray Wolves to the Olympic Peninsula, Washington.*

Van Syckle, Edwin. 1981. *They Tried to Cut It All: Grays Harbor—Turbulent Years of Greed and Greatness.* Seattle: Pacific Search Press.

Vermeer, Kees, K. Briggs, K. Morgan, and D. Siegel-Causey. 1993. *The Status, Ecology, and Conservation of Marine Birds of the North Pacific.* Ottawa: Canadian Wildlife Service.

Vitt, Dale H., Janet Marsh, and Robin Bovey. 1988. *Mosses, Lichens and Ferns of Northwest North America.* Vancouver, B.C.: Lone Pine Press.

Washington Department of Fisheries, Washington Department of Wildlife, and Western Washington Treaty Tribes. 1993. *1992 Washington State Salmon and Steelhead Stock Inventory.* Olympia.

Wertheim, Anne. 1984. *The Intertidal Wilderness*. San Francisco: Sierra Club Books.

Wessen, Gary. 2006. "Archaeological Site Testing Activities at 45CA400, Makah Indian Reservation, Washington." Neah Bay, Wash.: Makah Cultural and Research Center.

Whitlock, Cathy. 1992. "Vegetational and Climatic History of the Pacific Northwest during the Last 20,000 Years: Implications for Understanding Present-Day Biodiversity." *The Northwest Environmental Journal 8*.

Wickersham, James. 1961. "A National Park in the Olympics . . . 1890." *The Living Wilderness*, Summer-Fall.

Williams, Hill. 2002. *The Restless Northwest: A Geological Story*. Pullman: Washington State University Press.

Wood, Robert L. 1967. *Across the Olympic Mountains: The Press Expedition, 1889–90*. Seattle: University of Washington Press.

——. 1976. *Men, Mules, and Mountains: Lieutenant O'Neil's Olympic Expeditions*. Seattle: The Mountaineers Books.

——. 1984. *Olympic Mountains Trail Guide*. Seattle: The Mountaineers Books.

——. 1995. *The Land That Slept Late: The Olympic Mountains in Legend and History*. Seattle: The Mountaineers Books.

Wray, Jacilee. 1997. *Olympic National Park Ethnographic Overview and Assessment*. Port Angeles, Wash.: Olympic National Park.

——, ed. 2002. *Native Peoples of the Olympic Peninsula: Who We Are*, by the Olympic Peninsula Intertribal Cultural Advisory Committee. Norman: University of Oklahoma Press.

Wunderlich, Robert, B. Winter, and J. Meyer. 1994. "Restoration of the Elwha River Ecosystem and Anadromous Fisheries." *Bethesda* 19, no. 8.

Wydoski, Richard S., and R. Whitney. 1979. *Inland Fishes of Washington*. Seattle: University of Washington Press.

Yates, Steve. 1998. *Marine Wildlife from Puget Sound through the Inside Passage*. Seattle: Sasquatch Books.

Yorath, C. J. 1990. *Where Terranes Collide*. Victoria, B.C.: Orca Publishers.

Zwinger, Ann, and Beatrice Willard. 1972. *Land Above the Trees: A Guide to American Alpine Tundra*. New York: Harper and Row.

Index

Page numbers in italic refer to illustrations.